CARNAL SPIRIT

CARNAL SPIRIT

The Revolutions of Charles Péguy

Matthew W. Maguire

PENN

UNIVERSITY OF PENNSYLVANIA PRESS

PHILADELPHIA

Published by
University of Pennsylvania Press
Philadelphia, Pennsylvania 19104-4112
www.upenn.edu/pennpress

Printed in the United States of America on acid-free paper
1 3 5 7 9 10 8 6 4 2

A catalogue record for this book is available
from the Library of Congress.
ISBN 978-0-8122-5095-4

CONTENTS

Introduction   1

Chapter 1. Modernity, Antimodernity, and Beyond   25

Chapter 2. His Youth   65

Chapter 3. An Answer to the Question: What Is Modernity?   83

Chapter 4. The Revolution of Critique   94

Chapter 5. Revolutions of the Body and Work   117

Chapter 6. Continuity and Revolution: War and Honor   132

Chapter 7. Universal Particulars, Particular Universalities   151

Chapter 8. Mysticism and Politics   164

Chapter 9. The Style of Infinite Reality   176

Chapter 10. The Christian Revolution   191

Chapter 11. Despair and Exaltation   216

Conclusion   224

Notes   233

Index   273

Acknowledgments   285

INTRODUCTION

Born into a provincial family of modest means, Charles Péguy became an internationally famous intellectual in the years before the Great War; he was killed in that war at the age of forty-one. As a poet, journalist, and philosopher, for generations his writing prompted fascination, awe, fury, scorn, searching criticism, laughter, wonder, little imitation, and no indifference.

Among Péguy's most abiding enquiries was the question of what it means to be modern. We are often modern, thought Péguy, in two different ways. One way advances an inexorable becoming; another opposes it.

Credentialed, procedural, and managerial in affect, the advocates of a new, entirely immanent becoming, thought Péguy, work to transform institutions patiently from within rather than seeking their overthrow. Sustained in ways great and small by the ultimate assumptions and insatiable expansion of global markets—with the market and its technological artifices as the ubiquitous and paradigmatic form for all human relations with others and with the world— this process brings the imperatives of negotiated, contractual exchange and profitable consumption to all our experiences, guided by the ongoing labor of sciences natural and social. Human being is increasingly encompassed by an ever more uncompromising immanence, from which the transcendent appears only through cracks in locked doors of long disuse, the unceasing glare within obscuring prospects without.

These advocates sense by no means an unreserved concord of discrete practices or ultimate purpose, but rather, a profound and ongoing *alignment* between their aspirations and the general direction of a society propelled forward by a technological market. Hence they express a deep if occasionally irritable confidence that their triumph is assured. While they work within free republics, they are not always or even often sympathetic to notions of individual free will, or sovereignty of the people; they wish supremely to see their shared idea of the future vindicated, which, they assume, will require the persistent and expansive guidance of accredited specialists in diverse fields of enquiry and policy.

The adherents of this way are generally sympathetic to determinism, in either material or social forms. As long as there is history, science and technology will always allow human beings to remake our world continuously (often in ever more complete accord with science itself). They assume the ultimate reality of an experimental becoming against the illusions of a persistent (or worse, eternal) being. They tend toward agnosticism or atheism, to the desirability of practical arrangements among persons and societies governed by continuous negotiations about contingent "values" that often "cash out" to some increasingly self-concious, increasingly pervasive validation of material and social interests, even if a diminution in communal meaning and purpose is the object of abstract speculation.

For most of their advocates, these assumptions should generally *not* be positively defended. Rhetorics of indirection, irony, and above all, applications of putatively dispassionate method are much to be preferred to making direct claims about the ultimate nature of reality that inevitably elicit pointless and tedious but—annoyingly—not refuted counterargument. Direct disagreement with the supereminent assumptions underwriting their historical advance is hence embarrassing. Set directly before a person or persons who insist on such disagreement, it is generally best not to engage with them at all but to continue one's work with the like-minded, secure that one's own positions are and will be sustained by a deeper and inexorable logic working through political economy, culture, scholarship, technology, and institutions.

The specifically scholarly advocates of this immanence often complement the progress of technology and of the social sciences with a highly developed if selective historical consciousness. A methodical and comprehensive "contextualization" regularly falls with force upon philosophies of life and the world different from their own; the injustices that might or ought to be attributed to these views receive close attention, and the injustices that might or ought to be attributed to the scholar's views are passed over in silence. It is assumed— and thus unsurprisingly concluded—that alternative meanings and accounts of the whole ultimately owe their existence to atavism, and with it more intellectually limited, cruel, fearful, credulous, and scarcity-addled pasts, decisively produced by transitory and often unhappy circumstances, upon which the meticulous scholar can now perform distinctively modern disciplinary operations.

Whatever their walks of life, the advocates of this immanent, expansive becoming are at home in universities. Their sense of self is entwined with them, and the order of merit and prestige attending them. Befitting their professional status, an appropriate zeal for their own advancement and that of their allies is suitable, even praiseworthy. To pay dearly in order to live honestly in a flawed world is regrettably still necessary elsewhere; but through the expansion of perpetually negotiable becoming to which they have contributed as scholars and students, there is no longer a tension between being honored by one's contemporaries and telling the truth without reserve. To claim otherwise is to open the way for archaic economies of sacrifice, in which the desire to sacrifice for truth often produces the oppositions that themselves create the need for and legitimacy of sacrifice. It is thought better to examine that dangerous economy from a secure scholarly distance, or to avoid it entirely.

Among these judgments often rests the assumption that most of the long-standing particular forms of human conviction, belief, and allegiance that mediate between individual persons and universal humanity—in particular, notions of communal continuity, of peoples, and perhaps above all of religious faith—should be allowed to dissolve inexorably, consumed by the irresistible velocity of media and scholarship, and the general liquefaction of identities in the flux of increasingly self-conscious becoming.

It is likely, and desirable—a kind of immanent justice—that these older forms of being human will be altogether absorbed in that continuous, perpetually contemporary negotiation and exchange, issuing in a cumulative equanimity of perspective set loose from all particular fictions, all arbitrarily inherited and given commitments. For the daring, this will ultimately include the great given of being human. Human being may only be a transitional moment in becoming's perpetual advance. Perhaps most important, a straightforwardly two-dimensional linear time, moving neatly from past to present to future, will vindicate this immanent and ultimately universal becoming.

Such was the intellectual world Péguy saw coming to be in early twentieth-century Paris.

Alongside it a faction comes to be, this one self-consciously particularist, populated by the avowed enemies of expanding becoming. Furthermore, in a truly universal humanity, universal rights, universal hopes, and perhaps above all the work of universal justice, these enemies see only the triumph of the expansive immanence they oppose. To block its triumph is their foremost purpose and end.

For the advocates of this particularist order, both immanent becoming and the universally human are alleged to be the instrument of an inexorable exsanguination, set against vital and positive action, that cuts itself off from the chthonic power inhering in the limiting forms of particular peoples, a particular traditional culture, in traditional forms of order and prejudice that, in their account, themselves give ultimate limiting coherence, purpose, and above all strength to being human. They have an idolatrous awe for this strength, often serving as self-appointed champions of some portion of the culture identified as its true and ultimate origin, its putative "heartland." This heartland is set in contrast to modern urban life, and perhaps especially the universities beloved by their adversaries; for self-conscious and resentful particularists, the world of learning is simply a base for an opposing ideology.

The partisans of this order often claim to love the past, but most reliably express not a love or gratitude for its givenness; rather, they give vent to an inexhaustible anger over its present alteration, whether or not those alterations are just. Their rhetoric abounds in invective. To strip their opponents of respect is a task to which they warm with alacrity—even as they express a longing for the forms of mutuality, respect, and dignity that the new order of perpetual negotiation sweeps away. For all that, they often present the past they claim to love only in evocative outline; at intervals it appears as the necessary MacGuffin for the expression of antagonisms, hastening the way to an allegedly clarifying agon.

These wrathful particularists often intimate a loyalty to older notions of transcendence—including religious faith and its avowal of abiding truths—but they conceive of that which transcends time only as an *arrested* immanence. They often present an amalgamated past as a unity, the final and definitive form for flourishing for themselves and their community, in which a comprehensive fulfillment was possible, and which now must be reinserted mechanically into the present, without creativity or surprise. Within their arrested immanence, they express contempt for their learned adversaries but also hope—once more the captives of their opponents—that "science" will confirm their particularism and its prejudices.

The champions of willful particularism show themselves ready and often eager for collective sacrifice—often for others in their self-identified community—in relation to enemies. Yet they stand in unmistakable disaccord with many of the exalted truths they profess to defend and proclaim worthy of sacrifice. In its most conceptually assertive and self-aware forms, the sacrifice particularists are most eager to make is a sacrifice of truth. They assert that faith should be upheld, though they do not believe it true,[1] that long-standing prejudices and brutal forms of scapegoating should be affirmed regardless of the facts of the case, that illusions are more compatible with human and historical drama and collective power than truth.

Péguy opposed *both* an immanent becoming and the particularist, arrested immanence that accompanied it in the early twentieth century. The partisans of each group were not the same, and they required different forms of opposition. For the partisans of "the intellectual party"—whatever their politics—that opposition took the form of written argument.

To oppose the most enraged and violent anti-universalists, however, would require direct defensive action in the streets as well as words, as in the defense of Alfred Dreyfus—a Jewish officer in the French Army falsely accused of treason—during the Dreyfus affair of the 1890s and early 1900s, in which Dreyfus and other French Jews were subject to an increasingly vicious and pervasive anti-Semitism.

It was an integral part of Péguy's work to see both ways of being modern as they were; to see, at various speeds and levels and in different ways, the profound and consuming *inhumanity* that subsisted in both immanent, inexorable becoming and reactionary particularism.

Reactionaries tended to cohere enthusiastically around immediate threats to both the dignity and the physical safety of other human beings, especially those belonging to small and vulnerable groups, and to find a malicious glee in their suffering and degradation.

The other side was solicitous of the physical safety of persons but, in Péguy's account, sought no less to put an eventual end to human dignity, and with it to the notion of human being as something distinct from material mechanisms, or units of social function, or the comprehensive products of impersonal historical processes. This end would be directed not only at accounts of the soul—religious or secular, aesthetic or moral—but also often to the very possibility of human freedom as something other than an increasingly complete repudiation of the past and of all not subject to becoming. (The advocates of immanent becoming were decidedly chary about arguments advancing free will or the possibility of substantive human creativity.) They pursued their own project with a sweaty partisan zeal that made its way under an amusingly ill-fitting carapace of judicious calm and meticulous neutrality of method.

Péguy would insist upon another way—related differently to the past, present, and future alike—in which the particular and the universal, being and becoming, were equally indispensable to human flourishing. He insisted

further that the political obsessions of both continuously becoming immanence and arrested immanence were most important as a visible sign that life-
giving dimensions of human experience were suffering from neglect and an
intentionally cultivated ignorance, often produced by a severe misunderstanding of time.

For Péguy, neither of these forms of culture and politics could serve to
substitute for a free, continuous, and living relation of diverse pasts with the
present and diverse futures, and ultimately to the transcendence of linear
time in eternity, prompted by love and sustained by lucid hope. For him,
those truths that move at once within and beyond time participate imperfectly in the fullness of any historical moment, because eternity cannot be
encompassed by any moment. The moral improvement of human affairs in
time was a real (if neither an automatic nor final) possibility, but this required
metaphysical freedom and the free expression of abiding convictions. The
freedom and integrative creativity opened by an encounter with different dimensions of time could in turn open the way to a renaissance of republican
freedom and of Christianity, to a positive encounter between Judaism and
Christianity, and to a renewed understanding of our embodied lives. Surrounded by moderns and antimoderns, Péguy set out upon a path that could
be called amodern.[2]

It is unwise to ignore the unique historical specificity of Péguy's situation.
Yet it is also unwise to ignore the contemporary resonances of Péguy's observations and arguments. As the events of the early twenty-first century have
shown with piercing clarity, Péguy's animating questions and insights
have not "ended" historically, in the manner of arguments for the claims
of the Guelfs and the Ghibellines. Péguy writes repeatedly about certain dilemmas in late modern culture, some of which have recently reemerged with
great and disquieting force throughout the West. To claim that one does not
see these resonances, or does not take them into account—while in fact ar-
ranging one's sources very assertively to vindicate certain conclusions, leading the reader with words like "nostalgia" and "anxiety"—is tedious and
dishonest. This is all the more true if one affects the self-consciously flat,
stagily sober rhetorical style weighing upon so much contemporary scholarship. Genuine sobriety is far more interesting and insightful than its counter-
feit. It is the unsober person, trying to win the approval of wary authorities,
who assumes a sonorous monotone.

Yet why else should you read a book about Charles Péguy? If Péguy—
particularly in the Anglophone world—is now a figure often overshadowed

by his contemporaries and near-contemporaries like Émile Durkheim, Max Weber, Marcel Mauss, Friedrich Nietzsche, and others, this occlusion was nowhere in evidence through the greater portion of the last century. For generations, Péguy inspired thinking and action across all manner of political, religious, academic, and national boundaries.

The literary critic Walter Benjamin, for example, wrote enthusiastically and at length about Péguy, finding in his work a "friendly togetherness" and continual dialogue, a sense of touch absent in Proust.[3] Benjamin also claimed admiringly of Péguy's politics and life that the phrase "enemy of the laws, indeed, but friend of the powers that be" is one that "applies least of all to Péguy."[4]

Benjamin's friend, the great scholar of Judaism Gershom Scholem, also wrote in highest praise of Péguy, defender of the unique and mystical character of Judaism. Near the end of his life, Scholem said that Péguy "has incisively understood the Jewish condition to an extent that has been rarely achieved, and has never been surpassed by non-Jews."[5]

For the twentieth-century Catholic theologian Hans Urs von Balthasar, Péguy transcended the characteristically modern tendency to assume a disjunction between the aesthetic and the ethical.[6] The theologian Henri de Lubac wrote that Péguy "will save us from Nietzsche,"[7] because he responded to similar questions and dilemmas in decisively different ways. Following the same path, for the philosopher Charles Taylor, Péguy is a "paradigm example of a modern who has found his own path, a new path," to faith.[8]

In political life, Péguy long enjoyed a similarly varied and enthusiastic readership. Charles de Gaulle—the single most influential person in twentieth-century French politics—acknowledged, "No writer marked me as much" as Péguy.[9] Yet a quite different political figure—the Senegalese intellectual and politician Léopold Senghor—also took inspiration from Péguy for the Négritude literary movement, with its emancipatory hope of bringing together traditional African cultures and modern ones.[10]

Immediately after World War II, Hannah Arendt clarified her disagreements with Péguy, but she counted him unhesitatingly among the champions of "freedom for the people and reason for the mind."[11] In the same postwar moment, the literary critic Rachel Bespaloff wrote that Péguy transformed the language that would later be used by fascists by directing it toward entirely different ends; he "had a mind whose true significance is just beginning to be recognized."[12] In a very different way, within the pages of *Difference and Repetition*, Gilles Deleuze finds in Péguy an indispensable thinker about time, who evokes the possibilities of repetition as something other than an assimilable concretion of similitudes and iterations of identity.[13]

Yet why have the depths and insights of Péguy been cast in relative shadow? In part, many scholars wish to explain the tragedies of the twentieth century from within the security afforded by the seemingly inevitable advance of immanent becoming. They simply assume—to quote Margaret Thatcher—that "there is no alternative" to continuing with the same project *in saecula saeculorum*. Part of their task is to preclude a vivifying encounter with lives and thoughts that cannot be assimilated into their account of the past.

Their scholarship does not always draw conclusions from close reading, or even from especially attentive reading. Hence the reading of Péguy in many recent books, including Christopher Forth's *The Dreyfus Affair and the Crisis of French Manhood*.

Forth claims that Dreyfusards, while working to free and exonerate Alfred Dreyfus, participated wholeheartedly in accepting and disseminating a hypertrophied masculinity that would ultimately prove useful to or even partially constitutive of fascism, in an effort to avoid, in his concluding words, the "feminizing pitfalls of modernity."[14] While a historical account from the mid-twentieth century would look to the Dreyfusards as harbingers of the Resistance to fascism, this dangerously naïve reading needs to acknowledge the gendering of their work, and the Dreyfusards' deeper affinities with the forces that brought Europe not simply to the persecution of a single innocent man, but very likely to the Holocaust.[15]

Péguy is among those who Forth argues—to move toward traditional Marxist language—were "objectively" proto-fascist even if they were "subjectively" opposed to anti-Semitism and worked to secure Dreyfus's exoneration. (Or to modulate the claim into an alternative hermeneutics of suspicion, an apparent antifascism and its progenitors had a *latent* but deep affinity with fascism, even if they were *manifestly* opposed to proto-fascism and fascists.) The evidence for Péguy's participation in this fascist-tending masculinist discourse is, first, that he, "from his bookshop near the Sorbonne," would reportedly say "fall in"[16] to gather allies in order to defend Dreyfusard professors threatened by anti-Dreyfusard groups. Péguy also said that Dreyfusards "were heroes" and had "military virtues" nowhere in evidence among Dreyfus's persecutors on the General Staff.[17] Finally, as part of the "sporting enthusiasm" that contributed to fin-de-siècle masculinism, the adolescent Péguy "successfully lobbied the headmaster of his lycée to permit the older boys to play football [soccer]."[18]

Péguy indeed used the phrase "fall in" to exhort others to protect the victims of antirepublican and anti-Semitic aggression; but that is perhaps less an indication of nascent fascism than of the ways in which language about war and sex is a particularly fertile domain for metaphors, ones that cross the most varied domains of human experience, and have done so for a very long time.

This claim could be established with abundant references to Homer, Herodotus, and the Bible—or simply to the corridors of twenty-first century universities, in which a host of perfectly kind and good-natured contemporary academics have, in this author's direct experience, referred to a student being given a "warning shot," or our need to "fight" for a new course to be approved, or someone's candidacy being "torpedoed," or needing to fight a "battle" and form a "united front" in relation to an inconveniently obdurate dean or another department. If we are to admit this evidence, then it appears that liberal-arts academia in the twenty-first century is awash with masculinist triumphalism and subliminal fascism.

There is an important argument to make about Péguy's changing reflections on violence and war, and it will be a significant factor in this book.[19] Yet calls to fall in during the Dreyfus affair give no plausible purchase upon it. It might also be said that in an age when "calling security" was not an option for institutions of higher learning, Péguy's clearly defensive work, as the proprietor of a bookshop, to protect intellectual freedom for university faculty and students against gangs of violent anti-Semites is rather implausibly stretched toward proto-fascism.

Péguy does refer to the Dreyfusards as "heroes" in his essay *Notre Jeunesse* ("Our Youth"). But his supreme example of heroism in that essay is the intellectual and anarchist Bernard-Lazare, who was an advocate not of Dreyfusard masculinist violence but of a universal justice that encompassed Dreyfus and the oppressed around the world, and who, seeing the world clearly despite his spectacles,[20] ill health, and considerable avoirdupois, devoted himself to exposing the lies that brought about Dreyfus's conviction in hopes of a future and quite expressly judicial vindication. Péguy praises him for his "gentleness" (*douceur*), as well as his "goodness" and "even-temperedness."[21]

Furthermore, the "martial" virtue in question for Péguy in *Notre Jeunesse* is courage—but courage for him was not, as it was for fascists, supremely expressed in a nihilistic and racist confrontation with death that finds its paradoxically debased *Aufhebung* in collectivist, industrial violence and domination. For Péguy, loving self-sacrifice, persistent devotion to carefully thought-out and established truths in the face of rejection by power, and voluntary poverty compose the true courage of the Dreyfusards (as Péguy argues throughout the essay). Moreover, Péguy's preeminent example of heroism throughout his life's work is not a man but a woman—Jeanne d'Arc.

It is certainly true that the idealization of a chaste woman who ends her life as a sacrificial victim was part of the masculine-obsessive's palette in early twentieth century culture, and it is equally evident that these tableaus could perceptibly constrict the lives of living women. Yet within Péguy's rendering in both prose and poetry, Jeanne is in no way a passive, abnegating, willowy damsel in the manner of fin-de-siècle representations of "delicate" or "neurasthenic" women; nor is she an emasculating virago in the manner of some women in the work of male artistic contemporaries like Gustav Klimt or Richard Strauss and Hugo von Hofmannsthal, nor an exalted romantic or erotic ideal (illusory or not) in the manner of Henry James's Madame de Vionnet, Villiers de l'Isle-Adam's Sara de Maupers, or the variously idealized or "fallen" women that appear in the paintings of Paul Gauguin or Félicien Rops.

In his extensive writings about Jeanne, Péguy describes her body's actions but never describes her physical appearance, nor does he dwell on her physical suffering or her death—in his most famous poem about Jeanne, her death is entirely absent, as are any scenes of battle or violence. It is a challenge to find in his Jeanne a modern male fixation on the sacrificial death of a beautiful young woman, because her death is mostly set aside, and her appearance goes entirely unmentioned.

Instead, Péguy's Jeanne is a hero at once acutely intelligent and contemplative, and intensely ambivalent about war. She reluctantly leads men into battle as a way to create justice and peace even as she agonizes over the mistreatment of soldiers—including enemy soldiers. Her most characteristic gesture is not violence but her ongoing anguish at the thought that anyone should be in hell[22]—a concern that was also Péguy's. She is eager to help others and repeatedly argues with men to do so; she is willing to give her food to children in need (though she displays no desire to starve herself and is generally presented as healthy and readily, assertively disputatious with men and women alike). The actual poems do not offer themselves to now-standard interpretations exposing dehumanizing and instrumental accounts of women's lives.

In short, to sustain Péguy's appearance in Forth's masculinist, proto-fascist discourse, we are really left with the evidence that a teenaged Péguy persuaded his headmaster to allow for broader student participation in soccer games. While this claim offers a neatly symmetrical (if ghastly) parallel to the Victorian cliché about the Battle of Waterloo and the playing fields of Eton, this "evidence" does not give the author any grounds to draw historical connections between the soccer fields of Péguy's lycée and fascist blitzkriegs, let alone the moral abysses of Sobibor and Auschwitz.

It could be said that Forth's purpose is to write not about Péguy, but about a masculinist discourse in which Péguy participates. Yet the argument for his inclusion in this discourse is not established by anything resembling careful, patient reading. Vladimir Nabokov's sound if rakishly daunting injunction for interpretation that holds well beyond specifically literary reading—that it should passionately attend to details[23]—is often brazenly flouted by historians seeking explanations for the cultural trajectory of late modern European history. It often binds together a wide range of sources in sheaves of very short and selective quotations in order to establish a series of "anxieties," not in order to prepare the way for careful reading of particular sources (a perfectly legitimate task in the absence of infinite time), but as a substitute for a careful, patient reading of any sources.

In this way, the tendency of a certain strain of modern history writing to argue or imply that historical selves fail to self—that is, they are set within a matrix of linguistic and cultural practices that determines their position, or at least the historical efficacy and relevance of that position—is all too often sustained by a prior commitment by the historian not to inquire about individual differences in the first place.

This type of argument—of which Forth's book is only one example—has become a kind of standard model for a great deal of writing about late nineteenth- and early twentieth-century Europe. In it, it is claimed, or assumed, that the public, civic culture of the West in general, and Europe in particular, labored to prolong with only minor or at most gradual adjustments the presumed (as we understand, a selectively muted and amplified) culture of a premodern, traditional society with origins in the early modern or even the medieval period and its classical inheritance.

In this account, this culture artificially prolonged and intensified often rigid distinctions of gender and caste, a sense of beauty and morals and metaphysics and honor, accompanied by other aspirations, prejudices, and hierarchies from its past. It dimly perceived but refused to accept that this public, civic culture had been stretched beyond the technological, social, economic, material, and cultural imperatives that gave it its suasive power. This disjunction produced "crises" and "anxieties" about decadence and decline that led the defenders of this composite "traditional" culture to something like a mannerist caricature of the already edited, selectively reduced, or amplified castes, hierarchies, and aesthetic and moral codes it sought to uphold, and sometimes to their pseudo-scientific rationalization in medicine, psychiatry, and social science.

Working within this model, for some time many cultural and intellectual historians of Europe have shown how, at the beginning of late modernity (say, from the closing decades of the nineteenth century to 1914) a new, larval order began to fashion itself in aesthetics, politics, new notions of gender, sexuality, and social change. Not all of this is rendered in bright hues: still following Michel Foucault, the period's more imperial forays into science and social science are often the object of criticism, explicit or implicit, on the grounds that they limited their universality by, for example, importing traditionally European, masculinist assumptions into their notion of universality, or imposing a coercive, homogenizing immanent eschaton (as in Marxism) upon the apparently spontaneous unfolding of becoming. But above all, historians trace the pathologies that sought to freely combine a steroidal enhancement of sundry limiting atavisms with the distinctive technological, ideological, and (often pseudo-) scientific possibilities of modern culture. It was this pathological response to an emerging late or postmodernity that brought Europe—or at the least, left Europe vulnerable—to the hecatombs of 1914–1945.

Like all standard models, this model encompasses a variety of emphases and qualifications, and thus, if its advocates wish, it can deny its own existence. Something similar happened in economics at the turn of our own century, where "efficient market," fresh-water economists for many years claimed they were "just doing serious work" in different corners of economics, with various intricate models that allowed for gratifyingly piquant scholarly exchanges, until the global financial crisis disclosed a remarkable unanimity of conviction—in the face of some decidedly jarring developments—about the putatively "serious" or "sober" principles of economics.

The writing of history is rather less open to immediate contradiction by events. Yet while certainly not without the capacity to adapt and integrate disparate sensibilities and interests at various levels of abstraction, the commitments of this historical standard model have been expressed with some clarity and consistency for at least a generation, sometimes among those who acknowledge their limitations.[24]

What ultimately rests behind these commitments? While a given historian can deny that his or her models have morals, the choosing of ordering argumentative principles, or of criteria for the selection of evidence, or of emphases in argument, imply notions of what is true, about what is and what should be, or at least about what is "good in the way of belief" or "a desirable state of affairs."

This reality is generally—if rather discreetly—acknowledged by historians. Peter Gordon, for example, claims that while an "ethic of neutrality partially occludes" the presence of "strong normative frameworks" in the writing of history, an account of what should be enters into the formulation and development of historical arguments: "The discerning reader can usually grasp without difficulty what political or moral judgment may have animated the historian in her work and guided her toward certain conclusions."[25]

One moral of the standard model of late modern Europe tends to assume the following, applying its truth of immanent becoming to the origins of the twentieth century's catastrophes: the notion of a rigorously ethical, integral, strong, persistent, and sacrificial self is not a source of resistance to fascism but rather and ultimately is a precondition and enabler of fascism. Following Foucault and others, advocates of the standard model have implied and asserted that resistance to fascism, and more generally to modern tyrannies of either a bluntly political or a more subtle kind, can be attributed to a refusal or repression of discontinuous identities, desires, and forms of expression.[26]

Given this account of fascism's ultimate inner hold upon us via our very notions of self and self-command, it is rather awkward that resistance to fascism in the twentieth century was often carried out by those with a robust attachment to some considerable portion of the aesthetic, moral, and metaphysical commitments that many contemporary scholars consider to be, as it were, incipiently fascist in their internal logic. They include integral selves making deliberate moral decisions at great personal cost, founded in what is often a mixture of quite traditional and quite modern notions of virtue and civic good associated with solidarity, courage, equality, integrity, independence, duty, socialism, Christianity, Judaism, humanism, and so on.

An open encounter with Péguy's thinking meets another obstacle in a different prevailing model, this one more closely associated with intellectual history. It is less political than the standard model and operates at a higher level of abstraction. It tends to emphasize how ideas in history often work within an immediately contextual matrix, one that allows for apparent differences to be set within conceptual, social, and linguistic structures of which participants were generally unaware, or only dimly aware, and from which they cannot escape. This is often accompanied by a conscious effort by historical agents to "negotiate" contemporary institutional and intellectual expectations in order to secure intellectual credibility and status. For this model's advocates, to focus upon thinking by a given person without assigning priority to these structures and negotiations veers dangerously close to humanist nostalgia. Often the very attempt by a given thinker to move beyond various social, conceptual, and professional constrictions is treated ironically, though it may well be a tragic or melancholy irony that intimates an unspoken wish for an impossible escape from what contextually bound both the thinker and the thought.

Whatever the rhetorical hue of the argument, this ready-made form of historical understanding allows the scholar to devote him- or herself to structures of assumption and inquiry, to what "shows up" as "knowledge," or the immediate, inescapable contextual boundaries of intellectual work.

For example, in Sarah Hammerschlag's *The Figural Jew*, Péguy is a thinker who tries to subvert cultural assumptions, especially anti-Semitic preoccupations with Jews' putative "rootlessness" and "disloyalty" to affirm an ongoing prophetic vocation. Yet in her account, he failed; his writing does not really escape the anti-Semitic discursive historical matrix from which it is said to emerge. Péguy's Judaism remains racial—if not racist—in nature, it is "dehistoricized" and reduces Jews to being the exemplary suffering servants of Christians, or as edifying examples in a Christian typology.

For Hammerschlag, Péguy's very praise of his friend Bernard-Lazare is not, as it was for George Steiner, the best account of friendship since Montaigne;[27] rather, it is itself veering close to anti-Semitism, since it also claims that Jews were not Dreyfusards as Bernard-Lazare himself was, and thus that most Jews were disloyal to, put baldly, one of their own, in part because of a besetting anxiety. Even when Péguy sought justice for Dreyfus, he did so for the honor of the nation, not for "some universal law."[28] A more promising remedy for the exclusions of modern identity politics must await the theoretical transposition of simultaneously figurative and defigurizing language from literature, via the ministrations of Maurice Blanchot and Emmanuel Levinas, which finds especially promising expression within the French student movement of 1968.

Hammerschlag's reading does not always condescend to read with care. For example, it is not true that Péguy finds in "most of the Jews"[29] a refusal to support Dreyfus that suggests their alleged distinctive "failings" as a people. First, Péguy observed at the time that most Jews indeed defended Dreyfus's innocence.[30] He also repeatedly refers to a limited and initial reluctance to get involved in the campaign to vindicate Dreyfus as a natural human tendency, applying to *human beings in general*. Many people do not wish to get involved in costly and difficult campaigns that do not immediately affect them. When it did occur, this was manifestly a universal human trait for Péguy, not a "Jewish" one; here, as Péguy repeatedly puts it, the Jewish people are "like all peoples" (and Jewish voters are like other voters).[31]

"Anxiety" is for Péguy a human experience, uniquely inflected in Judaism but not uniquely a Jewish one: "Man" as such is a *"puits d'inquiétude"* (a well of anxiety), as he puts it in one of his most famous lines of verse,[32] and Jewish anxiety is "grafted" into Christianity by Jesus himself.[33] Hammerschlag's explicit antihumanism[34] leaves her unmoved by these repeated references to cross-religious affinities and universal human situations, but that does not relieve an author of a need to acknowledge what is clearly and repeatedly in an author's work.

It is also not true that Péguy sees Jews serving only as a typological example for Christians. He expresses his conviction directly that in the Dreyfus affair, Jewish, Christian, and French mysticisms were engaged in "coming together"[35] and "mutually tested," one another[36] in which all three distinctive mysticisms brought out what was best in one another and made it possible for them to work toward the common end of justice.

Furthermore, these identities were in no way mutually exclusive: for Péguy, Bernard-Lazare is not simply or only Jewish—he is also and simultaneously French, and Parisian, and secular in his sensibilities.[37] If there is "essentializing" in Péguy, it is relational and multidimensional, both within individual persons and among different religious, national, and extranational groups.

Similarly, the "dehistoricizing" to which Hammerschlag refers can only be made plausible if it is meant to mark Péguy's failure to be a doctrinaire contemporary historicist. For Péguy, the forms, even the beliefs, in which those elected to fulfill the best (mystical) imperatives embodied by a given historical group can be starkly different according to very diverse historical circumstances, while enjoying an unforeseeable but profound continuity. Péguy, the impoverished anticlerical Parisian writer of 1900, expresses French chivalry in ways very different from Jeanne d'Arc or Louis IX's chronicler Jean de Joinville. As Hammerschlag herself observes, Bernard-Lazare is an atheist[38] (and an advocate of universal justice—things to which Péguy gives unmistakable emphasis).[39] Within the poststructuralist canon, Hammerschlag might have consulted Deleuze's account of repetition in Péguy to avoid a misreading of this kind. Péguy assumes, however, that regardless of historical period, participation in and fidelity to a mysticism generally entails poverty, weakness, and a distance from established institutions, whether those institutions are French, Jewish, Christian, or some mixture thereof.[40]

For Péguy, Jewish, Christian and French (or again, some combination thereof) participation in the Dreyfus affair—what he calls an *"elected affair"*[41]—is a kind of election that cannot be chosen, but can be refused. This way of thinking about election can be harsh in Péguy, but is neither racial nor dehistoricizing. For example, Péguy thought that the mystical-historical role of Dreyfus in the Dreyfus affair was to refuse his pardon and insist on his being declared innocent no matter what the cost, on behalf of all the mysticisms that sought his vindication. A judgment like this one would be a much more promising basis upon which to criticize Péguy's thinking.

The Dreyfus affair in Péguy's account was also not simply an affair of national honor. As Péguy wrote explicitly in *Notre Jeunesse*, it is precisely the universality of injustices that must be fought against, wherever they appear, and in that universal moral rigor, honor may be found. Péguy directs his readers' attention to Bernard-Lazare's willingness to castigate *both* Muslims and Christians for their anti-Semitism and persecution of other minorities whenever it appears around the world, rather than (as many did) speaking of Ottoman "tyranny" and expediently ignoring Christian anti-Semitism.[42]

Another recent history testifies to a similar tendency to assume inescapable, tightly bounded social and linguistic fields in the past. Given the abundant citations of Péguy in a host of twentieth-century Catholic theologians, and specifically his appreciation of Judaism, one would assume that a recent historical account of changing attitudes toward Judaism among Catholics would include Péguy. This would be all the more true given the appreciative comments by Jewish thinkers about Péguy (for example, by Scholem and others). Péguy's close friend Jules Isaac—who later wrote *Jesus et Israël*, in part a thorough accounting of the ways in which Christian anti-Semitism ignored and contradicted Christianity's own Scripture[43]—participated in many organizations and meetings for interreligious dialogue between Christians and Jews, including the Seelisburg conference of 1947. These efforts helped to open the way for the Second Vatican Council's *Nostra Aetate* and other affirmative statements about Judaism in twentieth-century Catholicism. In John Connelly's *From Enemy to Brother: The Revolution in Catholic Teaching on the Jews*, this history is swept aside.

Of course, it is both legitimate and important to research, as Connelly does, Catholic thinking about Judaism in German-speaking Europe, especially in the middle decades of the twentieth century. But Connelly hopes that this partial history of a dense, interconnected contextual *network* of thinkers, in a very specific and recent historical context, can serve as a complete history. Péguy is a sacrifice to this commitment.

Péguy first appears just short of the book's halfway point, where he is mentioned very briefly as a "figure from an earlier generation who might be counted" among those who engaged in respectful, substantive dialogue with Jews and Judaism. But this was not a true and fully articulated commitment on Péguy's part; like Hammerschlag, Connelly assumes that Péguy could not partially yet meaningfully and creatively reconfigure an ambient matrix of discourse. While he was opposed to anti-Semitism, his opposition was prompted by his "personal affection for the Jewish writer Bernard-Lazare." It expressed itself in a statement "written in private to a friend" that Jews were not responsible for the suffering of Jesus, but rather all of human sin was so responsible.[44]

In fact, Péguy wrote at length against anti-Semitism in a host of very public and widely published writings, writings that were read extensively during the interwar years and afterward. It is untrue that a single statement in a letter represents Péguy's full authorial protest against anti-Semitism, or his protests against Jews being unjustly blamed by Christians for things they did not do. It is also not true that the notion that Christian sin as the true cause of the Passion does not appear in any formal writings by Péguy. It can be found in his posthumously published *Clio, Dialogue of History with the Carnal Soul*, in which, among other things, the Christian sinner Péguy is told that through the evil he has done, it is "Jesus that you crucify."[45] Additional remarks to that effect were published by Romain Rolland—a Nobel Prize–winning author and then a figure of international renown—in his memoir of Péguy, published in 1944.[46]

Similar and still more forceful objections to anti-Semitism, and of an ongoing positive relation between Christianity and Judaism, can be found in *Notre Jeunesse* (Péguy's best-known prose writing) and *The Mystery of Jeanne d'Arc's Love* (one of his most famous poems), among others.

Under the heading "The Troubling Origins of the New Vision," Connelly appears to make a major argumentative concession. He acknowledges that a

convert to Catholicism at the center of his history—Ottilie Schwarz—
attributed the origins of her and others' work for a change in Catholic attitudes toward Judaism to the work of "Catholic Dreyfusards" like "Jacques
Maritain [and] Charles Péguy" at the turn of the century. According to Connelly, "other pioneers from the anti-Nazi struggle concurred."[47]

In this way, his own historical protagonists appear to contradict Connelly.
But he adds to the names of Maritain and Péguy that of "their teacher, the
antimodern apocalyptist Léon Bloy."[48] It may well be that some of his sources
conflate these authors; but Connelly endorses that conflation, joining the
"Catholic Dreyfusards" with the "dark and troubling sources"[49] of their
"teacher" Bloy's profound anti-Semitism.

Yet Péguy was not in any way Bloy's student. In fact, Péguy intensely disliked Bloy, took no instruction from him, formally or informally, did not
know him personally, refused to answer letters from him when the anti-Semitic
writer tried to establish a connection with Péguy,[50] and did not cite his work
in thousands of pages of published and unpublished writing. Further, in an
unmistakably dismissive reference to Bloy in conversation, Péguy told his
friend Joseph Lotte in 1912 that Bloy was one of several apocalyptic "idiots."[51]

For Connelly, Bloy opens up distant possibilities for Jewish-Christian reconciliation despite his own ugly anti-Semitism; but those possibilities are
only given their full life, free of poisonous hatred, by the network of interconnected figures at the center of his own, later history. That Péguy had done
so in less "networked" circumstances decades before has been ruled out, above
all by posthumously enrolling him into a "network" to which he clearly did
not belong. To call him Bloy's "student" is a description accurate neither as a
fact nor even—given Péguy's direct and sustained rejection of Bloy and his
work—as a cavernous metaphor.

One might imagine going further than Connelly or Hammerschlag, "sit-
uating" Péguy in a still more conceptually ambitious contextual matrix. One
could argue that his writing is one symptom of subtly shared conceptual commitments manifest in, say, thinking about temporality, alterity, and ethics, at
work in apparently diverse and opposed figures, for example, Péguy, Marcel
Mauss, Paul Claudel, Henri Bergson, Henri Poincaré, and Émile Durkheim.
One could traverse disciplinary boundaries to show, for example, how certain
ideas associated with their different bodies of work were connected to a certain phenomenology of time, simultaneously working through different status networks (say, in universities as opposed to the world of independent writers
in Paris).

It is certainly a possible if radically incomplete and partial project. Among these diverse and often opposed philosophers, scholars, and artists—as we shall see—there is a common fascination with the repetition or the singularity of events in accounts of historical time, in which an "ultimate" knowledge reveals itself by variously affirming either repetition or singularity. There is also a related ethical engagement with two apparent disruptions of modern self-fashioning, generally oriented toward acquisition and self-advancement: sacrifice and the gift.

One might offer some sort of "deft" inversion at the argument's end: for example, Mauss's account of the gift as entrapped by cyclical, interminably immanent repetition could be initially contrasted with Péguy's account of the gift as a primal event, an eruption of eternity into the present, and then both could be referred to the presence of their opposite in one another, so that there is a concluding indeterminacy about the gift as eternally recurring reciprocity in time (Mauss) and the recurrent event of eternity entering time as an infinitely gratuitous gift that can never be reciprocated (Péguy). The distinction between Mauss and Péguy could then be described as one of subtle emphasis within the phenomenological architecture of early twentieth-century European culture—rather than something that requires an understanding of distinct, consequential, and mutually exclusive possibilities.

The appeal of shared conceptual preoccupations is not to be forsworn. But it is also not to be taken as self-evidently "serious" in relation to all other forms of knowledge, including consciously embodied ones—particularly in history.

Conceived somewhat differently, it is a good thing that many contemporary histories are suspicious of heroic, promethean subjectivity. But calcified into an ideological commitment to affirm its opposite, this suspicion itself becomes implausible, and can only sustain itself by tendentious and peremptory readings, ones determined not to see that distinct and consequential events of thought and action indeed happen within complex and unique historical moments. This in turn discloses a striking professional contradiction: from their graduate student days forward, historians are often evaluated supremely on the basis of their ability to do individually distinctive and original work, and yet a principle underwriting a great deal of that individually distinctive and original history-writing assumes either that individual singularity and originality do not exist, or that they are not historically significant.

Péguy is a practitioner of distinctive thinking, and hence he does not fit neatly into our historiographical models. He is not easily collapsed into the standard model of late modern history or the technocratic historicism that accompanies it. He is indeed always inflected by and in conversation with the history around him, but is not encompassed by it.

We shall have to look elsewhere to understand this history—and that is a rare and precious historical opportunity. As the philosopher of science William Wimsatt puts it, "When testing philosophical theories [or historical explanations, one might add] look for the tough cases; ones capable of producing deep and rich counterexamples we can learn from."[52]

In this way, instead of contemporary scholarly guides precluding a free encounter with Péguy and his singular writing, we shall remember those thinkers—Christian, Jewish, and nonbelieving, European and African, men and women alike, from Bespaloff to de Gaulle, from Deleuze to Senghor, von Balthasar, and Benjamin—who were able to read Péguy before the preeminent contemporary models for historical thinking emerged as obstacles to that encounter.

The meeting with Péguy in these pages will take life from the following commitments. First, both the partisans of an immanent becoming and a mechanical, arrested immanence are still very much with us, more than a century after their emergence. Given that reality, simply repeating the predictable, inexorably immanent "contextualizations" in ever more sweeping terms will do precisely nothing to improve our historical understanding—nor will it improve our ability to discern the needs and possibilities of our own historical moment.

Deep historical understanding is not the same as airless, rigidly contextual historicism, in which diverse, one might say, pluperfect pasts only become present as "representations" in circumambulated linguistic, discursive, social, or institutional fields. Péguy's thought draws deeply and creatively from immediate contemporaries, the philosophy of Henri Bergson in particular, as well as the general tendency of thinking in philosophy of science and history associated with Émile Boutroux, Henri Poincaré, and others, not to mention the evanescent cultural and technological opening for intellectually ambitious philosophical journalism. But he is also indebted to, for example, a careful, sustained, and creative reading of Blaise Pascal—he is by no means always repeating the representations of Pascal's thought among his teachers and contemporaries.

The possibility of an encounter with pluperfect pasts may seem odd, given our present intellectual commitments and their penchant for modular, linear time. Yet the possibility of noncumulative, not immediately contextual historical influence is at work well beyond political thought, metaphysical reflection, and literature; it is at work in the most rigorously cumulative and demonstrative disciplines. It is this, as it were, "spooky action at a distance" that allowed Gödel's Platonism to deliver such an extraordinary mathematical riposte to the prevailing logicism of David Hilbert,[53] or that allowed the cataphatic theological commitments of the Moscow school of mathematics—drawn from long-standing prayer practices in Eastern Orthodox Christianity—to open the way to different paths in twentieth-century set theory, beyond those dreamed by French-Cartesian mathematicians.[54] In this way, the present—which is of course simultaneously connected to the recent past and more distant pasts—can also encounter a given distant past as a source of surprising renewal; what Péguy called, in his own very influential neologism, *ressourcement* ("going back to the sources").[55]

Péguy's life and writing offer us a rigorous conversation between past and present, where one can test the tensile interplay of historical contact and distance, inquiring about whether our received categories are truly able to fathom the past and the present alike.

The list of Péguy's distinctive allegiances and positions is remarkable in variety and depth. To start cautiously, Péguy was a socialist, but an anti-Marxist. In France at the turn of the last century, that was not remarkable in itself,[56] but he also refused to align himself with any party, even as he insisted on his socialism and a robust critique of capitalism. To this end, in 1900 he founded his own journal, the *Cahiers de la quinzaine* (Fortnightly Notebooks), for which he refused all advertising in order to guarantee its complete editorial independence. The decision to strike out on his own—before he had earned a university degree, while renouncing expected sources of funding—led him to pursue a life of at times oppressive poverty, occasional if never quite total intellectual isolation, and sometimes resented marginality.

Yet for all that, Péguy was able to bring his work into the life of French and ultimately global letters. In its fourteen years of publication, the *Cahiers* could count among its subscribers the philosopher Henri Bergson, the politician Raymond Poincaré, and the novelists Anatole France, André Gide, Romain Rolland, and Marcel Proust, as well as Alfred Dreyfus and many famous Dreyfusards.[57] Many of them also contributed articles—notably Rolland and France—as well as Julien Benda and Georges Clemenceau. Péguy edited and produced the journal regularly until his death on the eve of the Battle of the Marne.

Within the pages of the *Cahiers* and elsewhere, Péguy was a critic of the emerging intellectual and institutional power of social science, and an advocate of an education dedicated to Greek and Latin, as well as the classics of France literature as they had been gathered into a canon in France over the course of the nineteenth century. Yet Péguy's own poetry often in no way comports with the formal rules of prosody, and it owes a great debt to an incantatory encounter with a very earthy world redolent at once of French peasant culture as well as the meditative, suspensive qualities of compositions by early modernist artists like Claude Monet and Claude Debussy.

Similarly distinctive commitments can be found throughout Péguy's life. Péguy was a great admirer of Émile Zola as a political activist, but not as a novelist. He criticized parliamentary corruption, and the modern ambitions that he believed sustained it, in intemperate language, but was convinced that the countries that had long offered freedom to their citizens were representative democracies like France, Britain, Switzerland, and the United States.[58] He admired both the pastoral serenity and the silent grandeur of the countryside and also his beloved Paris, with its ceaseless bustle and crowds. He could be a turn-of-the-last-century polemicist against modern culture and also an unwavering supporter of the French Revolution and its universalism, as well as a lifelong, very public opponent of anti-Semitism, assuring Bergson months before his own death that he alone could best defend Bergson against the anti-Semites who attacked him.[59]

In those same years, Péguy exhorted his readers to ready themselves for what he wrongly believed would be its world-historical destiny to fight a short, defensive war against a German invasion, in which France would be vindicated as an agent of liberation. Yet he had for some time been skeptical about European imperialism, both in his own writings and by publishing in his journal famous critics of imperialist injustice like E. D. Morel.

Péguy's religious convictions also confound easy preconceptions. In 1907, Péguy returned to Catholicism and became fascinated by what he called "the Christian Revolution." Yet he remained anticlerical and volubly, caustically suspicious of ecclesiastical politics to the end of his life. Upon his death, he was in a remarkable position: he was a vigorous opponent of theological modernism who was simultaneously in danger of having his writings placed on the Vatican's Index of Forbidden Books.

Even this short list of affinities and commitments shows that Péguy does not neatly fit our received categories. That these distinctive commitments existed in the same, at times defiantly anti-institutional person—and above all in a person who was at pains to affirm the essential continuity of his thinking[60]—makes him an intriguing and remarkably revealing historical case.

Finally, his writing took its shape from what was a favorite term; that is, from "revolution," understood comprehensively and with its full range of meaning in French. In this way, Péguy's revolutions of thought are at once an attempt to achieve radical and thoroughgoing change, an act of revolving around an orienting center that repeats a cyclical action in linear time with intimations of constancy and eternity, a return to an origin through perpetual motion, and the process of organic regeneration that allows a forest or field to regain its full depth and vitality, extending itself deep into the soil in order to grow.[61] This organic, earthy fecundity leads naturally to Péguy's affirmation of the "carnal" (*charnel*), and with it the blessings of a spiritually embodied and carnally spiritual life.

Above all, through Péguy's work, it is possible to understand the cultural and intellectual life of Europe's late modernity with fresh eyes, and to understand our own cultural and intellectual world differently.

We shall begin by surveying the range of prominent forms of assumption and inquiry into knowledge, time, truth, the self, and meaning available to him in the Belle Époque. These will be variously adopted, refashioned, and recreated in Péguy's revolutions. Since contexts are porous and multidimensional, a wide variety of conversations are possible, in which the boundaries of different contexts can be opened for exploration.

To sound the fullness of Péguy's thought we shall also have to be God botherers, and there are those who will find that very bothersome indeed. But for those tempted to lament a "troubling nostalgia for the Big Other," or a "dangerous return to the metaphysics of presence," I can offer only a friendly greeting, and be on my way.

A century after his death, Péguy's contrarian life opens our understanding of intellectual and cultural worlds in Europe before the onset of horrifying violence. Those years must never be set aside. Yet it must not also be assumed that absolutely all historical alternatives other than immanent becoming are, after a rapid survey of sources, to be condemned as subtly or overtly responsible for those catastrophes. Still less must we conclude that only an ever more immanent becoming can serve simultaneously as prosecutor, jury, and judge for all alternatives to itself.

Through a historical reading of Péguy—through this singular test case—we can ask different questions of the past, not to enforce the answers of the currently prevailing metaphysics (whose supporters, like their forebears among Péguy's contemporaries, claim with rather touching presumption to stand "after" or "beyond" metaphysics),[62] nor to indulge in the vandalism and malice of their reactionary adversaries. We should free ourselves to wonder whether there are possibilities available to neither of them, an originality disclosed through origins recently obscured that await us still.[63]

CHAPTER I

Modernity, Antimodernity, and Beyond

The standard model of historical explanation for turn of the last-century European culture proposes an amalgam of traditions and long-standing hierarchies, sunk in crisis, defensive, beset by anxiety, forced to fit within an emerging and very different order of things, in which those hierarchies and traditions had become dangerous. At the least, this amalgam left late modern Europe vulnerable to the catastrophes of the twentieth century.

A technocratic historicism has long sought for lattices of social and institutional practices, linguistic patterns, and phenomenological and conceptual structures that decisively shape and often determine thinking and its reception. We have already seen that contemporary scholars assume Péguy cannot partially and meaningfully break free from constrictive notions of identity and cultural "discourses" (often prejudices) that saturate his historical moment, despite his attempt to think beyond them.

To venture out toward this history without the usual assumptions requires us to alight upon popular understanding and rarefied learning and, not least, their attempted reconciliation; to traverse something of politics, culture, philosophy, and science, and sound some tensions in their depths. A few long-standing tendencies will allow us to orient ourselves as we embark.

France had long been considered a or even *the* preeminent culture for certain kinds of "high" or refined expression in the arts and in learned enquiry—not least by the French themselves. It was often assumed that France's intellectual and political culture led the world, or served as a prophetic example for others.

Given the ongoing prominence of intellectual life at the center of French culture, and never far from politics, France's humiliation by Prussia in 1870–1871 was a comprehensive shock, affecting the world of learning, education, and ideas no less than that of military strategy and ministerial politics. The young republic that followed immediately upon that shock was obliged to secure its legitimacy by negotiating the terms of defeat rather than victory, and to rule in the name of stability rather than revolution. That this same republic, in May 1871, brutally crushed a revolutionary insurrection in its own capital immediately after negotiating an end to the war with Germany severely complicated its relationship to France's revolutionary past.

Yet the disorienting defeat to Prussia would not have had the cultural, social, and intellectual power it had in France—even accounting for the long-standing entanglement of political power, intellectual life, and elite culture in France, and especially in Paris—were it not for unsettled questions in the life of the nation and its educated citizens in particular. What is modernity? How modern ought France to be? Was France a revolutionary nation or not? Did France stand for a tradition of cultivated learning and a traditional and integral humanism, or was it dedicated to science and, in the achievement of beauty, an aesthetic of transgression? Was France the secular nation par excellence, or was it at heart Christian, even Catholic?

The answers to these questions in France since the Revolution had swung back and forth, and in recent decades had settled upon an unyielding commitment to ambiguity. The Revolution of 1848 drew inspiration both from the insurrectionary *journées* of the French Revolution and a Christian commitment to the least of these and the life of Jesus;[1] Napoleon III was an advocate of modern technology and industry, the practitioner of a conventional, accommodating piety, and yet by force of arms the defender of the Vatican under Pope Pius IX.

In only partial contrast to that partial piety, Auguste Comte's "scientific" positivism had begun to exert considerable influence on French intellectual life, but Comte's "religion of humanity" struck many of its sympathetic readers as too close to a substitute Catholicism, even as actual Catholicism had a vital ongoing presence in French life.

Within the world of letters, a reader of Charles Baudelaire's great *succès de scandale, Fleurs du mal*—or of his *The Painter of Modern Life*—could be forgiven for thinking that modern art must transgress to say something powerful to its audience. Yet France was also an international capital of traditional artistic techniques and methods, in the visual arts and in monumental architecture, most notably at the École des Beaux-Arts in Paris. That in the middle decades of the nineteenth century, the dominant philosophical movement in the French educational system was Victor Cousin's revealingly named "eclecticism"—itself freely drawing upon Immanuel Kant and German idealism, English and Scottish empiricism, and Cartesian philosophy—expresses a willingness in speculative thought to affirm a combination of philosophies rather than to develop a rigorously unified philosophy, or in Cousin's case, to open the way to a genuine pluralism of diverse and distinct commitments.

Many intellectuals whose careers took shape in the final decades of the nineteenth century believed that under the Third Republic the long-established tendency toward carefully maintained tensions, tactful mixtures, and studied ambiguity about France and the precise nature of its modernity had to end. Émile Durkheim said that the "shock" of defeat

> was the stimulant that reanimated men's minds. The country found
> itself with the same question as at the beginning of the century.
> The organization, or rather the façade, which constituted the
> imperial system [under Napoleon III] had just collapsed; it was a
> matter of remaking another, or rather of making one which could
> survive other than by administrative artifice—that is, one which
> was truly grounded in the nature of things. For that, it was
> necessary to know what this nature of things was: consequently,
> the urgent need for a science of societies made itself felt without
> delay.[2]

The stakes were high, not just for the survival of the French Republic, but also for the fundamental moral order and social cohesion of modern societies. Among others, Durkheim saw his age as one where, as he wrote in 1893, "our faith has been troubled; tradition has lost its sway; individual judgment has been freed from collective judgment . . . if this be so, the remedy for the evil is not to seek to resuscitate traditions and practices which, no longer responding to present conditions of society, can only live an artificial, false existence . . . [yet] it is not a new philosophical system that will relieve the situation."[3]

Durkheim believed that France required nothing less than a science that could in turn lead to a new ethic: for "our first duty is to make a moral code for ourselves."[4]

Many French intellectuals and political figures sought not only a new scientific and moral foundation for French education, but also a new emphasis upon learning of immediate economic and political utility. As Raoul Frary put it in *The Question of Latin* from 1885, in a democratic age when France faced a formidable military enemy across the Rhine, "The cult of the beautiful must not make us neglect the culture of the useful."[5]

Where utility and a new ethic was sought, a very broad educational, political, and ethical inheritance was assumed to be no longer plausible. With that assumption, a desire for distinction and novel thinking entered even elementary moral education.

To trace this change, it is instructive to read two letters by two different ministers of education. Some forty years before the declaration of the Third Republic, in 1833, the education minister at the time, François Guizot, wrote a letter to teachers to accompany an educational reform law. In it, he takes for granted that these teachers will accept a given moral order distinct from but compatible with sacred order, founded upon "virtue and honor" that includes "faith in Providence, the sanctity of duty, submission to paternal authority, the respect due to the laws, to the prince, and to the rights of all."[6]

In 1883, the republican minister Jules Ferry wrote a similar and yet very different letter to teachers. He thinks it necessary to say that there must be a kind of moral instruction "common and indispensable to all," drawn from the common ethical teachings of parents.[7] But, he tells the teachers, in fact "some say" that "your task of moral education is impossible to accomplish," while others say "it is banal and unimportant." He finds himself compelled to warn them away from the cliffs of theory, philosophy, and *dissertations*, and to encourage them to share simple and edifying moral precepts and examples proven by the broadest experience.[8]

Guizot writes an appeal to politically divided instructors who nonetheless cohere around a loose, eclectic moral and cultural consensus. Half a century later, Ferry writes to teachers who are tempted to introduce thoroughgoing forms of moral critique and innovation in primary and secondary schools, or simply to be indifferent to moral instruction as such.

Ferry himself had no doubt what ethics and politics he wished not just for France but for the world. He dedicated himself to secular education and a new French Empire; he told the socialist leader Jean Jaurès that his ultimate purpose was "to organize humanity without God and without a King."[9] Republican leaders and authors repeatedly sounded similar themes and pressed for far-reaching reforms of French education, weakening its connections to classical languages, Christianity, and humanism in favor of a secular education connected to science, modern commerce, and industry.

Not surprisingly, for Ferry and for others, the positivist Comte was a great influence; a fellow leader in the early Third Republic, Léon Gambetta called him "the most powerful thinker of the century."[10] In the same period, the positivist politician, lexicographer, and intellectual Émile Littré affirmed his support for a positivist science of humanity and society but renounced Comte's "religion of humanity."[11] As universities oriented toward specialized research flourished, in accordance with a pruned positivism in the manner of Littré, a statue to Comte was dedicated in 1903 in the Place de la Sorbonne.[12]

It was certainly not the case that Comte stood as some singularly exalted prophet of the new order of things, in some alleged "positivist age." Durkheim among others was well aware of Comte's limitations, including his assumption that history would end neatly with his "positivist" stage.[13] In fact, two other French thinkers loomed very large in the consciousness of those who aspired to create a new settlement for France and, in time, for other nations and peoples..

The first of them was Ernest Renan, the scholar, ex-seminarian, and celebrated author of *La Vie de Jésus*. In the same year that Comte's statue appeared, the town of Tréguier dedicated a statue to its native son Renan, with the novelist Anatole France as the featured speaker.[14] In 1890, his *The Future of Science* had at last been published (Renan had written it in 1848, more than forty years earlier). For Péguy himself, Renan was a crucial figure; while Péguy expressed some early sympathy for him,[15] he later became a sharp critic of Renan's ambitions. For him, Renan was nothing less than "the leader, the boss, and the saint" of the "intellectual party" in modern universities, this party devoted to "modern superstitions" and the "superstition of science."[16] *The Future of Science* constituted the "very book of institution for the modern world."[17]

For Renan, science is the source of all real, nonimaginary knowledge: "Without science he ['Man'] loves only chimeras."[18] Renan claims that the childhood of humanity—especially its ancient past, but for Renan, really any past prior to a modern skeptical, critical turn associated with the eighteenth century—is most powerfully expressed in its myths and religions, which can be beautiful and charming. But the modern scholar understands that they are not true, except as a portrait of humanity's own projected desires and quandaries in a purely human, *historical* time. Hence "the beauty of Beatrice belongs to Dante, not to Beatrice, the beauty of Krishna belongs to the Indian genius, and not to Krishna, the beauty of Jesus and Mary belongs to Christianity, and not to Jesus and Mary."[19]

If until the eighteenth century it was "caprice" and "passion" that ruled the world, now "science contains the future of humanity." In fact it will "organize humanity scientifically," and with humanity, God.[20] "Science is therefore a religion . . . science alone can resolve for man the eternal problems for which his nature imperiously demands the solution."[21]

With its advance, modern criticism will "destroy every system of belief marred by supernaturalism."[22] While religious orthodoxy "petrifies" thought, science is open to constant progress. Words like "decadence" have no meaning, and absolute meaning is found only in reason and science.[23]

For Renan, the triumph of this "reason" will be accomplished neither by demonstrable proofs, nor by philosophical argument, nor by polemic in the manner of Voltaire, but by a kind of persistent indirection and suggestive rhetoric. He says,

> [When] I want to initiate young minds into philosophy, I start by any subject, I speak in a certain sense and in a certain tone, I take little care that they retain the positive information to which I am exposing them, I do not even try to prove it to them; but I insinuate a spirit, a manner, a turn; then, when I have injected [*inoculé*] them with this new sense, I leave them to look for what they please, and to build their temple following their own style. Here begins individual originality which it is necessary to respect supremely . . . there is a religious way to take hold of things, and that way is mine.[24]

If Renan's manner of "scientific" instruction is allusive, gestural, and insinuating, the actual progress of science and learning will be secured by the bourgeois, rigorously specialized scholar. Renan has little use for aristocratic dilettantes, and for an unlettered "people." They can be prepared for enlightened participation in public life and learning in some indeterminate future.[25] The meticulous scholar is a champion of "critique," ready for the work of analysis[26] rather than creation. Critique can be applied anywhere and is often superior to its object, which may be a piece of culture without claims to artistic greatness: "a frivolous novel" or "a madrigal."[27] Critique is quite pointedly not a form of rigorous philosophical skepticism but rather a continual examination of prior assumptions, toward a "more pure and advanced truth."[28]

Instead of seeking some creative synthesis—or an unfortunate declaration of first principles—the modern research scholar, Renan continues, should devote himself to a well-defined subdiscipline (it becomes "a little world where he encloses himself stubbornly and scornfully") and produce specialized monographs within it, even as he shares his work with other scholars to produce further knowledge.[29] The scholar should *not* hope that his work will outlast him. He should be pleased to have, with a life's labors, added "an obscure stone . . . without name" to the great "temple" of secular knowledge.[30]

For Renan, the numberless monographs of modern scholars will be of inexpressibly greater use than a metaphysical statement about the nature of the world or being. The nineteenth century, claims Renan, is not a century of metaphysics, and certainly not of religion. In a circular thought, he believes that the historical moment demands critique, above all through historical and philological scholarship; they are the replacements for both religion and metaphysics, and should be.[31]

As the foregoing suggests, the argument of *The Future of Science* is not always remorseless in its rigor. After announcing that belief in God is implausible and discredited, Renan offers a conclusion that recalls the loss of his own faith with only a measure of irony, and plays with the possibility that he may be wrong to reject it.[32] He claims there is nothing special, unique, or true (or, if one prefers, "true") about classical civilization but then defends its contested prominence in education on linguistic and cultural grounds.[33] He writes boldly as a herald of the age of reason, but renounces speculative, philosophical reason, and commends insinuation as the most effective pedagogy for the emerging scientific age. Perhaps above all, despite the declared absence of metaphysics in modern thought, he also announces the very metaphysics to which he and other modern scholars have pledged and should pledge themselves. They work "to substitute the category of becoming for that of being, the conception of the relative for the conception of the absolute, movement for immobility."[34]

For Renan, the destination of this scientific world was entirely open; it would not serve or fulfill the human but perhaps transcend it entirely. The progress of knowledge might lead to a future in which humanity itself is superseded—in which "humanity will have disappeared"[35]—a prospect he proposes with equanimity.

In addition to Comte and Renan, there was a final, more distant philosophical forebear who appears with considerable regularity among the writers, scholars, and publicists of these new settlements of culture, society, and politics in the Third Republic: René Descartes. For Durkheim, readers must remember that France is "the country of Descartes." Hence France must, Durkheim says, "bring things back to definite notions."[36] The search for a science of society must "systematically discard all preconceptions," as Descartes and Francis Bacon did.[37] Descartes' physiological speculations were still respectfully (if critically) addressed in articles about neuroscience as well. In January 1897, an academic journal usually dedicated to scholarship—the *Revue de métaphysique et de morale*—went further, and published a poem by Sully Prudhomme entitled "Descartes." There the philosopher appears as hero, his "glory forever without rival / Tomorrow we will build, with all your writings / With the hands of France a triumphal arch / Through which the august army of minds will pass!"[38]

Descartes, Comte, and Renan served as points of reference and inspiration for those seeking to build a new, self-consciously modern and scientific order in France in the late nineteenth century—but why? What possibilities did they hold within their work that other thinkers did not, and what was drawn from each of them?

For various scientific and social-scientific theorists of the Third Republic, Descartes in particular offered the assumed example of a radical break with a discredited past. Whatever intellectual historians might make of that dubious assessment, it clearly inspired Durkheim and others. To cast away assumptions in search of secure and certain knowledge was assumed to be an enterprise of immediate relevance.

Still more than in Descartes' *Discourse on Method*, the break with the past would now be collective in form. Its rhetorical affect was that of meticulous exactitude in accord with consensual disciplinary boundaries, not bold and distinctive metaphysical argument, and it would vindicate its authority through the work of specialized scholars. For Descartes, Renan, and Comte alike, advances in the sciences would come through the accumulation of many individual studies, leading to a magnificent edifice—what Descartes called his rebuilt "house" of secure and certain knowledge, above all of medicine, that would be built while he lived provisionally by a more conventional morality,[39] and what Renan (as we have seen) called a "temple." At the turn of the last century, some sought a science of society, others a physcial science of human being as such, as in psychomotor research and the workings of the brain. But for all their differences, the social and intellectual form for the acquisition and accumulation of knowledge—immanent, collaborative, credentialed, specialized—was assumed.

Yet Descartes was not quite the thinker to vindicate that change in every particular. Comte provided the means of exit from philosophy into the social sciences, above all via sociology. Durkheim remarked, in a Kantian turn of phrase, that sociology began under the "tutelage" of philosophy,[40] and his-

.torically, it was Comte who offered the path from that tutelage to a discipline that could in turn master philosophy. Durkheim certainly believed that sociology would be required to renew or even refound philosophy: "Nowadays it is universally agreed that philosophy, unless it relies upon the positive sciences, can only be a form of literature."[41] As for ethics, "it is social science that takes up the problems that up to now belonged exclusively to philosophical ethics."[42]

Similarly, through Renan, many writers, scholars, and theorists could find an expansive account of what science was and how it could best assure its progress. The days of Cartesian argument against radical skepticism, first principles, and metaphysics should serve as inspiration for precisely no one. In the "scientific" world Renan saw coming into being, one would simply assume that individual human agency counted for very little, that the idiom and methods of the modern bourgeois scholar were the best or at least the most lucid possible expressions of human understanding, that becoming and the relative were real, and that being and the absolute were superfluous or illusory.

These thinkers gave overlapping ambitions for many of the new intellectual and cultural settlements of the Third Republic. France—and ultimately the world—were ready to be organized by communities of scientists natural and social, and they were ready to enter into the domains of society, culture, humanities, the mind, the soul, and God.

These projects were loosely allied with one another but by no means the same, in method, cultural and political views, and in discrete professional ambitions. Durkheim was not a materialist, as many contemporary partisans of a fully naturalist account of the mind were; Marcel Mauss and others were socialists, Durkheim was not. Durkheimian sociology confidently asserted its authority over social facts without historical or geographic boundaries; but Durkheim also believed the nation-state to be a modern communal form especially well suited to address the problem of anomie, while Renan predicted the eventual attenuation of that same nation-state.

Amid all these differences, however, these thinkers tended to share certain assumptions. Important among them was an abiding sense that conscious experience, free will, and individual agency were of little import. As Durkheim put it on behalf of his own disciplinary commitments, "Individuals are much more a product of common life than they are determinants of it" and "the duties of the individual towards himself, are, in reality, duties toward society."[43] For "everybody knows how full the consciousness is of illusions . . . every causal relationship is unconscious."[44]

Furthermore, in their scientific anti-pathos, they no longer spoke freely and rigorously of love, as so many of their freethinking predecessors had. It is this change that makes most sense of Péguy's remark in 1913, "The world has changed less since the time of Jesus Christ than it has in the last thirty years,"[45] and that, "The free thinkers of that time were more Christian than our devout Christians of today."[46] He perceived a sea change in modern secular notions of human fulfillment.

While different forms of modern skepticism and progress generally denied the possibility of divine revelation, through the middle decades of the nineteenth century, many Deist and atheist philosophies settled their ethics and philosophical anthropology upon assumptions drawn from Christianity, above all by affirming the ultimate importance of an at once personal and universal love, or charity.

At the very origins of modern philosophy and philosophies of science, the motives for modern ambitions are said to be charitable ones. The demands of Christian charity explicitly justify Bacon's scientific investigation and call to complete the conquest of nature,[47] just as it is the goodness of God and the care of the body he has created in love that justify Descartes's claim to acquire medical knowledge above all, since the health of the body is the "first of all human goods" and further, it is "greatly sinning" against the supreme commandment (that is, love of God and one's neighbor) not to occupy ourselves with medical research.[48]

During the eighteenth-century Enlightenment, even a vehemently anti-Christian materialist like Julien Offroy de La Mettrie carefully keeps open the possibility of personal immortality in *L'Homme machine*, as well as emphasizing the possibility of a natural reconciliation with one's enemies through love and virtue.[49] In a different way, Kant argues that practical reason demands that we believe in an ultimate reconciliation of happiness and justice in a world where death is no more, guaranteed by God, in an infinite movement toward the Highest Good.[50] When Kant does reflect (with a certain playfulness upon a forbidding theme) upon the possibility of an eschatological end to history, it is possible, he says, only "should Christianity ever reach the point where it ceases to be worthy of love."[51]

The Deist or atheistic desire to relate to a positive infinity, in the sense of a historical horizon that represents the complete fulfillment of human aspiration through benevolence to and love for others, reaches its apogee in the most eminent atheists of the mid-nineteenth century: Auguste Comte and Ludwig Feuerbach.

Feuerbach declares the advent of a new "religion of humanity," whose acceptance would inaugurate an age of fully human flourishing, in which justice, creativity, and science would dwell as one upon a newly sacred earth, tended by an ultimately unified humanity freed from its ancient alienations, united by love.[52] Similarly, Comte foretold an era of humanist priests attending his own religion of humanity, in which true knowledge of human beings and society would beget universal well-being and fraternal happiness founded upon "altruism,"[53] to use Comte's neologism.

By the end of the nineteenth century these ordering temporal and humanistic unities—which sustained non-theological but exalted notions of positive, even infinite human flourishing through universal love—were decomposing in philosophy and the more exacting, elite forms of political and cultural criticism. It is not only that Émile Littré could defend Comtean positivism while repudiating Comte's religion of humanity as an embarrassment. In his notebooks, Nietzsche mocked Feuerbach and others as thinkers who "reeked of theologians and Church Fathers,"[54] and elsewhere exhorted his contemporaries not to hold timidly to Christian morality and anthropology without faith in Christ, but to repudiate root and branch Christian notions of self, goodness, people, and purpose as well as Christian faith (even if one built upon their ruins, that is, upon the inward turn of will to power accomplished by Judaism and Christianity).

In Durkheimian social science, religion was not the gradual entry to some more "total" or "real" universal, even mystical or exalted love, nor did it require comprehensive study of the ongoing history of religion as a whole, as Benjamin Constant, Hegel, or Feuerbach did. It became an object of fascination for prominent sociologists through a meticulous, detached, putatively objective inquiry that methodically disassembled its most "primitive" forms and rejected mysticism.

Early sociology often occupied itself with religion; Durkheim remarked in a memorable turn of phrase that in the mid-1890s, the study of religion "was a *revelation* for me."[55] For Durkheim and others, religion disclosed its essence in its most primitive states: it was first and finally a social, entirely immanent phenomenon, that was not on its way to some more perfect and expansive love. For the sociologist, there is no relation of love toward one's subject, or toward the purpose of the enquiry: the same sort of objective method could be applied to locate elemental religious structures elsewhere, properly cleansed of their particularity, and allow them to be understood as general, social facts and forms. Social facts were common things—and things for Durkheim were "any object of knowledge which is not naturally penetrable by the understanding." They had to be studied as such in a rigorous science of societies, which would rigorously dispense with all "preconceptions."[56] This science would "avoid" all "mysticism," with "constant care," and even those sociologists ambivalent about the more robust Durkheimian assertions did not waver upon this question.[57]

It is his study of religion among especially "primitive" peoples—the Aborigines of Australia—that (Durkheim believed) permitted him direct and objective access to the original essence of religious life, that is, as a social phenomenon dealing with the sacred and the profane. For Durkheim, "whenever we try to explain something human viewed at a particular point in time—whether a religious belief, a moral law, a legal precept, an aesthetic practice, or an economic system—we must begin by returning to its simplest and most primitive form."[58]

Whatever the possibilities of primitive religion, the organic, messy contingency of narrative history, with room for meaningful agency and free will, was for many sociologists no less suspect than mysticism or universal love. For example, the sociologist François Simiand (who worked closely with Durkheim) took to the pages of *La Revue de synthèse historique* in 1903 to criticize the practice of history precisely for its failure to consign events and personal agency to its own disciplinary past. For Simiand, historians should seek regularity and "if possible, laws" along with other "positive sciences."[59] Durkheim and other social scientists agreed.[60]

In his essay "Historical Method and Social Science," Simiand instructs historians that, along with sociologists, we are to "clear our minds of these metaphysical relics" that lead them to assume that there are material facts but not social facts.[61] The realm of the objective is that which is "independent of our individual spontaneity,"[62] and thus social life can be considered objectively. All sciences use abstractions, but Simiand believes that "fortunate abstractions"[63] are those that lead to the establishing of regularities and ultimate laws—of natural science or social life. The notion of individual agency as a cause of change was naïve, and itself a late historical product of "social development"; the historian should be willing to apply an assertive skepticism (it seems almost an assumption of error) to the testimony of individuals in history trying to explain the reasons for their own actions. That is to introduce "explanation by final causes," which is an "illusion" not acceptable in the "positive sciences."[64]

For Simiand, it may be true that particular historical events or the decisions of individual human beings in time can be unpredictable—and in that sense contingent—but Simiand believes that true history must not tarry over them. He scolds the historian Charles Seignobos for arguing that the political history of France—for example, in an account of the Revolutions of 1830 and 1848—had anything to do with the work of "obscure republicans" and "democratic and socialist agitators," who, according to Simiand, are present in different nations and historical epochs without revolutions.[65] The scientific causes were the "social disintegration accomplished by the [French] Revolution" as well as, with the Restoration and July Monarchy, "the maladaptation of reestablished governments to new social tendencies, [and] a collective disposition of minds."[66] While history cannot ignore events entirely, it must seek to obtain "stable and definite relations" independent of events,[67] and thus laws independent of temporal specificity or historical singularity.

In his ambitions for a comprehensively scientific account of the human in history and beyond, Simiand did not speak only for sociology. By the early years of the twentieth century, a scientific turn had left few disciplines untouched, from political economy to the humanities to psychology.

Léon Walras—who would later be lauded or condemned as one of the founders of efficient market economics—wrote a book attempting to reconcile his sympathies with liberalism and socialism[68]—his *Studies of Social Economy*—in 1896. Among his goals was to abandon the moral and qualitative arguments of traditional political economy in favor of a rigorously demonstrable "scientific truth"[69] of economics.

Others would make even more expansive claims, as a "scientific" ethos spread to the humanities themselves. Gustave Lanson wrote that for reasons of intellectual honesty and national security alike, the scientific "esprit" should "predominate everywhere, even in literary education," since "science alone imparts the taste and the sense of the truth." Following a similar logic, historians like Charles Langlois and Seignobos rejected any role for aesthetics in history: a kind of denuded knowledge was the only purpose of their work.[70] Lanson went further: "The true modern humanities are the sciences."[71] In fact, Lanson said he had "no difficulty" in acknowledging that in contrast to those who work upon "the construction of laws and generalizations" above, those who "do literary history" properly "work in the basement of science."[72]

The natural sciences themselves—if one inexplicably persists in the puerile hope that the true humanities are the humanities—flourished in the New

Sorbonne and the research institutes of Paris. In particular, they promised imminent breakthroughs in the study of human beings as scientific objects. For
example, a breathless article by the biologist Alfred Dastre of the Sorbonne,
entitled simply "The Nervous System," was published in April 1900 in the
widely circulated and intellectually prestigious journal *Revue des deux mondes*.
Dastre declared, "One day, we can hope to know the laws that regulate the material states of the brain, the relations that exist among them, their sequences
and their reciprocal influences. They will be the same laws, the same relations,
the same sequences that will allow us to go to the other side of the ditch, into
the psychological domain, to illuminate the functioning of the soul."[73]

According to Dastre, a host of findings from scholars around the world
would take modern science to this seemingly ultimate materialism, in which
the soul would be understood above all as matter in motion. Some excitedly
reported results could seem rather modest: an uncharitable observer might
conclude that the notion that frogs whose brains are removed have a sort of
consciousness in their spinal fluid[74] and that degrees of consciousness ascend
to voluntary movement, stands at some considerable remove from a materialist eschaton. But Dastre assures his readers that "no other scientific field is more
investigated," with "so many publications and papers." One "could fill libraries with the ones that appear each year."[75]

Yet Dastre not only declared his confidence that materialism would only
grow in explanatory power. He also, somewhat more discreetly, acknowledged
his *assumption* that questions of volition and consciousness must be bracketed
out of the field altogether (though the field was itself fascinated by consciousness). Dastre acknowledged this undemonstrable commitment. He wanted
"to avoid entering into philosophical controversies" by limiting the discipline
to physical motions and objects.[76]

Similar projects that aspired to collapse mind into brain enjoyed considerable prominence in the early decades of the Third Republic. In 1881, Théodule Ribot published *The Diseases of Memory*,[77] in which memory was assumed
to be an entirely physiological phenomenon: by 1906, it had gone through eigh-
teen editions,[78] and by that time Ribot had long been a professor at the Collège de France. Other research in Paris—following some of the work done in
Germany by Wilhelm Wundt (whose own positions were relatively nuanced)—
became fascinated by the possibilities of physiology as a way to investigate
the brain, itself the focus of an international community of researchers.[79] Consciousness was not a reliable or especially interesting witness to experience;

rather, the trained scientist could disclose what personal, qualitative experience had long hidden.

Throughout higher education and educated commentary, the prestige of natural and social science, and their imitative forms in the humanities, had undergone a meteoric ascent between 1870 and 1900. Altering Péguy's term slightly, one could speak of an intellectual *coalition*—less unified than Péguy's own term "party," more cohesive than a tendency—that had achieved great prominence at the start of the new century.

For all their differences, the members of this coalition conceived time in unwaveringly linear terms, and history as material, moral, social, and above all scientific progress along that temporal line. It inclined strongly to reject both religious revelation and "high" metaphysics as incredible artifacts of a more primitive past ("really" belonging to earlier points along that temporal line), and believed that accompanied by a scholarly affect of meticulous bourgeois sobriety—adopted by trained specialists engaged in the Cartesian crowdsourcing of knowledge—a generally positivist notion of science would lead humanity forward. Freedom was not to be found in an affirmation of free will (now understood to be not only inflected or constrained but severely restrained or even determined entirely by either material or social laws); rather, it was to be found through a cumulative critique and repudiation of the past and its "illusions" in favor of brain studies and neurology, social fact, mathematically driven economics, history, and literature as scientific disciplines, and so on.

By pursuing these ends, both national and global society would embark upon a course of perpetual reformation, more just, more rational, and faithful to fact. New laws of nature and society—variously of history, technology, and money—would be the fundaments of novel and uncompromisingly modern orders of things. In particular, with rare exceptions, the thought and culture of all ages prior to the late eighteenth century now serve primarily as *raw materials* for academic industries of scholarship and science, rather than seeking out the work of a more distant history as a dialogical partner in understanding. In Renan's radical forms of a "future science," if human beings must eventually become raw materials in turn—for a science that conquers human nature as the last frontier in the conquest of nature—so be it.

Beyond their stated intellectual ambitions, the members of this broad intellectual coalition held very considerable influence over academic appointments, as well as ambitious reforms of French education, from primary school through university. This was especially true for Durkheim and his students.

The social sciences in particular began to institutionalize themselves in French education in the thirty years before the Great War. The theology faculty in French universities was abolished in 1885.[80] The next year, the École Pratique des Hautes Études founded a "fifth section" dedicated to the study of "religious sciences," in which sociologists associated with Durkheim were soon appointed in significant numbers.[81] The fifth section assumed the unique legitimacy of modern research methods and applied them to explain a past in modern social-scientific terms; in this sense, it was altogether different from a theology faculty, which tries to interpret an exemplary or revelatory past, through which the present can better understand itself.

Sociology positions had been almost nonexistent in French universities, and students trained by Durkheim and his circle began to occupy posts in "law, education, linguistics, religion," and other disciplines, as well as teaching philosophy in lycées.[82] This led many advocates of other disciplines to conclude that Durkheim and his circle were academic conquistadores, building their movement at the expense of their own.[83] The fact that there was a formal requirement for the president of the French Republic to approve academic appointments[84] gave the rapid ascent of Durkheimian sociology a political cast.

The ascent of Durkheim and his allies was particularly striking: by 1902, Durkheim was appointed to the chair for the science of education at the Sorbonne, and eventually his course on pedagogy was required for any student seeking certification as a teacher at the Sorbonne or the École Normale Supérieure.[85] Along with his friendships with national educational administrators like Paul Lapie, it was difficult not to perceive Durkheimian sociology as quite deliberately on the march: a sympathetic scholar like Steven Lukes concludes that Durkheim's "overriding project was an imperialistic sociological penetration and co-ordination of the various social sciences."[86]

Since 1897, French universities had been free to create degrees in various disciplines, including social sciences, at a time when universities in Paris and elsewhere also began to reward specialized research rather than knowledge of the humanities and teaching.[87] It was a period for founding new professional associations and journals, most famously the *Année sociologique*, which began publication in 1898, intended for both scholars and educated general readers. The task of the journal demanded a grasp of developments in international scholarship, especially work published in English, Italian, and German in addition to French.[88]

These changes were associated with the emergence of the New Sorbonne, dedicated to research and often to positivist methods of research and, in history, to what was thought to be a meticulously objective account of historical context. For example, the literary historian Gustave Lanson's work on Voltaire's *Lettres philosophiques* in 1909 was a pure instance of its kind; Lanson claimed to want only to present "a commentary from *sources*, nothing more."[89] In this way of thinking, the idea of historical differences made legible by referring any portion of it to a continuous human experience or "nature" was assumed to be implausible, unscholarly, and inclined toward a naïve aestheticism.[90]

Alongside these changes in higher education, reforms in 1902 created a sequence for secondary education that allowed students to avoid Greek and Latin entirely, in favor of a heavier emphasis on the sciences and to some extent modern languages as well. In terms strongly reminiscent of Frary's exhortation seventeen years earlier, the instructions accompanying the decree made it clear that these changes would give to any student "the instruction most useful in view of his future career."[91]

This intellectual coalition constituted the disciplinary mainstream in diverse and prominent academic fields, it changed the shape of secondary education, and it enjoyed some considerable purchase and prestige in the more ambitious reaches of generalist intellectual journalism. Of course it was not the only sort of vibrant intellectual enterprise—or orienting constellation for experiences of culture, art, and life—available in an age of neo-Kantians, socialists, and anarchists, not to mention symbolists, impressionists and post-impressionists, naturalists, and many others. But this intellectual coalition enjoyed an unmistakable civic and institutional pride of place in the Third Republic and to some considerable degree in an emerging international scholarly community as well. Others took their bearings from it, in appreciation or protest.

Reaction

The intellectual coalition found an adversary in an intensely political reaction. It self-consciously opposed the commitments of that coalition, as well as its association with the nascent egalitarian, positivist rhetoric of the Third Republic. It was directed against the intellectuals associated with that republic, and it did not hesitate to indulge in vitriol. "Agathon" (the collective pseudonym of the young Henri Massis and Alfred de Tarde, both of them admirers of Charles Maurras) referred to Durkheim's "intellectual despotism" over the academic life of the Sorbonne.[92]

Much of reaction was in fact devoted to expansive condemnations; with them came a rejection of universalism in favor of an exclusive and sometimes integral nationalism. The front page of the right-wing, anti-Semitic newspaper *La Libre parole* (*Free Speech*), founded in 1892, carried the motto "France for the French."[93] In a campaign speech for the Chamber of Deputies in 1898, the author Maurice Barrès declared that France no longer needed "the Jew, the foreigner, the cosmopolitan"; the "foreigner, like a parasite, poisons us." Whatever new energy France requires, "it will find in itself," from its own "poorest [and] most downtrodden."[94]

In particular, reaction found a common anti-universalist cause in a pervasive anti-Semitism.[95] It allowed right-wing movements with exiguous political appeal to engage in demagoguery targeting a vulnerable minority,[96] it drew upon a still potent Christian anti-Judaism, and it created conditions in which every Jewish person who enjoyed some success in the new republic could be scapegoated, forced into the role of villainous archetype, representing everything about modernity that reactionaries disliked.

The rhetoric of anti-Semitic reaction was acidulous, and often inclined to scientific pretensions. For example, the putative Jewish "effect" on French life could be described by anti-Semites as analogous to the "breeding of microbes."[97] Édouard Drumont's *La France juive*—which sold over a hundred thousand copies within a year of its publication in 1886[98]—included frankly racist ruminations, even though these were not systematic in the manner of the mid-century French racist Arthur de Gobineau or of twentieth-century racist "science." Drumont claimed that the "Jewish conquest" was part of a transhistorical struggle between "Semites" and "Aryans," a struggle that required not just ethnographic and psychological comparisons but "physiological" ones as well.[99] Drumont's polemic careened from racism, to prolix reflection upon the allegedly baleful effects of Jews on French history (especially modern French history), to occasional moves in the direction of purported Christian grievances. Drumont variously implies and asserts that the Basque Ignatius of Loyola was a "pure Aryan," that Jews inspired Luther and the Protestant Reformation, and that German Jews "organized" the notorious "Culturkampf" [*sic*] against German Catholics.[100]

Anti-Semitism had a poisonous efflorescence with the great event of Péguy's youth, the Dreyfus affair. A distinguished young officer in the French Army, Alfred Dreyfus, had been falsely accused of treason in 1894; his Judaism motivated and sustained the campaign to convict him, to manufacture forged evidence against him, and to send him into solitary confinement on

Devil's Island, where it was hoped he would quickly die. Many associated with the republican intellectual coalition eventually became convinced that Dreyfus was innocent and worked as "Dreyfusards" to secure his release and ultimate exoneration. In contrast to them, French reactionary movements— including Catholic political conservatism, in the form of newspapers like *La Croix* (The Cross)—disgorged a torrent of anti-Semitic writing to vilify and calumniate Dreyfus, and in fact all Jews. The careers of far-right anti-Semitic intellectuals like Charles Maurras and Maurice Barrès were energized by the affair.

If anti-Semitic politics was a shared base for French reaction in the Belle Époque, the theoretical justification for right-wing politics aspired to reach for wider and deeper accounts of history, culture, and politics, with a revealing relationship to the arts, to political economy, and to science.

In *The Future of Intelligence* (1905), for example, Maurras, founder of the influential and extreme right-wing Action Française, rejects all manner of practices and commitments associated with the Third Republic. He has no use for democracy, and anticipates its end.[101] He turns to parody to denounce a "government of opinion" in contemporary France,[102] as well as a general, softening decadence he associates with romanticism, descended from traditions and authors "of foreign origin" like the Swiss Jean-Jacques Rousseau and Madame de Staël.[103] Quoting a contemporary critic approvingly, he finds French literary culture in need of "national discipline."[104]

For Maurras, France has a culture of letters corrupted both by romanticism and by modern capitalism; the latter has control of both culture and government,[105] and force and interests in French society are no longer aligned with intelligence.[106] Yet an ongoing freedom of opinion is *not* the answer to this problem. Rather, there must be a concerted effort to take over some "citadel" of money and use capital against itself.[107] Hostile to freedom of opinion as an ideal, Maurras was also explicitly opposed to feminism, and he found in contemporary women poets the dangerous expression of a "feminized" culture.[108]

Amid these denunciations, he lavished praise upon a thinker who was an "enemy of democracy" and "Protestantism," and who opposed the "doctrines" of the French Revolution.[109]

Yet here things become considerably more complicated: the thinker of these thoughts is Auguste Comte. *The Future of Intelligence* is Maurras and French reactionary politics at its most theoretically ambitious, and in its pages Maurras bestows praise upon Comte at almost every opportunity, as liberally as many of his contemporary "progressive" antagonists in universities and letters alike. At the outset of the book, Maurras declares that it is "the genius of Auguste Comte" that "instituted the magnificent rule" known by "the name of Positivism."[110] There is "no name that one must pronounce with a more lively gratitude."[111] For Comte sought a "science of societies"[112] and saw that the future must include the integrative, even supreme role of this science—sociology. He also understood that, in Comte's own words, glowingly quoted by Maurras, "man must be more and more subordinated to humanity" (which Maurras interprets as individual submission to particular collectives). There is indeed progress, but as Comte said, "Progress is the development of order."[113]

In a limited but surprising way, Maurras agrees with many of his adversaries in the preponderant intellectual coalition. For him as much as for Renan and Durkheim, the future is scientific, and social science is the key to realizing the possibilities of that future. Time, and with it history, is inexorably and progressively linear. Maurras quotes Comte in a manner that, absent the identifying source, would not have incurred the opposition of a sociologist like Simiand. There is no "freedom of conscience" in astronomy or physics, because there we have scientific principles established by "competent men." It is different in politics because the old principles are gone, and new ones have not yet been secured.[114] But Maurras, still quoting Comte, agrees that it is science that will find the principles of a new order and "reorganize society."[115]

Of course, the Maurrassian vision is distinct: Maurras seeks a polity without elections, in which those who rule designate their own successors.[116] Religion plays a prominent role, even without faith in God, in which humanity itself, in Comtean fashion, becomes an object of divine reverence.[117] The past is indeed a yoke upon the present, but a "noble" one,[118] integrated into the science of the future. Maurras, unlike someone like Littré, thinks that the late Comte was quite right to move in the direction of an allegedly scientific religion.

Maurras offers a reading of Comte in order to propose a future broadly "authorized" by Comte; many in the intellectual coalition warmed to the same task but emphasized a certain series of questions and methods extrapolated from Comte, rather than his discrete ambitions for an applied sociology instantiated in cultural and spiritual life. Their differences move amid many more affinities and homologies than one would assume. It is a disagreement about what precisely a truly scientific, truly modern future—drawn from and inspired by an inexorable sociological positivism—demands.

This should in no way be mistaken for the historically facile and morally irresponsible claim that in response to the immediate moral questions of their own time, right-wing reaction and the advocates of immanent becoming at the turn of the last century were the same. Among other things, the unifying importance of anti-Semitism among the acolytes of reaction is an enormous moral difference between the two groups, as is the clearly stronger commitment to due process among reaction's opponents. Upon questions of method and argument, there are other distinctions: Maurras wrote belles-lettres, a genre of inquiry and reflection that Durkheim, for example, had detested from his student days. But for all that, it is essential to understand that on questions of science, sociology, and time, the work of Maurras and, say, Renan, Durkheim, and Simiand participated in shared, profound, and eminently debatable philosophical and historical assumptions.

What is still more remarkable is that this Comtean, sociological fascination, spreading its wings to cast its shadow across the political and cultural spectrum, became in that very moment the target of penetrating criticism. Furthermore, this critique of the "received" positivist account of science—of flat, linear time, of cumulative scientific progress in the formulation of demonstrable laws, of science as methodically secure and perpetually, progressively liberating itself from contamination by the archaic, the subjective, the uncertain and the imprecise, intended to make a science of society and an ethics for modernity to replace what had been definitively superseded—did not arrive only in the form of artistic protests by Montmartre bohemians, prompted by absinthe-infused dreams, laboring *épater le bourgeois*. It came from within the labor and reflection of science itself—and at the very highest levels.

Science Questioning Science; Philosophy Unbowed

In 1898, the mathematician and philosopher Gaston Milhaud published an article in the *Revue de Métaphysique et de morale*, entitled "La Science rationelle." It expresses the unmistakable brio of a confident contrarian. Milhaud repeatedly emphasizes how science depends upon the given, including temporal givens. For example, we assume the notion of "succession in time" as when thunder follows lightning; we do not establish them in each instance.[119] We cannot make a precise comparison of "consecutive duration," nor can we know what "series of circumstances" would be required for perfect identities of temporal measurement.[120] (This is equally true in the twenty-first century: even with satellites and the Global Positioning System, time is a consensus among different time measurements, for "not all labs calculate their clock data exactly the same way." In truth, "the algorithm" now used to calculate exact time requires "individual mathematical artistry" that gives an "exact" Universal Coordinated Time, about a month later, in the form of a newsletter.)[121]

Then there are those nontemporal elements that, "*constructed*," are often "quite close to the *given*."[122] Nonspecialists assume that the planets move in a smooth ellipse around the sun, for example, but that depends upon the points used to chart a planet's trajectory. We must acknowledge "with astronomers that the immobility of the sun is still only a fiction, and that, in sum, the movement of the planets as we represent it today is always a relative movement."[123] Similar ambiguities surround the use of central concepts in physics, like "the proportionality of force to acceleration."[124]

Scientific instruments are assumed to endow measurement with perfect exactitude, but in actual experiments, instruments must be accompanied by "a host of corrections," for "temperature, atmospheric pressure, air density, etc."[125] There are theories devoted to standard formulae for correction, but absolute precision exists neither in the instruments themselves nor in the rules for their adjustment. Even the most rigorous experiments rely upon a mass of assumptions, postulates, and instruments that are all being tested in the experiment, rather than the test being confined to a single isolated variable or series of variables. Many different accounts of the same scientific observations can be given.[126] Given all these realities, the "postulates, concepts, [and] the constructions that we have indicated are indispensable to the understanding of these [scientific] laws" would "also well deserve the name of chimeras, if this word was reserved for all that is not directly verifiable."[127]

Milhaud awakens his readers from a Cartesian dream of demonstrable certitude, reconfigured by Comtean positivism and its descendants. Yet he calls upon a phrase in Comte's own writing to undo what Milhaud called "the exaggerated promises of positivism," since Comte once acknowledged that hypotheses are not necessarily a faithful, neutral representation of the real, and are chosen for their "advantages."[128] Hence Milhaud does not argue for thoroughgoing skepticism about all knowledge, but he insists that science must recognize the "active intervention" and "creative intervention of the mind" in scientific research and experiment.[129] Scientists must accept imprecision and uncertainty as they work—and that as part of that work, their own creative powers are indispensable and cannot be relegated to some earlier stage of scientific inquiry. In this account of scientific rationality, science can legitimately approach "other forms of thought"—in particular, those with an "aesthetic character."[130] In this way, Milhaud claims for physics an aesthetic attunement that Lanson, Seignobos, and others had sought to banish from the humanities themselves.

Milhaud's account of science finding inspiration in individual creativity and aesthetics is not easily reconciled with the assumptions about "science" found in the work of Simiand, Lanson, Mauss, Durkheim, Maurras, and countless others within the republic's intellectual coalition—or their reactionary enemies. Nonetheless, Milhaud was a philosopher, and, until 1909, a provincial one. When the renowned mathematician and physicist Henri Poincaré made distinct but congruent arguments, many unsettling possibilities entered broadly educated conversation, in France and beyond.

Around 1890, Poincaré's mathematical forays into the application of differential equations to celestial motions involving three objects exerting a gravitational attraction (for example, an asteroid in relation to the sun, the moon, and the earth) led him to a surprising conclusion: stable orbits for, say, an asteroid were only mathematically probable, not certain. Space did not appear to obey the order and regularity that Poincaré had expected,[131] a conclusion that quickly led him to similar conclusions about time.

In August 1900, Poincaré went further, claiming at a conference that "there is no absolute space, and we can only conceive of relative motion . . . there is no absolute time. When we say that two periods are equal, the statement has no meaning, and can only acquire a meaning by a convention."[132] Here, Poincaré in 1900 began to approach the theoretical innovations of Einstein. Whatever the precise extent of his prescience, that Poincaré found time to be a convention rather than an absolute had some troubling implications. What would become of the confident, at least broadly positivist metaphysical naturalism that gave many educated people the sense that a received materialism or a science of society, working in a commonsense time and space, was self-evident?

Taking his argument further in his popular *Science and Hypothesis* (1902), Poincaré repeatedly turned to the ways in which the fundamental assumptions of mathematical inquiry into space could be changed. He gave particular attention to the non-Euclidean geometry associated with Nikolai Lobachevsky, in which, setting aside a long-accepted axiom of Euclid, there can be more than one line drawn through a point B that will be parallel to line A, when point B is not on line A.[133] Drawing from the mathematical contributions of Bernhard Riemann, Poincaré goes on to show how our embodied experience gives us our given notion of space: in another world, with two-dimensional beings of circular shape living on a sphere, an arc would be the shortest distance between two points, and "in a word their geometry will be spherical geometry."[134]

In a neo-Kantian turn of phrase, Poincaré claimed that those who thought scientific reasoning gave access to things in themselves (that is, a kind of absolute and uniquely valid account of reality) were "naïve dogmatists," since the immense power of science was predicated on its ability to make suppositions only about the relations among things.[135]

Raising questions associated with the humanities as well as the sciences, Poincaré was also at particular pains to observe that the scientific emphasis on repetition (and with it, experimental confirmation) over time for the confirmation of hypotheses simply did not work as a way of inquiring about history.

For Poincaré, history deals necessarily with the unique and unrepeatable *event* rather than replicable experiments. Hence a secure science of historical development à la Comte or Simiand was impossible. As Poincaré puts it, moving from science to the world of Victorian letters, "Carlyle wrote somewhere something like this: 'Only the fact matters. John Lackland passed by here: here there is something admirable, here is a reality for which I would give all the theories in the world.'" Poincaré adds, "That is the language of the historian. The Physicist would say rather, 'John Lackland passed by here: it's all the same to me, since he won't pass by again.'"[136]

Like Milhaud and Poincaré, the theoretical physicist Pierre Duhem also argued against Cartesian, Comtean, and Renanian notions, most notably in his *Physical Theory: Its Aim and Structure.* Duhem said that "a physics experiment is the precise observation of a group of phenomena, accompanied by the *interpretation* of these phenomena; this interpretation substitutes for the concrete data actually collected by observation abstract and symbolic representations that correspond to them by virtue of the theories of physics assumed by the observer."[137]

For Duhem, scientists must take into account the limits of observation and measurement. Mathematics may be exact, but neither human perception nor the scientific apparatus and instruments that assist that perception can be exact. Hence "the results of a physics experiment are only *approximate*."[138] These conclusions naturally lead to a revision of scientific certainty in Duhem: as he puts it, "The goal of all theory in physics is the representation of experimental laws; the words *truth, certitude* have, in relation to such a theory, only one meaning: they express the agreement between the conclusions of the theory and the rules established by the observers."[139]

Certainly Poincaré, Duhem, and Milhaud were distinct thinkers: for example, Poincaré was careful to create a tiered protest against positivist accounts of science, arguing against Duhem that some hypotheses are, as Anastasios Brenner has said, "more conventional than others."[140] Furthermore, Duhem, Milhaud, and Poincaré were not saying that all science is unreliable or a radically constructed fiction. They were saying that scientific work and experiment participates in a multiplicity of realities and an expansive plenitude of variables and assumptions. Our scientific knowledge is integrally connected to our embodied being and environment (as Poincaré observed with his notional spherical beings), and—especially for Milhaud—our aesthetic sense as well. Working with diverse theoretical constructions, embodied experience and aesthetic sense, reason can be both creative and strikingly plural in its accounting for all the scientific data upon different questions (the questions themselves being cooperative work involving creativity). Furthermore, unique, unrepeatable historical events are simply not amenable to the creation of immutable "laws," which often are more mutable than advertised anyway, or at least dependent upon more assumptions and variables than is generally acknowledged.

In this way, Milhaud, Poincaré, and Duhem made several contiguous arguments about the construction of scientific knowledge, and attacked the notions of scientific certitude and objectivity within the natural sciences—notions that social scientists had assumed were "grounded" or endowed with "secure foundations" and could be straightforwardly transposed from the natural to the human sciences, from sciences of society to those of individual consciousness.

Péguy knew this work of critical reflection upon science and its methods well: he was an admirer (and near neighbor) of Henri Poincaré,[141] as well as a reader of what he called Duhem's "admirable work."[142] He knew that challenges to positivist assumptions popular with many of his contemporaries were not necessarily part of some "antiscientific" political reaction (a reaction that, as we have seen, could be frankly positivist in inspiration), but often came from scholars deeply engaged in new and demanding scientific and mathematical investigations.

From his student days, Péguy found his way to other sources of dissent, away from the regnant assumptions of the intellectual coalition. These included the neo-Kantian philosophy of Émile Boutroux, who had long been a prominent figure in French academic life. Among his earlier students was Durkheim, who credited Boutroux with teaching him about the nonreducibility of different forms of knowledge (not surprisingly for Durkheim, he came to this

realization with some assistance from his own reading of Comte).[143] Boutroux's own work went in a different direction: he presented another critique
of an all-encompassing science of human being, in part through a course he
offered on Pascal, which the young Péguy attended in the late 1890s.

In his *Pascal*, published in 1900, readers can find the Pascal taught by Boutroux. Péguy's teacher gave sustained and positive emphasis to the ways in
which, for Pascal, scientific knowledge, on the one hand, and moral and religious knowledge, on the other, operate in different domains of consciousness.
In his account of Pascal's thought, Boutroux argues that for Pascal, scientific
knowledge belongs to reasoning from the senses, and morality and theology
to an expansive faculty of memory.[144] Inquiry into matter in motion can dispense with precedent and provide its own ground through experiment to acquire knowledge cumulatively; but this form of knowledge cannot be applied
to memory, just as the authority of memory has no place in the adjudication
of scientific evidence.[145]

According to Boutroux, to confuse these orders of understanding is either
to make moral and religious knowledge impossible, or to stunt scientific dis-
covery by deference to what stands outside its animating imperatives.
Ultimately—and most important for Boutroux—our moral responsibilities
cannot be justified scientifically or simply by disinterested reason; it is charity, or love, that uniquely fulfills human nature and directs human action
toward the good.[146]

This emphasis on love—from a neo-Kantian philosopher—was part of a
deeper and broader current in French thought in the Belle Époque, very different from the positivist-inflected projects of Durkheim, Ribot, or Maurras.

The philosopher Félix Ravaisson, who found an appreciative reader in
Péguy's mentor Henri Bergson,[147] enjoyed, like Boutroux, a similarly intense
affinity with Pascal, and was no less attracted to Pascal's insistence upon a rigorous respect for different orders of knowledge. Pascal is unique, in Ravaisson's view, since "no other philosopher, in fact, has had a sharper awareness of
the difference of the two orders of things and faculties whose contrast corre-
sponds to that of matter and spirit."[148] Ravaisson appreciatively observes the
metaphysical interval that Pascal asserts belongs to knowledge as such, including scientific knowledge: for Pascal, it is "the heart" that gives us our sense of
time, space, and number, and these are the nondemonstrable *preconditions* of
scientific knowledge rather than their "proven" and "secure" foundation. Ravaisson is grateful that Pascal "reduces the very knowledge of first principles

to the heart."[149] Furthermore, Pascal, along with Plato, argued that "everywhere in the universe the inferior is an image of the superior."[150]

Yet for Ravaisson, this vertical ascent is a declaration of allegiance not to hierarchies of persons or peoples but to the exalted possibilities of being human, against those who would make a metaphysical desert and call it peace. Ravaisson's *Philosophical Testament* was quite forthright about the contemporary effort, "much in favor today," to become fascinated by the neurophysiological research that Dastre promoted, including "reflex movements, which would be absolutely machine-like responses of bodies fixed to impressions and solicitations from the outside . . . in such a way, everything in this world, except perhaps purely intellectual determinations, would be subject to an irresistible fatality, and there would be no point in invoking the mind."[151]

The ambitions of this movement involved nothing less than the death of philosophy: "The idea that philosophy, bound within ever-narrower limits, will disappear one day is becoming a majority view."[152] Ravaisson, like Boutroux, found the distinction between intellect and matter indispensable, but this independence found its end above all in service of a transcendence without equal, for "the will . . . [has] its most intimate root in what in us has the most force and efficacy, namely love."[153] For "we are in the world for no other reason than to love, Pascal said."[154]

Read within the rhetorical pathos of meticulous, secure scholarly distances, these enquiries into metaphysics and charity can easily seem rather like ungrounded *Schwärmerei* (passionate, undiscerning enthusiasm). But for Ravaisson, these questions are open: the secure, objective ground his opponents assume for their own views is not in evidence. In a clear allusion to Poincaré and others, he says, "The particular sciences prove with more or less convincing force, according to the nature of their objects: but of them it is true to say that they rest on hypotheses, or as the mathematicians often say today, on unprovable conventions."[155]

Bergson and the Freedom of Time

Above all, Péguy and many others owed the opening of their intellectual horizons to Henri Bergson. For Péguy, Bergson's philosophy had liberated his generation, or as he put it, Bergson exposed a "universal laziness"[156] and "broke our chains."[157]

At first blush, Bergson's philosophy appears to be another modern brief for the exaltation of becoming over being—and in some ways it is. But Bergson was not Renan or his diverse legatees. First, Bergson saw a vital absolute working through history, rather than upholding a purely immanent, linear historical becoming discoverable by the inexorable progress of "science." As he put it in an important letter to the American philosopher Horace Kallen, "It is the 'eternity' of ancient philosophers that I have attempted to bring down from the heights where it resided in order to relate it to the duration, that is, to something that swells, grows richer, and builds itself up indefinitely."[158]

Through this—at least in this stage in his thought—immanent "eternity," Bergson introduced into late modern philosophy a Neoplatonic strain totally foreign to Renan, Comte, Durkheim, and many others. It is in a certain sense cumulative but not "progressive"; rather, it integrated a continuous multiplicity of the past into the present. It was one dimension of Bergson's effort to transform the understanding of time among his students, including Péguy and Proust. By 1900, when Bergson held a chair at the Collège de France, his lectures had become public events for many intellectually curious Parisians; he became an internationally famous philosopher and a regular, friendly correspondent with luminaries in France, Europe, and beyond, including William James.

For Bergson, the decisive error in human experience was to confuse time with space. The two are distinct, even though intellect cannot resist conflating them, and in fact this conflation is a practical necessity, drawn from the demands of action.

Bergson's reading of evolutionary science took the opposite direction from the one taken by many of Bergson's contemporaries (and ours). It was not that Charles Darwin had shown that a "disenchanted" rationality, devoted to the documentation of processes in linear time, could reliably disclose natural laws divorced from metaphysical speculation. If one took evolutionary theory seriously, it meant that our intellects evolved for practical purposes, involving our own well-being and survival—in particular in order to *act* upon our environment. To this end, time would be transposed and plotted, measured, divided, and assembled as space. In practical terms, these operations were entirely legitimate. But they did *not* come to be in order to afford us an encounter with the multiple plenitude of reality, and they did not give anything but a very incomplete and often distorted access to that plenitude.

Many well-established movements in European intellectual life that identified themselves as scientific were hence not really the terminus of "sober reason" at last "set free" from theology, putatively archaic effusions about love, and, above all, "metaphysics." They were actually the latest iteration of a traditional, even primal misunderstanding of time, connected to the imperatives of practical action, which received its first philosophical expressions with Parmenides and Zeno of Elea.[159] For Bergson, "the elimination of time is the habitual, normal, banal act of our understanding."[160]

As long as the relation between objects remained the same in space, for the making of scientific laws, it would not matter if time drastically accelerated or slowed; it was as if time were not real at all. An encounter with time *as time*—that is, as *durée*, or duration—required a concentrated effort of intuition.

Bergsonian durée is an authentic temporality that does not involve measurement, juxtaposition, or stark separations. Rather, time is continuous and indivisible; it is necessarily mobile, and with it come both unity and qualitative (rather than quantitative) multiplicity, neither of which is prior to the other.[161]

Durée is difficult for Bergson to define, since spatial metaphors are irresistible to minds that have evolved to seek the fixed, homogenous, and manipulable (but not vital). He compares durée to the experience of hearing a melody: the melody can be experienced or understood neither as individual notes, nor as a succession of notes regardless of their temporal duration; its power and its reality as a melody depend upon its duration as a whole, its inescapably temporal flow, in which the past must be distinct yet continuous with the present for the melody to act upon us.[162]

Qualitative multiplicity in particular manifests itself in duration, as our experiences—and the different motifs, timbre, and tones of those experiences—relate to one another simultaneously, prompted by the same perception in the same moment, and are yet distinct.

Our emotions, for example, may be prompted by a certain kind of event—say, falling in love—simultaneously toward gratitude, joy, confusion, a sense of awakening, sadness at the departure of different real goods preceding the life changes aborning, thrilled and nervous anticipation of those same changes, doubt, a sense of peace and acceptance oriented variously toward the past, present, and future. They are mingled, simultaneous, distinguishable and yet never entirely distinct from one another. They can harmonize into a fullness of greater sympathy for others, a sense of lucid happiness for what is given to us through life with all its fragility, that integrates many different dimensions of this multiplicity. But none of these can be simply "reduced" to the other or presented as "nothing more" than material-chemical quantities in the brain, or as neatly separable states, or states that causally determine one another in a temporal sequence.

For Bergson, to apply an often mathematical, homogenizing instrumental rationality to all experience—not just inert matter but living things as well, in a spatially reduced temporality—distorted the real and rendered it lifeless. Above all, it deprived human beings of their freedom. Furthermore, Bergson was convinced that a careful review of scientific evidence in contemporary neuroscience, biology, and other fields would not refute but substantiate his own arguments. This was the primary task of *Matter and Memory*, published in 1896, a book Péguy greatly admired (he was more reserved about Bergson's later book, *Creative Evolution*).[163]

For Bergson, both philosophical idealism and materialism had estranged mental life from the body, and endowed either matter or mind with miraculous powers. Either (for materialists) matter could somehow create consciousness and memory "corresponding" to "an independent reality," or (for idealists) mind could somehow produce a "material world" that is "nothing but a synthesis of subjective and unextended states." Ultimately, both doctrines assume "that our representation of the material universe is relative and subjective and that it has, so to speak, emerged from us, rather than that we have emerged from it."[164]

Bergson believes that previous "spiritualists" (roughly, antimaterialist philosophers) had turned matter into a "mysterious entity" that prevented them from refuting materialism. To do so, it must be understood that "there is one, and only one, method of refuting materialism: it is to show that matter is precisely that which it appears to be."[165]

That is, matter is really there, and through our nervous system we have access to the Kantian *Ding an sich* (thing in itself). Our ability to perceive "images" of the material world is connected to our nervous system and processed by our brain, always in connection to potential action. But materialism fails to explain consciousness, because consciousness is always suffused with memory, which constantly participates in perception but is not itself material. Bergson reviews the neurological literature being published in great quantities around him and concludes that it fails to uphold either Kantian arguments, or the materialism that had claimed that research as vindication. Rather, his own distinction between perception and memory finds experimental confirmation.

As Ribot himself acknowledged, perception is integrally connected to movement, hence the motor apparatus of one's nervous system.[166] The research surrounding Ribot's Law (about the patterns of memory loss in amnesiacs) shows that there is often a grammatical structure to the loss of word memory: proper names are the first to elude consciousness, followed by common nouns, and then verbs last of all. Bergson concludes that verbs are "precisely the words that a bodily effort might enable us to recapture when the function of language has all but escaped us."[167] This suggests powerful connections among perception, memory and action, rather than some abstract idealist capacity of "representation" through, say, Kantian forms of intuition.

Bergson's inquiry into other neurological research proves no less troubling for materialist explanations of consciousness. It does not appear that memories are localized in the brain (what is called cerebral localization—a claim received skeptically in critical accounts of contemporary trends in cognitive neuroscience as well).[168] In cases of aphasia (when one loses the ability to speak or understand speech), a "lost" noun can often be found by paraphrase, sometimes alighting on the noun itself. In other cases, a certain letter is lost—say, the letter F—but it is highly unlikely that such a precise incision into personal memory of the alphabet could be made without unconscious knowledge of that very letter and its exact place in countless words.[169] The "destruction" of memories is understood in closer alignment with evidence if it is understood not as a destruction of some part of the brain "in which memories congeal and accumulate" but rather as "a break in the continuous progress by which they actualize themselves."[170]

For Bergson, the brain has evolved to serve the needs of bodily action—those needs are "so many searchlights, which, directed upon the continuity of sensible qualities, single out in it distinct bodies."[171] Memory, however, retains a plenitude of experience; it finds itself slimmed and sharpened by the demands of possible action, but that immaterial plenitude remains.

At first, this suggests that Bergson has merely returned to older, rigidly dualist arguments, in which perception and the body work on one side and a remote, immaterial memory on the other. But Bergson turns to experiments by R. F. Müller and others to show that memory constantly participates in the instantaneity of the present rather than standing apart from it. For example, Bergson cites research establishing the fact that readers decipher words not "letter by letter" but through memory filling in what letters and phrases have followed from a similar prompt or pattern in the past.[172] The immediate present is where memory and material perception constantly meet.

On the nature of the present, Bergson strikes notes that are characteristically attuned to both philosophy and contemporary scientific research. In the manner of Augustine in book XI of the *Confessions*, he writes that "when we think this present as going to be, it exists not yet, and when we think it as existing, it is already past."[173] Yet he also observes that recent investigation has established that the smallest interval of a perceived present among human subjects is ".002 seconds."[174] In such an instantaneity, there is no development of thought and no fulfilled intentional action, which always requires perception suffused with memory.

It is in this suffusion that body and soul are reconciled. The body is responsible for "directing memory toward the real and binding it to the present." Memory is, through the combination of sensations and movements, "ever pressed forward into the tissue of events," though as memory it remains "absolutely independent of matter."[175] Memory is spirit, and can "unite with matter." Idealism and materialism alike cannot think the "reciprocal influence" of mind and matter, and thus "sacrifice freedom."[176] But for Bergson, once they are properly understood, we see "with memory, we are, in truth, in the domain of spirit," and that our "past" is an indispensable part of our freedom. It is "that which acts no longer but which might act, and will act by inserting itself into a present sensation from which it borrows the vitality."[177]

Why has the unity of body and spirit not been obvious to us? Beyond philosophical errors, the shaping of the brain by the imperatives of security and control over our environment leads our minds to constantly posit "homogenous space." If this space is immediately assumed to be the theater of all experience, it is because it allows us to be "masters."[178]

Once movement is turned over to space, it "abandons that solidarity of the present with the past which is its very essence."[179] Yet when we escape the habitual assumption of homogenous space, we see that body and spirit meet temporally. There is always a certain durée in which memory participates, and hence we are able, with Bergson's philosophy, to "compress within its narrowest limits the problem of the union of soul and body."[180] (Though Bergson's compression is not the same as a definitive resolution.) What is clear to Bergson is that the proposed solution on offer from many of his contemporaries does not hold: the collapse of conscious experience into material or sociological suppositions no longer appears as a bold extension of scientific reasoning but as the latest error in a long historical procession of errors designed to give human beings power rather than truth.

For Bergson, the intuitive knowledge of durée in turn relied upon a profound, participatory immersion in temporal mobility and flow (including but not limited to intuiting its presence in one's self) that brought the intuitive mind in immediate and direct contact with reality and the multiplicity of things and states that participate in it.[181] Durée afforded an encounter with something beyond the habitual or interested relation of the self to other selves, to society, to the world, and to itself.

Bergson argued that the self, drawing its life through durée and in memory, is constituted not as an object or discrete qualities or drives but as a mobile totality of its whole existence in time. As he put it in his first book, the *Essay on the Immediate Data of Consciousness*, for Bergson the "fundamental self [*moi*]" can only be recovered by "vigorous analysis" in large part because "language cannot seize it without fixing the mobility of it."[182]

In Bergson's account, the mind, like life itself, allows the present to express radical creativity from a real if discursively elusive multiplicity, a creativity whose profound continuities with the past are real but unforeseeable. According to the early Bergson, "Durée in all its purity is the form that the succession of our states of consciousness takes when our self lets itself live, when it abstains from establishing a separation between the present and anterior states."[183] "A free act" is accomplished in such a state, when "the self alone will have been the author of it, since it will express the entire self . . . we are free when our acts emanate from our whole personality."[184]

In *Matter and Memory*, freedom is similarly manifest in moments where we live "with an intenser life" in which we, "creating acts of which the inner indetermination, spread over as large a multiplicity of the moments of matter as you please," are able through memory to "pass the more easily through the meshes of necessity."[185] Matter "repeats the past unceasingly" because it is subject to this necessity. But memory is "not a regression from the present to the past" but a "progression from the past to the present": it is "spirit [that] borrows from matter the perceptions on which it feeds and restores them to matter in the form of movements which it has stamped with its own freedom."[186]

In this way, freedom for Bergson is unpredictable, and is much more than the ability of the will to choose from different options.[187] Rather freedom is a kind of unifying integrity that draws upon the whole temporal reality of the self to express the new in surprising, sometimes even shocking continuity with the past, that expresses itself in and transforms the material world through the free meeting of matter and memory.

Bergson opened a spectrum of possibilities for his readers and his audiences radically distinct from those of both the intellectual coalition and of French reactionary politics. Evolution should lead us to question the "commonsense" habits of mind we bring to experience, since we understand them to be shaped by the imperatives of survival and control rather than the full expanse of reality. The Cartesian and popular-Comtean assumptions about "science" are not supported by actual scientific research, and the attempt to transpose these assumptions into "human sciences" is misbegotten and superficial. Determinism in particular is precisely what is vindicated neither by meticulous review of scientific literature nor by careful philosophical understanding. Properly understood, past and present, body and soul are integrated in our experience. Our freedom is temporally integrative and reconciles origins and originality; it is not finally transgressive and supersessionist.

Learning and Time

The philosophical differences we have explored logically entailed different positions within the white-hot debates about learning in the Belle Époque.

Specialized research had taken secure hold of the New Sorbonne in the Belle Époque. As we have seen, Lanson among many others praised the "faculties of specialists and scholars"[188] who were bringing the Third Republic's educational system into a new century assumed to be ruled by objective methods drawn from science, particularly in its universities.

Bergson's position was different. In 1882, Bergson gave a Prize Day speech at the lycée in Angers, where he then taught. While he argued that "the division of the disciplines is a natural thing" and its accomplishments in the arts and sciences demand "eternal gratitude," he thought that it is "specialization [spécialité], that makes the scholar sullen." For "in contact with the specialist, everything becomes dry and sterile." Instead, we should remember it is animals who are specialized; "since the variety of abilities is that which distinguishes us, let us remain men." Bergson ends the address with a warning against the peril of following specialization, et propter vitam vivendi perdere causas ("and for the sake of life lose the reasons for living").[189]

Bergson's openness to nonspecialized inquiry remained a living possibility throughout the age. A leading socialist politician like Jean Jaurès could write a highly regarded multivolume history of the French Revolution,[190] and independent persons of letters like Salomon and Théodore Reinach could also make contributions to archaeology.[191] For Bergson, nonspecialists often had a vitality and freshness of perspective that the professionally trained, bourgeois scholar often too quickly set aside.

Sometimes the dissenters from the broad intellectual coalition around the Sorbonne presented more pointed critiques of their opponents' positions on education. Given his prominence as a mathematician and scientist—and as a graduate of the École Polytechnique—Henri Poincaré appeared to have little reason to involve himself in debates about liberal learning. But in fact, along with other members of the Académie Française, he joined the Ligue pour la culture française, in order to fight, in the words of the group's manifesto, secondary education's "corruption by the utilitarian and professional spirit."[192] Poincaré aligned himself firmly against Simiand, Durkheim, and other educational reformers—but for expressly scientific and mathematical reasons.

Poincaré wrote a brief for his concerns in his 1911 essay *The Sciences and the Humanities*. He argued that while an education in the humanities is not necessary for scientific achievement, in his experience it was extremely helpful. For Poincaré, the "spirit of analysis"[193] in, for example, the study of classical languages required a precision and mental agility that was very helpful for high-level mathematics, one that could be taught to children and adolescents in a way that high-level mathematics could not. For biologists, instruction in the development of words from different languages allowed for a morphological consciousness of reality useful for understanding the subtleties of biological development.[194] For Poincaré, the careful study of the liberal arts trained the student in conceptual dexterity—that is, moving concepts and ideas from one conceptual language to another. This dexterousness had a powerful relationship to scientific creativity.[195]

As for Bergson, an education in the humanities was neither an act of dutiful reverence for the past nor an "objective" supersession of the past, but rather a living encounter with the past that opened new possibilities. In his speech "Good Sense and Classical Education" (delivered at the Sorbonne in 1895),[196] Bergson describes foreign tourists in Paris gathered "in front of our monuments and in our museums" reading guidebooks. He then asks the assembled students: "Absorbed in this reading, do they not sometimes seem to forget for its sake the beautiful things they had come to see? It is in this way that many of us travel through existence, eyes fixed on catchphrases [*formules*] that they read, neglecting to look at life."[197]

For Bergson, this "guidebook" approach to philosophy, literature, and history was disastrous, whether the guidebook consisted of novel or venerable formulae. Whatever its historical provenance, the knowledge of a single language or a single way of thinking (including "scientific" assumptions in a given discipline) created intellectual habits that made the infinite richness of reality a ready-made, easy-to-read—but dead—text. Such habits were lazy, very partial, and reductive—but once acquired, very difficult to break.

Bergson finds "precisely in classical education, before everything, an effort to break the ice of words and to find again beneath it the free flow of thought."[198] He argues that foreign languages—especially ancient ones, with very different ways of "carving" the real—free us from "our conventions, our habits and our symbols," all of which dull creativity and an interest in a living precision.[199] They require an intense effort to learn, and thus associate understanding with meticulous effort rather than the indiscriminate application of a few basic abstract ideas to the most diverse phenomena—those "ready-made" and "dead" ideas of which he is always skeptical.[200] Among them, he writes, is a "serious error, which consists in reasoning about society as if [one were reasoning] about nature, to discover there I know not what mechanism of ineluctable laws, to in the end misunderstand the efficacy of good will [*bon vouloir*] and the creative force of freedom."[201]

For Bergson, a classical education "attaches no value to knowledge passively received." It "dishabituates one from a certain excessively abstract matter of judging."[202] For Bergson, classical education has an almost Aristotelian capacity to adjudicate between different kinds of judgment, allowing a discriminating *bon sens* to determine the sort of reasoning and degree of precision appropriate to it. It requires an attentive, free mind, analytically at work and yet also engaged by feeling, including and above all "the passion for justice."[203]

Bergson's emphasis on the unity of learning and feeling through classical education—and significantly, a passion for justice—was what had worried Thomas Hobbes earlier in the modern age: an emphasis on classical and sacred learning was likely to produce a desire for heroism, goodness, or sanctity that would lead to civil conflict and pervasive instability. But for Bergson, a classical liberal-arts humanism was an education in what Bergson would elsewhere call qualitative multiplicity, compatible with flourishing living and thinking—and, as he mentions with reference to France, "tolerance."[204] A hard-earned sense of the real (that is, not "ready-made ideas") joined to "generous passions" is not a threat to peaceful coexistence but in fact its spring.[205]

It is anything but a coincidence that the opposite sides in the debate about educational reform were also on opposite sides of contemporary debates about the nature of time, including historical time. Whatever the possibilities offered by the study of ultimate origins, Durkheim, Simiand, Mauss, Lavisse, and others who favored "modernizing" educational reforms were happy to think of time as a linear, homogenous kind of space in which theoretical, "scientific" explanations account for events and change, in which the past was neatly differentiated from the present, which bore responsibility for the ultimate stop on the temporal line—"the" future.

Those unpersuaded by proposals to "rationalize" education and to make it "relevant" thought much more carefully about time. Henri Poincaré's argument that there was no such thing as absolute time, and that history could never be a science, left the question of "relevance" far more open than many of his opponents assumed it to be. For a linear account of history and supersessionist progressivism, on the one hand, and backward-looking reaction, on the other, Bergsonian durée posed distinct but related problems. If our experience of time has been gravely damaged by confusing it with space, Bergson was more than willing to have deep, continuous, and distinct linguistic and temporal origins open up our durée, the fullness of time, and with it what he called "the free flow of thought," in pursuit of a freedom that integrated different pasts with a present instantaneity. It could offer different possibilities for diverse futures. In various ways, Poincaré and Bergson—and Péguy—understood that different accounts of time produced different kinds of history, education, and culture.

Telling the Truth in Time

For all of Péguy's acknowledged debts to scholars like Duhem, Poincaré, and above all Bergson—Péguy was a singular composite of philosopher, poet, and journalist. His was very different work from that of established institutional figures. Why did he devote his life to the *Cahiers*?

To understand Péguy's ambition takes some mental effort for an educated person of the twenty-first century—it requires entering into the variety and intensities of temporal experience in the early twentieth century. Our experiences of time, or at least the ones most easily discussed in our culture, are often resolutely linear and intensely contextual historically (often subdivided by decades as one approaches the present).

This was not the case in the two decades before the outbreak of the Great War. As the possibilities, experience, and understanding of time underwent rapid change in the Belle Époque, many of the characteristic ways in which human experience had created a distinctively modern order in the seventeenth, eighteenth, and early nineteenth centuries were beginning to be the subject of intense questioning among educated persons and intellectual subcultures. What was learning for, and to what end? How should we know the world, and ourselves? What was the relation between historically rooted communities and universal humanity? Were notions of personal or communal honor an integral part of being human, or archaic excrescences? What place was there for universal love, or for religious belief in an allegedly "mature" modern culture? In short, what did it mean to be modern, or antimodern, and was it possible to be something else altogether? The future appeared to many to be unsettled and therefore open to decisive human thinking and action.

It is not that Péguy would simply "choose" this or that position in the cultural, political, and philosophical worlds in which he worked; rather, he would try—in Bergsonian fashion—to integrate freely, to synthesize, to create, to draw upon distant and different pasts in order to open up futures different from the ones expected by the eminences of immanent becoming and from reactionaries. That attempt would in turn open up possibilities that others could fashion in their present toward still other futures.

Something indispensable can be grasped of that historical moment if we attend to a single thinker in Paris—one of the most energetic and vital points on earth for so many changes associated with the early twentieth century—engaged simultaneously with changes in culture, literature, daily politics, theology, and philosophy. As a way of thinking through and with these possibilities, Péguy would come to insist upon founding his own journal to give form to his thought.

In France, an ambition of this kind was made especially plausible by social and material circumstances at the turn of the last century. In the Belle Époque, the vast majority of the French population could read, an unprecedented situation in the history of the country. Throughout the second half of the nineteenth century, a profusion of newspapers became available in Paris and elswhere, as advances in printing and typography (and the Third Republic's relaxed censorship and lower taxes on newspapers and journals) made possible the daily purchase of newspapers of diverse opinion even by very modestly compensated laborers.[206] Paris in particular was soon flooded with newspapers: by the autumn of 1910, more than sixty daily newspapers were published in Paris, a startling increase from just thirty years before.[207]

Yet the hope that Péguy would live out through a journal had long been a venerable dream in France (and in Europe: the Viennese Karl Kraus was

Péguy's contemporary). For example, In *Sentimental Education*, Gustave Flaubert's great historical novel of the 1848 Revolution, the friends of the protagonist hope to found a journal that would allow them to speak the truth hidden by established powers and secure for France a fully just and free regime. The dream foundered quickly because it had to work *within* the corruption of the present to tell the truth *about* the corruption of the present. In Flaubert, the hoped-for journal required a great deal of money, and honest wealth was not easy to find; what is more, those who dreamed of the journal were unwilling to make the daily sacrifices necessary to tell the truth. The time and treasure the journal would require to be something more than a dream were spent upon the social whirl of Paris and would-be lovers, squandered in the pursuit of more selfish ambitions, until the merest hope of the truth-telling journal was dead. At the end of the novel, the protagonist and his best friend are adrift in middle age, fondly reminiscing about an abortive early adolescent visit to a brothel.[208]

The dream remained in the 1897 novel *The Uprooted* by Maurice Barrès. There the protagonists leave their native Nancy (in Lorraine), and several of them ultimately work for a journal in Paris that they believe can transform France and realize their ambitions, fittingly bearing the title *La Vraie République*. Their ambitions meet with disaster as politics, love affairs, and persistent poverty lead several of them astray, even into crime. Amid Barrès's anti-Semitism and denunciations of both Kant and Parisian corruption (in contrast to the "purity" of a traditionally "rooted" life in Lorraine), the "true" republican newspaper can barely be mentioned without references to the sums of money required to keep it going.[209] But in a novel aspiring to express the dilemmas of a generation—written almost thirty years after Flaubert's *Sentimental Education*, and set a half a century later—it says a great deal that the hope that through a journal the young intellectual could tell the truth to the present was as alive, and as futile, as ever.

For Flaubert and Barrès alike, the dream *cannot* be made real. The gravitational tug of greed, status-seeking, and egotistic passions will leave it inert or transformed into the opposite of what it was intended to be, so that in the end the dream is forsaken or one surrenders it, providing contemporaries instead with the expedient and reassuring falsehoods so many of them yearn to hear. Flaubert and Barrès leave room for little more than the notion that a true journal might be made real through a constantly renewed renunciation; a renunciation that for a young person would be without drama and color, and would offer instead only a life of grinding, relentless work.

Yet to give a different account of the present, without seeking to flatter ready-made ideologies, intellectual cultures, and coalitions, and to learn properly not just from Bergson and others but to integrate the fullness of Péguy's own experience, and that of France, and that of philosophical argument, political reflection, and Christianity—these forms of integrative argument and creativity would inspire Péguy's own journal. The *Cahiers* would be "inserted" (as Péguy would put it) into a unique historical moment, but with resonance in diverse pasts, and for different futures. It would be more than an intellectual proposition or a professional project. By his own principles, it would require him to wager his life.

CHAPTER 2

His Youth

Before Renan and Durkheim, before the Sorbonne and Alfred Dreyfus and Henri Bergson, there was the Loire. It runs both through Orléans and through Péguy's life. One of Péguy's early pseudonyms was "Pierre Deloire," and there is in his writing about the river and its surroundings a palpable sense that the river expresses many of the qualities Péguy hoped would become his own. His Loire runs through "the large and intelligent and liberal valley of courtliness and of nobility, of ceremony and festival, the valley of pavanes and of a perfectly intelligent goodness . . . the river [is] not only royal, but kingly, the majestic river, but majestic with a politeness, an ease, with inimitable contours . . . it lingers only to look at the most beautiful province in the world."[1]

Charles Péguy was born steps from the Loire's banks in early January 1873—the same week as Thérèse de Lisieux. Many prominent modernists and intellectual innovators of the early twentieth century were born just before or after him. Marcel Proust, Serge Diaghilev, and Bertrand Russell were born in the two years before Péguy; by the end of 1874, they would be joined by Karl Kraus, Hugo von Hofmannsthal, the philosopher Max Scheler, and Gertrude Stein.

In comparison to his philosophical and artistic contemporaries, Péguy had very modest origins. He was born in a neighborhood of small, low houses in the faubourg Bourgogne in Orléans, often inhabited by traditional artisans,[2] dotted with small flower boxes leaning outward from the sills of the front windows.[3] His father had been in poor health following his service in the Franco-Prussian War of 1870, and he died before his son's first birthday. Péguy was raised by two women—his mother and his grandmother—who earned their living by mending chairs.

Both women worked harrowing hours: Péguy's mother for sixteen hours a day,[4] beginning at four in the morning.[5] His grandmother worked along-side her and told Péguy old peasant stories, folktales among them, including tales about the damned.[6] The vivacity of her telling gave him a lasting memory of what she said. Péguy was struck by the fact that he had learned his mother tongue from a peasant grandmother who could neither read nor write.[7] He later wrote of how a past of "unlettered souls" in a culture were like a "reserve," an "immense ocean," and a "secret treasure."[8]

His childhood offered Péguy a sort of security, since his mother earned a limited but steady income from her work, one that allowed her to buy some small buildings in the neighborhood. The work left little time for sentiment, however: Henri Roy, a friend and future minister of the Third Republic, wrote of Péguy's boyhood as one "without joy . . . between these two women for whom gestures of affection were a forbidden weakness, and for that matter, wasted time."[9]

Péguy earned excellent grades at school, even as he began to work at home, helping his mother with her chairs. In his circumstances, it would not have been surprising for him to finish an impressive if resolutely local education and become a grammar school teacher, and it seemed that without unforeseen intervention he would have done precisely that.

Péguy's prospects may seem surprising. But they were not out of place in late nineteenth-century France. For all its meritocratic ambitions, lycée education in the early Third Republic was generally reserved for children from families far wealthier and more socially established than Péguy's own. Less than 3 percent of French boys attended a lycée. Nor would educational and social mobility improve before the Great War: the number of students entering secondary schools in France actually dropped in the years between 1880 and 1914.[10]

In these circumstances, Péguy was, in social terms, an unlikely candidate for an elite education. Yet the principal of the local école normale, Théophile Naudy, thought his abilities required such an education, insisting that Péguy take Latin and enter the Lycée d'Orléans with the help of a scholarship.[11]

For Péguy, this was a wonder, and to begin learning Latin was "the opening of a whole world." For "the grammarian who, one day, for the first time, opened the Latin grammar to the declension of *rosa, rosae*, never knew what beds of flowers he opened in the soul of the child."[12] This ancient language opened up the world to Péguy in a new way, at once deeply, numinously ancient and surprisingly alive. He would later come to read German fluently as well, but never spoke of his enchantment with German as he did with Latin.[13]

Many of Péguy's generation—those whose names would be remembered in the foremost ranks of modernism or social-scientific innovation—experienced a nineteenth-century classical education differently. It was part of an expected social, cultural, and familial inheritance, sometimes a musty or even an oppressive one in need of transformation in order for it to have new meanings divorced from its recent past. For Péguy, the opening to the world of the classics was an unexpected, invaluable, and unlikely gift. He would later say of Naudy that he was "the man to whom I owe the most in the world."[14]

Yet even as his imagination blossomed amid Latin declensions, Péguy lived in an industrial town in an industrial age. Daily and weekly newspapers were easily available to him, and Orléans was a well-established stop on the French railroad system throughout his childhood.[15] Péguy's youth was thus a study in unusual contrasts. He inhabited a liminal moment between a preliterate culture drawn from a soon-to-fade but still-extant peasant and artisanal culture, as his mother and grandmother—and he himself—worked as manual laborers. Yet he began to inhabit a culture that still placed considerable emphasis on classical education for its elites, amidst a modern culture of ubiquitous print and topical information made obsolescent in days, or a day.

There was a similar distinction at work in the moral and metaphysical background of Péguy's youth. A communal Catholic culture possessed considerable energy, and the church had adapted quickly to an industrial age. Péguy attended catechism classes in Orléans. In his early years, the bishop of the Orléans diocese was Félix Dupanloup. He was a passionate admirer of Jeanne d'Arc, and introduced the cause of her beatification in 1869.[16] He wrote against Renan's antitheological speculations, and successfully so—Dupanloup was eventually elected to the Académie Française. But he had also opposed Louis-Napoleon's coup against the Second Republic in 1851 and expressed vigorous skepticism about the views of Ultramontane Catholics like the journalist Louis Veuillot—though he also resigned from the Académie when it elected the positivist and atheist Littré. He famously worked to refine and bound the potentially sweeping antimodern theses presented by Pope Pius IX's *Syllabus of Errors* in 1864.[17]

Throughout his life, Péguy retained vivid memories of Dupanloup's Catechism, published in 1865.[18] This catechism—certainly Péguy's own—

expressed no hostility to Jews, the "faithful people" who had lived by God's covenants. It did not impute guilt to Jewish people for the death of Jesus but instead emphasized the demand that all Christians live in and by charity with others.[19]

Dupanloup was a spirited and convinced orthodox Catholic, but he clearly did not belong to reaction, or to its Ultramontane Catholic wing. Though he died well before the Dreyfus affair, it is telling that while Orléans had anti-Semites, as did the rest of France, it had no anti-Semitic riots during the affair, while other cities did.[20]

Yet alongside this Catholic culture lay a developed, civic secularist culture upheld from Péguy's earliest education forward—and often it was the schoolmaster who was the champion of *laïcité* in communities throughout France. Péguy himself remarked that the priest and the schoolmaster were dominant forces in his moral formation, and while he came to believe that they shared far more than they acknowledged (in this provincial setting, he was less worried about the fraying of moral consensus than Ferry), they certainly perceived themselves as presenting two incorrigibly distinct, even irreconcilable accounts of God and the modern world to their charges.[21] The simultaneous existence in provincial towns both of a vibrant and distinctively modern Catholic culture and of a convinced and explicit secular culture was (at least from our vantage point) available only for a small number of generations, of which Péguy's was one.

There is no question that the Third Republic's educational mission aspired to unify the heterogeneity of late nineteenth-century France and its history while disavowing the history of civil violence associated with intranational differences. A standard primary textbook of the early Third Republic, *Le Tour de France par deux enfants*, testifies to this profound yearning for national unity. In *Le Tour*, two boys who ultimately lost their father to his wounds in the Franco-Prussian War, travel around France, learning about the ancient Gauls, the chief ministers of the Sun King, and the Jacobins. They are all heroes, France is as truly French in the upbringing of horses as it is in its factories and railroads, no less French among its artists and generals than among its scientists. These different lives are all contributions to the unique genius of France, to which the boys pledge their lives at their journey's conclusion.[22]

Péguy's own circumstances gave him the opportunity to understand the unitive ambitions expressed in *Le Tour* with unusual sharpness and force, since they were not simply part of a national or a regional history but part of Péguy's direct personal experience. Of the boys who read *Le Tour*, no doubt a good number were pupils in both catechism class and the laic schools of the Third Republic, but considerably fewer were personally and simultaneously acquainted with peasant life, manual labor, and the classical education required of French elites. More, Péguy was one of those who, like the book's protagonists, really *had* lost his father in the aftermath (and as a consequence) of the Franco-Prussian War.

For Péguy, these different aspects of his experience were also different aspects of himself, and the desire to unify these disparate origins and energies without effacing them would become one of the most persistent imperatives in his life as an author. It was an imperative that both led him to and found itself fortified by Bergson's philosophy of integrative time, and of freedom as an act expressing the whole self, past and present.

In the fall of 1891, Péguy entered the Lycée Lakanal outside Paris, a school from which many students studied for the admission exams to the École Normale Supérieure. It was a grim institution: there were defined periods for speaking to other students, and students could shower only once a month.[23] Yet it was here that he met his lifelong friend—later the renowned historian of the French Revolution—Albert Mathiez, as well as the future politician Henri Roy, and another lifelong friend, Albert Lévy, the son of a rabbi.[24]

Péguy was at Lakanal for only a year; perhaps his most memorable essay there was on the question, "Morality: Is It Independent of Metaphysics?" He answers that the moral law is immediately apparent to consciousness, before reason. In this way, "reason only intervenes later, when we are brought to choose between two or several acts that conscience has arranged in the class of acts that ought to be done."[25] That moral intuitions require reason but cannot be deduced entirely from—or reduced to—reason alone would be a conviction that Péguy would hold throughout his life.

Péguy took the examination for the École Normale Supérieure at the end of his year in Lakanal, and failed. He accepted his one-year military call-up, and by all reports enjoyed the training. At the end of his year, he came closer than he had before to passing, but nonetheless again failed the exam for admission to the École Normale.

It seemed Péguy's attempt to build an academic career might come to an end. But friends prevailed upon the Collège de Sainte-Barbe to give him a scholarship while Péguy took courses at Lycée Louis-le-Grand. In these days, Péguy's thought took on a more determined tone. He decided that he was no longer even a nominal Christian but an atheist and a socialist—though he continued to work with a St. Vincent de Paul society to undertake charitable work at the request of his friend (the future monk Louis Baillet), appearing at the society's meetings only after the opening prayer had been said.[26]

His socialism was more focused upon the telos of socialism (say, the socialism of Marx's brief reflections in *The German Ideology*) rather than a thoroughgoing materialist socialism or a more general revolutionary immanence that required a break with previous notions of morality. For Péguy, ending material deprivation was instead a prerequisite for true freedom and morality.[27] When he was still a young man, he had already concluded that "the social revolution will be moral, or it will not be."[28]

On his third try, Péguy passed his entrance exams to the École Normale and became a student there in the fall of 1894. When it was proposed that he, along with the other first-year students, would have to submit to some hazing from an upperclassman, Péguy made it clear that he would under no circumstances participate. Upperclassmen who tried to haze him should be ready to come to blows. The following year, no longer a first-year student himself, he ran for student government on a platform of eliminating all first-year hazing. He lost, but something of his character had been expressed.[29]

The École Normale in those years was starkly divided between "talas" (for *vont-à-la-messe*, that is, Catholic churchgoers) and religious skeptics, but that did not preclude varied friendships. One of Péguy's contemporaries, an assertive skeptic, called himself the "Personal Enemy of God" and used to read out passages from Voltaire's *Philosophical Dictionary* during thunderstorms. A close friend of Péguy's—an enthusiastically Catholic friend—would look on, smiling.[30] The battles of Péguy's youth over religion and politics burned hot, but they did not always or even usually provoke ill will.

Péguy continued to hope for a "universal intellectual emancipation" that must be preceded by a "material" emancipation, as he put it in a letter to his fellow student Paul Collier in 1895. But Péguy had no doubts that the ultimate end of this liberation would be "the superior work of humanity: philosophy, arts or sciences." In keeping with those hopes, he spent his days reading Kant, and regularly going to concerts and plays.[31]

Péguy's friends were mostly socialists, and their study area was known as the "turne Utopie." There was every sign that Péguy had a promising career as a socialist writer and activist, and perhaps a professor as well (he also retained his not uncritical interest in Kant: some of his fellow students nicknamed him "the Kantian").[32] The then-famous labor strikes at Carmaux had already led Péguy to collect money for the strikers. He began to be close to Lucien Herr, the university librarian and an influential socialist among students. Herr held discussion groups for students about politics and had already served as a mentor to the young Jean Jaurès, who later became leader of the French Socialist Party. Through Herr, Péguy met Jaurès, of whom he was initially in awe. There is every indication that his esteem for Herr and Jaurès was reciprocated, and that he was their protégé.

It was through this connection that the young atheist Péguy began to learn about the power of mysticism. This may sound odd. It is tempting to assume that Péguy's own later references to "mysticism" are drawn from a putative "rejection" of reason that, for example, found its way into Georges Sorel's writing about myth, and from there into Péguy's own thought, baptized with a term more pleasing to the inner ear of a Catholic convert. The actual history is far more interesting.

For Sorel, Péguy's account of "mysticism" was disappointing: it was too vague and too associated with Christianity to evoke the precise and yet expansive powers of myth as Sorel understood it;[33] he grasped that his own notion of myth was very different from mysticism.

In fact, a positive account of mysticism within politics was planted in Péguy's thought through the socialist Jaurès—and even if indirectly, here too the influence of still "another Comte" finds its way into the early twentieth century. In an article in *Action socialiste*, which Péguy reprinted in the February 1900 issue of *Cahiers de la quinzaine*, for example, Jaurès dismisses the "narrow positivism" that had become dominant with Littré. In contrast to it, in the article reprinted by Péguy, Jaurès singles out for praise the "great positivist mysticism of Auguste Comte."[34]

This was not the only occasion in which mystery and the mystical became a charged and distinctly favorable term for the socialist skeptic Jaurès. As early as his doctoral dissertation of 1892, "On the Reality of the Sensible World," he wrote that "it is the unity of act and power in the infinite that gives to being this depth and richness; and thus, the manifestation of the phenomena of the world that participates in being, extension, movement, also takes on strange depths of truth and of mystery from the outset."[35]

Jaurès was committed to a critique of what he called "this superficial materialism that claims to explain everything by this supreme unknown called matter." It is the inability of materialism to respect the depth and scope of human desire and human aspiration, whose religious expressions cannot be resolved into a series of superstitions, projected communal needs, or calculated frauds designed to obscure material exploitation or social functions. Jaurès presents a rejection of mysticism as an error no less serious than the "infantile and governmental spiritualism"[36] of Victor Cousin, so congenial to established elites.[37] Religions are false, Jaurès claims, but they are also profound and, despite their confusion, point the way toward future human possibilities and their ultimate and mystical fulfillment in history itself.[38]

Surrounded by an anti-mystical positivism and an emerging "scientific" Marxism, the thought of Péguy's mentor Jaurès included the notion that politics was not a science, in a Cartesian, Durkheimian, or Marxist sense, or in the manner of positivism à la Littré. Rather, mysticism made possible social, political, and properly human achievements that allowed humanity to encounter its own depths and express its ultimate desires. It was through this Jaurèsian opening that mysticism could open new possibilities for thinking about the relationship between mysticism and political reasoning in a new century, in substantial part through Péguy's thought.

Yet even in those early days, as a protégé of Jaurès and Herr, Péguy was not an unreserved joiner of groups and an enthusiast for their demands. As he enjoyed the camaraderie of student life with the other residents of the "turne Utopie," he kept a trunk in their study space that was labeled with a warning that it should not be opened. In it were the pages that would come to be his first poetic drama about Jeanne d'Arc. Despite her extraordinary cultural prominence in the Belle Époque, it was a strange task for a young political intellectual at the École Normale—with a promising career in journalism, politics, and perhaps university life—to make his own.

The young Péguy was also a faithful if distinctive kind of friend—and this was an ambiguous predilection. He tended to believe in his friends to excess and yet narrowly, telling them that a great destiny would be theirs in some profession or some cause, in a way that assumed that their best possible selves as he understood them would naturally become their actual selves.[39] Even in his student days he was taken with the aspiration to embody convictions without reserve, making the body and the mind one through vigorous fidelity to one's most exalted hopes.

Yet that concord of mind and body could also be a heavy and often unjust demand to make of friends. Péguy was tempted to see life as something like a drama from his beloved Corneille, in which fundamental convictions were vindicated by lucid, forthright action regardless of cost.[40] Yet as he was demanding of others, so Péguy sought to live what he believed in uncompromising ways. The Catholic Louis Gillet wrote to the well-known Catholic Marc Sangnier of the then-atheist Péguy, "[He is] so filled with love for the poor that he gives away the little he possesses."[41]

Péguy's personal life expressed a similar resolve. In the summer of 1896, Péguy's friend Marcel Baudouin died of an illness during military training. Péguy was briefly convinced that his friend must have died at the hands of a malicious superior. He immediately rallied his friends to seek out the offending officer and challenge him to a duel. It was only when they arrived that he came to realize the death was the fault of no one. He parted on good terms with the officer who had explained the situation to him. Soon afterward, Péguy married Marcel's sister, Charlotte Baudouin.

The Baudouins were a formerly Catholic family that had become staunch anticlerical Socialists and deeply sympathetic to the Paris Commune of 1871,[42] despite having acquired some modest wealth that made them middling bourgeois rather than working-class. Péguy's political sentiments were similar to those of the Baudouins, but though he had served as her Latin tutor, Péguy did not know Charlotte particularly well.[43] The proposal seemed to have been prompted above all by his grief at the death of his friend, though Péguy was not insensible to her charms and the strength of her political and laic convictions. Their marriage would often be a trial for both of them, in which it appears that neither and both were at fault.

As he and Charlotte settled into plain lodgings on the Left Bank, Péguy found himself very much at the center of the Dreyfusard movement, seeking Dreyfus's immediate exoneration and release from prison. He spoke to Zola after he wrote *J'accuse*,[44] and met and befriended the famous champion of Dreyfus's innocence, Bernard-Lazare, with whom he became fast friends.

Péguy very quickly became an important Dreyfusard in the Latin Quarter, leading protests in the streets while writing pro-Dreyfusard articles in left-wing journals like *La Revue blanche*. Throughout, he expressed a certitude about the Dreyfusard cause and other causes that others (sometimes from moment to moment) found alternately off-putting, imposing, compelling, and inspiring; there was in his force of conviction an unusual mixture of material selflessness, intellectual and personal pride, moral seriousness, loyalty, conversational affection, and social energy. Whatever their reactions, the defense of Dreyfus was the defining experience of Péguy's youth.

Amidst other things, there was considerable evidence available to confirm Péguy's anticlericalism in the Dreyfus affair. For many French Catholics—including clergy—French Jews were responsible for the perceived villainy of secular republicanism. While there was no shortage of secular anti-Semitism in France, certainly many French Catholics expressed anti-Jewish sentiments

with regularity and energy, appointing Jews as omnipresent scapegoats for anything that prompted their considerable spleen—or their wrath.

In some ways, not only Judaism but also Catholicism were often interpreted by Catholics through the events of modern French history rather than
through a continuous and international history over nearly two thousand
years. A poisonous anti-Semitic bigotry was fortified with something far less
than historical exactitude with the oppression of the Dechristianization Campaign during the French Revolution, as well as with the shooting deaths (one
accidental, one intentional) of the archbishops of Paris during the 1848 Revolution and the Paris Commune of 1871. In this haphazard assortment of
grievance, resentment, and hostile ill will, religious prejudice and integral
nationalism played a strong part.

This "respectable, bourgeois, French conservative Catholicism" would
leave Péguy cold throughout his life. Yet just as he had received his first introduction to Christianity in the Orléans of Dupanloup, his young adulthood
brought an orthodox but quite different Catholicism into view.

While portions of Rome and the media of the Vatican were themselves
clearly connected to right-wing political movements in French Catholicism,
French Catholics were also encouraged not only to accept but also to work
harmoniously for the good of the nation with secular republicans. Pope Leo
XIII's exhortation for French Catholics to undertake a *ralliement* to the republic in his encyclical *Au Milieu des sollicitudes* of 1892[45] built upon his endorsement of labor unions and economic justice in his encyclical *Rerum
Novarum* from the previous year. At the height of the Dreyfus affair, the pope
would give a front-page interview to the center-right *Le Figaro* that expressed
strong sympathy with Dreyfus, comparing his sufferings to those of Christ.[46]

A number of French Catholics followed Pope Leo's lead by founding new
associations within the church. Groups like Marc Sangnier's "Sillon" and other
Catholic social movements arose, including *semaines sociales*, where Catholics
could discuss the social questions of the age with workers and other citizens.[47]
These were held in considerable suspicion by those Catholics sympathetic to
an intensely Rome-oriented Ultramontanism, including the circles associated
with Maurras's growing Action Française. At the height of the Catholic-skeptic
divide in the first years of the century, the Sillon had 640 members' groups in
France. Opposition to its work came above all from politically conservative
Catholics, who, after Leo's death in 1903, often had the ear of Rome. In 1910,
the Sillon was condemned by Pope Pius X.[48]

In intellectual circles, conversion to Catholicism was a compelling possibility for persons of letters, including those from nonbelieving and atheist backgrounds. Before and after the Dreyfus affair, formerly secular intellectuals and members of the cultural elite—with a broader purchase on the ambient culture than theologians—converted, including J. K. Huysmans, Paul Claudel, and several of Péguy's friends, including Ernest Psichari (Ernest Renan's grandson) as well as Jacques and Raïssa Maritain.[49]

Yet for Péguy, the cause of Dreyfus came first. Even his ventures in book selling and socialism tended to serve the cause of the Dreyfusards. On May Day 1898, Péguy opened a socialist bookstore in the Latin Quarter, under the name of his friend Georges Bellais (the store could not be under his own name, since it would preclude his scholarship at the École Normale). He ventured his wife's entire dowry—amounting to thirty thousand francs—to go into business.[50]

On many days, Péguy's primary task at the bookshop was not to sell books but to organize groups of students to confront anti-Dreyfusard students who tried to intimidate Dreyfusard professors at the Sorbonne, including the historians Alphonse Aulard and Charles Seignobos.[51] Some of these confrontations turned to exchanges of shoves and punches.

In the store, an impressive pile of unsold copies of his now published *Jeanne d'Arc*—which had been greeted upon publication with total silence—were formed into chairs. The drama's poor sales did not discourage Péguy, despite that he fact that he had poured into it his unrestrained artistic and moral ambitions (manifest in its proto-modernist blank pages,[52] as well as its opening dedication to those who sought to heal "universal evil").[53]

While socialists were slow to turn toward the Dreyfus case, Péguy was no less a socialist for his Dreyfusism: he believed that socialism inspired "the best forces of the nation," and in 1898 he published his socialist dream in the form of a meditation entitled *Marcel: First Dialogue of the Harmonious City*. In it, he imagined a political community in some ways like an ancient polis (significantly not a modern nation-state), but one where work would secure not only universal prosperity but also universal dignity for all persons of all nationalities. In this frankly utopian youthful composition, he shows an early fascination with the proper combination of the particular and the universal in human experience, in which both relate to each other without subordination. For "all the men of all the cultures, all the men of all the different interior lives, all the men of all beliefs, of all religions, of all philosophies . . . all the men of all conditions, all the men of all the nations" come together in this city, for "it is not proper for there to be strangers [*étrangers*] there."[54]

Péguy's *cité* has a faintly Jacobin flavor; it was also influenced by a French socialist tradition that takes as its starting point the question of how to conceive of a universal human flourishing that makes a harmony of individual differences without suppression or coercion. It does not rely upon, and often emphatically rejects, the reification or quantification of human experience—for the young Péguy, a tendency manifest even in vote counting.[55] The cité embodies a harmoniously inclusive community, at once individually differentiated yet characterized by a comprehensive and foundational fraternity. Even in its earliest formulations, Péguy's socialism, like that of Jaurès, was thus already in tension with a pragmatic, often materialist positivism that had become popular among French Republicans since the 1870s.

Péguy believed the stakes of affirming or rejecting materialism and mechanical accounts of consciousness were very high. He remained devoted to the struggle against anti-Semitism throughout his life, and the Dreyfus case was for him an occasion for acting with complete moral clarity. He was no less certain that many of his Dreyfusard allies were, like many of his socialist comrades, inclined toward a philosophical anthropology that, to his mind, vitiated their shared moral commitments—including their commitment to Dreyfus. It was through this opening that the philosophy of Bergson first appears in Péguy's writing.

Péguy started to attend Bergson's lectures in the late 1890s, and was quickly a fascinated student, with evident sympathy for Bergson's conceiving human being as something other than a material, positive, socially, or physically quantifiable thing. The first mention of Bergson in Péguy's published writing occurs in a November 1899 article for *Le Mouvement socialiste*, which had started publication the same year. Bergson's psychology appears first in Péguy as a critical foil for Zola's psychological associationism, in which ideas are connected to one another in a rote, mechanical fashion reminiscent of positivist psychology.

The "mechanical" notion of psychology in Zola—contrasted unfavorably with the "recent theories" of Bergson—is criticized by Péguy precisely for what he understood to be its constrictive implications and their consequent failure to provide grounds for Dreyfusard activism. According to Péguy, this positivist psychology is not a natural ally of justice and universal rights: it left Zola's novels with a complacent anti-Dreyfusard readership dramatically at odds with the political allies he acquired as a result of *J'accuse*. As Péguy concludes, "The circle of those who fought with Zola [i.e., in the Dreyfus affair] had few men in common with the circle of those who usually read Zola."[56]

Another of Péguy's early citations of Bergson also enlists Bergsonism in political arguments. Here observations "not unknown to Bergsonian philosophy"[57] are made in support of an account of time, memory, and history that emphasizes the accumulation of impressions and the living, morphologically vivid, and mobile presence of events in the memory. Péguy argues from these remarks that a "true internationalism" should "enlarge" upon nationalism and the history that sustains it, rather than aspiring to an internationalism that rejects national and local attachments.[58]

In these early articles, Péguy expressed one of his most sustained convictions: victories for universal justice are only possible if substantial portions of different pasts are received and reconfigured with a living, integrative openness.

Yet even as he contemplated his utopian city and found in Bergson a critique of mechanical, materialist accounts of human motivation and experience, Péguy had concluded that there were decidedly practical barriers to the universal emancipation of human beings, perhaps above all the press. Like many of his contemporaries—real and fictional—he looked to the press as an agent of political and cultural transformation in service of truth.

In the late 1890s, Péguy remarked to friends that he hoped to found a "Journal Vrai." His journal would not publish professional journalists but instead publish those with experience in the relevant inquiry, including workers. It would appeal to all; not only to workers but to the educated as well, not just to men but also to women, and children too.[59] For Péguy, unlike for the fictional journalistic aspirants of *Sentimental Education* and *The Uprooted*, the journal in question would not turn to wealthy and powerful political patrons and hence founder upon inevitable compromises with power—quite the opposite.

The journal he and his friends would found would start with the premise that "the bourgeois spirit is in the midst of destroying everything in France: honesty, the family, France itself. Now there are workers and poor people who are more bourgeois than certain rich people. The press contributes, more than any other power, to the progress of the bourgeois spirit."[60]

The false universality Péguy perceived in the *embourgeoisement* of society would be a perpetual spur for his thinking. This perception also implied a practical question: How did the press find itself as the principal advocate of a global embourgeoisement, opposed to the universal emancipation of a humanist socialism? The root was the relationship of media to their readers: "At present all newspapers live by their readers, [and] are slaves of their readers."[61] Socialism would flourish in a regime of lucidity and honesty; embourgeoisement thrived in a regime of sensationalism and flattery.

To prevent this "enslavement" to a portion of the reading public, Péguy intended to start a journal by voluntary contributions, one that would allow it to challenge its readers with articles that did not confirm what they already believed or wanted to hear. Nor would it address the diversions and sundry entertainments of modern life: as Péguy sharply put it, "In the place where newspapers insert racing tips [e.g., for gambling] it would be written: 'We do not give tips on racing, because those who lose [money] there are imbeciles, and those who win are thieves,' etc."[62]

It is hard not to smile at Péguy's tone; so accustomed are we to the ubiquity of entertainment and the ingratiating tone of marketing as the signal tone of efficacy and practical success that the scolding of readers in search of racing tips can seem comically, quaintly severe, much like the monitors of the Lycée Lakanal allowing student bathing only once a month, or perhaps an earnest nineteenth-century Kantian's disdain for the blandishments of hypothetical maxims. But there was in this commitment of Péguy's something that would give shape to his life, and inspire others.

His intellectual development continued apace, even as he began to dream of his journal. Not only did he attend Bergson's lectures at the Collège de France in the late 1890s, he also, as we have seen, followed a course of lectures on Pascal given by Emile Boutroux at the Sorbonne in 1898. Boutroux's introduction to Pascal as a person—not simply as a thinker—would help to shape Péguy's commitment to distinctive work.

His interest in Pascal was one of the defining intellectual events of Péguy's life; in 1900 and while still an atheist many years away from returning to Christianity, Péguy wrote of him, "I have kept for this Christian a singularly anxious admiration."[63] For Péguy, Pascal would become "the greatest thinker."[64] Perceptive observers would note that Péguy's admiration for Pascal created the possibility of a distinctive kind of action in a very different historical moment: Anatole France recognized it, and called Péguy "the Pascal of the socialists."[65]

For Boutroux, Pascal as a person was a genius with at once an iconoclastic, obsessive, and sacral approach to work. He expands at length upon Pascal's ceaseless work as a child, a devotion to work that continued throughout his life. Pascal preceded writing with prayer[66] and despite his genius applied himself devotedly even to the most menial tasks connected to his work.[67] Yet this work is, in Boutroux's account, invariably collaborative work with others, for others (for example, in scientific research and invention with Descartes or Fermat, or in exchanges about theology with Pierre Nicole).

Boutroux's Pascal is also committed to a writing that is accessible yet rigorous.[68] It is a form of authorship that rejects technical terminology[69] because it easily corrupts thought and debases the work of writing to serve the vanity and intellectual pretensions of the author rather than the reader. Pascal's writing speaks with unswerving directness.[70]

Boutroux is at pains to emphasize the persistently difficult and at times confrontational relationship Pascal's work provoked between the author and the institutional leaders of Catholicism, including those in Rome and in France,[71] even as Boutroux admires Pascal's refusal to identify himself with the Jansenist movement centered around Port-Royal.[72] For Boutroux, it is by standing outside the institutional church and its most prominent alternatives that Pascal gives to others an extraordinary and indispensable service. He is a person of integrity, who is compelled by that integrity to take positions that contemporary factions and parties cannot fully understand or support, but that ultimately issue in writing that is at once independent, rigorous, demanding but without obscurity, and devoted to the truth.

Péguy's encounter with Pascal by way of Boutroux helps us to understand Péguy's shocking break with socialist solidarity soon afterward, breaking friendships and (it was widely assumed) destroying his career as an emerging socialist intellectual. It is from this break that the *Cahiers de la quinzaine* would emerge.

In the most practical terms, the origin of the *Cahiers* can be traced to the fact that Péguy's socialist bookstore was a failure. When it had visitors—generally not customers—they were often rather déclassé left-wing foreigners, whom Péguy was happy to have despite their failure to buy anything. He also kept a stray cat that he refused to expel from the premises (fittingly, animals were also "citizens" of the Harmonious City, endowed with "adolescent souls").[73] The bookshop was a deeply human place, universal and diverse, without exclusion. It also made no money.

It was soon clear to leading socialist intellectuals like Herr, Jaurès, Léon Blum (the future French prime minister), Mario Roques, and the sociologist François Simiand that there had to be changes to Péguy's bookstore if it was to be useful to French socialism. The store was put under their administration, with Péguy as a shareholder. He was saved from a dismal financial situation by their intervention, without which he would have been penniless. He had no other resources, having squandered Charlotte's dowry on the shop with startling alacrity (that in turn would help to sour his relationship with his wife and his in-laws).

The socialist intellectuals coming to Péguy's rescue made it clear that their help did not come free. The foreigners were no longer welcome to lounge there, and they banished the cat as well.[74] They announced their intention that Péguy would create a socialist journal that would help to support the Socialist Party and himself (and the bookstore). But in accordance with party policy, they made it clear that all socialist journals had to conform to the party's decisions, as articulated by a central committee.

Péguy refused. According to Jérôme and Jean Thauraud, Péguy understood their offer as an invitation to lie for the Socialist Party as other newspapers and journals had lied for the government during the Dreyfus affair.[75] They did not ask him to be a journalist or a writer but to be a publicist. Péguy proposed an independent journal instead, which would print varied articles about socialism, including records of socialism's internal debates and disagreements.

The Central Committee would have none of it. Simiand scoffed at the proposal; Herr told Péguy that he was an "anarchist" and that if he proceeded to create his own journal, "we'll go after you with all our strength."[76] Péguy took it as a challenge and decided to found his own journal by himself.

Herr's anger was hardly incomprehensible: he saw Péguy as a protégé whom he had just saved from financial ruin, and he was given nothing in return. Yet Péguy's reaction was also understandable. Péguy had been deeply committed from his earliest youth to personal independence and integrity, and Herr had asked him to become a mouthpiece for the party's official apparatus, assuming that he was bound to obey not out of honest conviction but out of financial need.

Péguy's task would not be an easy one. Péguy would remain a socialist, but his journal would have no formal funding or support from the Socialist Party. Amid his activism for socialism and for Dreyfus, he had left his degree from the École Normale unfinished, and he had no formal credentials.

Yet he was certain that—in keeping with his dream of the "Journal Vrai"—his journal was not to be compromised, whatever his personal situation. Hence it would have to accept no advertising of any kind. He simultaneously believed that, in fidelity to the craft of printing, it would have to make use of elegant fonts and heavy, high-quality paper.[77] In this way, he would rely entirely on subscriptions to keep the enterprise going, and to support his family.

He chose for his journal the name *Cahiers* (notebooks), or to use their full title, *Cahiers de la quinzaine*. The reference to "notebooks" suggested something unfinished, writing still in the making even as it was published—and the title would eventually become one of the signal rhetorical moves of twentieth-century French intellectual journalism. *Cahiers* for cinema, culture, and politics began to emerge with some regularity in the decades that followed. Yet for Péguy, the second term was no less important.

His journal would be notebooks of the *quinzaine*, or "fortnight." "Fortnight" suggests something in between an immediate impression (say, drawn from the daily rush of events in newspapers) and a fully developed conceptual contribution (say, a philosophical argument). At first, the *Cahiers* often included bulletins on Socialist Party congresses, along with essays on politics, culture, and art; but soon the essays came to predominate. Often an entire *Cahier* was devoted to a single work: an essay on Nietzsche, Pascal, Renan, or Tolstoy, an installment of a novel by Romain Rolland, or an article on the status of oppressed peoples—among them Russian Jews, Poles, and the people of the French Congo or Madagascar. Other issues would offer a theological or philosophical reflection on time, grace, and hope.

This distinctive ambition to mediate between the quotidian and immediate and the temporally expansive firmament of philosophy, theology, art, and history is itself a product of a distinctive liminality in Péguy's own experience, and in the circumstances that surrounded him. As a student of Bergson, he was convinced that present perception is always suffused with memory, whose recesses are deep and full of possibilities for those willing to enter into them without regard for immediate and convenient action. In one of the earliest issues of the journal, he claimed that he worked "in *quinzaines*; I am attached to the present,"[78] even as he called upon the philosophy and literature of ancient Greece, upon Christianity, medieval history, Pascal, and many other possibilities within a broad cultural and philosophical patrimony to interpret and reform that present.

The *Cahiers* would be no more profitable than the bookstore. Having run through his wife's dowry, Péguy would run down his brother-in-law's fortune, not to mention the financial support he received from Bernard-Lazare, Henri Bergson, and his friend Geneviève Favre.[79] His friends very often remained loyal to him, but in what often appeared to be desperate bids for an increase in importance or income, he could test that loyalty. In 1903, for example, he published an extended excerpt from Bergson's *Introduction to Metaphysics* in the *Cahiers* without the author's permission. Bergson was understandably displeased—he did not want his philosophical writing to appear in what he understood to be a political journal[80]—but it did not break their friendship.[81]

Continuous financial hardship, and Péguy's adamant refusal to accept advertising, made the *Cahiers* an unceasingly parlous enterprise. He would never have more than thirteen hundred or fourteen hundred subscriptions a year,[82] a number that rose and fell according to the degrees of enthusiasm and offense that an issue prompted in his readers.

The bookshop continued. It eventually moved to the rue de la Sorbonne, where it would attract many remarkable conversationalists, especially on Thursdays, when Julien Benda, Georges Sorel, or Romain Rolland might participate.[83] But no more than the journal would the shop ever afford Péguy and his family more than a minimal living, leaving Péguy struggling to feed his family, living very modestly in the suburbs of Paris.

Péguy would certainly be poor. But he was also free to publish whatever he liked, including his own writing, without concessions to editors, advertisers, or parties. His independence would come at a real cost—both to his personal standing and for his well-being—as he fought against those who had taken more commodious paths in the world of letters and learning. But Péguy, whose personal resentments could become protracted, nonetheless never ceased to hold an authorial dialogue with that world.

The first issue of the *Cahiers* appeared in January 1900. It was the month he turned twenty-seven years old. He would continue to publish them—as few as six, as many as twenty-two issues over the course of an academic year—until, at forty-one, he left for the Front in 1914. While he edited the contributions of others with meticulous precision, it was his own contributions that would make for the most controversial, resonant, and lasting of the *Cahiers*.

CHAPTER 3

An Answer to the Question: What Is Modernity?

If a single assumption underwrites very different formulations and definitions of the modern, it is that modernity is an unprecedented, decisive event in world history. Furthermore, even if it is vulnerable to the recrudescence of some form of atavistic cruelty or prejudice exploiting modern social conditions or technology, it is a great change that is ultimately irreversible.

The notion that modernity is a novel and comprehensively transformative event has a long history. It was the conviction of Descartes and his admirers—including Auguste Comte—that the modern promised a fundamentally new beginning for knowledge and progress in knowledge.[1] The profound newness of the modern was an integral, animating notion of the quarrel between ancients and moderns in the seventeenth and early eighteenth centuries, in both France and England. Jean-Jacques Rousseau, who saw the consequences of Enlightenment as in some sense new, final, and baleful, found the emergence of modern society (for him, at best) only provisionally meliorable and certainly irreversible.[2] Alexis de Tocqueville was anxious but hopeful about the modern future, and also thought it was both new and irreversible.[3] Ernest Renan in *The Future of Science* affirmed (as we have seen) that there was no retreating from a distinctive and thoroughgoing scientific future. On the question of "going back" from the modern, Nietzsche concurred with Rousseau and Tocqueville, speaking into the ear of a conservative that he could not go back from the new dispensation.[4]

Given that Péguy once referred to the modern world as something like a "natural disease," his readers can be forgiven for assuming that he is an anti-modern, and that he too acknowledges modernity's thoroughgoing and comprehensive irreversibility.[5] But when one reads him closely, it becomes clear that something very different is afoot, because the modern is defined as supremely *metaphysical* in nature, the "historically modern" is often celebrated, and metaphysical questions admit of different answers in any historical period.

The great polestar of antimodern thinking, to some extent throughout the West and certainly in France, had long been opposition to the French Revolution. Péguy refers to the ways in which some of his contemporaries assumed that the world before 1789 was "an abyss of shadows and ignorance," and that suddenly with 1789 there was abundant "electric light" cast upon history and humankind.[6]

Péguy could reverse the modern account and, in the manner of Joseph de Maistre, rail against the champions of modernity from Rousseau to the Jacobins: it is 1789 that ushers in an era of darkness. Yet Péguy is a convinced admirer of the French Revolution. Still more remarkably, for him the French Revolution is not modern at all; "the revolution is eminently an operation of old France."[7]

The problem grows only more tangled from this starting point. Péguy makes repeated references to "modernity" as a specifically *ancient* metaphysical possibility. He claims with provocative insouciance that Aristotle is a modern philosopher,[8] and that Euripides is more modern than Racine. He concludes with equal ease that in Charles VII, Jeanne d'Arc faced a modern king—in fifteenth-century France.[9] In a manner that would fail to gratify the reactionary panegyrists of throne and altar from Bossuet to Bonald, for Péguy it is the monarchy of the absolutist ancien régime that bore "the power of the modern world" into France[10]—even as the Revolution that displaced that ancien régime was *not* modern. Péguy himself, given to argument against a (singularly configured) modern sensibility, makes no protest as Clio, muse of history, tells him that he himself has in part a "modern soul."[11]

Hence to understand Péguy's account of modernity, one must first discern the governing logic behind an implicit definition of modernity that includes Aristotle, Euripides, Charles VII, absolute monarchs like Louis XIV, Ernest Renan,[12] Emile Durkheim, and at least partially Charles Péguy, but that with equal vigor excludes the French Revolution, and in many ways both Cartesians and Kantians as well,[13] not to mention many committed Dreyfusards, the resolutely secular schoolteachers of the early Third Republic,[14] and Henri Bergson.[15] Similarly, modern socialist political parties are modern, but universal social solidarity is not; Judaism is ancient, but anti-Semites are extremely modern, for "they are much more modern than us. They are much more modern than they want to be. They are much more modern than they believe."[16]

Even when an explanation for these classifications—in Péguy's playful, wry style, one can kindly call them eccentric—appears, the question of a relationship between the account of modern commitments Péguy gives and modernity will require careful thinking. But for now, it must be emphasized that however bracing his denunciations of the "superstitions" and "empty pride" besetting many of his contemporaries may be,[17] his status as an "anti-modern" cannot be taken for granted as some form of reaction, or even of political conservatism. Péguy clearly does not wax nostalgic for established powers, for mythically unified and hierarchically arranged peoples, for the indiscriminate affirmation of venerable authority against the alleged destruction accomplished by the Enlightenment or the French Revolution or notions of religious toleration, equality, and rights—all of which he supports.

In fact, Péguy refuses to limit his thinking to a linear, successive temporality, progressive or regressive. From his early writings to his late works, few words are more consistently pejorative for Péguy than "reactionary," applied to Maurras and others.[18] Yet he also was altogether willing to observe that "one will never know what acts of cowardice among our fellow French will have been prompted by the fear of not appearing sufficiently progressive."[19]

So what is Péguy's modernity? For Péguy, the modern refers above all to certain kinds of philosophical commitments and the practices that accompany them. Often, it refers to certain insistent assumptions about knowledge and the ends that knowledge ultimately serves. For example, Aristotle as well as, for Péguy, contemporary neo-Thomist enthusiasts are modern because, in his reading, Aristotle and his followers want everywhere to systematize and intellectually categorize, and thus, as he puts it, leave knowledge "immobilized" in a kind of fixed relation or "network" (*réticulation*).[20] They forsake the seeking of knowledge, in Bergsonian fashion, as something living and mobile that cannot be easily assimilated to the mechanical conveniences of the intellect.

Yet Péguy's modernity is not simply an epistemological or metaphysical project, but a series of political and rhetorical practices. When Péguy acknowledges being modern himself, the passage refers specifically to his penchant for a peculiar kind of "demagoguery" that he fights in himself even as he succumbs to it.[21] Euripides reveals another dimension of what Péguy means by modernity; he manifests an inclination for "cunning" and "cavils," even a certain "malice" that reveals itself in "perpetual trials."[22] Jeanne d'Arc went to the royal court to secure the king's throne and to lead the French to victory against their English occupiers, but she found a "modern" king with little interest in justice, who was "calculating" and a "dealer" in businesslike fashion, obsessed by politics, surrounded by clerical and secular politicians.[23]

For Péguy, socialism and modern solidarity with working people draw from deep human imperatives connected to hospitality, supplication, and fraternity,[24] and thus is ancient; Marxist-inspired socialist parties aspire to a totalizing monism prone to bureaucratic instantiation and control, and thus are modern.[25] Judaism's antiquity is obvious,[26] but the precise *reason* anti-Semites are exceptionally modern is because for them the world is governed by a duplicitous, loveless machination—in Péguy's words, they believe themselves ruled by "a forgery, a fabrication," of, or "invented" by, "the Jews"[27]—that allegedly lurks secretly "behind" the authentically mobile, organic, incorrigible diversity of the real.

Hence Péguy's modernity is not singularly modern, and it is not the modern age or modern people as such that Péguy opposes. Rather it is a series of related epistemological, metaphysical, rhetorical, and political orientations that he designates as modern, but that for him appear in a very wide range of historical periods and cultures. Moderns are often metaphysically "premodern" within distinctively modern societies, and metaphysically "modern" people sometimes wielded great power and influence in premodern societies.

If that is so, why call these orientations and points of departure modern at all? Furthermore, aren't fixed ideological commitments, sinuous administrative maneuvers, demagoguery, and encompassing philosophical systematizing something of a sloppy hodgepodge of undesirables?

For Péguy, the answers to these questions follow an often implicit but striking logic. "Modern" metaphysics and rhetoric is for him a way of calculation, self-interest, and above all control, in which the highest and most demanding truths are sacrificed. For a certain kind of reader, that clarification will be nothing but an obfuscation on top of a hodgepodge. Let us see if we can go further than that.

For Péguy, "modern" metaphysics and rhetoric inclines toward emollient (and often passive-aggressive) interested suggestion over direct argument about truth, loving the truth, or direct, reasoned argument; in another form they veer toward totalizing demagogueries (like anti-Semitism) that have a deranged or calculated contempt for truth. All of them aim for a spurious "mastery" of reality, in variously gradual or immediate terms. In each mode, moral, civic and spiritual integrity are forsaken for something more interested, and more easily consumed or controlled. Above all, for Péguy a desire for a kind of regular, assured control leads "modern" persons (again, "modern" like Aristotle and Durkheim but not, say, Henri Bergson) to seek systematic and abstract accounts of reality that, once they enjoy widespread acceptance, impoverish the encounters of human beings with an inexhaustible and infinite reality, both within and without themselves, conceiving a world of surpassing conceptual and technical mastery devoid of love.

Here Péguy expresses his convictions with supreme clarity. The modern world, whenever it appears in history, is founded upon an inversion he conceives through his reading of Pascal. Even as a young religious skeptic, he remarked that as part of "the confused memory that we have kept of Pascal" his readers may see that in modern culture, "the relation of mind to love, entirely injurious to mind, is veiled before the relationship of the body to the mind, advantageous to the mind; the modern world is essentially the glorification of mind against love."[28]

Modernity, in Péguy's distinctive definition, is unmistakably drawn from his creative reading of the "three orders" of human being in Pascal's *Pensées*; here it is not Boutroux's Pascal, but Péguy's own, that speaks.

As the methods of modern science were taking shape, Pascal had identified a "carnal" order of social, corporeal, material, political, and financial ambition and desire; an "order of mind" or conceptual understanding and genius; and finally, an "order of love," or charity.[29] For Pascal these orders encompassed human experience, and the soul can move through them in an order of ascent, with the two lower orders finding their proper boundaries when understood from within the ultimate order of love. For Péguy, what is essentially modern is the ambition to achieve a loveless mastery and control over others and over experience through intellect, but without an organic, charitable relation to what is known and mastered, including one's self.

This "glorification" of intellect against love begets further reflection, and brings Péguy to a greater level of precision. It is not, for him, the mind as mind that is glorified against charity. This would affirm an antimaterialist position, and Péguy also repeatedly remarks upon the powerful tendency toward materialism in metaphysically modern thought (again, regardless of its historical moment).[30] Rather, since the mind cannot fathom itself, this glorification is bound to seek its end through the intellectual mastery of the material and social world—that is, the world immediately, habitually apparent to the senses.

For Péguy, this ambition will—in the manner of the epistemological boxout championed by Renan in *The Future of Science*—also rule out an experience or desire that eludes full (and, at least in aspiration, definitive) intellectual explanation, or reduce incompletely explained phenomena to that which can be comprehensively understood and rendered manipulable by the intellect. To that end, for Péguy modern metaphysical sympathies incline easily toward reductionism. In his notes for an unwritten doctoral dissertation, his own list of these reductionisms includes "the metaphysics of atheism, of materialism . . . above all universal determinism."[31] It is often accompanied by the assumption that theories about the productive ordering of the human world through disciplined self-interest and utilitarian morality are evidently correct and fit for all purposes: "The morality of interest and the utilitarian moralities are presented as given, as automatic."[32]

These commitments are in turn complemented by a theory of "indefinite" historical progress defined as a procession of improvements in technology, material well-being, and freedom in relation to both nature and history sustained by the assumptions of a market economy (as he puts it, "a theory of capitalization, and from the age of capitalization").[33] They are in turn supplemented by accounts of the past developed through a magisterial historicism, in which the possibilities of diverse human pasts are, as it were, marooned on their own far-flung contextual islands. There is a powerful tendency to emphasize the incommensurability of a given historical moment with the desires and needs of other places and times, and to engage the past from a safe and secure distance.[34] In this way, the possibility of drawing creatively from different pasts to seek diverse futures is weakened, in favor of a single future secured by "modern" metaphysics.

Yet none of the foregoing answers our persistent question: Why call modern metaphysics and rhetoric "modern" at all, if it is at once ancient, medieval, and modern?

If Péguy's modernity is a revolution, it is a revolution in *intensity* and *ambit* but not in *essence*. Its fundamental metaphysical possibilities have been available in different forms and combinations, to varying degrees, in very different and often distant historical epochs; modern metaphysics is neither new nor final. But the increasingly comprehensive scope and intensity of modern metaphysics at work in historically modern societies vastly increases human power over nature and over other human beings, including one's self, and one is almost obliged to participate in this metaphysics (that is, to live as if this metaphysics was the true one) to live in modern society. Hence for Péguy, by the end of the nineteenth century, the spectrum of metaphysical possibilities that had always been modern were preeminent in a way that they had not been heretofore.

Here we enter some of the most forceful and carefully expressed passages in Péguy's writing. When God speaks to human beings in his poetry, or parents speak of children, or when he creates a dialogue with friends in his writings about culture and politics, Péguy turns easily to words of gentle, affectionate humor, tinged with melancholy, sometimes with a subtle joy. That wistful, tender if weighty note is present but comparatively muted amid his reflections on the historically late modern triumph of "modern" metaphysics. If Péguy's prose elsewhere can strike a tone of intimate, serene restraint often found in Mozart's piano concertos, these observations tend toward an intricately contrapuntal yet floor-thrumming *Dies Irae*.

Péguy believes that the venerable and very old theses of modern metaphysics have, in the modern age, built a new social and economic order, which in turn has made this metaphysics ubiquitous and immediately plausible to the subjects of this order despite its equally ancient elisions and ambiguities, ones that, for Péguy (as we shall see) afflict any metaphysics that attempts to place itself beyond doubt. He calls this new order "the reign of money."[35]

For Péguy, modern persons, whatever their manifest political loyalties, oriented themselves to human experience above all through the motivating forces and metaphors of the market as the increasingly ubiquitous medium of exchange, consumption, and desire in modern life, and this has underwritten the dominance of "modern" metaphysics in modern societies. Of course, only slightly before Péguy, Nietzsche too would observe that money was the final repository of value in an increasingly nihilistic culture. Yet Nietzsche interprets this repository as merely a debased version of will to power,[36] without describing its philosophical boundaries or consequences. Péguy is more precise than that.

Péguy's diagnosis is not a condemnation of money as such: he takes pains to emphasize that money is "highly honorable" as a means to live honestly by selling what one makes or does well for one's straightforward needs,[37] and that it should be spoken about honestly and without coyness.[38] His critique is also not an endorsement of economic determinism. Péguy believed instead, in Bergsonian fashion, that the market had become a source of extremely powerful and increasingly pervasive "ready-made" intellectual habits, analogous to—and a logical extension of—the way that for Bergson, human beings came to conceive time as space. For Péguy, self-interest is not the most powerful motive for the triumph of modern metaphysics, since explanations with reference to immediate personal interest are "narrow and infertile," whereas explanations that reveal the habitual (for example, habitual assumptions and ideas) are "much more interesting and much more profound."[39] In this way, "economics is like a vulgarization of morality, and morality is like a codification of certain aspects of psychology and metaphysics."[40]

Péguy hence finds within the "reign of money" the constant incentive to adopt certain ethical, psychological, and metaphysical positions in living and thinking. To use Weberian language congruent with the market, every "value" can be a subject of equivalence and negotiation, exchanged for another one. The very rigidity of rationalism and comprehensive "theory" in relation to life produces a kind of "liquefaction" of other possibilities for being human,[41] which allows them to be shaped and reshaped by the framing assumptions of the market. The fixed, ubiquitous assumptions of a universal obsession with comfort, safety, and acquisition make all other motives and aspirations appear (and often indeed make them) uncertain, ineffective, and weak. What Péguy calls "economic automatism" is assumed to be an imperative that rules human beings in aggregate, whatever consequences it has for life.[42] Human being also becomes subject to pervasive quantification. There are ever-fewer commitments and human possibilities that are not quantified—and made exchangeable with other ones. In Péguy's words, "The modern world considered negotiable values that the ancient world and the Christian world considered nonnegotiable. It is this universal negotiation that has made this universal debasement."[43]

With the reign of money, Péguy claims that many people within its orbit begin to habitually conceive of time and history in new ways. Ongoing metaphysical commitments beyond an immediate temporal, social, and material horizon appear to be too inflexible and demanding in a world of rapidly changing technology, potential profits, and negotiations, and they are set aside in favor of "progress," understood as an accumulation of immanent, temporal goods (in every sense). Human progress is no longer easily perceived as the outcome of individual initiative and action, but perceived as an inexorable if mostly impersonal force that is assumed to encompass all aspects of possible experience. It is not the same as a progress associated with the legal protections and rights connected to the Declaration of the Rights of Man, where Péguy thought progress was possible[44]—although for him, such progress relied upon individual initiative and keen-sighted, devoted action.

Following a comprehensive notion of accumulating progress, "the judgment of History" comes to be the supreme arbiter of goodness, justice, and truth. As Péguy's Muse of History puts it, "Yes, the modern world has made of me a pitiful idol."[45] For Péguy, if modern metaphysics labors to ensure that diverse pasts are comprehensively contextualized and kept separate from one another, "the" future replaces God as the source of ultimate vindication.

For Péguy, modern metaphysics—or the world assuming that metaphysics as true—had not only a predilection for the determinative force of historical time and the homogeneity of experience but also "a secret shameful taste for the inorganic" over the organic.[46] Inanimate things and tendencies—or "objective" social forces—were assumed to be the motive force and the ultimate foundation for knowledge. For Péguy, all these lifeless forms and forces were given far more prominence under the "reign of money" than they had enjoyed before.[47]

According to Péguy, this new dispensation of practice and reflexive assumption—though not of real and reasonable metaphysical possibilities—increasingly blocks out metaphysical alternatives to produce a particular kind of alienation, what he calls a "horizontal anxiety" and an "interior dispersion." That is to say, people increasingly do not experience anxiety supremely for, to take two long-standing outward-oriented forms of anxiety, the standing of the whole person before gods or God, or for their failing before an abiding standard of justice, or for how they should face an external enemy. One feels instead an anxiety born of instability within oneself.[48]

This reign, in Péguy's account, also changed the personal horizons of time that directed the course of life and its ultimate end. Under the reign of money one prepares and sacrifices primarily not for eternity and gods or God, but for a comfortable retirement.[49]

If human life was thus much more pervasively organized around the promise of a material or professional security, giving boundaries to an increasingly uncertain and wobbly sense of self, Péguy believed that it also circumambulated the self in a kind of metaphysical security that did not permit an opening to possibilities that challenged an increasingly habitual, allegedly "post-metaphysical" metaphysics. As a sort of palliative solution to modern anxiety, an increasingly doubt-filled, fragile self sought a refuge from alternative ways of life that would demand risk, commitment, sacrifice, and above all an abnegating love. Amid this movement, individual human beings increasingly sought not to give themselves beyond themselves but to be secure and comfortable, without venturing the self upon any truth. It encourages the formation of "the world of those who have nothing left to learn. The world of those who try to be clever. The world of those who are not dupes, not imbeciles. Like us. *That is to say*: the world of those who believe in nothing, not even in atheism."[50]

In this way, ongoing attachments to a person, a group of persons, or a culture—especially if they could be perceived as exceeding "modern" reason and utility, or were an unchosen inheritance—were set in opposition to quite distinct notions of "freedom" and "success." For Péguy, this was true even as contemporary attachments to distinctions of professional status and social class entirely retained and even fortified their hold over minds, ambitions, and actions.[51]

For Péguy, under the reign of money, many have begun to make an implicit or explicit claim that modern persons have left metaphysics behind, and that their own metaphysics is uniquely evident to reason. For him, just as in other and very different, earlier regimes of metaphysical order, "modern metaphysics" are increasingly "presented naturally as physics."[52]

Péguy repeatedly broaches the possibility that this modern metaphysics will ultimately, by its inner logic, aspire to what he calls a purely temporal "second creation" or "decreation"[53] that accustoms more and more human beings, through the habits of daily life as well as daily reading, writing, and action, to incline automatically toward certain ultimate assumptions about human being, the world, and their meaning. For Péguy, unlike modern metaphysics (which can be ancient), this replica creation is new and already present in the accelerating information flows of his time—ones that give shape to daily experience. They create an increasingly complete horizon for daily life in late modern societies.[54]

What is this replica creation? For Péguy, the new social sciences "repressed" the real, by creating forms of knowledge and of social organization that embed and hence confirm their assumptions about human motives and actions.[55] For him, moderns generally prefer abstract myths (made of theories, say, in social science), or what he called mythic "systems," to the vivid narrative particularities of ancient myths,[56] and often attempt to live in accordance with the mythic abstractions that they themselves have created, in order to make their experience of the world conform to their (often unspoken) metaphysical convictions.

Both historians and social scientists (in particular, sociologists) claim a power to make a replica creation,[57] through scholarship, one that will banish the unpredictability of events and try to fashion persons according to the postulates of social and natural science, in which the totality of human experience is no longer free or open to the new, but mastered and disciplined by abstraction. These assumptions are in large part not vindicated through the test of varied lived experience; they are vindicated in a factitious regime of opinion, as modern persons increasingly experience the world through media and textual mediation. These would include the exchanges of labor and commodities in markets, diverse forms of manufacture and technology, and—what was especially important for Péguy—by a daily diet of expository prose that describes, redescribes, and interprets the world each day.

In this way, the daily newspaper is not for Péguy, as it was for Hegel, the daily prayer of the realist; rather, Péguy claims it is "the beginning of decreation." It gives people "ready-made thought" and with it a "ready-made soul" or a "habituated soul,"[58] shaped both by the immediacy and seductive topicality of what it reads, and by the selective account of reality within it. Like modern history and modern sociology, journalism works toward a "second creation" that will vindicate a certain construal of the world, even though the world of one's own stubbornly complex and multidimensional experience does not. For these purposes, media and scholarship describe a constantly renewing cascade of events and experiences from the same metaphysical vantage point—while assuming that metaphysics itself is not "relevant" or otherwise suitable for discussion.

His unique account of the modern allows us to understand why modernity can be for Péguy analogous to a natural "illness." It takes certain legitimate, abiding human possibilities and aspirations and allows them to undergo indefinite expansion, while trying to diminish or even immobilize other legitimate, abiding human possibilities and aspirations. The cure for that illness is not to return to some previous historical epoch but to reopen the full metaphysical horizons that he believed had been ominously constricted very recently, in the late nineteenth century.[59]

Whatever constrictions were in place within modern culture, for Péguy metaphysical alternatives are inevitably, persistently alive. For him, there is no age in which a preponderant metaphysics can honestly rule out its most profound alternatives.

Péguy was convinced that in his own time, the reign of money should have found its natural opponents among those devoted to the lives of rigorous intellectual and spiritual integrity. Yet he saw that far too many priests and professors—including the devoted socialists among the latter—were in fact very often devoted to the metaphysics underwriting the reign of money. For him it was a source of protracted and outraged astonishment. In particular, professors increasingly formed what Péguy would call "the intellectual party." Their sway in the world of learning would be broken only by a revolution of critique.

CHAPTER 4

The Revolution of Critique

In *The Future of Science*, Renan had used the word "critique" for the pervasive sensibility he claimed for modern scholarship, and for the methods and the distinctive rhetorical style that accompanied it.[1] Péguy made the term his own, but saw in it an effort to preclude criticism of its modern metaphysical commitments rather than a true intellectual freedom. In his words, many of his opponents at the Sorbonne and elsewhere "very much want for us to critique everything. But they don't want us to critique critique."[2] For "they want everyone to be subjected to their method except themselves, and the results of their method."[3]

Yet how does one turn critique so that it can itself be criticized? How was the "critique of critique" forestalled? Péguy was convinced that an indispensable claim of metaphysically modern persons was to deny that modernity had a metaphysics: that is, assumptions and convictions in relation to ultimate questions about the nature of being, knowledge, history, goodness, justice, beauty, and truth that are not demonstrably certain. Whatever the answer, the responses to these questions transcend the findings of "physics" in the Greek sense and exceed what can be known by inquiry into nature by science, even if science were entirely "grounded" and without the elements of interpretation and convention explored by Milhaud, Duhem, and Poincaré. This reality was being assertively obscured. In Péguy's words, the "great cry of the modern world" is that metaphysics can be dispensed with entirely. "What one opposes is metaphysics; what one defends is never metaphysics."[4]

To this end, metaphysics was increasingly defined not as a series of ultimate convictions connected either to materialism or idealism, either to theism or atheism. Rather, metaphysics became something necessarily "religious" or Platonic in nature, a "high" concatenation of projected ideals onto a purely material universe, or one subject to objective social laws. Nondemonstrable affirmations—claims that science would inevitably replace philosophy, that religion was first and foremost a social fact and function, a hermeneutics of suspicion toward love, giving, generosity, and so on—were said to have no metaphysical status, and somehow to lie "beyond" or "after" metaphysics. They rejected not only a "Platonist idea," or that of Judaism, and Christianity, but also Hindu, Buddhist, and other sources. In Péguy's account, modernity—in some ways in the ancient and medieval worlds but openly and pervasively in the age of Nietzsche, Weber, Freud, Durkheim, and Mauss—belonged to those who claimed there is no unseen dimension of meaning, and that there is no labor of transcendence worth one's commitment, or even worth seeking.[5]

For Péguy, modern metaphysics is, as we have seen, often not new. Materialism, a comprehensively "debunking" metaphysics of all high motives, and related claims had been in various forms available well before the late nineteenth century. Second, this "post-metaphysical" metaphysics found itself facing a perennial temptation that, for Péguy, confronts all successful philosophical, religious, or ideological movements. Once a metaphysics has taken hold of a certain preponderance of influential persons and respected institutions, it begins to claim that its own metaphysical assumptions stand beyond serious question—they become the assumed template for all respectable thinking, with the same claim to consensual assent as replicated scientific findings. It is this that makes them "unbearable."[6]

Péguy's critique of critique is an argument that no metaphysics should be exempt from the challenge of reasoned argument, and no metaphysics should assume that it is simply and demonstrably "rational." Yet Péguy perceived a gathering rhetorical consensus among at least an effective plurality of educated people that such a challenge was no longer necessary, or even possible. One's arguments no longer required philosophical defense; they simply reflected the way things really are, or the integral boundaries of what we can really know.

Péguy believed that a broad swath of professors in the new research universities, above all the professors associated with the New Sorbonne—including social scientists like Durkheim and Mauss, as well as historians and historically minded scholars like Ernest Lavisse, Gustave Lanson, Charles Seignobos, and others—constituted a kind of party, the "parti intellectuel." They shared what he called the "superstition of the modern intellectual party . . . after so many others, like so many others, before so many others. [That is,] that they have said the last word about the history of humanity, that they have put the final period upon the history of human thought."[7]

Péguy's critique of the intellectual party is not therefore a nostalgic cry to "go back," since the intellectual party was guilty of precisely the same failing as the representatives of other dominant forms of metaphysical order in history. Yet Péguy uses a comparatively new term to describe them: "intellectual" was a term of recent vintage, and given its steady employment during the Dreyfus affair as a term for scholars and writers who intervened on behalf of Dreyfus (including Péguy himself), it seems the word would have strongly positive connotations for him.

In fact, when broaching the subject of the intellectual party, his emphasis was on the second word; Péguy acknowledged that he himself and a great many of the people he admired were intellectuals.[8] It was quite specifically a "party" of intellectuals that worried him. He concluded that a certain convergence of metaphysical convictions and ambitions had begun to dominate universities and a broader intellectual culture, not because of the force of its arguments, but because of its institutional and political power.[9] This made it ultimately more dangerous than political parties: "Intellectual parties—themselves political—are more dangerous than political parties . . . because they reach into man much more deeply."[10]

The intellectual party was of course not a formal party, not did it enjoy unanimity on questions of method, fields of inquiry, or political allegiance. For Péguy, the intellectual party upheld a certain set of related if not identical metaphysical postulates. Above all, its members were committed to "the essential thesis of modern intellectual metaphysics . . . [which] comes back essentially to this proposition: that man, or that humanity . . . we can know, we can achieve and seize or embrace an integral knowledge, with an exhaustive grasp, real, metaphysical, the entire event [événement] of reality, of man and of creation."[11]

The primary manifestation (in importance if not in chronological sequence), of this commitment, according to Péguy, could be found in modern academic history; secondarily, it manifested itself in sociology.[12]

In the notes for his prospective doctoral thesis, Péguy writes: "Historians have dominated."[13] This may come as marvelously gratifying news to historians, who do not generally see themselves that way. But Péguy means something quite specific; for him, historians compose the only one of the disciplines within the humanities that is able to have something other than a "secret shame" in relation to science.[14] For the diversity of human experience in time (which science struggles to explain entirely by itself) is preeminently their expertise. It is their responsibility to explain why the past is so various and multiform, and does not look immediately, scientifically explicable.

For Péguy, a careful, often erudite encounter with the past was indispensable for human beings. Yet he claimed that the historians of his own historical moment were precluding an authentic encounter with the past.

From his earliest writings on the subject—around 1906—Péguy identifies Renan as the master of these new historians, and with him as model, they desire to vindicate the modern age (defined by modern metaphysics) as the apex of human achievement.[15]

In the years that followed, Péguy accused the historians of the Sorbonne of failing to respect the unique and unrepeatable power of human events, in all history, modern or no.[16] The writing of history is accomplished by "the method of the indefinite exhaustion of historical detail"[17] and the Brobdingnagian accumulation of documents that make the extraordinary events of history seem pedestrian and entirely predictable. Such was the technique, for example, of Gustave Lanson's work, as discussed in Chapter 2.[18] The sole exception to this rule, for Péguy, is the intellectual party's account of the French Revolution.[19] In more general terms, he claims that the new historians want a "reprise of creation," a complete reproduction that would be able "to exhaust reality" and deprive time of its real creative power, collapsing all possible new action into a chimera of exhaustively historical, comprehensively contextual knowledge.[20]

Yet if all claims about human experience were *entirely* historical, and had to be fully understood with prodigious contextual erudition—not just in part, which Péguy believed was important, but entirely—then only a scholar could learn from the past and allow others to learn from it. Their method excluded the educated and attentive reader who did not accept their guidance. Furthermore, establishing such a context by stupefying quantities of contextual detail aspired, in Péguy account, to make it impossible for human beings to enter into a lived understanding of the past, and to be inspired by the past in consequential ways. Through the methods of modern historical research, metaphysical differences became contextual differences, with the metaphysics of the present passing judgment on the contextual limitations that prevented preceding ages from recognizing the evident legitimacy of the currently dominant metaphysical configuration.

Péguy claimed to be supremely interested in the possibility of learning diversely from diverse historical moments, and he finds these totalizing historicist accounts implausible on their face, even in his early attempts to critique critique. These often took the form of *humani nil a me alienum puto*, rendered in an unmistakable French accent.[21]

More precisely, however, Péguy accuses the new historians—in contrast to a historian like Jules Michelet[22]—of having little sense of events, peoples, and persons from previous historical epochs as potentially something more than prosaic occurrences and persons in an unending human round of often small, petty, even squalid motives and compromises. The possibility (crucial for Péguy) that individual lives included free and consequential decisions was set aside as tired and naïve, in favor of apparently secure generalizations or theories about the aggregate practices of groups, or of society as a whole.[23]

In his later years, Péguy claimed that the historians of the New Sorbonne had an aversion toward the very possibility of meaningful historical agency, in individual or sometimes collective terms. Historians like Langlois were "equally opposed to pagan and Christian grandeur."[24] Among them, writes Péguy, it is "grandeur itself that they cannot bear . . . they really want that man and humanity always lose."[25] In order to appear "liberal, equitable, shall I say, *objective*," modern historians engage in a quarrel with all heroes and saints. It was a quarrel of convictions that promised advancement as well, since "there will always be a Chair at the Sorbonne for the one who declares that the saints were fit for an insane asylum [*Charenton*]."[26]

For Péguy, historical persons now dead cannot defend themselves, even as they are consumed by condescending commentary, by "archivists of the world . . . [who] waste [*dilapider*] archives."[27] Historians of this kind level experience indiscriminately, depriving human beings of their dignity,[28] in an empty, homogenous space and time: the spatialized time that his teacher Bergson had repeatedly argued robbed enquiry of an encounter with life.

Through history, for Péguy the modern metaphysics of the intellectual party served as the basis for an antihumanism, rejecting both the partial, contextually-turned and inflected but nonetheless real continuities in human experience over time, as well as the possibilities of individual agency.

Péguy sometimes hoped to turn these prevailing methods against their practitioners, say, by applying their methods in different contexts ad absurdum. After being criticized by the historian Langlois, Péguy argued that Langlois could not criticize him until he had exhausted all the documentation and literature on Péguy himself, since he was also a person in history.[29]

Péguy thought that genuine historical understanding and novelty emerge from an organic relation to the past. For him, memory makes this organic relation possible; it is the distinctive method of writing history at the New Sorbonne that precludes it. For Péguy, the writing of (metaphysically) modern history refuses to participate in the past as a fellow human being learning about human beings in the past. In the name of objectivity, for historians of the intellectual party, both subject and object disappear in "serious" clinical disengagement. In the words of Clio, the muse of history (in *Clio, Dialogue Between History and the Pagan Soul*), the historical methods of his contemporaries move alongside time like a "railroad" placed parallel to the past, discreetly observing it from a distance:

> History is this long, longitudinal railroad that passes lengthwise all along the coast (but at a certain distance) and that stops at all the stations one wants. But it does not follow the coast itself, it doesn't coincide with the coast, for on the coast itself, on the coast there are tides, and men and fish, and mouths of streams and rivers, and the double life of the land and the sea.
>
> Man, she [Clio] says, will always prefer to measure himself rather than see himself.[30]

For Péguy, late modern history observes the past but will not take the risk of entering into its organic complexity, in part because it presents to human beings their own limits, their own mortality, and their own perpetual incompleteness.[31] Representation confines the real into manipulable, inorganic space: the map is preferred to the territory.[32] Taken to its extreme end, it finally ceases to be "objective"; rather, it is "not subjective or objective,"[33] it is simply removed from the reality of what it claims to address. In contrast to history, for Péguy memory insists on an opening in one's self in relation to human things and human beings in the past: "History is essentially longitudinal; memory is essentially vertical. History consists essentially in *passing alongside* the event. Memory consists essentially in being inside the event, in above all not leaving it, remaining there, and in ascending back from within."[34]

The turn toward memory requires participation and vulnerability, and so it is not for those who wish to remain merely secure: "To descend into one's self, that is the greatest terror of man."[35] Memory, in Péguy's formulation, enters into the past and understands its unique questions and tensions as ones that demand a human response that includes risk, and a patient discernment. It is a multidimensional, exacting, carefully critical receptivity on the part of the author who recounts and investigates past events.[36] For Péguy, if Michelet is the foremost example of a researcher into the past who draws upon the memory of events and allows his humanity to relate to the humanity of the past,[37] Ernest Lavisse and other representatives of the New Sorbonne renounce the task of memory and of understanding unique events in favor of a fantasy of objective distances and control.

Yet "events" are not simply historical or present "happenings" for Péguy. Events were the unpredictable, startling transformative developments that altered the horizons of possibility for a person, a people, or history itself—it is in this way that the contemporary philosopher Alain Badiou thinks of events, with Péguy as forerunner.[38] Nassim Taleb's "Black Swan" also has some of the connotations Péguy places on "the event"—but in Péguy's case, there is more emphasis on the event that inspires or constitutes transformative happenings in the history of a culture or civilization, including the ultimate meaning and purpose of politics, science, metaphysics, and revelation.[39]

The present opacity of the event was of great moment for Péguy. With the turn toward an "objective" understanding of human being, the perpetually unpredictable quality of the transformative event was no longer a respectable entrant into thought. For Péguy, the event eludes all predictive, putatively "scientific" or "realistic" or comprehensively "contextual" models of human behavior. It has myriad relations to its own past, but it comes as a shock: "What is always most unforeseen, is always the event."[40]

In Péguy's account, the Christian Incarnation, the French Revolution, and the Dreyfus affair all stand as events. These events are unique and have an uncanny power, disrupting both the aspiration toward expansively, predictively calculated experience and infinite abstraction that partisans of modern metaphysics so desired. For Péguy, events brought to ruin the most diverse attempts to formulate any complete explanation of historical change or a predictively secure social science of human being.[41] They became the reference points for understanding an entire epoch, even as they fundamentally violated the conventional wisdom of the age in which they happened.

Events are sometimes political for Péguy, sometimes spiritual; they can also be philosophical and scientific. He argues that philosophy and science alike rarely change in the manner of capitalist investment, accumulating resources and investing toward a desired, foreseen profit. Rather philosophical change and scientific discoveries alike often appear as an unexpected "intellectual revolution."[42] For that reason these transformative discoveries are generally not only unforeseen but unwanted as well: they "have almost never been desired by contemporaries."[43]

The leaders of the intellectual party believed that with modern metaphysics they had found clear, foreseeable patterns and meanings. They tended very strongly to believe that human beings can anticipate a final historical judgment—toward universal freedom or equality, or the conquest of nature affected by human beings for themselves. It was an idea that for Péguy appears with much *greater* power in the modern period than in any of its predecessors. It was no longer an eschatological judgment but drawn from history itself, a "laicization" of divine judgment. The future verdict of history is passionately sought, for it has become a substitute for the judgment of God or gods.[44] But for Péguy, this hope of validation from history is founded upon an "illusion of perspective."[45]

Many of his contemporaries imagined future persons and generations smiling attentively upon their epoch, or their own lives, or perhaps simply their opinions, and sanctioning their most important decisions in an ongoing future that intimates eternity without taking leave of history. But Péguy observes tartly that futures (for him there is no singular "future") will have their own constantly changing priorities, as well as their own futures and their own posterity to think about. Not only are there multiple futures, these futures will doubtless have their own flaws that make their judgments partial and flawed like the judgments of one's own time: posterity, he says, "will have other fish to fry."[46] It is also impossible to predict those futures merely by extending the predilections of the present, which is what people living in anticipation of future vindication want and expect, assuming that "posterity is like themselves . . . [but] later."[47]

Yet if one actually believes that the judgment of one's life will come from posterity's approval, then one's expectations of history's "direction" take on a heretofore inconceivable strength. They become the subject of an almost religious awe and concomitant obedience in return for a purely temporal salvation, bestowed upon the elect that were "faithful" to *the* future (with the definite article) before it had fully realized itself. It is a futile if poignant hope: for Péguy the notion of a single "tribunal of history" or "judgment of posterity" is quite "touching."[48]

The illusion of an extended and continuous vindication in time never becomes real. Amidst the future's own distinctive hopes and anxieties, if a given historical moment turns its gaze backward at all, it has a great host of persons and epochs demanding its attention: "It is *each* judging generation, each future generation" that must decide what it wishes to judge "in the presence of *all* the past generations."[49] Rather than the host of future humanity gazing upon one's moment in history, there is stiff competition simply to be noticed, by a constantly changing and constantly distracted group of imperfect and unknown judges, who—if they are metaphysically modern in Péguy's sense—are also hoping to be noticed, quite possibly for very different reasons.[50]

Through the event, history turns and returns, giving no epoch, method, or person the comfort of subjugating surprise. History cannot even be trusted to move clearly forward. Péguy thus has Clio, the muse of history, warn his pagan soul: "One must distrust even me. I am altogether capable of turning around again what had been turned away before."[51]

For Péguy, beyond the anticipated vindication by a perpetual future that it had deliberately prepared or created, there was another way that the "intellectual party" could avoid reckoning with the event: through the postulates of social science. His notes for his doctoral thesis develop his thoughts about how "the sciences inspire much more respect than letters, arts [and various] philosophies," and that departments of letters even felt, as noted above, "a secret shame" in relation to science.[52] He believed that a modern metaphysics wished to identify itself with modes of enquiry into nature that made continual progress in subjugating nature, and that were therefore considered the supremely valid form of knowledge, in relation to which the humanities' own traditional paths of posing questions and encountering the world appeared weak, quaint, and arbitrary.

The attempt to systematize, rationalize, and mathematicize reality—to make human being and human experience purely scientific objects—had inspired Péguy's articulate opposition from the very beginning of his career. His first published article was a review of a book by the economist Léon Walras for *La Revue socialiste* in 1897. Péguy pointed out that Walras made remarkable and by no means self-evident assumptions, set forth in simplified examples, rendered in mathematical abstractions.[53] For Péguy, Walras depended upon a radical estrangement from (and simplification of) "the real" to make his system work.[54]

This convergence between mathematics, science, and a certain variety of metaphysics was for Péguy often a complex, awkward, and implausible one, but he clearly feared those ambiguities and complexities had been cast aside in favor of a spurious pathos of objectivity and distance, in frank imitation of the natural sciences. For instance, in a draft manuscript of 1906, he wrote: "The original Darwinism, the Darwinism of Darwin[,] . . . was a truly scientific hypothesis, a hypothesis of true science, like so many others, verified."[55] But by what Péguy calls a "metaphysical extension," a *methodological* naturalism quickly became a *metaphysical* naturalism: "By a first usurpation . . . this scientific, naturalist, modest hypothesis was made into a metaphysical, supernatural, universal, proud, total, absolute, infinite thesis."[56]

Above all, modern metaphysics—along with the intellectual party—deployed a ubiquitous if subtle evasion when it wanted, in Péguy's formulation, to present its metaphysics as a secure body of knowledge. It aspired to create methods and systems, but these inevitably relied upon an "as if" (Péguy made this claim before the publication of Hans Vaihinger's famous book on the subject). For Péguy the "as if" involved a series of assumptions that animate the discipline or resolve the enquiry that are themselves uncertain, and require some metaphysical decision that is masked as a procedural necessity or a dictate of disinterested reason. For example, a modern discipline operates on the assumption that human beings are fundamentally motivated by rational self-interest, that religion is supremely or exclusively a social act, that human experience can be satisfactorily quantified, and so on. No argument is made; the discipline functions on the grounds that it acts *as if* these claims were true.

For Péguy, "the real absolutely can in no way welcome [or] accept this *as if*" that represents the forgetting of "organic memory."[57] The "as if" becomes a "perpetual miracle" and "monstrous" ("in the etymological sense of the word"). It allows a science of human being to exempt itself from reality.[58] For Péguy, human sciences aspire to bypass lived human experience [expérience]. Actual experience, he wrote, "as it is, as it comes from the womb of nature, earthy experience . . . not at all sanitized . . . one would almost dare say anarchist," is set aside for "experience as it ought to be . . . washed experience, shaved, clad, dressed . . . sanitized, presentable." This experience is "the sole object of truly scientific knowledge," but it can never be more than an incomplete and abstract rendering of reality.[59]

For Péguy, the miracle of the "as if" was everywhere in the rapidly expanding and ambitious social sciences, above all by way of Durkheimian sociology—and often at the expense of philosophy. In Péguy's account, Durkheim sought to replace metaphysical inquiry with what Péguy calls "socio-therapeutics," or "sociometrics."[60]

Sociology had interested Péguy early in his career: he had written a generally positive if not uncritical review of Durkheim's *Suicide* for *La Revue socialiste* in 1897. Péguy found the book insightful but by method "condemned to study only exterior manifestations, always a little broad [*grossières*] and inexact."[61] But he became more critical as Durkheim's power grew (and especially as Durkheim became an intellectual opponent of his mentor Henri

Bergson). By 1907, he referred to Comte as a kind of god for the scholars of the Sorbonne, and to Durkheim as the "greatest of his saints."[62]

Sociology in general, like other disciplines based upon modern metaphysics, depends for Péguy upon suppressed, unacknowledged metaphysical decisions,[63] and sought to suppress a more widespread recognition of those unacknowledged decisions by casting philosophy to the margins. Péguy singled out Durkheim for particular criticism: "Durkheim is not a patron *of* philosophy, but a patron *against* philosophy," expressing "this terror that the Sorbonne has at present for everything connected to thought."[64]

Péguy made no secret of the fact that he rejected the tacit modern metaphysics of the sociologists, historians, and others who constituted the parti intellectuel. At one point he calls the party "vulgar" for, among other things, "having not only no sense of beauty, but as not having even, at bottom, the sense of nature."[65]

For all that, Péguy was certainly attuned to variations in cultures and radically distinct possibilities in nature. Yet he was very skeptical about the notion of a decisive caesura or epochal break in human history, in which permanent changes to the fundaments of human nature were possible, or had in fact already been achieved. When he began to think about the intellectual party in 1906 and 1907, he spoke skeptically of "the new or allegedly new humanity" of the modern world.[66] To assume that metaphysical modernity was both fundamentally different and decisively superior to all its alternatives reflected what he believed was a deeply implausible assumption that, as he put it in his *Zangwill* of 1904, "humanity begins with the modern world, that the intelligence of humanity begins with modern methods."[67]

It could be that the positing of a "nature"—even one of larval capacities, proclivities, and ends rather than of some comprehensive and fixed order—was by the time of Péguy's writing an impossible task. Just a decade after Péguy's death, Virginia Woolf famously wrote: "On or about December 1910, human character changed."[68] Péguy was not convinced by these sorts of increasingly prominent and widely accepted claims. Historical change for him was real and powerful, but he did not find it supremely powerful, as his thinking about metaphysical modernity as a premodern possibility suggests. Even the changes in "sympathy" with which Woolf is concerned are for Péguy distributed in part by historical epochs and circumstances, but also by many other factors, not least one's own metaphysical intuitions and questions.

In Péguy's way of thinking, a claim like Woolf's was itself a metaphysical decision that had been available for a long time, that is, to decide that human nature was so fungible that it could change suddenly and decisively with the move from one historical epoch to another, driven by historical changes in mores, technology, politics, and so on. To deny a metaphysical claim (that is, that there is such a thing as human nature) is almost inevitably to affirm another one,[69] (for example, that no such nature exists, but is always, constantly, and invariably constructed and reconstructed by a few carefully selected "forces" working in history).

Péguy could be rather sharp about the tendency for a given age to exult in its overcoming of some path of life or way of thinking in the past. When various forms of metaphysics leave us behind, "we flatter ourselves with the belief that it is we who have left them."[70] For "a mind that has begun to *go beyond* a philosophy is simply a soul that is beginning to get out of joint with the tone and the rhythm, with the language and the resonance of this philosophy."[71]

If the controversy was simply about professors committing themselves to a series of metaphysical assumptions, for Péguy they always have the right to affirm the metaphysics they find most plausible.[72] But it was difficult to oppose a metaphysics that would not acknowledge itself as such; for Péguy, it made it possible simply to ignore critics and criticisms of critique. If someone called attention to the modern metaphysics behind their positions in a way that implied disagreement, the response was often to ignore the objection until the author departed from the scene, demoralized from lack of recognition and isolation.[73]

The tendency to ignore disagreement was by no means entirely attributable to malice. The members of the intellectual party struggled to live appreciatively as equals among those with whom they disagreed. This created a culture of constrictive and sterile politesse, which often meant silence in the face of substantive difference, and imposing a remarkably constrictive boundary around substantive dialogue.

In one passage, Péguy describes this impasse by using the term "modernism" for the new putatively post-metaphysical or "low" metaphysics, and opposes it to what he describes as freedom. In this way, "modernism consists in not believing what one believes. Freedom consists in believing what one believes and in admitting (in the end, demanding), that one's neighbor also believe what he believes. Modernism consists in not believing one's self so as to avoid offending the adversary who doesn't believe either. It is a system of mutual decline. Freedom consists in believing. And to admit, to believe that one's adversary believes . . . modernism is a system of politeness. Freedom is a system of respect."[74]

Whatever awkwardness might accompany a modern encounter with others who think differently, here as elsewhere the metaphysics of critique is protected from all critique and takes shelter in an exclusive sociability of implied agreement, congruent with Renan's sinuous if not always forthright acts of suggestion.

Yet above all, it was the attempt by the members of the intellectual party to institutionalize their metaphysics as a kind of science that incurred Péguy's fiercest objections. As Péguy wrote in *On the Situation Made for the Intellectual Party in the Modern World* of 1906, "The modern intellectual party has the infinite right to have a metaphysics, a philosophy, a religion, a superstition as vulgar and stupid as is necessary to please them . . . the legal right . . . but what is at question . . . is to know if the modern state . . . has the right . . . to adopt this metaphysics, to absorb it, to impose it on the world and put at its service the enormous means of governmental power."[75]

For Péguy, the task of placing critique beyond critique took the form above all of government-approved curricular reform. It is for this reason that he locates a fundamental modern change not in 1517 or 1789, but in a less universally remembered date: "The decisive date is found around 1881."[76] This date marks a revolution, with the accompanying capture of opinion and institutions: the passage of the Ferry Laws of 1880 and their application to primary education the following year.

In his references to the Ferry Laws and many other similar changes in education, Péguy gives little attention to the most famous provisions of these laws—an education that is universal and free, an extension of mandatory primary education to girls as well as boys. He strongly objects, however, to a perceptibly heavier emphasis on contemporary knowledge and learning through new education schemes that sever the study of science from the humanities.[77] Not least, he vigorously opposed the diminution of instruction in Latin and Greek.[78]

For Péguy, since the Ferry Laws, the supporters of modern metaphysics had worked continuously to reduce the place of disciplines that might lead students to stand outside their own favored metaphysical horizons. Sociologists associated with the intellectual party favored additional courses in social science, less work on ancient languages, and a smaller place for philosophy. They had, in his words, sought to "abolish" both Hellenism and Christianity from secondary education.[79]

For Péguy, the diminution of classical learning and the thoroughgoing rejection of earlier accounts of the person and moral duty represented an attempt to enact the epochal break to which modern metaphysics in the modern age aspired. The modernity of the intellectual party—understood metaphysically—runs counter to Jewish and Christian sources, and from earlier but distinctly modern sources: it is "against the Platonists, against the Cartesians, against the Kantians."[80] In this new order, if one's education involved premodern or early modern sources offering an alternative metaphysics, they would be carefully filtered through late modern methods, for example, as sources defined by "prescientific" or naïve, incredible metaphysical positions that must be contextualized.

Péguy is insistent upon this point: modernity must be understood *not* as a return to paganism but as an attack on pagan, Jewish, and Christian cultures, in fact upon all the cultures that preceded its own creation of a world in which metaphysical modernity is not one option among others but an intellectual, metaphysical sovereign that simultaneously insists upon its non-metaphysical, non-sovereign character. This sovereignty demands the contextualization in particular of claims that persons have lived different kinds of exemplary lives in diverse cultures.[81] Students would now meet an encompassing spiritual, historical, and cultural horizon in late modernity itself. In one passage, Péguy claims that a new intellectual order, believing in a world of technical, credentialed experts presiding over an increasingly comprehensive immanence, has created in universities like the Sorbonne—and increasingly in education as such—a "materialist scholasticism."[82]

By the summer of 1914, Péguy—writing the *Note conjointe* that would be unfinished when he left for the Front in August—was still very much concerned not simply with Germany's mobilization, but about the victorious advance of modern metaphysics through the habituating powers of capitalism, and its ongoing hostility to metaphysical diversity:

> This modern world has made for humanity such conditions, so entirely and absolutely new, that all that we know from history, all that we have learned from preceding humanities cannot help us, cannot make us advance in knowledge of the world in which we live. There are no precedents. For the first time in the history of the world, the spiritual powers have been altogether oppressed not by material powers but by a single material power: the power of money. . . .
>
> For the first time in the history of the world, money is master without limitation or measure . . . for the first time in the history of

the world money is alone before God . . . that which ought to serve only for exchange has completely invaded the value to be exchanged.

The instrument has become the matter and object and the world . . . it is as if the clock began *to be* time. . . .

In these conditions . . . I consider criminal and gestural, all politics that tend to divide the spirit from itself and to turn it against itself, all politics that tend to divide spiritual forces.

Because it will not be other spiritual forces that will win out. It will always be money. . . .

All that one will take to a spiritual force, *whatever it is*, all that one will remove from it, and that one will withdraw from a spiritual force, it is not another spiritual force that will gain it, it is money.

I have said it twenty times: the struggle (and it is a mortal struggle), the debate, the struggle is not between the Christian world and the ancient world. (And in the ancient world I put naturally all the worlds of philosophers.) The struggle is between the modern world, on one side, and on the other side all the other worlds together.

All the other worlds (other than the modern world) have been worlds of some spirituality. The modern world alone, being the world of money, is the world of a total and absolute materiality.[83]

In these lines, Péguy argues that under the "metaphysical option" of modernity, the acquisition and spending of money is no longer an indispensable support for life. It has become the preeminent activity of life and the foremost criterion of judgment—and hence its unprecedented power justifies a broad front against modern metaphysics (but not one of indiscriminate alliances, as his constant opposition to reactionary and Marxist politics shows). The threat he sees before his culture is nonetheless conveyed with urgency: "Everywhere thought is targeted, metaphysics, freedom, fecundity. It is the soul itself that it wants to reach, and lower it once and for all."[84]

This project finds itself advanced enthusiastically by cultural and intellectual establishments: "All that was made responsible for, officially made responsible for, maintaining culture, all that is constituted, all that has been instituted to maintain culture and the humanities betrays culture and the humanities. Betrays them officially, formally, and takes glory and honor from it."[85]

Openings leading to other metaphysical possibilities—for Péguy, plastered over by historicism and the social-scientific "as if"—always remained available. But for his opponents, methodological sleights of hand like the "as if" themselves had a kind of concealed religious function tending toward a distinctive end of history. As Péguy put, the "as if" was the "missionary of redemption, the father of the Trinity," since "all this modern scientific certainty is wagered upon this evasion [*démission*], upon this metaphysical abdication."[86]

Since the reign of money so easily habituates persons to certain metaphysical conclusions, Péguy argues that with the help of social scientific "as ifs" supporting that metaphysics, modern societies are in some important ways *more* homogenous—metaphysically—than their premodern predecessors. Though modern societies are certainly more complex in relation to the logistics of production or exchange or distribution, they are simpler in regard to ways of life, in which a homogenizing metaphysics (drawn from, say, capitalism, materialism, utilitarianism, social-scientific theories, or a popularized positivism) is universalized to all persons or cultures. They can make fewer allowances for a true interior diversity—both individual and communal—of motives, aspirations and purposes.[87]

Within education itself, Péguy also found a characteristic way of reading among members of the intellectual party, a way of reading that precluded receptivity to the text, or to working with what one reads. He writes that texts expressing compelling metaphysical alternatives, from Homer to Hugo, are not read but rather stand "accused."[88] In this way, for him the intellectual party has turned living thought available through reading into an inert object of study, where libraries and similar places become "intellectual necropolises."[89] Books are no longer part of an ongoing conversation but are preserved on library shelves for scholarly specialists—which is "an existence of the dead."[90]

Yet if Péguy gives an account of how the horizons of knowledge and wonder are being metaphysically closed at the beginning of the twentieth century, what—or better, how—should people know? Péguy's answer to that question is in fact an opening to two questions: given that for him metaphysics does involve uncertainty and uncertain answers, how can one address uncertainty, beyond remarking upon the uncertain commitments of one's metaphysical opponents? If one is thus made metaphysically "open," how should one read?

The deference to science at the New Sorbonne and elsewhere relied upon the unmistakably Cartesian notion that demonstrable certitude is the ultimate and legitimate master criterion of truth, and hence that mathematical and scientific knowledge is the supreme, paradigmatic, and true knowledge. Péguy's own method of returning to origins to deal with very contemporary dilemmas—that is, to think in "fortnights"—leads him to return to Pascal's quarrel with Descartes, and to find there the starting point for his own answers to questions of liberal learning and metaphysics.

First, Péguy argues that metaphysics is as natural and necessary an experience of being human as laughter—in a revealingly Rabelaisian allusion, the earthy example that Péguy himself gives—or language, eating, aging, love, sex, art, death, parenting, or any other fundamental human experience. That is to say, "metaphysics is also of man and of humanity."[91] Just as these human activities are not foresworn before demonstrable certitude is secured, so it is with metaphysical enquiry.

On the question of demonstrable certitude and metaphysics, Péguy affirmed without hesitation that no philosophy (or elsewhere, theology) can decisively resolve its own "difficulties"[92] and thus demonstrate its own validity. But for him, there was a crucial, even infinite, logical gap between the statement "this is not demonstrably certain" and the statement "this is purely subjective," or still more assertively, "this must be considered false."

In this way, Péguy claimed that imperfections and vulnerabilities are a necessary part of finite beings making any attempt to describe and explain the inexhaustible plenitude of reality.[93] A truly consequential metaphysics is thus an adventure, what he called a "an exploratory voyage of the real"[94] that sets people on unpredictable, diverse, and always incomplete paths of thinking and acting.

Since metaphysics is not a historically contingent practice that can be set aside without abandoning an indispensable dimension of being human,[95] the attempt to supersede it is unnatural. Yet it is not the case that all metaphysical possibilities are impervious to rational investigation.

Metaphysical decisions should be beyond conclusive demonstration *and* be accompanied by reason—and, at least at their outset, by uncertainty as well. Péguy follows Pascal carefully, though with a certain vivacious, Corneillian buoyancy quite different from Pascal. That buoyancy is simultaneously endowed with a stronger sense of the risk and sacrifice involved in wagering one's life upon a way of truth, rather than upon initially accepting a truth for the purpose of individual salvation. Working through Pascal's thought in his own way, Péguy concludes that to think through truly ultimate questions, one must think very carefully and critically in order to be free to take a risk upon an answer to them, an answer that after all of one's thinking appears most likely to be true. One's spiritual or philosophical way of life can then be undertaken reasonably and boldly as a "wager"[96] amid what he calls elsewhere the "glorious incertitude of metaphysics."[97]

Far from being a shortcoming, this "glorious" uncertainty in which human beings must place a metaphysical "bet" is a guarantor of our freedom, a gift from God himself.[98] In theological terms, Péguy argues that the God of Jewish and Christian revelation allows himself to be freely questioned, lowered into a seeming kind of equality or near equality with other metaphysical possibilities for thought, with (in the manner of Corneille's writing) a disarming sense of honor and love.[99]

Rather than refuse a metaphysical venture until a final, demonstrable security of metaphysical conviction—forever unavailable to human beings in history—arrives, Péguy recommends discerning which metaphysics appears to open toward the truth. Péguy's metaphysical wagers include both careful reasoning about and the embodiment of the truths one affirms. Here the desire to invest is put to a very different use from the prevailing reign of money, because the self is freely spent and given in honest metaphysical ventures, rather than securely hedged, saved, and withheld.

For Péguy, there is no linear progress in thought, especially in metaphysics: philosophies do not "surpass" one another. Descartes did not strike down Plato, nor did Kant strike down Descartes. For him "great metaphysics" are "languages of creation." Atheism is a legitimate metaphysical response to theistic metaphysics, but it in no way surpasses it,[100] as his adversaries believed. Péguy argues that a rigorous, careful thinker "can enter in his turn" and add "his voice to the eternal concert."[101]

Readers enter into and participate in this concert through the very act of reading. Péguy repeatedly calls for a way of learning that cooperates with metaphysical, historical, and cultural difference rather than forcefully (often, to his mind, with a passive-aggressive violence) subjugating metaphysical and historical difference to an unstated but ubiquitous metaphysics that wants to present itself as a comprehensive, final account of the real.

While interpreting a passage from Pascal, for example, Péguy argues that we should read texts as if they have been sent "in a package by postal express for us."[102] The method of reading can legitimately draw upon contextual historical knowledge,[103] but it does not allow previous historical and philosophical uses of the text to dictate our response to it. Péguy believed this way of reading gives the reader a "frightening responsibility." In what to contemporary ears sounds like Levinasian language, he writes: "The works [of past cultures and civilizations] are in our hands like hostages."[104]

The work of reading and seeking understanding through reading is end-less: for Péguy, no author can foreclose diverse future interpretation. Yet this ambiguity is a good and living indeterminacy. The act of interpretation should generally take the form of cooperation between author and reader[105] rather than serving *either* as matter for an accusation on behalf of metaphysical mo-dernity, or as a marmoreal act of reverential reaction.

The dangers of habitual reverence are real for Péguy. To read Homer, Clio instructs Péguy: "Don't say to yourself, he is great . . . don't tell yourself: it's Homer."[106] Péguy goes still further: Homer's poetry should be read in the same way one reads "a volume released last week by Émile Paul" (a popular French publisher).[107]

These words that make the past present come from Clio herself, and that is important. The reader must acknowledge in some sense that the text is *both* present to oneself and historical, rather than turning into a flawless monu-ment, even as the reader must also avoid an "objective" historicism in which the present consigns the past to irrelevance in order to seek the approval of "the" future.

This responsibility includes the responsibility to learn about the context of a text—its language, the historical circumstances of its creation, and more. Péguy's position on history was nuanced: he understood the importance of reading and thinking about history, and recognized that it was something that could never be explained or recounted definitively. He praises historians, those "true historians" who "passionately search for the truth of past events, espe-cially human events, and who most ordinarily find it, to the extent . . . that it is possible to find it."[108]

For Péguy, the truth of past events could not be found by placing undue emphasis upon a monadic greatness divorced from the lives of ordinary people. In one of his late writings, he called for a history that would show how the daily life of a people shapes its mores, and how it is related to the exceptional events, movements, and persons that are always connected to the original people and conditions from which their originality came.[109] To understand the people around "thinkers" and "republican leaders" and the "great founders of the Republic" one needs to understand "an *ordinary* repub-lican family," including "what they did . . . how they married, how they lived . . . how they raised their children," which would form "the history of every day of the week."[110] In this way, history would be connected to the egalitarian aspirations of modern history at the Sorbonne, but without a ready-made metaphysics that levels gradations of quality and importance so that all historical action and agency becomes disembodied, ready to be sub-jugated to prevailing patterns of abstraction.[111]

Rather, different levels of reality participated in one another subtly and multidimensionally. Péguy was quick to affirm the notion of genius and ex-traordinary persons, but he also remarked that Homer, Plato, Beethoven, and Jesus all came from a certain irreplaceable place and time, which does not de-termine or comprehensively circumscribe their life and work, but is integrally connected to their work and to their lives.[112]

In Péguy's critique of critique, there was no question of secure epistemo-logical or metaphysical foundations—whether they acknowledged it or not, that was his opponents' ambition, not his own. Both the author and the reader were "perpetually incomplete." The stakes for Péguy were high: "A bad read-ing of Homer has a resonance on and in the [that is, Homer's] work."[113] We as readers "are free to hold the opinions that we want, alas, that is to say to bring, to introduce the collaborations that we want. We are free to say and to do all sorts of foolishness that we want."[114] A reader must cultivate a certain mea-sure of vulnerability, even a kind of precise, lucid, cooperative love, in the act of reading: at one point, Péguy even suggests a mild illness that does not af-fect one's intellectual powers opens the mind to a truly careful reading, while maintaining the required energy to avoid an unthinking passivity.[115]

For Péguy, a work read honestly and collaboratively could come alive, and matter, in a way that the most urgent inventory of contemporary happenings from a tacit, ubiquitous metaphysical starting point did not. "Homer is new this morning, and perhaps nothing is as old as today's newspaper."[116]

The encounter with metaphysical possibilities and embodied ways of life through reading can only come once both the reflexive tendencies of late modern "critique" and of "monumental reverence" are set aside. For the latter, the exhortation to revere past achievement mechanically precludes exacting judgment and intellectual honesty; for the former, human nature is suffi-ciently discontinuous that ways of reading that hope for any kind of living engagement with the past through memory rather than history are impossi-bly naïve. For Péguy, a full education does not demand the subordination of the mind to a single abstract system in order to "mummify reality"[117] but in-stead does so to offer what he calls "a system of dignity." He adds "of indig-nity" as well, since he, Péguy, could be judged unworthy in his "system" of "culture and humanity," whereas, a system of knowledge that denies au-thentic human achievement or agency cannot discriminate between goods—and degrees of excellence—in human action and thinking.[118]

When history, literature, and philosophy were read this way, they entered memory. Following his teacher Bergson, Péguy believed that it was the participatory, integrative, organically cumulative properties of memory that made freedom possible. Memory allowed the creative self to act freely in the present in surprising continuity with the past. Memory also opened the distance of time so that it became a living distance. According to Péguy, it is very much like aging,[119] which allows persons to turn to memory to encounter the meaning of their lives anew; it is what gives persons and peoples both their depth and their creative possibilities.

Metaphysical Federalism

For Péguy there is no question of a tidy metaphysical progress, determined in turn by material and technological progress. Humanity "will constantly invent various -graphies and -copies and -phonies, that will not be less 'tele-' from one to the other, and that will make it possible to go around the globe in no time. But it will never be anything other than this temporal earth . . . [for] no man ever, nor any humanity, in a certain sense . . . could intelligently boast of having surpassed Plato."[120]

Of course, Péguy's claim is absurd if one assumes that "to surpass" means to "know facts" or to "master nature" in the manner of a scientific society, or to further the nature-conquering ambitions of early modern scientists like Bacon and Descartes. But Péguy is interested in learning above all as a way of thinking, sharply and freely questioning others before and along different metaphysical paths.

Péguy proposed that modern metaphysics, despite its frequent (though not universal) sympathy for philosophical liberalism in politics, was in fact deeply illiberal, and would, in the very moments of its greatest success, eventually betray free questioning, and with it an indispensable insight of liberalism: that is, that the imperfectibility of human beings requires a mixture and separation of powers in order to prevent systemic corruption and oppression. For Péguy, this applied no less to metaphysical paths and ways of learning than it did to political institutions and the distribution of political power. He served as an advocate of what might be called a philosophical and cultural *meta-liberalism* of learning.

Previous historical epochs and regimes had counterbalanced the persistent power of money and the metaphysical habits it engendered in a way that late modern life did not.[121] With all their flaws and injustices—and their own inevitable metaphysical triumphalism—a certain *fatras*, or jumble, of living intellectual and cultural possibilities[122] was often available at diverse levels of learning and station. This fatras was for Péguy, "le petit nom" of freedom itself.[123] For him, a "living jumble is worth more than a dead order."[124] He hoped for new ways of ordering culture that would revive, extend, and affirm the need for a cultural distinction of powers within and among different orders of human experience.

For Péguy, these powers would include a mixture of those persons devoted to prosperity and wealth, persons devoted to civic vitality, and persons devoted to chivalric honor, as well as those whose lives were shaped by forms of etiquette and public ritual, others by religion and spiritual life, or by life with their kindred and their people.[125] In Péguy's account, it is this diversity that finds itself threatened in an increasingly global order, one that seeks to subordinate these different ways of life to the regnant assumptions of a universal bourgeois culture.

This diversity could be secured through a "true federalism" that is not limited to nation-states and legal prerogatives—not being merely "territorial and formal," it allows freedom for different ways of life and paths of mind.[126] This metaphysical balance did—and presumably would—not preemptively exclude the market or the intellectual consensus that draws its plausibility from the habits of mind encouraged by the market, but rather, open more room for other ways of work, thinking, and learning to thrive without, alongside and within it.[127]

Péguy proposed distinctive ways of reading, of turning to memory, of venturing one's self and relating to the past, ones that drew upon diverse origins but offered no imposition of some single way of thinking or being in the past. Péguy offered a much more relational approach to learning. He wanted to set the past and the present in an open, ongoing, and unpredictable conversation, in which individuals honestly explore and wager upon different metaphysical possibilities, alive to their own freedom and respecting the freedom of others.

It is not clear, however, that material and technological change can be so easily set apart from an account of human action and metaphysical wagers, as Péguy believes. Might the very nature of persistent human desires and durable forms of human action require changes once technology transforms their relationship to human life as a whole, and to the world that human beings inhabit? These are questions that Péguy engages—and also fails to engage—as he ponders revolutions of honor, and questions of war. But he engages them as *embodied* questions. For his quarrel with the intellectual party and the modern metaphysics it championed did not end with the critique of critique. He concluded that his opponents had also committed themselves to a misunderstanding of the body—in fact, an ostensible exaltation of the body that expressed a latent but pervasive contempt for it, manifest both in the carnality of the body itself, and in its relationship to solidarity, love, and work.

CHAPTER 5

Revolutions of the Body and Work

For many decades, historians have given copious attention to the body in the Belle Époque. The erotic body, idealized male and female bodies, the medical body, the body of the citizen—these topics have prompted an abundance of research and reading.[1] In these terms, a fascination with the body—variously desirous of liberation and control, its capacities for work and sexual expression—elicits intense interest.

Péguy understands the body differently. For him, the exclusion of the spiritual from the body by both Christians and a secular, nascent "post"-Christian culture reflected a misunderstanding of the relationship between soul and body. It expressed what was for Péguy a characteristically bourgeois misunderstanding of nature. This conviction put him at some distance from his contemporaries, believers and skeptics alike.

The gender of "nature" in Péguy's thought is, not surprisingly, feminine, but her season of life is not at all what it would be for many eighteenth-century pastoralists and nineteenth-century Romantics, with their idealized and ravishing "natural" youthful woman nursing her children at the breast. This idealized nature was often defined supremely by fertility and by a hazy moralism that expresses itself most easily in mute and preferably fatal sacrifice by the woman representing nature, usually on behalf of her children or her own sexual virtue, as in Rousseau's *Julie* or Bernardin de Saint-Pierre's *Paul et Virginie*—or, in a slightly different key, Auguste Comte's idealization of Clotilde de Vaux.

For Péguy, nature is quite strikingly an old woman, "an old mother," of exuberant life. Maternal Nature is "cleverly, basely, dirtily, nobly, humble and haughty, boiling and drunk, full and starving, sated and parched, all atremble and full of eternal fermentations, universally triumphant and inexhaustibly victorious."[2]

The mixture of reason and instinct, baseness and nobility, is both striking and clearly sympathetic. In the hands of another author, this rendering of nature might speak of feminine "caprice," but for Péguy a certain exuberant messiness, what he calls a fatras, is very much a precondition for free and flourishing life,[3] for both men and women. In contrast to his own rendering of nature, he finds in the social scientists around him a nature that is an object of theoretical speculation and is supposed to submit to their ceaseless probings, just as the demure young mother of romanticized domesticity submits to her "duties." Sociologists, for example, want to replace a reasoning and uproarious nature with a submissive "skinny little miss."[4] She is a perfect specimen of what they believe nature should be, without ambiguity or aging.

In contrast to modern notions of a perpetually youthful nature, Péguy's nature appears to owe more to an earthy and older notion of Mother Nature: it is closer to the nature of Chaucer than it is to the nature of either eighteenth-century philosophes or nineteenth-century Romantics, or to the nature that is ready to have herself "explained" by the social and natural sciences.

Nature as an aged, exuberant, fertile, and messy abundance appears repeatedly in his poetry, where Péguy encounters "a world drunk with sap and with vitality."[5] His accounts of the human body also show a marked fondness for the earthy, peasant body. It is the body of the man or woman who lives within the decidedly untidy experiences of embodied life, who also passes easily into melancholy at the gray hairs and weakened body that signal his or her aging and stand as silent harbingers of death. Men and women find a melancholy but also invigoratingly hopeful peace in the youth of their children and youth in general rather than in their own indefinitely continued youth.[6]

Such images can quickly become kitsch if they are referred immediately to the prospects and putative easy happiness of the young, to which the aged give tribute and from which they derive vindication (as they did in some of the popular writings of Rousseau, the paintings of Jean-Baptiste Greuze, and their many imitators and epigones in the eighteenth and nineteenth centuries). But kitsch—as Milan Kundera put it in one of his good novelistic essays[7]—that posits a false eternity by narcissistically denying real suffering, aging, uncertainty and death is precisely *not* what Péguy has in mind. On the contrary, for him, aging must be part of all our experience, "aging being the human itself."[8]

In his late writings, Péguy recounts how people at different moments of life relate to experience differently, but with an increasing awareness of limits, especially aware of both the beauty and the inevitable futility of youthful illusions. It is a tendency perhaps most visible in his reflections upon the "secret" of the "man of forty."[9] The secret is a paradox that animates the life of a father's relationship to his sons, in which the father's own aging body and (at a distance) approaching death lead to an at once painful and tender lucidity. It may be revealed to some who are in their thirties, but it is impossible to explain to those who are younger than thirty. The secret is that no man is happy—in the sense of the unambiguous, complete, and continuous fulfillment of expectations and dreams that people generally await and work for in their youth.

The paradox of the secret is that this "same man" with a "fourteen-year-old son" has only one thought: "that his son [will] be happy." With that, "he wants only to read the future in the eyes of this son."[10] He knows intellectually that his son must come to the conclusion that all come to know by forty—that the unqualified happiness he expected of his life at fifteen or twenty or even twenty-five will never come—but he wants and even convinces himself that this one time, for one person—his son—there will never be a time when he will have to learn the secret. The middle-aged are animated by hope of a miracle for the children they love, and, this hope is itself miraculous. As Clio puts it, the expectation will in some sense be disappointed, but "nothing is so beautiful, and . . . nothing is so disarming before God, and that is . . . the ordinary miracle of your young hope."[11]

Yet this young hope will not be realized: the aging of one's own body cannot be "made right" by the young. For Péguy, there will be a time where the memory of one's existence will be forgotten, with the death of one's own children, and one's presence on earth will enter the minds of few, and then of no one;[12] in this there is little room for sentimental evasions, only a joy that is never far from suffering, and a suffering that perpetually allows joy to enter suffering. Things will "be fine" as one is forgotten.[13] As one of Péguy's poetic protagonists remarks, he will have been "in the cemetery for a long time now," while his children are thriving without him.[14]

Péguy's earthy, often peasant body is often a dogged, aging, melancholy, and beloved "brother Ass,"[15] and yet it is also a powerfully, necessarily spiritual body. This is true not just for the individual but for the community as well. In antiquity, the physical city "house[d]" the spiritual city,[16] just as among persons it is the spiritual that "lives" in the carnal.[17]

For Péguy, it is this embodied spirit that the "second creation" of modern metaphysics wishes to deny: to deny its passage in time toward death, and to deny the spiritual power of the body, the full earthy and spiritual dimensions of the "carnal" (*charnel*—it is one of Péguy's favorite words). As Péguy's Clio—the muse of history, in which moderns seek progress and their own vindication—tells his pagan soul: love, hope, and faith are spiritual goods, and therefore "it is these spiritual [things] that are carnal, not me."[18]

In this way, Péguy's poetic descriptions of the body do not "anxiously" avoid the body, but neither do they work with the increasingly scientifically disaggregated body that serves as an object and instrument of "objective" reason (which translates the body into space, divisible and inanimate for purposes of understanding) or the body that serves as a mere instrument of imagined desire (say, the body of erotic fantasy).

Péguy is especially interested in political and cultural life—and thus collective bodies—but data like fertility statistics elicited no essays or articles from Péguy. Medical investigations of the body are not of special interest to him either: in Péguy's oeuvre, Jean-Martin Charcot and other famous medical investigators of the age are passed over in silence. Péguy occasionally talks about fallen warriors—but only in relation to the justice or injustice of their cause, or the conviction that invigorates them. The soldier's disposition of body in life and death receives no description, and hence it does not inspire the mixture of homoerotic and violent imagery common in early twentieth-century literature, that has been the subject of incisive comment since Paul Fussell.[19]

Beyond the individual body, bodies in the Belle Époque were also often assigned to collective biological "races," with "respectable" claims about their "traits and characteristics." In a similarly striking relation of proximity and distance to the preoccupations of his moment, "race" for Péguy simply is not—and in many ways cannot be—a biological category that designates collective bodies. At times, it appears that he means something like "race" in the collective, biological sense, at least potentially. In late 1905, for example, he claims in what appear to be then drearily conventional racist and nationalist terms that the "French race" is the "only visibly chosen [*élue*] race of all the modern races."[20] From this remark alone, Péguy could easily be joined with those who spoke of the "Teutonic race," the "Anglo-Saxon race," and so on, and of their "destinies" that allow them to transcend historical change and expand a collective life through centuries and even millennia.

Yet there are some formidable barriers to assigning Péguy to the odious band of racist "theorists." The reference in this passage to the "French race" grows out of a discussion of the "Jewish race" and its fidelity to the notion that "the temporal salvation of humanity has an infinite price." But the entire paragraph is placed "under the invocation of the memory that we have kept of the great Bernard-Lazare"[21]—who is both Jewish and French. Péguy presents him implicitly as both Jewish and French in this passage, and explicitly as both Jewish and French in his essay *Notre Jeunesse*, five years later.[22] If "the French race" was a biological category for Péguy, contemporary assumptions about racial difference would have almost certainly excluded Bernard-Lazare from it, as contemporary anti-Semitic polemicists like Drumont would have been very eager to inform him.

Péguy also refers in the passage from 1905 to "the modern races."[23] If "races" is meant to denote collective participation in a biological essence that transcends historical change, it isn't clear how biological races could be "modern," since for him and many of his contemporaries an ascendant modernity (for Péguy, a now dominant mode of being human that has from antiquity been a possible mode of being human) starts in the seventeenth and eighteenth centuries and, in Péguy's account, triumphs only in the late nineteenth century—to be precise, 1880. Hence in Péguy's account, multiple biological "races" would had to have been formed over a few very recent generations.

Late modern European racists tended to be far more inclined to extravagant pseudo-archaic grandiosity than this, claiming that this or that race emerged from some primeval Eurasian mist—like the Aryans in the imaginings of Drumont and others—or at least from suitably crepuscular and archaic Teutonic forests, or the verdant plains of ancient Gaul. A race that found its portentous *Entstehung* in the generations of Newton's *Principia* and the calculus, Montesquieu and the Dutch East India Company—let alone the age of telephones and Henry James—would be deflatingly close to hand.

Other references to "race" in Péguy are not, one might say, excessively biological in implication. There was for him a "race" of true scholars devoted to the humanities.[24] In 1906, Péguy wrote that Renan, despite his skepticism, belonged to the "Catholic race," since Catholicism continued to mark his thought after he abandoned his faith.[25] Elsewhere he writes of "the race of professional moralists"[26] or even the "detestable race" of self-conscious letter writers, writing private letters for eventual publication, whom he calls "épistolaires."[27] In a designation that—understood biologically—would have vertiginous philosophical implications, he refers to the "immense majority of the Kantian race."[28]

For all that, personal and collective bodies are indispensable for Péguy's writing. It is simply not the—if one might so call it—late modern "racial" or "medical" body or the modern or postmodern "erotic" body that interests Péguy. Nor, strikingly, is he taken with some aggrandizing masculine *virtù*— quite the opposite is true.

In some of his earliest work for the *Cahiers* in 1900, his writing is shaped by an extended, at times amusingly absurd, consistently humbling encounter with weakness and illness. Three of his earliest essays for his own journal—written at the age of twenty-seven—draw upon his immediate experience to reflect upon the body's vulnerability, entitled "On the Flu" (*De la Grippe*), "The Flu Again" (*Encore de la Grippe*), and "Still More on the Flu" (*Toujours de la Grippe*).

Péguy expresses a certain penchant for irony about his (less than serious) illness: "Sick for the first time in a very long time, I am a little bit childishly amused about my new situation."[29] Yet it prompts him to reflect on the same page, as he so often did, upon Pascal.[30] A suffering body is a source of humor and philosophical insight, and the suffering, humor, and insight run with rather than against one another.

In an enfeebled body, Péguy discovers—as is generally the case in his writing, the text is presented as an occasional, informal dialogue—that the body's limits and vulnerability affect the mind, but that that very vulnerability is an opening to understanding, since life must be not only lived, but understood under the sign of mortality. Sickness and fragility are an indispensable portion of life, among persons and peoples.[31] But like persons and peoples, Péguy discovered that "incapable of all work" he broke the hold of a constrictive and lifelong illusion: "I had always lived according to this idea that I would never be sick."[32]

By acknowledging the body's imperfections and frailty, the mind can cooperate with the body's condition, honestly working through the commitments of one's life. Here the body does not appear as a subject that must conform to some contemporary ideal of "health" (though health is certainly desirable); nor is the body made to speak its mute secrets through hypnosis or psychoanalysis. Rather, Péguy seeks to experience the flesh in both strength and weakness, seeking health but not denying that illness and vulnerability— "*sub specie mortalitatis*"—allow him to reflect upon what matters most: he discovers that for himself, the supreme priority of life is justice.[33]

Perhaps because many people sense and fear the paradoxically limiting and liberating power of our carnal fragility, Péguy claimed that there was an almost insuperable tendency for different cultures to deny either the earthiness of carnal life or the spirituality of the carnal. Yet for him modernity itself offered the most thoroughgoing denial of the carnal and embodied spirit—not, say, an intensely ascetic Christianity.[34] For Péguy, there are many forces and metaphysical positions that seek to render the modern body spiritless and denude it of its distinctive dignities, absurdities, pains, and joys.

He preferred his own aging and flawed body, his own "sinful hands," to disembodied being of any kind.[35] His affirmation of the body includes sacrifice, as the body must embody love, faith, and hope, which inevitably ask for sacrifice (as his poem *The Portal of the Mystery of Hope* emphasizes). It is through the organic that spiritual enters a world of finite time.[36]

For Péguy, one indispensable way we affirm love in particular through our temporal, carnal lives is through work. His poetry often turns toward the working body, not as part of an industrial process, but through a respectful participation as human hands work with tools and nature. His depiction of Jeanne d'Arc—as well as the work of his mother and grandmother to earn their living by their hands—may well have inspired the quatrain in his poem *Ève*, with reference to woman as "eternally thrifty, eternal worker." It continues, "O medical woman and nursing woman, you wipe up the blood, after it has flowed."[37] Few early twentieth-century men versified upon the possibility that the work of women's hands in healing might actually go beyond the work of a nurse. Work could be masculine as well, and in similar ways: one thinks of the abundant reference to the tools of the woodsman, "made for his hand,"[38] in Péguy's poem *The Portal of the Mystery of Hope*.

For Péguy, however, modern metaphysics brought great changes to experiences and notions of the body at work. The work of the modern world took its forms from the animating goals of bourgeois life. Péguy assumes that his readers will think of a bourgeois as someone who does not devote himself to a spiritual life of prayer, or a physical life of regular physical labor or bodily risk-taking, but rather engages in work with writing and reading, often in a profession or business oriented toward respectable, secure acquisition and advancement. In this sense, Péguy is himself partially bourgeois, though his early work with his mother and grandmother in manual labor—and his care with the physical production of the controversial *Cahiers* amid his poverty—make him only partially and conditionally so.

Even as a critic of bourgeois life, Péguy insisted upon its legitimacy. In his essay *Victor-Marie, Comte Hugo*, of October 1910, he engages in dialogue his "dear Halévy" and tells him that "the bourgeois world, that stands [*se tenir*], that exists, is good."[39]

If this life is also an urban bourgeois life—and for its partisans and crit-ics in the Belle Époque, bourgeois culture was often associated with the town or the city rather than the countryside—Péguy affirms the sensorial buzz and whir of urban life with unbidden enthusiasm. In fairness, in his late writings he claims that urban and rural experience have their own unique forms of "depth" and "beauty" that are for him distinct but equally valuable.[40] But if anything, he seemed irresistibly attracted to life in a great modern capital like Paris. In a passionate encomium from 1907, Paris is simultaneously a distilla-tion and an intensification of the human and the most varied human aspira-tions, embodied in a single city: "Unique city in the world, modern city, ancient city . . . the most royal city in the world . . . the most republican . . . the most serious, the most frivolous city . . . city of the body and city of the mind [esprit]." It is the "city of commerce . . . [and] when one wants, of the greatest solitude."[41]

Yet elsewhere Péguy assumed that the bourgeois occupies a social, eco-nomic, cultural, and metaphysical position bound to the reign of money, with serious implications for work and for the body that works. For him, the bour-geois assumes the ubiquity of markets and the imperative of self-interest and self-advancement, where material goods, material pleasures, and comforts are of explicit and often preeminent importance.[42] It is perhaps still more impor-tant that modern, broadly bourgeois cultures strongly prefer both abstract theories (and elsewhere, material things and technology)[43] to the narrative, spiritually embodied particularities of living persons[44] and groups of persons.

In this way, Péguy had long argued that late modern bourgeois culture was in fact quite hostile to the body in its unabashed, aging, fecund, ener-getically generative carnality, whatever affirmations it made to diverse (medi-cal, erotic, aesthetic) ambitions, needs, and desires that turned to the material body for their successful expression, for which the body was preeminently a vehicle or a specimen. As he put it in an unpublished essay from 1906 with a biblical allusion, "These are now bones of my bones and flesh of my flesh: words without resonance for the modern world."[45] The language becomes stronger in the summer of 1913, when he remarks that the "modern world" (of "bourgeois capitalism") "is distinguished, uniquely, from all other orders . . . according to a law (of sterility) that we have encountered so many times, as having a secret, shameful taste for the inorganic."[46] For him, this was a secret, even repressed antipathy toward carnality with serious consequences. It af-fected even Kant, whom he admired: Kant's imperatives, demanded of all autonomous rational beings (embodied or no), without solidarity, left him cold. As he put it in his own emphatic capitals, *"Kantianism has clean hands,* BUT IT HAS NO HANDS."[47]

Péguy perceived in his own capitalist and industrial age a worrisome transformation. As he wrote in 1913, at best, "If the bourgeoisie had stayed . . . the economic arbiter of market value, the working class would only have asked to be what it had always been, the economic source of market value."[48] But now he saw a world where "everyone is a bourgeois," including the former aristocracy and the working class.[49] The peculiar assumptions of bourgeois life were increasingly becoming the universal, habitual way of encountering and interpreting the world and others, and he thought that was a loss—not because these ways were pernicious as *a* way of being human, but because they were increasingly accepted without question by nearly everyone, not as *a* way but as *the* way of being human. He was certain that institutional socialism would not offer modern peoples a respite from the presiding assumptions of bourgeois life, since "the *political* socialist party is composed entirely of bourgeois intellectuals."[50]

His concerns about the embourgeoisement of work and the world are revealingly compared with his praise for the professions that Péguy loves most. As he wrote in 1913: "The most beautiful métier in the world, after the métier of being a parent (and moreover, it is the métier most closely related to being a parent), is the métier of a school teacher or a lycée teacher."[51]

Parents and teachers engage in the best work—provided they do their work well by respecting their children's and their students' freedom, that is, they work among and for "a free people."[52] They know that their charges, whom they love and respect even if they are inevitably exasperated and frustrated by them, will live quite different lives, separate from and beyond the limits of their bodily life. They want them to do so, and so they give them the knowledge and love that will allow them to lead free and flourishing lives.

As long as they avoid the corruption of trying to spiritually and temporally "govern" minds and spirits—a temptation to which Péguy says the priests of France generally yielded, and hence lost the love and respect of their congregations[53]—the work of parents and schoolteachers is of the best and highest kind. It is hard work, but done well it is not without a certain rhythm of minds and persons that allows the self to abandon its egoism and participate in life with others, endowed with personal meaning and dignity that does not shrink from acknowledging one's own limits and finitude even as it works with confidence.

According to Péguy, the modes and horizons of work, and relations to work, favored by bourgeois culture are very different from those of a good parent or a schoolteacher. For example, the intrinsic quality of work, and of the objects of work, matter less than the primarily selfish advantages derived from working, especially those connected to money, often very imperfectly connected to honest and good work. Work done in this dispensation no longer permits a profound sense of temporal continuity—in letters and learning, or trades. It valorizes the "disruptive" forces that continually subject work to competition and rivalry motivated above all by egotism and greed.

Furthermore, the self that works no longer anticipates an encounter with eternity that awaits his or her life of work, since, as we have seen, "as the Christian prepares himself for death, the modern prepares for . . . retirement."[54] Work becomes the "preparation" for a comfortable retirement in a marketized, bourgeois society.[55]

The felt need for perpetual, uninterrupted income—not a solid security of life from one's community, which, as we shall see, he believed to be an imperative of justice—was for him an extraordinary challenge to living truthfully. For in order "to have a secure retirement (that is to say some assured money when one is old), one does not say, one does not write what one thinks, what one really has to write and to say, and that everyone knows, and that nobody dares to say or to write."[56]

For Péguy, the bourgeois culture of work finds nothing so important as acquisitive security, but that form of work constantly refers work back to the self and its ongoing, often bodily ease, comfort, and safety, in a way at odds with the work of a good parent or schoolteacher, or anyone who lives fully with and for others. It is not only the work and the worker who suffer but the truth. Hence late modern bourgeois culture may congratulate itself for its devotion to medical and psychological research that discloses the secrets of the body and psyche, but for Péguy, the social and political imperatives of bourgeois culture preclude telling the truths that one knows and lives out with one's body and one's life.[57] Telling those truths requires one to pay for them.

In contrast to his own notions of work, for Péguy the bourgeois solution to modern work is either (for those on the right) to justify the misery of many persons by the increasing abundance of material goods and services theoretically available to them or (on the left) to seek foremost the advance of material equality. His own position is complex: he is skeptical of placing a supreme emphasis on material equality, and yet scathing about the conservative complacency toward profound poverty, or destitution.[58]

For Péguy, there is an indispensable and lasting distinction to be made between poverty and misery (or destitution)[59] and their effects on our spiritually carnal lives. In his account, poverty requires modest living, but he and other poor people do not have to worry about enjoying the necessities of life as long as they or their family can work. The poor as Péguy understands them are economically secure, with lasting employment but without a great deal of money. Work that is truly theirs allows them to enjoy their work and to participate in the pains and joys of life as full persons within and beyond their work, in at least a potential relation of trust with their neighbor and (after Péguy's conversion) with God. Péguy clearly has in mind generations of craftsmen and peasants in France.

Misery, or destitution, is something entirely different. It is always precarious—without steady employment, or reliable shelter, or a steady supply of food, or of attachment to and trust in other human beings. Even if these things are currently at hand, they could be taken away at any moment. For Péguy, misery breaks people—it fills them with pain, mistrust, and fear, and it is a way of life largely bereft of ongoing fraternity and solidarity.

While the peasant or craftsman of modest means can inhabit communities with real cultural vitality, enjoyment, and dignity, the destitute only desire to escape their circumstances and (generally) not look back. When they do escape, they are among the happiest of people; often they become conservative and parsimonious with money, seeking to draw as sharp a line as they can between their old and new circumstances.[60] When Péguy was still a religious skeptic, he drew upon religious terms to impart to his readers the depths of destitution: while poverty could be like purgatory, destitution is hell, and "purgatory is about life; hell is about death."[61]

As a socialist, Péguy was scandalized by those who did not understand the sufferings of the destitute—and who did not seek to help them. To acquiesce in any instance of their suffering was to call an entire regime into question for if only a single person is "knowingly left in destitution," it is enough "for the entire social pact to become void."[62]

Péguy was also critical of how the bourgeois and a bourgeois economic order had changed the life of the poor, as he defined them, but in this case, for primarily supra-material reasons. Above all, modern bourgeois culture asked workers—though materially better off than the destitute—to expose themselves to constant *insecurity* in order to maintain their modest way of life. Péguy concluded that this was an unconscionable violation of civilized order, whatever the flaws of the different civilizations that have instantiated that order. "This," he wrote, "is perhaps the most profound difference, the abyss that has been placed between these great ancient world[s], pagan, Christian, French, and our modern world."[63]

In very diverse previous cultures, there was a certain security and safety in poverty: at one point he called it "a silent contract between men and fate."[64] Workers would remain in modest circumstances, but they would not be deprived of their livelihood. Péguy failed to add that in exceptional circumstances nature could withhold its bounty (as it could obviously do in, say, times of famine, with very few ways to protect one's self and one's loved ones against that withholding). For him, assuming some basic means of sustenance was available to the community, the poor would be able to feed themselves and their families. In return for accepting "the limits of poverty" they would enjoy the "security" of having basic needs met and a basic "happiness" that comes with that security.[65] Poor persons were free to break this "silent contract" and pursue a higher place, but if they did so, they risked falling into misery. "It was indeed the principle of ancient wisdom that the gods struck down without wrongdoing the one who wanted to escape his condition."[66]

In Péguy's account of the (certainly metaphysically, to some extent historically) modern world, however, the life of the peasant or craftsperson, lived in secure if simple well-being, was destroyed. The many among the working poor who worked but were not eager to advance themselves, who were not willing to move in close coordination with the movement of money, eagerly "adaptable" to circumstances, conditions, and perhaps even in character to better accord with money and technology—it was *they* who were punished with deprivation and failure. In striking contrast to the ethos of diverse premodern cultures—it was the one who did not "play" or "bet" on the roulette wheel of material advancement who was threatened with destitution, and punished if prompt conformity to the prevailing economic system and its motives was not forthcoming.[67]

It is not that Péguy recoiled at the thought of gambling, properly understood: we have seen that for him human life required a "wager," in spiritual and metaphysical terms.[68] But he favored a kind of fundamental, universal material security that afforded people the freedom for free and distinct *metaphysical* wagers, that is, wagers on certain distinct ways of life with various but persistently real costs and aspirations, and with them various accounts of ultimate reality. The wagers of modern capitalism were often purely material wagers, set against an oppressively monochrome metaphysics sustained by the pervasive habits of the market. The price for those aspirations, in Péguy's account, was an erosion of meaningful work, of the vitality of attachments to others, and of the time and stability available for the choosing and living out of free metaphysical wagers in a spiritually carnal life. That was to get the goods of life precisely backward.

Péguy was convinced that while a comprehensively bourgeois culture was now associated with work, it is in fact hostile to different ways of work, just as it is hostile to metaphysical difference and the carnal, aging body. Perhaps the most pressing disagreement he has with the "bourgeois intellectuals" of the Socialist Party was that they believed that a quantifiable equality would solve the modern problem of work. Work, and the withholding of work, became a means toward the end of a more complete and thoroughgoing material equality. Péguy supported better wages for poor workers as well as for the miserable, but he treated their situations quite differently.

For him, there is a distinctively modern preoccupation with equality that excludes genuine solidarity. Care for the destitute is different. He sees this imperative at work in many civilizations, from the ancient world to late modern Europe. Care for the miserable had been "one of the most ancient cares of noble humanity, persisting through all civilizations." This is true of fraternity "from age to age . . . whether it is clothed in the form of charity or the form of solidarity, whether it is done in the name of Zeus hospitable, or whether it is done in the name of welcoming the poor as a figure of Jesus Christ, or whether it is done to establish a minimum income for workers."[69]

Whatever its form, fraternity with the destitute was a "living, human and imperishable sentiment." It was simultaneously a "profoundly conservative and profoundly revolutionary sentiment,"[70] conserving the communion of humanity across time and, as fraternity changed form, expressing the need for people to express this abiding unity in new and living ways in different times and places.[71]

Péguy turned to the motto of the French Revolution to clarify his thoughts about fraternity. While he endorsed all the ideals of the Revolution, "liberty, equality and fraternity are not on the same level." Equality is often a "blended, mixed, often impure sentiment, where vanity, envy and cupidity contribute." That is, it looks more like a praiseworthy ideal that nonetheless is easily reduced to the dimensions of bourgeois life. It "often only reaches men of the theater, of representation, and men of government."[72] It does not necessarily require action—including difficult, sacrificial action of solidarity on behalf of universal justice and to relieve the suffering of others, as fraternity does. It can too easily satisfy itself with vain, theatrical self-expressions of virtue. Fraternity is less easily satisfied with self-regarding gestures, and gives life to the work of equality, justice, and freedom in the world: it "unsettles, moves, and impassions profound, serious, hardworking, modest souls."[73]

Péguy's criticisms of bourgeois culture prompt an important question: How might fraternity and work be reconciled with the achievements of modern technology and with bourgeois equality and efficiency? In his notes for his unfinished doctoral dissertation written in 1909, Péguy proposed a future path through which the achievements of modernity (and its bourgeois character) might be integrated with other ways of life: he called it "the age of competence." It was both a continuation and a successor to the cité harmonieuse of the late 1890s. Here Péguy provided a countermove to the tripartite account of history in Comtean positivism, in which the theological age gives way to the metaphysical age and then to the final, "positive" age, where scientific knowledge reshapes the natural and human worlds in accord with its own methods and ends.

Péguy identified an age of "empiricism"[74] when human beings cultivate and interact with nature in limited and fairly intuitive ways. It is succeeded by a scientific age that is a close analogue of Comte's positive age, when science transforms the relationship of human beings to the world, to themselves, and to one another, apparently without limit or respect for our nature as carnally spiritual persons. But for Péguy, Comte's final age—that is, the age in which science triumphs—is only a propaedeutic to the age of "competence," which will succeed it in turn. Here the intuitive understanding of the world and the gratitude for the given are restored, not by repudiating science, but through a recognition of both the virtues and the limitations of science for human flourishing: it has "absorbed the scientist" and "the scientific," and is a "restitution of the organic."[75]

In the "age of competence," science once again respects the full scope and depth of human aspiration and inquiry, including spiritual, moral and aesthetic experience, governed by a now truly universal and mutual fraternity. The good and justice are rightly restored to the ultimate depths and to the summit of human reflection, rather than (as they do in the scientific age) serving supplemental or ornamental functions, assumed to be inferior and uncertain in relation to scientific knowledge and its applications to the world of matter in motion, to technological mastery, perhaps above all to control and mastery of the human body. In this way, for Péguy, the age of competence will be the age of the "qualitative" rather than of quantity.[76]

Above all, the age of competence will place its hope not in the final overcoming of suffering through technology, but in creating the moral, aesthetic, and material conditions for an abundant, transitory, and therefore irreplaceable organic life. Such a life is lived with the respect of the aged for that which has preceded them,[77] alongside the manifold contributions of science.[78]

Péguy thus often looked to a future age of integration. He sometimes saw the domination of the market, of materialism, and of technology—and, more profoundly, of the metaphysics that underwrote them—as one useful, partially legitimate but also limited epoch in history, rather than the "end" of history. He sought a socialism that would work toward the age of competence and overcome the embourgeoisement of work. It was a revolution in the sense that it is committed to revolving "back" even as it affirmed what had been acquired since, as it went "forward." Péguy concisely brought together these hopes for work in particular in *Notre Jeunesse,* where he writes: "Our socialism was essentially . . . a philosophy of the organization and reorganization of work, of the *restoration* of work."[79]

Yet what was Péguy to do before the advent of his "age of competence"? He tried to live his answer: it was to inhabit with one's body and mind an integral unity in which the carnal self, inspired by love and justice, is given in work rather than withheld (that is, for future promotions, for a comfortable retirement). Having rejected that comfort in words, he would not enjoy it in life.

CHAPTER 6

Continuity and Revolution

War and Honor

War and peace were hotly contested terms—and possibilities of human experience—in the years of Péguy's *Cahiers*. These tensions were inherited above all from the eighteenth-century Enlightenment and the French Revolution.

At the turn of the eighteenth century, François Fénelon—who figures prominently in any account of European pacifism's origins—wrote in ambivalent fashion that "a great deal is saved" when there is "a little blood shed seasonably."[1] Later in the century, the avatar of the late Enlightenment, Condorcet, was an active supporter of France's war of choice against Austria in 1792.[2] His Girondin ally Madame Roland wrote after the king's flight to Varennes a year earlier, "It is a cruel thing to think, but . . . peace is taking us backwards. We will only be regenerated by blood."[3]

Further from revolutionary turmoil, Kant famously wrote of "perpetual peace." But in the *Critique of Judgment*, he also found in a long peace "debasing selfishness, cowardice and weakness." He claimed that "war, if it is pursued with order and sacred respect for civil rights [*bürgerlichen Rechte*] has something sublime in itself."[4] The notion of war as holding something "sublime in itself"—not simply the virtues to which it testifies, or its reasons, or hopes for peace—is one expression of a new and immensely dangerous way of thinking about war.

Such a change *ad bellum* was accompanied by idealizing atavism *in bello*. David Bell has observed that within the French Revolution, both Girondins and Hébertists disliked fighting with modern weaponry, separated in space from the foe. They preferred to trust to "the strength and courage of individual warriors," as medieval knights had "at the start of the gunpowder age."[5]

Wilhelm von Clausewitz himself knew that this form of warfare was an anachronism in modern conditions: no longer was war conducted in the manner of "a pair of duelists" who "battled with moderation and consideration;" rather, war was fought as "a war of all against all."[6]

In this way, the eighteenth century becomes, as Bell has argued, both the source of modern "enlightened" limits on war and the moment in which war becomes more than a witness to character, a source of temporary excitement, or as a path to some general political goal. Rather, war was now an initiation into revelatory depths that bestowed new life and a kind of transcendence (Madame Roland's "regeneration" or Kant's "sublime") through collective violence.

Yet the hope of a lasting, even a final peace remained. After the horrors of the French Revolutionary and the Napoleonic Wars, Benjamin Constant argued very differently, and hopefully, that war and commerce were two different means toward the same end. The ceaseless growth of modern commerce would hence eventually bring the age of war to an end.[7]

In Péguy's own time, many were entirely persuaded by Constant's claim that war is motivated above all by commerce. They were prepared to apply those arguments to twentieth-century Europe, and to create an unprecedented mass following for arguments about a lasting end to war that had enjoyed a more modest scope a century or two before. In Great Britain, *The Great Illusion*, by Norman Angell, argued that war was now very unlikely among advanced industrial economies, since all powers stood to lose much more from fighting a war than they would gain by winning it.[8] Internationally, a broader pacifist movement took hold, with Universal Peace Congresses held almost yearly from 1890 to 1914. One of their champions, Bertha von Suttner, won the Nobel Peace Prize in 1905.[9]

In France, pacifism had more than one political orientation. Middle-class reformers founded pacifist organizations grounded in international law, like the Association de la Paix par le Droit in 1887.[10] But there were also French socialists (most notably Jean Jaurès, but also his young admirer Charles Péguy) who believed that antimilitarism was inevitably entwined with social justice, and that mass strikes might avert a war.[11] Péguy's friend from the Lycée Lakanal, the famous historian of the French Revolution Albert Mathiez, advocated reconciliation with Germany and accepting the loss of Alsace-Lorraine.[12] In the years before 1914, Jaurès and German Socialist leaders met to agree that the working classes of both countries would not participate in a war between their nations, devoting their energies to the peaceful transformation of their countries from capitalism to socialism. Yet when war came in 1914, French pacifists mostly assembled to support the *union sacrée* and the French war effort. Perhaps the most prominent exception—who remained pacifist at the peak of war fever—was Péguy's friend and contributor to *Cahiers de la quinzaine*, the novelist Romain Rolland.[13]

Nonetheless, fantasies of war as a transcendent event flourished alongside hopes for permanent peace. There were spaces within modern culture, from the late eighteenth-century forward—especially intellectual culture—that showed a palpable fascination with organized violence as a source of vivifying cultural action, and even the agent of regeneration for a whole civilization.

In the twentieth century, some of these tendencies, in France and in Europe, belong to the intellectual genealogy of fascism. These would encompass the frantic expostulations of Marinetti (whose *Manifesto of Futurism* was published in Paris in 1909)[14] and other Futurist exhortations to destroy civilization in order to create a new one. It would also include the lurid fascination with the violent powers of crowds in Gustave Le Bon's *Psychology of Crowds*, as well as the often enthusiastic emphasis on violence and organizing myths that motivated grand historical action in Georges Sorel's *Reflections on Violence*.

Yet in less familiar places one could find a similar fascination at work, often blended with a frankly idol-fashioning nationalism. There was something of this sensibility in *Le Tour de France par deux enfants*. The two boys in the textbook come close to praying to France at the end, greeting the dawn with the declaration, "Beloved France, we are your children, and we want to become worthy of you!" There is no question what the highest form of that worthiness might be; the eldest boy "will soon be under the colors, he will soon be a soldier of France."[15] Presumably the effort to be "worthy of France" would entail more than well-turned drill on provincial parade grounds.

Throughout the Belle Époque, schoolchildren and adults alike would have found many places to indulge a fascination with soldiering and war as forces of moral resolve and unity. An extremely popular book in the Third Republic was Paul Déroulède's *Chants de soldat* of 1872. It went through many editions and was widely known for its poems dedicated to martial glory and the stirring, unifying lyricism of fighting and dying for France, some of which were taught in schools. The book was popular among supporters of the republic and its foes, and until his wan, abortive coup in 1899, Déroulède was a kind of trans-partisan figure of patriotic virtue. After his star began to fade, he was partially replaced by Ernest Psichari, grandson of Ernest Renan, whose *L'Appel des armes* of 1913—dedicated to Péguy, with whom he would later have a falling out prompted by political and religious disagreements—gave lyric expression to the soldier's life. For Psichari, soldiering opened upon a unity of natural beauty, physical excellence, and meditative spiritual composure. This meant that soldiers belong to an eternal vocation, with a "purity" and "barbarous simplicity" that casts aside all notions of progress, and "Americanism."[16]

Yet Psichari's ideas were not far from at least the musings of far more established, posthumously respectable writers. Before the war, the liberal political essayist Alain (given his later, very prominent postwar pacifism, very incongruously) struck similar themes, writing on several occasions on the ability of war to unify action and thought, in a way that brought a release from the difficulties of their separation in modern society. As he wrote in 1913, war was for him "an admirable game, in which one comes to see more magnanimity than ferocity: what is ugly above all in war is the servitude that prepares the way for it and that follows it."[17] In other essays, Alain goes further than this, claiming that even as he firmly opposes war, "there is . . . a poetry in war" attributable not simply to danger but to an "intoxication with freedom."[18]

Intellectual life in France before the war often turned toward disturbingly fascinated and very ambitious thinking about war, colonial domination, and violence. Long-standing convictions of (at least) broad public consensus—that sacrifice had some legitimate means of access to spiritual truths associated with love and justice through Christianity, that war could be thought exciting or revolting but not transcendent, that war was not inevitable but sometimes unavoidable—had fragmented. The still-forming motives and thoughts that proposed to take their place, starting in the late eighteenth-century—that war would soon vanish from the earth or that war was a preeminent source of vitality and renewal for whole societies—were in intense and not necessarily fruitful tension with one another.

The issue was made all the more urgent since war—and failure in war—was the beginning of Péguy's political consciousness, as it was for many children of the early Third Republic. The humiliation that followed France's defeat by Germany was, as he put it in 1905, "for the men of my generation, this mother knowledge" created "in the aftermath of the defeat."[19]

Yet that "mother knowledge" found variable expression in Péguy's writing. It is not quite right to say that the young Péguy was a pacifist, but he was far closer to pacifism than to militarism. In his *Harmonious City*, there were no violent conflicts among nations.[20] In practical terms, Péguy expressed no enthusiasm for the wars of conquest waged by the French Army to acquire its empire, and for the wars and abuses of all European powers toward what he called at one point "suffering [*misérables*] colonial populations."[21] He published criticisms of French colonial educational policy in Madagascar in the *Cahiers*,[22] as well as a long essay cowritten by E. D. Morel condemning the exploitation of the Congo by Belgian colonizers, and then others on the plight of the Congolese under both Belgian and French domination.[23] His accounts of war in his early poem *Jeanne d'Arc* spare nothing of war's capacity to debase: Jeanne quickly realizes that French soldiers are as capable of brutality as English soldiers, and that their commanders often motivate both themselves and their subordinates by tantalizing them with the prospect of plunder and cruelty.[24]

Yet with the First Moroccan Crisis, in 1905 and 1906, Péguy concluded that Germany might invade France at any time.[25] He claimed that in the space of a morning, "a new period had begun in the history of my own life, in the history of this country, and assuredly in the history of the world."[26]

In the aftermath of the crisis, Péguy claimed that war was Prussia's "national industry" even as it has become the "national industry of almost all peoples."[27] He began to speak of war at greater length and with greater zeal, a zeal compounded by the Second Moroccan Crisis in 1911. Yet even with this change, he carefully distinguished between "ancient" and "modern" war, and opposed the latter with gusto. As is very often the case in Péguy, the "modern" is in fact often ancient as well, and the "ancient" can very easily be modern. In practice, these two forms of war are always mixed in political and military history. Different cultures and epochs have placed a preponderant emphasis on one or the other.[28]

Honor articulated the boundaries of the metaphysically "ancient" notion of war. In this kind of war, "a dishonoring victory (for example a victory by treason) is infinitely worse, (and even the idea of it is unbearable) than an honorable defeat."[29] The ancient notion of war as an operation of honor—evident as early as Homer, but according to Péguy dominant into the early modern period—conceived of combat as a series of duels,[30] where soldiers fight other soldiers, often on the same patch of earth, strictly bound to fight in a limited space for a limited time, both of them well prepared to fight and fighting only other soldiers. In Péguy's account, this form of war flourished in Celtic civilization, in medieval chivalry,[31] and sometimes in the history of modern France.[32]

Through his final writings during the summer of 1914, Péguy argued that the ancient notion of war is in explicit conflict with the modern idea of war, which is preoccupied with "hostility" and temporal "domination."[33] Modern war is often not a war of self-defense or of proportionally righting grievous injustice to others—permissible in terms of chivalry and just war—but aspires to conquest and empire.[34]

In contrast to (metaphysically) "ancient" war, the "modern" war of domination and success at all costs has a literary origin in the (historically) ancient machinations of Odysseus, and a historical origin in the brutal tactics of the Roman legions that conquered and patrolled the empire.[35]

In the early modern period—here the French patriot Péguy criticizes France—it is Richelieu and Louis XIV who led France to fight characteristically modern wars of domination with their neighbors.[36] In these wars, there are no limits or respect for persons that constrain the craving for success: deceit and betrayal are no disgrace, civilians are not spared, and the vanquished are humiliated and exploited. Nonetheless, Péguy believed that France often but not always (that is, not under Louis XIV and Richelieu) represented the (metaphysically) "ancient" way of war, and Germany at times succeeded with the methods of (metaphysically) "modern" war.[37]

In a certain fashion, Péguy started to transpose the strictly limited notion of war as an "ancient" duel into modernity itself, as one more dimension of human carnality. It is revealing that in 1909 Péguy calls war a kind of "carnal . . . communion."[38] It seems here that a strictly limited war of honor, without injury to civilians and waged for a just cause, is one more experience in which he found that modern abstraction and rationalization had disembodied, even disincarnated vital dimensions of human experience.

In his later years, these distinctions remained in force, but his personal distress drove Péguy to less measured expression, seeking some release from the tensions both of his life and of France's vulnerability. In January 1912, he wrote in a private letter to the socialist Alexandre Millerand, just appointed minister of war, that since 1905 an upcoming war with Germany had been "his only thought." He added: "I would give my complete works, past, present and future, and my four limbs to enter into Weimar at the head of my good regiment [section]."[39] The reference to marching into Weimar rather than, say, Berlin—and thus raising inevitable associations with Goethe and Schiller rather than Bismarck and the Kaiser—is remarkable. By the summer of 1914, he claimed: "*To have peace*," is "the grand phrase of all civic and intellectual cowardice."[40] At first, the context of the quote softens it significantly, since he is talking about a cowardly and false comity in *intellectual* life rather than in situations in which physical violence is at issue; but he then explicitly extends its meaning to "civic" life, a more ambiguous—if still not explicitly military—political category.

In a related change, whereas once Péguy was volubly dubious about European imperialism, including French imperialism, he began to soften perceptibly though not to abandon these criticisms in his final years. In the summer of 1914, he wrote (very dubiously) that Napoleon spread French liberties to conquered lands rather than imposing an empire of exploitation. He conceded that the French "are not always good masters" but claimed "we are always bad dominators."[41] He returned to the notion a few paragraphs later: "The Empire sometimes crushed freedom. By these means freedom has constantly worked upon the Empire," since "the one who wanted to be just has sometimes been found the strongest."[42] Perhaps—but Péguy elsewhere shows no enthusiasm for this kind of quasi-Hegelian negative labor, rather than serving as a forthright champion of justice as he sees it.

In his late writing, Péguy repeatedly casts war as an extraordinary and enticing interval where opposites come together. In 1913, he wrote that he was "a good republican" and an "old revolutionary." But the combination rests upon an allusion to the French Revolution: "In time of war, there is only one policy, and that is the policy of the National Convention. But one must not conceal the policy of the National Convention: it is Jaurès in a tumbril and a rolling of drums to drown out his great voice."[43] The Declaration of the Rights of Man, he wrote, was not a declaration of peace, any more than the life of Jesus, who comes to bring not peace but a sword. They both demand a universal justice and love, and to demand universal justice in a world of oppression and cruelty is to prepare one's self for war.[44]

His endorsement of the imagined execution of Jaurès (clearly modeled upon the execution of Danton in 1794) did not exhaust Péguy's late accommodations with the prospect of war. War and death are specifically commended elsewhere as a kind of purgative for the aspects of modern life he liked least. In a 1909 passage raising the possibility of revolution and war, he wrote: "Our positivists will learn metaphysics like our pacifists will learn war. Our positivists will learn metaphysics from rifle shots."[45] War is now a "carnal communion" that forces the alignment of the body with living convictions—though not by first changing convictions (and hearts) but by *compelling* the body to submit to war, and blithely assuming a different metaphysics will follow mechanically from this material condition, in the metaphysically modern way that Péguy elsewhere resolutely condemned.

Despite his commitment to a metaphysically "ancient" mode of war, his acknowledgment that he had a "modern soul" is in this case a revealing confession: Péguy began to conceive of war as a rather mechanical method of turning the metaphysical tendencies of his culture away from those sustained by the reign of money. As we shall see, he left abundant room for an argumentative verbal duel with his metaphysical antagonists—much more in keeping with his principles—but was nonetheless tempted to anticipate war as an agent of metaphysical transformation, in a way that (as Bell observes) would have been a very eccentric view before the eighteenth century. In these passages, Péguy hopes that the experience of war will impel metaphysical change, without attending to the metaphysical diversity through which that experience could be freely interpreted (and of course, the Great War most certainly did find people willing to draw wildly different metaphysical lessons from it).

Even when this modern metaphysics is not in evidence, war appears— appears—to be affirmed in the late Péguy. For example, in late 1913, he famously wrote: "Happy are those who died for the carnal earth" (that is, in war).[46]

If one stopped here, there would be nothing less than a volte-face in Péguy. He moves from being an antimilitarist to an author boasting of a "taste" for war, his desire to march into Weimar, the happiness he as a poet assumes for those who die in war, and so on. Yet the judgment of a total discontinuity is substantially altered by Péguy's full body of writing, even within those same passages. He indeed wrote "happy are those who died for the carnal earth" (in war) but then immediately added: *"But provided that it was in a just war,"* repeating for emphasis later on the same page, "happy are those who died in a just war."[47] The sustained emphasis on justice is not to be set aside. It makes it impossible to place Péguy within a trajectory of late modern exultations in war and violence "beyond" or indifferent to good and evil—and beyond justice—whether they appear in Nietzsche, Sorel, Marinetti, or Ernst Jünger.

The *Note conjointe* as well as prose and poetry on other topics testify that whatever he wrote impulsively in private correspondence, war was not Péguy's "only thought." His published writing also includes far more measured reflections on the possibility of a European war. As he wrote in the summer of 1913: "I am the most liberal man in the world, provided that liberalism is not *ignavia* [indolence, cowardice] . . . I do not say that one must believe that there will be a war, but I say only that it is madness to *guarantee* that there will not be a war."[48]

Within the *Cahiers*, Péguy continued to publish those who opposed war on principle. In the same year that he announced his abrupt turn away from antimilitarism following the First Moroccan Crisis, he wrote an introduction to a featured essay in the *Cahiers* entitled "Peace and War" by the famous physiologist and polymath Charles Richet (he would win the Nobel Prize for Medicine in 1913). For Péguy, Richet stood for "a pure pacifism . . . an integral pacifism" untainted (as Victor Hugo was, according to Péguy) by a hypocritical fascination with war.[49] His readers, he believed, needed to consider that integral pacifism.

Péguy's thinking about war also did not veer toward an embrace of war for its own sake, or perceive organized violence without moral stakes and moral ambiguity. It was *after* the First Moroccan Crisis that Péguy wrote not of conquering Germany but of justice, and the possibility that France could wage an unjust war against Germany. If a French "caesarian government of military reaction" invaded Germany, he wrote, German socialists would be right to fight against France. Péguy went further: if France invaded Germany, French socialists—including Péguy—would consider it a crime, and "would be the first to give not only the precept, but the example not only of desertion, but of insurrection and revolt."[50] He would never retract or qualify that promise.

In this way, Péguy's reflections on war are very close to those of Madame Roland's "regeneration" in a just war to defend the universal principles of the French Revolution, and of Kant's praise of the enlivening, purifying effects of just wars in the *Critique of Judgment*. In some ways Péguy's late thinking about war is actually more irenic than reflections about imperial war in nineteenth-century liberal imperialists, like Tocqueville's reflections on French imperialism in Algeria, an imperialist sensibility broadly supported by John Stuart Mill.[51] Péguy's late argument certainly cannot be reconciled with Italian Fascism or German National Socialism. In fascism, organized violence is understood apart from justice, both in its justification and in its manner of fighting. A given *ethnos* and its nation-state arrogate to themselves the right of conquest, and one cannot countenance the possibility of any legitimate protest against the injustices committed by one's own nation and people, let alone declare an "insurrection" and "revolt" against one's own government and its military in the name of universal justice.

Doubtless it is true that if—even with his commitment to justice in going to war, and fighting a war—Péguy had held these views about a specifically total, industrial war after he and his nation had experienced it, they would rightly be interpreted differently. But because he died in the earliest battles of the summer of 1914, he did not have this totalizing experience, and so his thinking about war must be judged with reference to the historical sources and experiences that were available to him. Yet that is a little too simple; for here too there was both insight and a failure of vision.

Péguy certainly believed that modern wars would be characterized by their distinctive "speed."[52] Like many people before the end of 1914, he struggled to imagine an extended, brutal conflict in an age of cars, planes, telephones, and express trains. War promised to be a brief affair of honor, in which an ancient duel of combat, sparing civilians, would be fought to defend his country against a German invasion. Specifically, Péguy believed the war would be over soon, requiring his own sacrifice and, he hoped, sparing his eldest son, who would be eligible for the draft in 1916.[53] Ultimately, for him the war would accomplish a truly lasting peace and, as he put it, a "general disarmament."[54]

Given his commitments to an "ancient" way of war fought on behalf of revolutionary freedoms, it is scarcely surprising that as a French army officer in 1914, Péguy believed that he and his fellow soldiers would duplicate the victories of the French Revolutionary Armies in 1793.[55] But he simply did not consider the notion that industrial military technology would make a repeat of those victories impossible, even though he saw that technology was changing the organization and conduct of war.

Such a change in modern warfare was hardly an unthinkable notion to Clausewitz a century before. Péguy seemed to have a subtle intimation of the same conclusion. In his remarks about his own military maneuvers, for example, he criticized the "scientific" experience of twentieth-century military life, in which there is an attempt to provide equipment for all contingencies, as if all could be foreseen, while paying no attention to the human being who must carry it all.[56]

Intimations aside, Péguy's failure to recognize what sort of war was in the offing was a mistake. As he put it, "One must always say what one sees. Above all and what is more difficult, one must see what one sees."[57] Here that indispensable "second sight" was absent.

The failure of sight—and above all its compromise with a modern metaphysics of habitual compulsion as a "method" of metaphysical transformation, in which "positivists" would change their metaphysics thanks to "rifle shots"— is real. It was not without connection to Péguy's own grinding years of sacrifice.

Yet through that sacrifice, Péguy pursued an ideal of personal honor without violence, that was simultaneously old and new.

Honor in Revolution

For all his talk of an honorable, "ancient" war as a duel, Péguy never fought one. Given the fierce criticism he received throughout the history of the *Cahiers*, there was certainly no shortage of suitable affronts for his honor to avenge. Péguy could easily have found some plausible expedient, and issued a challenge in fulsomely archaic fashion.

Such a decision by Péguy would hardly have been out of step with his culture: Belle Époque France saw the revival of the duel. Banned and sometimes unpopular, by the turn of the last century dueling returned to prominence, especially in Paris,[58] where they were widely tolerated and prosecution for dueling was rare.

The professional and political scope of dueling showed remarkable breadth. Given the acidity of his wit, journalist and politician Georges Clemenceau regularly fought duels, and he kept his pistols ready for use. Another politician and journalist, Joseph Reinach, fought thirteen of them.[59] Journalists were particularly prone to fight duels: the tendency in the 1880s to have French journalists sign their names to their articles gave those offended by their writings a precise target for a challenge.[60]

Political figures from the Left and the Right alike fought duels: the socialist leader and intellectual Jean Jaurès fought a duel against the nationalist and anti-Dreyfusard Paul Déroulède.[61] Artists also participated: Marcel Proust—who, unlike a number of others, did appear directly motivated by issues of "manliness"—fought a duel as well.[62] As film began to penetrate daily life, the duel was a promising subject: YouTube preserves forever in the ether a duel fought by Charles Maurras, founder of Action Française, against the journalist Paul de Cassagnac.[63]

Women sometimes participated in debates about outraged honor, and contemplated a similarly violent settling of accounts. The feminist Arria Ly, for example, proposed that women could duel men, and others argued that women could fight duels with men who had left them with child and without support.[64] Women might also turn to a more general physical vengeance for an insult. In 1914, after the newspaper *Le Figaro* published unflattering information about her husband, the Radical politician Joseph Caillaux, Madame

Henriette Caillaux walked into the office of the editor and shot him dead. She made no attempt to flee the scene.[65]

The popularity of dueling revealed a deeper assumption about persons: Paris at the turn of the last century had no shortage of educated people who conceived of the relationship between the words one spoke and one's body as one of mutual accountability. A verbal insult gained force if one maintained it by risking one's body (if for the most part not ultimately; most duels were not deadly).[66] Similarly, protest against an insult became more credible if one's body were wagered in the pursuit of the objection.

Yet while Clemenceau, Reinach, Maurras, Proust, and countless others followed the general vogue, taking to the Bois de Boulogne and other favored spots, thrusting rapiers and firing pistols through the morning air, Péguy remained at his desk, scrawling his loopy letters across correspondence, manuscripts, and proofs in his cramped office on the rue de la Sorbonne. It was not a question of courage, given that he would insist upon his readiness for active combat in his forties. It was also hardly the case that he was indifferent to honor, or for that matter, that he took slights well. As he wrote in 1913, he supported the "Cornelian system," in which "*honor is dearer than life.*"[67] Rather, it was that he understood that in personal terms, the accord between reasoned conviction and embodied experience now had to be lived out differently.

Péguy's reference to the seventeenth-century playwright Corneille gives us an entry into Péguy's thinking. In his work, to refer to Corneille is above all to refer to his play *Polyeucte*. It was Péguy's favorite play.[68]

Polyeucte is an ancient Armenian nobleman who is married to the beautiful and prominent Pauline, daughter of the leading local Roman official. Upon converting to Christianity, Polyeucte immediately resolves to defy official practice and interrupt a public, ritual sacrifice to the pagan gods, calling his fellow Armenians to worship the God of the Bible and to become Christians. The act of defiance is done without any violence to others. Polyeucte is sentenced to death for blasphemy; his father-in-law, his wife, and his esteemed erstwhile romantic rival for Pauline's hand successively try to persuade him to renounce his own action—to introduce an expedient fissure between his actions, his words, and his convictions in the name of continued life, influence, success, power, and respectability. Polyeucte refuses to rupture the unity of his embodied convictions with his words and actions, and goes to his death.

Polyeucte dies happily, having fulfilled his calling and satisfied his sense of honor. After his death, his wife refuses to marry her old love (Polyeucte's·

rival), in memory of Polyeucte's greatness, and his wife, his father-in-law, and her former suitor convert to Christianity.

As the foregoing suggests—and as Péguy observed—Corneille was not a tragedian in the strict sense, any more than Péguy himself. He said of Corneille, "His tragedies always end well. Heroism, mercy, forgiveness, martyrdom always end with a coronation."[69] For Péguy, Corneille's plays were not, in the manner of Racine, about intense if subtle inner conflicts or a painful disclosure that brought about agonizing self-knowledge at the end of a rigorous authorial plan.[70] Polyeucte, for example, expresses an entirely lucid and profound sense of self, and knows exactly to what and to whom he wishes to devote himself (and to what degree, and in what order). The outward expression of his inner unity sets him against others, but eventually brings about a general reconciliation, prefigured by the constant intercession of the characters for one another within the play itself, in what Péguy calls a "communion."[71] It is most important that this "communion" is achieved through honorable sacrifice, but without that honor being secured by committing violence against another person. Polyeucte's honor is an honor of lucid, loving, sacrificial constancy in speech and action.

The logic of Péguy's sense of personal honor developed in similar fashion. First, honor put into accord the convictions of the mind with the actions of the body. For Péguy, honor was expressed supremely not by becoming violent when subjected to insults, but by permitting one's body (that is, in poverty) and spirit (in rejection, in marginality) to suffer at length for one's convictions by refusing to soften or silence them for the comfort of the physical body, or the approval of social and professional bodies that could secure one's material prosperity and status. In Péguy's account, it is only when this personally embodied love for the truth is realized in word and action that one has personal honor, an honor that can *then* affirm the differences one has with others without reserve, and enter into honest communion with very different people.

In this way, Péguy participates wholeheartedly in the culture of personal honor in the Belle Époque, but very much on his own terms. His reconfiguration of honor required several crucial changes.

First, it was an honor more easily upheld by the poor than by the privileged—in contrast to the duel, it was quite specifically not an imitative ritual aping aristocratic culture. Péguy had concluded that the "modernists" (in his peculiar sense of the term) of the intellectual party believed themselves to be liberal and free, but they were not: as he wrote in *L'Argent*, "To be liberal is precisely the contrary of being modernist."[72] It is in precisely this sense that he identified "modernism" as "a system of politesse," and "freedom" as "a system of respect," where "modernism is the virtue of society people," and "freedom is the virtue of the poor."[73]

That the poor could be exceptionally free, lucid, and faithful to what one sees was one of the foremost lessons Péguy took from his participation in the Dreyfus affair. The heroism of Dreyfus's "poor" and "obscure"[74] defenders appeared not in a record of duels but in their work for the truth that they upheld. This honor was worth more than any expedient compromise or tactful silence could give them. For Péguy, to qualify his support for Dreyfus, or to soften his socialism, or his Dreyfusism, or his Catholicism for a group of ready-made patrons and allies[75] would be a failure of integrity and honor, since along with his readers and contributors, through the *Cahiers* he had maintained a "Dreyfusard honor" that others had found too costly.[76]

As Péguy reflects upon the Dreyfus affair later in his life, the honor in question is for him distinctive. It is like military honor and requires "military" virtues of courage and sacrifice, but it is not the same. This ultimate courage is not the "vulgar courage" ("already difficult") to stand up for one's moral convictions within a larger social or cultural world but an "interior courage," a "secret courage" to remain faithful to justice even when one's friends do not.[77] Hence Péguy says that, with the true Dreyfusards, he is able to say, "I will render my blood as I have received it." It is a strange turn of phrase, and hardly mitigated by the preceding reference in the same paragraph to the "historical honor of our race."[78] But the entire point of the passage is not to speak of collective affirmations of blood but to affirm the absolute necessity of individual rights and a people's responsibility to uphold them for human beings as such.

The reference to "rendering my blood" is from Corneille's *Le Cid*,[79] and here Péguy claims it for the cause of Dreyfus. The importance of legal protection for individuals, respect for rights and individual justice, is not there simply by implication (that is, as part of an essay about the Dreyfus affair) but by declaration, since in the same paragraph Péguy asserts with reference to Dreyfus's persecution: "A single injustice, a single crime, a single illegality, above all if it is officially recorded and confirmed, a single insult to humanity, a single insult to justice and law [*droit*], above all if it is universally, legally, nationally, conveniently accepted . . . ruptures the entire social pact, the entire social contract . . . [and] suffices . . . to dishonor an entire people."[80]

In this passage, to claim fidelity to the blood one has "received" is not an instance of an at once pseudo-mystical and pseudo-scientific racism that defies the demands of justice and respect for individuals as individuals, but a "return" to the honor culture of the *grand siècle* in a distinctively late modern context: that of civic action and protest in defense of rights at once individual and universal (as Péguy puts it in the passage above, "humanity"). The honor in question is also not that of Rodrigue, Corneille's aristocratic duelist, but an affirmation of justice as a charge for the members of the community that perpetuated an injustice—all the more so when those individual rights have been previously defended in equally or more difficult circumstances by one's own people.

Honor became in Péguy's *Cahiers* a personally costly but patiently borne embodied honor of the poor, which could live as an alternative both to antiquated extravagances and to an expedient career in the modern "market" of letters. Péguy found that market at work both within the culture of the modern university and in the court of public opinion, in which an established community's approval (or the approval of one's friends and colleagues) took the foremost place, and honorable justice and difficult truths had to be set aside to preserve career prospects, or even an easy comity with professional and social peers.

In contrast to those who tell the truth without regard for its cost, he claims that the members of the intellectual party "go naturally to the side of power," not the side of "justice or of truth."[81] The prospects of comfort and respect from the powerful usually occlude one's ability to see, and in Péguy's terms, to see what one sees, in late modern no less than in premodern cultures. The intellectual party fails to put into accord its members' minds and bodies, and prefers to disincarnate history. As Péguy puts it, they want diplomas, and promotions at the École Normale Supérieure;[82] they serenely deprive other human beings of their dignity in their scholarship, but greatly desire their own dignity.[83] Péguy claimed that like many Catholic clergy given to clericalism, the members of the intellectual party believe fundamentally in not having to pay ("ne pas payer") for their convictions.[84]

For Péguy, the purpose of the *Cahiers de la quinzaine* was to offer occasions for a new form of honor. The "fundamental principle of our *Cahiers*," he wrote in 1905, "is that they are respectively autonomous, free among themselves, mutually free, free the one from the others, each born, living, and moving in a free company of free *cahiers*."[85] For him, the willingness on the part of author, editor, and reader to challenge others—and yet to be ready to open space for the challenges of others—was explicitly the "honor"[86] that the *Cahiers* offered to its readers and writers.[87]

In his words, while "we [that is, those associated with the *Cahiers*] have the taste and respect for freedom,"[88] that freedom requires an embodied honor. The *Cahiers* would ask rationally reflective, deliberative selves to engage freely with other, perhaps very different rationally reflective, deliberative selves. Péguy thus demanded that the *Cahiers* be filled with direct disagreement among authors, between the editor and contributors, between contributors and readers—without pseudonyms (though he himself had used them in his youth) or anonymity. In this way, he sought to *transpose* honor culture into the modern intellectual life and letters.

This transposition could take different forms. Individual *Cahiers* were often devoted primarily to a single author; Péguy believed "every *Cahier* author is sovereign master in his *Cahier*."[89] It would inevitably give offense to readers, but Péguy never relented on this point. As he wrote in 1913: "A review is only living if it makes a good fifth of its subscribers unhappy. Justice consists solely in that they shall not always be the same fifth."[90]

The notion of honor that Péguy upheld was embodied in his own life—but not always, and the exceptions reveal the tensions in himself and his historical moment. Above all, he could excoriate Jaurès with polemics that sometimes culminated in ad hominem psychological attacks in the pages of his journal (in one unpublished manuscript from 1907, the "social" Catholic Marc Sangnier received somewhat similar treatment, despite Péguy's and Sangnier's often shared aspirations—and as noted, Alfred Dreyfus was scolded for accepting a pardon rather than continued imprisonment in the years before his acquittal).[91] *Notre Jeunesse* substantively criticized Jaurès's support for the punitive anti-Catholic policies associated with Émile Combes[92] (in which many nonpolitical, often educationally focused orders of Catholic clergy were forced out of the country), but the criticism quickly turned to excurses on Jaurès's putative self-hatred, his tendency toward the "cowardly"[93] and self-abasement, in which Péguy presumed to speak in Jaurès's own voice to sustain a wicked personal attack on his character: "I scorn my friends because they love me."[94]

Péguy's subsequent, vehement musing on how a critic of war like Jaurès would be publicly executed in a time of national emergency and war[95] is at painful variance with his own principles (manifest in his friendship and intellectual support for the pacifist Rolland throughout his life). It is difficult to see how this writing was honorable, in Péguy's own terms—that is, how it expresses the "honor" of the *Cahiers*.

It is true that in 1906 (after he and Jaurès had fallen out, and Péguy had begun to criticize him sharply in print), Péguy considered inviting one of his readers to write a defense of Jaurès, which he would publish "immediately" as a "duty" and even a "secret pleasure," but that invitation was never published, and the defense never appeared.[96] In 1910, he asked his readers to consider what would be said if Jaurès were Jewish[97]—and thus that anti-Semitic bigotry produces unjust, vicious judgments—but the purpose of the passage was to comment upon the insidious workings of anti-Semitism, not Jaurès.

Péguy articulated the ideal of a sacrificial life of writing that included mutual respect for writers and colleagues with whom he disagreed, but his departures from that intellectual code of honor give his readers a glimpse of the pain he felt at his own intellectual marginality (at least until the final years of his life) and precarious livelihood (to the very end of his life).

It would be a mistake, however, to focus exclusively upon Péguy's failed struggles against his own spleen. Péguy did not spare himself the prospect of making himself less than happy through the publication of views divergent from his own. These included political disagreements after 1905, as in the case of Charles Richet's pacifism, or Romain Rolland's; but it also included direct and personal criticisms of Péguy himself.

For example, in a 1913 issue of the *Cahiers*, he included in full a scathing review of his own work published in *La revue critique des livres nouveaux* under a pseudonym (Péguy identified its author as the historian Charles-Victor Langlois).[98] In it, Langlois accused Péguy of having "little taste, no wit, but [he is] very bitter . . . [with] a simmering and unbounded pride."[99] Péguy offered a brief rebuttal of the more personal charges but let much of the criticism go unanswered in the pages of the *Cahiers*. In this way he embodied the conviction he expressed in 1911 while responding to another criticism: those who made it "had a hundred times the right to criticize my texts."[100]

The failure to give respect to one's enemies was one of Péguy's most forceful and consistent criticisms of his age. Speaking of modern royalists like the members of Action Française, he wrote, here in the manner of a gradualist conservative rather than as a liberal or (as he did most frequently) as a socialist, "They are reactionaries, but they are infinitely less conservative than we are . . . they keep themselves busy as long as they can demolish respect, which was the very foundation of the ancien régime. It can be said literally that these partisans of the ancien régime have only one idea, which is to ruin everything good and healthy that we have kept from the ancien régime, which is still very substantial."[101]

Within the *Cahiers* and elsewhere, Péguy would not yield his honor for gain, even if he would bend it to accommodate his frustrations; a unity of conviction and action would be confirmed even when mores or institutions might offer an expedient escape. The prospects renounced could be very personal ones.

At times, for example, Péguy and his wife simply found it difficult to live in the same house, and their marriage approached being a disaster for both spouses. Clearly his recklessness with the generous dowry he received from the Baudouins played a role in their marital difficulties. That Péguy now had to support his mother- and brother-in-law—now living in very reduced circumstances, their savings gone—weighed heavily upon him.[102]

For someone of a passionate nature like Péguy, the desire for a romantic escape from the burdens of a difficult domestic life could spring promptly to mind. It comes as little surprise that entering his mid-thirties (around 1907) he fell in love with a young woman named Blanche Raphaël, from a middle-class, Jewish Parisian family. He told some of his closest friends about it, including Geneviève Favre, the daughter of the prominent Republican politician Jules Favre, who had herself ended her marriage. But he decided never to act upon it, and supported Blanche's decision to marry another man in July 1910.[103]

Given that he and Charlotte Baudouin had been married in a civil ceremony and not in church (and that his wife had refused to have their children baptized after his conversion), an opportunistic person with a gift for pious rationalization could have exploited his conversion to Catholicism in 1907 to try and have his marriage annulled. After securing a civil divorce to complement his annulment, he would have been free to pursue a new romance and a new marriage. But with several young children and many years of living together as husband and wife with Charlotte, he would not make expedient use of religious doctrine to break the vow that bound their lives together, and pretend that his marriage was anything other than a marriage.[104]

Upon his departure for war in 1914, he wrote Blanche occasional letters that whispered nothing of his affection, and asked her to pray for him when he was away. In the weeks before he died, he told Geneviève Favre about, as he saw it, the steady path of honorable abnegation he had pursued in relation to his love: his letters to Blanche were "no less pure" than the letters he sent to Favre, to his wife, and to his mother.[105] He had written Madame Favre years earlier that though it pained him to see Blanche married, "I would rather be a little sick from work than miss my vocation through an undisciplined heart [*un dérèglement du coeur*]."[106]

In intellectual terms, Péguy refused to use the development of his convictions expediently: rejecting any alliance with the Right, for example, when his poem *The Mystery of Jeanne d'Arc's Love* led some associated with Action Française to believe his return to Catholicism meant a turn to their politics, and with it their patronage. He insisted to the end that he was a Christian and a socialist, opposed to all forms of anti-Semitism and ready to fight for France against Germany, but many of his contemporaries on both the French Left and Right were ready to assume that the commitments he did not share with their own group were the decisive ones.

In these and other ways, Péguy took on the work of honorably embodying his own commitments and bearing their costs. While lapses and mistakes attended that labor, he configured the honor culture of the Belle Époque in a distinctive way and made sure that honor found expression in the *Cahiers*, through his own work and the regular publication of those who directly disagreed with him, or even denounced him. This honor of embodied conviction worked *within* a late modern culture of rapid communication and verbal conflict, and relied upon honest argument and observation rather than dueling pistols. The encomiast of Corneille found in the truthful practice of Parisian journalism, letters, and civic action a field of honor, writing the truth as much as he could see the truth—and live it among others devoted to convictions both like and unlike his own.

CHAPTER 7

Universal Particulars,
Particular Universalities

At the start of the twentieth century, there was no consensus about whether particular human communities, nations, or humanity as a whole could lay claim to the futures to come. For some, humanity had finally recognized its global unity, and that was a world-historical triumph; for others, humanity aspired to a global unity, and that was a foolhardy, demoralizing catastrophe. Nation-states were soon to pass away altogether; nations had an eternal destiny, the source and summit of common purpose, to be presented to schoolchildren as the foremost object of their devotion unto death. Communities were bound by suppressed memories of division, and selective memories of pain and violence; communities were bound by biological race, or by a unique and beloved language. Alternately, communities were bound by beguiling illusions that gave drama and a sense of purpose to history, or by moral solidarity, or *should* be bound by provisional utility alone. Regions bound persons to their native soil, gave them their true and unalterable character and their most immediate duties; individuals should be fundamentally autonomous, and all local, or collective, and intermediary attachments between the single individual and universal humanity were archaic fictions, best attenuated with speed in a new century of speed.

The reconciliation of the universal and the particular had long been a preoccupation of French and, more generally, of European thought. The German philosopher Johann Gottfried von Herder, for example—mediated through the appreciative readings he received in France throughout the nineteenth century, from Benjamin Constant to François Guizot, Edgar Quinet, Jules Michelet, and Ernest Renan[1]—was an inspiration for those inclined to

pursue a broad historical reconciliation between the particularity of the nation, or sometimes the collected peoples of a given historical epoch, and universal humanity. Each epoch and each civilization, expressing the genius of a
people, could add something unique to the tapestry of human achievement
in history, oriented not toward a final universality but toward a diversity of
cultural forms that need not stand in judgment of one another across time
and space. They presented themselves differently to the historical spectator.
Renan's remark, for example, that "nations . . . all bring a note to this great
concert of humanity"[2] has an unmistakably Herderian resonance. Cultures
are unique, but education and reason enable their achievements to be properly understood and appreciated by human beings as such.[3]

In the realm of popular sentiment and practical politics, European nationalists through the 1848 Revolutions often proposed a harmonious concord
between individual nation-states and humanity as a whole. For Giuseppe
Mazzini, Edgar Quinet, and many others, a truly liberal internationalism would
allow the free and independent societies of Italy, France, Germany, and Britain
to be fully themselves while forming a harmonious complementarity with other
nations. This could perhaps lead to a pan-European confederation of independent countries.[4]

After the failures of the 1848 Revolutions, this sense of complementarity
underwent a rapid decline. Some of Quinet's and Mazzini's spirit survived
until the Paris Commune, but even its advocates sensed that a patriotic universalism was fading. During the Commune, the journalist Jules Vallès criticized
the longtime revolutionary Charles Delescluze for his Mazziniesque, universalist sensibilities, and he conceded the point, saying in reply, "I represent the ideas
of another century."[5]

In direct political terms, Napoleon III sustained his domestic popularity
in France—in particular among French Catholics—by defending the all too
particular and extranational existence of the Papal States, thus preventing the
unification of France's neighbor to the southeast. Camillo Cavour in turn
would aspire to achieve Italian national unity through diplomatic and military maneuvers. Germany's unity was achieved through the ingenious manu-
facturing of wars by Otto von Bismarck, the last of which included a triumphant
war with France that ended with the seizure of territory in Alsace-Lorraine
and the humiliation of France. These developments toward an assertive, com-
petitive, and distinctly non-universalist nationalism generally elicited cheers
of triumph from German and Italian liberal nationalists, just as more than a

few French republicans, who identified themselves with the French Revolution, would come to hope for *la revanche* against Germany.[6]

The decay of a harmonious unity in difference between nationalism and internationalism was not always replaced by a dry-eyed nationalism founded upon realpolitik in the manner of Cavour and Bismarck, or even by dreams of revenge. In speculative thought, the second half of the nineteenth century saw the radicalization of both the particular (often if not invariably understood as the nation-state) and the universal.

An indispensable point of departure for understanding both uncompromising universalists and particularists was Ernest Renan's famous address, *Qu'est-ce qu'une Nation?* of 1869. For Renan, nations were not necessarily bound by language, political system, interest, ethnicity, or "race." Nations were the product of what he called a kind of preconscious "daily plebiscite"[7] in which the members of the nation decided to continue conceiving of themselves as members of a single community. The nation is for Renan a "spiritual principle" or a "soul," or a "moral conscience [*conscience*]."[8]

For Renan, however, the spiritual and moral affirmation produced by this plebiscite was very clearly prompted by glory and success, but above all by suffering and sacrifice, particularly the memory of painful, often violent collective suffering in the past.[9] Furthermore, the memory of suffering that had divided the community in the past—in French history, he mentions the St. Bartholomew's Day Massacre[10]—must be forgotten if not actively suppressed if the nation is not to undergo an inner fragmentation. A nation is often unified by memories of pain and violence inflicted upon it by others, and split asunder by pain and violence in which some portion of the nation served as perpetrators as well as victims. Memory will accentuate the former and artfully diminish if not entirely obscure the latter.[11] Thus for Renan, "the progress of historical study is often a danger for nationhood."[12]

Throughout his address, national cohesion depends for Renan upon a settled, semi-mythic past (far closer to myths than memories in the Bergsonian sense) rather than truth or shared hopes.

At the conclusion of his lecture, Renan rather nonchalantly informs his readers that in the future, Europe will "probably" lose its (at present) necessary national identities and become a confederation.[13] He does not appear to feel the force of any moral necessity to bring this state of affairs about.

Many of Renan's contemporaries and intellectual descendants would not—to use Nietzsche's terms—be content to be one of the "learned" who acts as a "mirror," who observes but acts cautiously, or does not act.[14] For some French and European socialists as well as anarchists and pacifists, particular communities were fictions, and pernicious fictions at that. Human universality had permanently exposed them as archaisms that must be consigned to history posthaste. Modern universality required putting national particularism to an end. For example, French anarchists often cut themselves off from their families and any loyalty to their own nations, devoting themselves to assassinations that targeted heads of state and the random killings of ordinary citizens, in hopes of destabilizing nation-states and bringing about their collapse.[15]

In a somewhat more irenic but similarly uncompromising mode, during the Dreyfus affair a socialist internationalist like Gustave Hervé would argue that if Dreyfus were guilty of treason, it would hardly matter, since the very notion of treason was founded upon the legitimacy of national communities and institutions, and nations had no legitimacy. Hervé, a member of the Antimilitarist Association and founder of the newspaper *La Guerre sociale*, declared that "our country is our class,"[16] and that it would be better to shoot one's officers than to fight against oppressed workers in the colonies.[17] A true universalism would require, if not the abrogation and eventual erasure of all national distinctions among peoples, at the very least the abrogation of all the political, legal, and economic forms that defined and sustained modern nations.

We have already seen that in contrast to this anti-particularist universalism, reactionary politics became aggressively anti-universalist and particularist. Maurras, Barrès, and many of their followers were contemptuous of foreign influence (at least modern foreign influences), and the prospects of international cooperation and harmony. For Maurras and those who sympathized with his movement, Action Française, the particular national community found its greatness in the repudiation of any form of international, reciprocal recognition among nations; "native traditions" were to be embraced, and the "modern abstractions" of, for example, the Enlightenment were opposed to all political and cultural coherence and vitality.

How did Péguy's writing move among these possibilities, and the contemporary cleaving of cultural and national particularity from universalism?

In his earliest days—as we have seen—Péguy sought a Harmonious City that would encourage the efflorescence of individual differences without exclusion (not only persons of different religions and races are citizens, but foreigners as well). He hoped that this Harmonious City would encourage lives of individual freedom and communal belonging.

Yet this is often not how he has been remembered in recent decades. Instead, he is remembered for a strident nationalism. It will indeed have occurred to his vigilant readers that he might be rather fond of France. In Augustinian language, he appears at times to blend the City of Man and the City of God much too freely. In 1905, he wrote of France during the French Revolution in a way that would not have been out of place in the salons of the Girondins and Jacobins themselves: "Our politics was always, at bottom, the politics of humanity, or better, let us say divine politics."[18] In Péguy's poem "The Mystery of the Holy Innocents" of 1912, God himself says, "I am a good Frenchman" (though a gentle, playful irony of a writer daring to speak in God's voice peeks through here, as it does with the reference to God being an "honnête homme" and "a good Christian" in the same passage).[19] But there are intervals in Péguy's prose that suggest not all of these references were intended entirely as gentle irony: in 1914, for example, Péguy wrote that the French are "the last of [the] elected peoples."[20]

The notion that the French are an elected people and that France has a providential mission of liberation exceeding those of other peoples has a long history, not only within the Revolution but beyond it. It could certainly be attributed to, among others, Victor Hugo. In *Les Misérables*, Hugo declares, "France is meant to stir the soul of nations, not to stifle it. Since 1792 all revolutions in Europe have been the French Revolution: liberty radiates from France. It is a solar phenomenon."[21] These words could have been Péguy's without alteration.

Of course, with intermittent adjustment, there could be other points of influence upon Péguy's account of France—among them Michelet's histories, or the oratory of war among the Girondins of 1792, or even Gregory of Tours's early medieval panegyrics in the *Historia Francorum* regarding the divine mandate of Clovis. But unlike Hugo and Michelet, and certainly Gregory of Tours, Péguy wrote when modern nationalism had become a form of mass consciousness in an age of industrial power and industrial arms, when the consequences of nationalist triumphalism could be felt all over the world.

Given the history of Europe in the twentieth century, some of Péguy's remarks about France could indeed be easily aligned with the nationalism of certain French republicans or, more broadly, with the bombast about an "eternal race" that punctuates European nationalism at the turn of the last century. Péguy could appear here in a way that the standard model might like: as a symptom, his writing mined for quotes that testify to the nationalist fever that would soon kill Péguy himself and millions of others.

Sometimes Péguy is indeed a nationalist; writing without revision, he succumbs to lazy thinking, veering toward a reflexive national pride, one that could indeed be found in several precincts of French society—and European culture as a whole—in the early twentieth century. An incomplete reading of Péguy could emphasize these passages.

Yet several questions remain unanswered. Did Péguy really think France was a kind of supreme nation-state, that God had a uniquely exalted mission for France? Was France, repairing to a Virgilian reference with which Péguy and his contemporaries were entirely familiar, destined to "spare the defeated and tame the proud"? What role was there, then, for a universal humanity, or for individual freedom, or for the aspirations of Péguy's own Harmonious City?

We can start with God and France. God speaks to France in Péguy's poetry; yet it is remarkable how he does so. For example, notwithstanding his earlier humorous line about God being a good French gentleman, in Péguy's "Mystery of the Holy Innocents," God is not French, since he lives eternally while the French cease to be. More importantly, Péguy's poetic invocation of God does not offer a God of Power but an affectionate and exasperated peasant *père de famille*, fully aware of the particular faults of French persons, history, and culture, but bearing them a particular but dry-eyed love. Above all, God, in Péguy's writing, affirms that France and the French—like all individual Frenchmen—will die. For

It's annoying, said God. When these French people are no more,
There are things I will do, and there will be no one
to understand them. . . .
Such are our French, said God. They are not without
faults. Far from it. They even have a lot of faults.
They have more faults than the others.
But with all their flaws I love them still more than the others with
    supposedly fewer faults.
I love them as they are.[22]

A perceptible patriotism flows through these lines. Yet it would require considerable hermeneutic ingenuity to find in them a proto-fascist, violent exaltation of national power, with God or "Providence" as the supreme force licensing that power. The poem has an unmistakable tone of wry, gentle peasant affection and inevitable human limits—including a tender, even loving sense of abundant human failings and inevitable mortality—entirely absent from the worship of undying national or "racial" strength that entranced the twentieth-century Radical Right.

Yet how exclusive is this love of his own nation in Péguy's mature and most influential writings? Did Péguy abandon his universalism? The answer to these questions opens up Péguy's fascinating attempt to *reconcile* the universal and particular in his writing, rather than to deny the universal (as fascism would notoriously do) or to deny the particular (as communism tended and, in a different way, liberal capitalism tends to do).

If one hastily looks for Péguy to somewhere express nationalist indignation, then it is easy enough to find "wounds" to his nation in the form of lost territory, and so on. For example, when the pacifist journalist and politician Francis de Pressensé gave a speech at a French Socialist Party conference, he spoke of Alsace-Lorraine and the "Pax Germanica" there.[23] Péguy thought little of Pressensé's willingness to countenance if not quite endorse this peace. But here as elsewhere, Péguy's reasoning is attuned not simply to justice for France, but also to questions of international justice.

Péguy includes a close paraphrase of Pressensé's speech in his essay *L'Argent suite* of 1913, remarking that for Pressensé "the *Pax Germanica* is hard" yet "it is all the same a peace." Péguy replied: "And in the same way the [Czarist] Russian peace is also a peace; and the [Ottoman] Turkish peace was a peace, and the Belgian peace in Africa and the Portuguese peace [in Africa]."[24] Opposition to imperialist domination around the world and the desire to liberate Alsace-Lorraine was for Péguy presented as the *same* cause, not a series of different causes. The reason some of his contemporaries protested the exploitation of Angola by the Portuguese and not of Alsace-Lorraine by the Germans was, in his words, that "we are not scared of Portuguese power,"[25] and presumably France was frightened of Germany.

At no point in his political trajectory does Péguy fail to affirm a universal morality that includes everyone: as he puts in *Notre Jeunesse*, "the most legitimate rights of peoples" and the need to protest even a single "insult" to "humanity."[26]

The year before he died, even as he worried that France could not survive a German invasion without the help of its colonies, Péguy affirmed his general anti-imperial commitments and his ongoing support for "the freedom of peoples," from Romania to Russia to Portuguese colonies in Africa, from Finland to the French Congo.[27] He continued to say that he had no interest in a deliberate or offensive war against Germany, only to be ready for a war if one came.[28] We have already seen that if a French "caesarian government of military reaction" invaded Germany, he would join the fight against the French government.[29]

In *Notre Jeunesse*, Péguy returns to a universalism that challenged an easy, respectable French self-regard. For him, the supreme embodiment of universal justice remained his friend Bernard-Lazare, who showed during the Dreyfus affair and afterward that he understood "real internationalism."[30]

According to Péguy, Bernard-Lazare saw clearly that French Christians were horrified at the treatment of Armenians by the Turks, but curiously silent about the treatment of Jews in Romania. For Bernard-Lazare and for Péguy, the reason for their silence was clear: French Christians identified with the suffering of fellow Christians (thus affirming their particularity). But they lacked a commitment to a truly universal justice; through a kind of silent "collusion" they allowed their fellow Christians to terrorize Romanian Jews.[31]

It might be argued that in these passages Péguy affirms only the universal rights of *collectivities* rather than *individuals*, and thus that a Herderian commitment to cultural diversity and distinctiveness trumps individual freedom. Péguy, however, thinks very differently. In fact, he claimed that he and other principled Dreyfusards had "experienced [*éprouvé*] fifteen years of hardship for the defense of private liberties" and for a regime founded upon "freedom of conscience."[32]

This devotion to "private liberties" and "freedom of conscience" from 1910 reaffirms Péguy's earlier assessment of freedom around the world. Péguy could speak very harshly of parliamentary corruption, and while he praised decisive elections in times of crisis—those along the lines of 1792 and 1848—his response to more quotidian elections was often a mixture of terse resignation, sarcasm, and frustration on the grounds of the venality and corruption associated with those elected.[33]

Péguy endorsed liberal nations as the world's free nations (some, like both the United States and France, with significant immigrant populations), without retracting his criticisms of their failings. In 1905, when he names the countries of the world that are meaningfully free, they are all liberal republics and constitutional monarchies: "France, England, Italy, America, Switzerland, [and] Belgium."[34]

In similar terms, in the fall of 1912, in a conversation with his friend Joseph Lotte, Péguy opined that Action Française should accept the legitimacy of the French Republic. He said that while parliamentarianism could be corrupt, it had recently produced admirable protections for workers,[35] and he praised the work of the practical socialist politician Aristide Briand.[36]

While he criticizes the failings of modern government, nowhere does he suggest a revision of his list of free countries or cease to support the Third Republic. In February 1913, he wrote in *L'Argent*: "I love nothing so much as freedom."[37] Not only was freedom "the irrevocable condition of grace," "life" required freedom.[38]

Yet if both human universalism and individual freedom remain important to Péguy, why raise the particularity of France—and other countries— so insistently?

For Péguy, free countries need to be particular, unique countries for their citizens to be free, to live freely and to defend freedom around the world. In 1913, for example, he distinguished between a praiseworthy "internationalism" that upholds "a system of political and social equality, of temporal justice and mutual freedom among peoples" and what he calls a "vague bourgeois cosmopolitanism"[39] that quickly compromises or capitulates to injustice in return for convenience, prosperity, comfort, and safety. For Péguy, there is a tendency in the modern world not to seek a true internationalism as he understands it; rather, it aspires to the "artificial, intellectual equalization of men and peoples, of individuals and peoples."[40]

For Péguy, the supreme lesson of the Dreyfus affair was precisely that universal truth and individual rights—including the legitimate rights of all[41]— needed to be embodied in continuous, particular communities to pursue justice and rectify injustice. In Péguy's account, socialists and other committed internationalists were slow to recognize why they should care about the fate of a single French "bourgeois officer," just as anti-universalist nationalists and anti-Semites were delighted to see him suffer, even when the case against him was obviously false. We have seen that for Péguy there was a broader tendency in what he called a "modernist" bourgeois culture to shrink from conflict altogether. Pressensé, for example, proposed that Alsace-Lorraine secure its autonomy from Germany on its own. Péguy's dry riposte was that he could conceive "nothing as bourgeois" as this proposal.[42]

On these questions, there is a very rigorous, exacting analyst in Péguy that, as war approached, struggled against his own urgent, expressive intensity: rigor and exactitude usually carried the day, but not always. He was always an advocate of the Declaration of the Rights of Man,[43] and its commitments to universal rights. Yet as would later be the case with his friend Albert Mathiez, the historian of the Revolution, that defense could lead him to praise a very dubiously "universalist" regime in frankly implausible terms. Péguy claimed, for example, that "in times of war it is the National Convention [that is, of

1792–1795] that is the regime of gentleness and tenderness." Further, regimes that avoid violence and surrender to the enemy are those that lead to the greatest massacres and civilian losses.[44]

Whatever judgments Péguy made about the different stages of the French Revolution, his writing about politics, particularity, and universality in both philosophical and more immediate political-historical terms demanded and generally received careful thought. If he concluded that embodied communities were required for the functioning of universal justice, they were also required for creativity. It might be said that community is here simply a polite contemporary word for "nation-state." But Péguy had a more nuanced account of community than this one, the one to which so many of his fellow early twentieth-century Europeans gave themselves without reservation.

In his later work, Péguy begins to talk about how all people require particular "countries" (*pays*). But here Péguy's thought makes a forceful move away from nationalism: it is clear that "countries" clearly does *not* serve as a synonym for "nation-states."

In his dialogue between Clio and the pagan soul from 1913, Péguy writes: "Paris is a country and [so is] every parish of Paris . . . the rue Mouffetard is a country . . . Versailles is a country, and the century of Versailles; Paris and the twenty centuries of Paris . . . a country, a country is a place with a bell tower." The reference to a bell tower might make it sound as if Péguy's countries are exclusively Christian, but his list of *pays* also includes archetypally pagan places in the educated historical imagination of the Belle Époque like Troy, Crete, and Argos. In fact, Clio tells him in more universal terms, a country is fundamentally—and simply—a local place and a community in a specific time, "un endroit dans le temps" (a place in time). The dialogue moves more boldly away from the modern nation-state with a move from territory to time: "There are not only local countries, there are also temporal countries."[45]

Péguy understands these various spatial and temporal "countries" as places of carnal life, that nourish the relation of human beings to others in shared experiences through daily work and leisure, and awaken them to diverse human possibilities in a distinctive common way.

Péguy urges his readers to consider it promising—not least for originality—that both the place and the time of our origin cannot be chosen, just as human beings choose neither their parents nor their native language. Even if human beings are later at a great—geographic, temporal, linguistic, cultural, metaphysical—distance from their origins, those particular origins nourish unique paths of seeing and perception that individuals may change, but without which neither creative affirmation, nor creative transformation, nor creative transgression is possible. For "the greatest genius in the world does not replace having had such a cradle, such a nation, having come from this or that landed race. The greatest genius in the world also does not replace having had such a friendship, at such a date, in this place, this cradle of friendship. Every man has, by temporal birth, by his temporal situation, by his place, by his temporal time, by his date of taking effect, a certain zone of friendship and no other, a certain zone where he works, where he can work, where the event works for or against him."[46]

Clio tells Péguy's pagan soul that Homer, Plato, Corneille, Rembrandt, Beethoven, and Jesus himself entered history in a distinct, robustly unique place and time (with Beethoven's upbringing, Péguy includes a German place and time, in the high *Aufklärung* no less), and their achievements are, inevitably, partially dependent upon these places and times. Bereft of specificity, an attempt to live in history "in general" neglects the creative, vivifying sap of specific places and times, specificity that can stain but that also colors and nourishes. For those who aspire to universal objectivity, life becomes a form of consumerism and spectatorship. As Péguy's Clio says, it becomes "a kind of universal exposition that never ends."[47]

These unchosen situations are not the subject of idealizing language in Péguy's account. An "endroit dans le temps" is not simply a geographic place but another occasion for Péguy to express a kind of gentle, slightly melancholy yet affirmative irony. These places are also "a time where you situate yourself, a time where you are a man, citizen, soldier, father, voter, taxpayer, author, all the inevitable, all the irreparable, all the sacred silliness [*sottises*]."[48]

It is not simply creativity and vitality that are at issue in the affirmation of these "silly" and yet sacred forms of particularity and obligation, but universal justice itself. For Péguy certainly believed that creativity, genius, political innovation, and divine revelation might fall upon some countries more than others. His list of such "elect peoples" includes not only the French but specifically the people of Paris, Jerusalem, Athens, Rome, and Florence as well.[49] (For Péguy great urban metropolises are once more described as nourishing and distinctive "countries," just as his list of "countries of liberty" mentioned earlier in the chapter also include cities of liberty, like Paris, London, Brussels, Zurich, and Geneva.)[50]

It is often argued that particularism inevitably comes to sacrifice individual freedoms and universal justice for all persons in the name of "the people" and its alleged greatness, power, genius, and destiny. Péguy saw it differently: individual freedoms and universal justice *require* particularity.

Péguy was skeptical of what Voltaire had called "the party of humanity," not because—like Péguy himself—it upholds human universality, but because it is a universality without an accompanying particularity through which both love and sacrifice are embodied by a distinctive group of human beings, and thus a universal justice that can act, move freely and live.

For Péguy, the idea of universality without particularity was shallow, its champions too willing to demand sacrifices of others and incapable of reasoned, lucid, substantive, patient sacrifice of their own, a kind of sacrifice that would always be necessary for truth and justice to make their way in the world. For example, we have seen that for Péguy's contemporary Hervé, Dreyfus should be released, but treason defined by false and arbitrary distinctions between peoples was not really a crime anyway.[51] This blithe dismissal of any attachment and obligations to one's community was a practical misfortune (it undermined the Dreyfusards' commitment to demonstrating Dreyfus's fervently-expressed loyalty to the nation). It was also self-defeating, since the movement to uphold Dreyfus's innocence required some shared community, with shared notions of right and wrong, of guilt and innocence, to undertake the work of common justice.[52]

Yet to affirm particularism without universality—the reactionary particularism of Action Française, for example—was mere chauvinism: as Péguy put it when he was about to go to war in 1914, "Nothing is so contrary to French mysticisms than the politicians of Action Française."[53] Its members offered demagogy, encouraging people to abandon themselves to some simplistic and often delusive collective affirmation, as anti-Semites urged their politicized followers to vent their violent hatreds upon French Jews.[54]

Péguy thus finds in particularity—certainly including but by no means exclusively national particularities—and universality two equally indispensable dimensions of individual and universal justice, as well as creativity. To affirm universality without inhabiting some meaningful, living, and loving particularity opens the way to persons becoming cynical, self-indulgent, cowardly, derivative, expedient, and compromised; yet to affirm particularity without a genuinely just and open universality opens the way to persons becoming blinkered, defensive, bigoted, pitiless, arbitrary, and cruel.

A particularity that upholds universal justice and dignity requires a universalism growing out of a vital *pays*, in Péguy's special, both national and non-national sense of the word. It persists in the courage and above all the love[55] that embodies and sustains truth, justice, and creativity.

For many late modern and postmodern persons, the categories of individual and universal humanity still have some immediate purchase, even if these categories are increasingly put in question by what Péguy would call metaphysical modernity. But what rational claim can be made for group identities that are not chosen, that are drawn from an immensely complex, often messy and ambiguous historical inheritance?

Péguy acknowledges the force of the objection, calling the particular, communal love that maintains a relation to universal justice a "mysticism." For him, this term carries with it a long range of associations, not least from his reading of Jaurès.[56] But now it has a remarkable consequence: Mysticism is the precondition for the rigorous and successful exercise of any fully human—and precisely reasoned—action on behalf of universal justice.

CHAPTER 8

Mysticism and Politics

Péguy lived amidst an intense conflict between advocates of a scientific politics and an irrational politics. In *The Future of Science*, Renan exhorted his readers to think of an ideal politics practiced as science,[1] and ambitions of this kind were hardly limited to his musings. As we have seen, sociologists boasted of being scientists, free of all mysticism.[2] The positivists of the Third Republic as well as Marxists and the reactionary Maurras were all eager to declare that with their own metaphysics and policy preferences, the age of a truly scientific politics had already begun.

They were fiercely opposed by those who found in politics a part of life resistant to scientific control. For Gustave Le Bon, Georges Sorel, and others, the source and end of political action was not suprarational but subrational. They variously appear to both condescend to and revel in analyses of irrationality in politics, above all, of the irrationality of political energies in history.

Péguy lived among these disparate historical possibilities, and he crystallizes his own thought in an apothegm: "Tout commence en mystique et finit en politique" (Everything begins in mysticism and ends in politics).[3] It became the most famous sentence he ever wrote.

To contemporary readers, the very words may appear to approach the present through clouds of incense, summoned into the modern world by de Maistre or some other apostle of reaction; perhaps to breathe a culpable heedlessness if not actual contempt for reasoned procedure and negotiation, for the affirmation of difference and the hard-won practical accommodations of inclusive politics.

Yet what does it actually mean to say everything begins in mysticism and ends in politics? As is so often the case with Péguy, the reader must go to work. Péguy establishes, develops, and evokes his concepts rather than setting them in sequential propositions that aspire to exhaust the real. It is a form of writing that requires effort from the reader, and is an act of fidelity to his unsparingly anti-systematic convictions.

Péguy's own sense of mysticism developed over the course of his life. For the young Péguy, mysticism had been a slightly positive if rarely used term, often mentioned in passing.[4] Several years into the life of the *Cahiers* he began to write of mysticism with care, if with considerable ambivalence, in terms reminiscent of Jaurès. Mysticism is now a special and legitimate aspiration of human beings—and the failure to understand that has led materialist socialists to diminish the appeal of socialism in relation to Christianity. In 1904, the still religiously skeptical Péguy claimed that "politics does not supplant a religion; politics does not supplant a mysticism." Only a robust, nonmaterial, moral, economic, and social ethic can "supplant a mysticism"—that is, one that offers nothing less than a "temporal salvation."[5]

For many of those involved in the Dreyfus affair—and especially for the passionate Dreyfusard Charles Péguy—it was the defining event of their lives. It is therefore not surprising that while Péguy wrote extensively on the affair in the late 1890s (that is, before and during the controversy's peak), his famous reflections on it and its relation to mysticism came later, after much thought. Above all, this was the task of *Notre Jeunesse*, published in 1910.

In the months and years before *Notre Jeunesse*, there were those close to him—most notably Daniel Halévy[6]—who expressed ambivalence about their youthful devotion to Dreyfus. There were also those who assumed Péguy, now a Catholic who was known to have quarreled with socialists and the clerisy of the New Sorbonne, was on his way to the Right. They expected him to ally himself with Action Française, or repudiate his Dreyfusism altogether.

As rumors swirled around him, Péguy began to write, repudiating nothing of what he describes as his frankly mystical devotion to the Dreyfus case. But what is the relationship between mysticism and politics?

First, Péguy argues that mysticism is not ideological, or irrationally devoted to abstractions, and furthermore, it is necessary for an enduring and just communal order of any kind. For "a regime that stands, that holds fast, that is living, is not a thesis." That a regime is not a thesis is for Péguy systematically misunderstood by intellectuals of both "progressive" and "reactionary" varieties. For him, they "make the same false attribution" because as modern intellectuals they think in abstract, theoretical terms and "in a certain sense believe in politics." They want to discuss the distribution and exercise of political power above all, and this is itself a misunderstanding; that which is built upon the foundation is mistaken for the foundation. It is analogous to believing that "the chateaux of the Loire make or do not make earthquakes."[7] Mysticism is thus connected to "infinitely more profound realities" that shape politics, rather than the other way around.[8]

This is not to say that deeper realities—at this point, it is not clear whether Péguy simply means "culture" or a certain set of Durkheimian "social facts" or a cultural "ideal"—substitute for or abolish politics. He writes of the practical, necessary adjudication of interests and of the political compromises required for common life in a community. He readily observes that legal procedures like the right of the accused to an appeal were indispensable for Dreyfus's exoneration. He speaks without hesitation about the rights of different peoples.[9] Furthermore, for Péguy, when "politicians, when those who make a vocation and profession of politics do their professional work . . . there is nothing to say. . . . To do politics and call it politics, that is fine. To do politics and call it mysticism, to take mysticism to make politics from it, that is an inexpiable misappropriation."[10]

As deeper realities shape politics, mysticisms have another and supremely important source of life: for Péguy, monarchies or republics—indeed, created beings and things—find their strength, worth, and dignity in "being loved."[11] This love can and should be analytically explored, developed, and expressed by reason, but it will always elude comprehensive explanation. It can never become a thesis, since demonstrable theses are not loved, and love necessarily opens upon an experience that transcends mastery, in any form of necessary demonstration or possession.

For Péguy, it is not—as it variously is for Renan or for Nietzsche—a memory of spectacular, mythologized moments of suffering, domination, and violence (as well as selective acts of memory and forgetting) that creates a mystical love. For him, love is prior to suffering, and generally testifies to what it loves quietly. It is propelled from an original truth and justice embodied in a particular community—in the case of the Dreyfus affair, Jewish, Christian, and French Republican embodiments—and that seeks to express the love of that truth and justice in the conditions of a particular historical moment. In his words, suffering "makes" or "sanctifies" or, in more limited terms, "sanctions" mysticism, but its true strength ultimately springs from and moves toward a faithful, persistent love.[12]

Here Péguy's thinking is strongly reminiscent of Augustine's argument in *City of God* that "a people is the association of a multitude of rational beings united by a common agreement on the objects of their love." Yet Péguy is more consistently willing than Augustine to acknowledge the positive contribution those shared loves make to the common good and to justice, even when they do not explicitly recognize the God of Abraham, Isaac, and Jacob.[13]

To understand what mysticism is, Péguy also wants to understand who lives out a mysticism. They are very often not clergy or members of any institutionally respectable educated coterie, for example. Rather, for Péguy, mysticism, including the mysticism of the Dreyfus affair, requires devotion to justice and truth among the members of embodied moral communities. Mysticism does not find its strength in associating state power with divine power—in fact the opposite is true. Péguy claims that the mysticisms of the Dreyfus affair were sustained by "little people, generally obscure, generally poor, some of them very poor"[14]—called to come to the defense of a defenseless man. The Dreyfus affair ultimately became the concern of respectable and even prominent people, eminent leaders of opinion, and so on; but for Péguy that was possible only because before that cause was respectable or even noticed, there were obscure people willing to give up everything in order to uphold Dreyfus's innocence. Mysticism, as the love of justice and truth, is thus "the invincible strength of the weak."[15]

Péguy had seen that many of the great and the good in French political and social life, on both the Left and the Right, were initially willing to accept that Dreyfus would suffer death and disgrace, or at best to protest weakly while seeking the fulfillment of their long-standing political ambitions, or simply to avoid controversy. In contrast to them, the "mystical" Dreyfusards were weak and without immediate influence but unswervingly devoted. It is mystical love that lucidly discerns and steadily participates in the work of justice, work that may later demand a response from the more principled members of far more influential groups.

Péguy's mystical love has several more indispensable attributes, within and beyond the Dreyfus affair. First, it pertains to all humanity through universal justice. The mysticisms of the Dreyfus affair relate to a "single crime," a "single injustice" that requires the devotion of French persons, Jews, Christians, and non-believers alike. Dreyfus as a supposed traitor is exiled from their shared community, yet they come to his defense not because he can invariably be claimed as "one of ours" but because he has suffered an injustice. In this way, Péguy's close friend, the activist Bernard-Lazare—the embodiment of Péguy's mysticism throughout *Notre Jeunesse*—inspired Péguy by seeing "the Bretons and the Poles on the same level" just as he saw Christians and Muslims on the same level.[16] He was "for justice . . . but in the sense of a perfect equilibrium, a perfect horizontality of justice" that sought justice for human beings everywhere.[17]

This love of universal justice cannot demonstrate itself by criteria outside itself, say, by its "utility" (though Péguy will argue that mysticism is indispensable, it is not useful in the quantifiable terms recognized by utilitarians). But a mystical love of justice directs, inspires, and sustains moral reasoning about the world, and the human universality that makes it possible to reason and to act justly on behalf of Poles and Bretons, Jews, Christians, and Muslims.

This universality does not mean idealizing any group of persons, or humanity as a whole. For Péguy, all the agents within various mysticisms are flawed, but precisely with their flaws, they participate in humanity. All of them must patiently pay the price to raise the standard of justice for each and all in a given historical moment.[18] According to Péguy, Bernard-Lazare's general equanimity gave way to frustration when he encountered those who wanted the Dreyfus affair to unspool like a melodrama, replete with pure and unfailingly charismatic heroes. They did not find Dreyfus when he returned to France for his retrial "as we had dreamed," wrote Péguy, and for Bernard-Lazare, some Dreyfusards required him to have "all the virtues." Bernard-Lazare's memorable reply came in Péguy's emphatic capitals: "HE'S INNOCENT, THAT IS ALREADY A LOT."[19]

One of the ways in which mysticisms avoid their own corruption is through the work of testing among and between different mysticisms. During the Dreyfus affair, Péguy found the cooperation and mutual testing among Jewish, Christian, and French "mysticismes."[20]

These mysticisms cooperated neither in unanimous synchrony, nor in relations of subordination. A campaign for Dreyfus that involved only one of these three mysticisms would, Péguy strongly suggests, have simply failed, since these three mysticisms were engaged in what he calls a process of "coming together" that allowed for the flourishing of their respective *mystiques*.[21] He writes of how he and his Jewish friends and colleagues had "mutually tested" one another, found one another faithful, and brought about a "truly mystical friendship."[22] For different mysticisms to bring justice into the world, they must both work together and readily challenge one another.

Yet for all the coming together and testing required among different groups, for Péguy, to participate in a mysticism is not an exclusive or totalizing identity. Mysticisms could coexist in the same people, notably (as we have seen) in Bernard-Lazare,[23] just as Péguy's years of work for the Dreyfusard cause drew simultaneously from French Republican, socialist, and Christian sources.

For Péguy, mysticisms may not oppose one another at all, and if they do, they are less likely to do harm to others than political disagreements, since they partake in a particular (in every sense) love of universal justice and truth that has no temporal or spatial boundaries. In his words, "Mystics are much less each other's enemies than politicians are, because unlike politicians they do not constantly want to divide up temporal matter, a temporal world, an incessantly limited temporal power."[24] The late ancient world, says Péguy, did not find nearly as keen an opposition between the mysticism of the polis and Christian mysticism as it did between pagan politics and a politicized Christianity.[25]

In different historical moments, harmonious mysticisms find their legitimacy first in the love for others and for justice that they evoke and sustain. This love is to be identified not with a sentimental emotional immediacy, or, in Nietzschean terms, with a falsifying "illusory" or "romanticizing power"[26] but with painstaking discernment and sacrificial if often quiet and anonymous— yet heroic—action.

Furthermore, the mysticism is both in deep continuity with the past and embodied in the present. The Péguy of *Notre Jeunesse* is a faithful Catholic drawing inspiration from the Gospels, but a fiercely anticlerical one that would have made (and in fact, did make) no sense to the partisans of a fiercely clericalist Catholicism, who had a strong, predetermined notion of what a pious Catholic should say and do, not just in reference to faith and morals, but often in relation to culture and politics as well. Péguy was a Catholic who was long estranged from its French institutional champions, never formally returned to the church, and remained a sharp critic of French clericalism.[27] Bernard-Lazare was proudly Jewish and opposed anti-Semitism everywhere he saw it, defending Catholics and Muslims as well, but as an atheist,[28] an anarchist, and a Zionist, not as a religiously observant Jew.

Yet for all that, mysticism does not glory in its differences from the group that nourishes the mysticism, but maintains an exacting fidelity to that mystical body. Mysticism thus requires a certain sacrifice of the joys of membership in a coterie, group, or sect, since it does not find its home in power or the powerful; justice and truth are always poor.[29]

In this way, Péguy differentiates himself from a dangerous and unreflective affirmation of particular origins or allegiances (chosen or unchosen), as they manifest themselves in a given moment. In its strength through weakness, often accompanied by a principled and partial estrangement from institutions, Péguy's mysticism is the antipode of politics, which is always engaged in the pursuit or perpetuation of power.

Of course, from Machiavelli to Hobbes to Rousseau to Nietzsche (and, in a different way, in Hegel), mysticism is always political, and has already been political whenever and wherever it appears. Mysticism, if not the mask of power, is its extending and stabilizing faculty, or perhaps a surreptitiously rational artifice required for the ordering of subrational political agents and subjects.

Péguy's mysticism, however, is quite different: in it inheres the conviction that one's embodied life is oriented ultimately by the good that one loves most, and allows for a truly rational understanding, as opposed to the irrational, enervating "rationalisms" of what Péguy calls modern (that can also be historically ancient) metaphysics.

It is in this context that Péguy—speaking here for himself and other "mystical republicans"—writes of what has changed in late modern culture, politics, and notions of self and meaning:

> Immediately after us begins the world we have named—that we
> will not cease to name—the modern world. The world of those
> who try to be clever. The world of the intelligent, the advanced, of
> those who know, of those who can't be shown up, of those who
> can't be fooled. The world of those who have nothing left to
> learn . . . the world of those who are not dupes, not imbeciles. Like
> us. *That is to say*: the world of those who believe in nothing, not
> even in atheism, who devote themselves, who sacrifice themselves
> to nothing. *To be precise*: the world of those who have no mysticism. And who boast about it.[30]

In Péguy's account, failing to ally themselves mystically with an embodied community and a mystical love—including in faithful estrangement from that community, which maintains the mystical communion despite its inevitable human failings—metaphysical moderns proselytize for an understanding of the world in which all mystical loves are illusions. For Péguy, since metaphysical moderns are supremely committed to *not* giving themselves—to practicing a continual suspicion before all invitations to self-giving—they move easily toward disembodied and often political abstractions, and struggle to make a meaningful, embodied sacrifice to fight injustice, or simply to

perceive a single injustice as such. A flourishing love requires careful thinking and sacrificial action; a ready-made thesis taken as self-evident is the subject of firm political opinions, not patient devotion to work in unique and often
difficult circumstances.

Of course, one could argue that modern anti-mysticism is a fundamentally rational position; one could say that all forms of self-giving are easily manipulated by the sinuous brutalities of powers embodied and disembodied (in
language, for example), and besides, none of them is true. Péguy's response to
this argument is not simply that nonexclusive mysticisms, properly relating
to universal justice, to quiet and loving sacrifice, to coming together and testing, participate variously in loving the truth, even if they can never claim to
definitively possess the truth as a demonstrable thesis. That is clearly his major argument, but it is accompanied by the argument that the refusal of all
self-giving does not improve the world: cumulative, uncompromising critique
or distinctively modern "critical thinking" will not save modern peoples from
being manipulated by power and allow them to be universally just.

The partisans of modern metaphysics refuse to acknowledge that the very
political, "practical realities" to which critique attends actually require mysticism to exist: "Every mysticism is the creditor of every politics."[31] Without that
mystical "credit," an embodied community will descend inexorably into an
alienated egotism inimical to any human flourishing and any genuine solidarity, including a constructively critical one, until some epoch of renewal.[32]
Péguy believed that something like that fragmentation had begun in the
French Republic: "Republican mysticism, that was when one used to die for
the republic; republican politics nowadays, one lives off it."[33]

The renunciation of embodied, mystical love on behalf of a universal
justice—rather than the continued existence of an inert principle—has created for Péguy an unprecedentedly widespread historical situation, in which
both an attachment to one's community and an attachment to God become
suspect as equally false forms of self-giving. For him, "the movement of the
derepublicanization of France is[,] in profound terms, the same movement as
the movement of its *dechristianization*. It is together an identical, a single profound movement toward *demystification*."[34] In fact, "one could almost say
that they [the people opposed to mysticism] no longer want to believe in idols
and that they no longer want to believe in the true God . . . an identical sterility dries out the city and Christianity."[35]

Yet even if a particularly embodied, universal love of justice is expressed
in secular French republicanism, in Judaism, or in Christianity, surely they

will inevitably undergo corruption. The mystical body of Christ degener-
ated into the Inquisition, the Tennis Court Oath of 1789 turned into the
Great Terror of 1794, and the generous patriotic internationalism of Mazzini
gave way to the expansionist, violent nationalism of second-wave European
imperialism.

Péguy agrees entirely that the moral and spiritual corruption of a mysticism is inevitable. Mysticism will, as he says, inevitably "end in politics."
He could write scathingly about what "clerical politics did to Christian
mysticism."[36] Similarly, among some Dreyfusards, the descent from mysticism to politics saw the Dreyfus Affair become matter for self-congratulation,
celebrating their own virtue[37] and using governmental power to avenge themselves spitefully upon broadly defined "enemies."[38] But Péguy's solution to the
corruption of mysticism is not the abandonment of all mysticisms (which for
Péguy will collapse upon itself without producing anything beyond itself)
but fidelity in one's unique present to the ultimate truth of a mysticism
(which will ultimately be corrupted before a new élan of demanding, self-
giving love oriented toward universal justice and truth). If a mysticism or
mysticisms are able to uphold a single act of justice, or protest against a single
injustice, they will have embodied a mystical love of justice in time,[39] a love
that will in turn be fruitful for many as yet unforeseeable futures.

Mysticism is also not without some modest hope of resistance to the gravitational pull of politics. In one passage Péguy writes in capital letters: "The
essential [thing] is that . . . MYSTICISM IS NOT DEVOURED BY THE POLITICS TO
WHICH IT HAS GIVEN BIRTH."[40] But even this exhortation concedes that mysticisms will give birth to politics; it is important only that mysticism not be
"devoured" by the politics that will inevitably betray it. What prevents a mysticism from becoming entirely consumed by its own politics?

The moment when one turns from a mysticism of loving sacrifice to a
politics, grasping for expedient compromise and the fruits of corruption, is
dauntingly difficult to spot, for "politics devours mysticism," and

> that is the perpetual and always recommencing history. Because
> it is the same matter, the same men, the same committees, the
> same game, the same mechanism, already automatic, the same
> surroundings, the same apparatus, the habits already adopted,
> and we see nothing of it. We don't even pay attention to it. And yet
> the same action, which was just, from this point of discernment
> becomes unjust . . . the same action . . . from this point of

discernment, becomes not only something else, it generally becomes its opposite, its own opposite. And in this way one becomes innocently criminal.[41]

Péguy argued that those who are able, with much difficulty, to discern the point at which mysticism becomes politics are put in an excruciating position. The politics that feeds off a mystical love, and eventually tries to consume it, is organized and supported by those who bitterly resent any suggestion that they are not the legitimate heirs of that original and fertile mysticism. It threatens their very existence, because "Every party lives by its mysticism, and dies from its politics."[42]

As for those who oppose the suggestion that they turned mysticism into politics, for Péguy this resentment is often morally sincere—hence their paradoxically "innocent" criminality. They are habitually prone to see certain causes or groups of people as oppressors and tyrants, and their own group as beleaguered defenders of truth and justice. For Péguy, this blinkered vision is often accomplished through a confusion of "orders," that is, among different levels of human experience. Mysticisms, he says, "must be compared with one another, and politics with one another." This respect for orders is generally not honored. Péguy observed that French republicans often "tirelessly compare royalist politics to republican mysticism," just as the reactionaries of Action Française generally compare "republican politics to royalist mysticism."[43] The honest work of comparing the political moves of one's own group to those of one's opponents, or better, comparing their respective mysticisms, is left undone. It is too hard, and too humbling.

Those who refuse to play the game of politics, and who thus can perceive that an original movement devoted to truth and justice has since become a political power that exists primarily to perpetuate itself, are called traitors by their former comrades.[44] In this way, those who have been faithful to a mysticism followed a rigorous analysis in love that often led them to "twice sacrificing their career, their future, their existence and their bread: the first time to struggle against their enemies, the second time to struggle against their friends."[45]

For Péguy, "an honest man must be a perpetual renegade,"[46] even as this rebellion is always in service of a more profound and consistent fidelity. The path of the mystic requires exacting, patient, and mobile discernment; the frames of modern metaphysics and modern political ideologies require only a ready-made, collective ideological assent.

There is a great deal of Pascal's different "orders" of experience in passages like these. But the exact point of discernment between mysticism and politics poses a great challenge, even if it is perceptible. Above all, when a mysticism becomes profitable (personally, professionally, financially), for Péguy it is in mortal danger of betraying itself, and becoming a form of politics.[47]

For all its difficulties and sacrifices, Péguy is certain that mysticism is required to bring the love of justice to life. It can certainly work within a clearly liberal political order, yet it is not simply *of* that order, and receives its imperatives from deeper sources, just as the chateaux of the Loire may well be politically, militarily, and culturally necessary but do not cause earthquakes (or the stability that allows them to stand at all). In this way, for Péguy, mysticisms sustain, work fruitfully within, and yet continually challenge the assumptions of liberal societies. For truth and justice to flourish, liberal societies need people who are willing to live within liberalism toward ends that transcend liberalism.

Péguy's account of the relationship between mysticism and politics can be difficult to understand in late modern cultures. For example, the philosopher John Rawls, in his discussion of an "overlapping consensus," assumed that extra-liberal metaphysics only functioned within liberal politics through a process of dilution and attenuation. At first "conflicting reasonable comprehensive doctrines" in modern societies[48] accept coexistence "reluctantly" because it provides "the only workable alternative to endless and destructive civil strife."[49] Eventually there could be a kind of convergence between, for example, liberal philosophical ideas and religious doctrines that include "lots of slippage" and allows "liberal principles of justice to cohere loosely with . . . (partially) comprehensive views."[50] Once they are seen to be "working effectively and successfully for a sustained period of time," they will tend to "encourage the cooperative virtues of political life: the virtue of reasonableness and a sense of fairness, a spirit of compromise and a readiness to meet others halfway."[51]

For Péguy, mysticisms do not "meet others halfway" so much as they simultaneously cooperate, challenge, and test one another on behalf of a justice that requires steady, difficult devotion in order to remain alive and embodied in history. Politics may then require compromise; but for Péguy, compromise and "slippage" are not the deepest and most important ways in which mystical "comprehensive views" meet political order and justice—and ultimately sustain them.

For Péguy, a political order without mysticism will lack the embodied love that enables one to persistently hold power to account, and the keenness of ethical and charitable perception that discerns even a "single injustice" as intolerable. To believe that "one does not lose a city, a city is not lost for a (single) citizen" sounds eminently reasonable to those without mysticism. In fact, that accommodating notion "is the language of reason"[52]—that is, of reason without love, not least a calculus that imperils the beloved practices and bonds of attachment among persons that the calculus assumes as more or less arbitrary "givens" that need not be affirmed except as provisional, subrational, occasionally useful historical legacies.

A mystical love inspires reason and is reasonable, but it is not nourished or sustained by reason alone. In this way, Péguy's account of mysticism strongly recalls his critique of modern metaphysics, where modernity is the revolt of the secondary order of intellect against the primary order of charity.[53]

To refuse participation in a mystical love of justice and truth in favor of an intellect that refuses all limits to its explanatory power is to take the first step toward politics and its abiding preoccupation with material, formal, and measurable (and thus, for Péguy, often superficial or at best penultimate) power in all its forms. This is, for him, not simply to risk a loss of moral and political energy, but to constrict drastically one's powers of perception.

The mystical love of justice, as Péguy understands it, must be pursued with total clarity about its cost. If the Dreyfus affair became a way to satisfy the need for "military glory"[54] for Péguy and others, this glory took forms and demanded action that never resembled a battlefield or a triumphal parade. For this glory manifests itself in the poor, "poor Jews and poor Christians" who "make our living as we can"[55] and entertain no illusions about their future prospects, from the Dreyfus affair or from anything else.

For Péguy, embodied and mystical particularities are ultimately the only reasonable way to recognize and to embody universal justice in the world. They require a more precise and agile rigor than any available to the systematic, ideological critiques associated with modern metaphysics—or with their alleged opposites, the partisans of "antimodern reaction" (but in fact, with their politically obsessed emphasis on critique and negation,[56] they represented an extremely modern reaction).

Mysticism for Péguy will indeed inevitably become politicized, and then oppressive. Yet a repudiation of all mystical love in the name of "objective" rationality will not end those evils, but make them much worse. For universal justice to live in the world, there must always be openings for the flourishing, cooperative, challenging mutuality of authentic mysticisms, both secular and sacred.

CHAPTER 9

The Style of Infinite Reality

Few styles of writing elicit more divergent judgment than Péguy's. Gilles Deleuze, for example, counts Péguy among those late modern philosophical stylists who—along with Kierkegaard and Nietzsche—affirm repetition, who "have a way of taking it literally and of introducing it into their style."[1] Péguy's "technique" is able to form "a before-language, an auroral language in which the step-by-step creation of an internal space within words proceeds by tiny differences."[2]

Deleuze was not inclined to Gaullism—and it seems forbiddingly unlikely that de Gaulle devoted any portion of his final years at Colombey les Deux-Églises to reading Deleuze—but de Gaulle, in remarks about Péguy, found himself similarly enthusiastic about his writing, not least for its repetitions. Claiming that "no writer has exerted upon me a similar influence," he said that he was attracted to Péguy by "his style, his taste for *formules*, his repetitions."[3] These exalted assessments of Péguy's style are not without contemporary defenders: the philosopher of science Bruno Latour, for example, said that Péguy is "the greatest French prose writer."[4]

Yet Deleuze, de Gaulle, and Latour do not speak for, one might say, a unanimous consensus. Marcel Proust thought very little of what he read by Péguy. In a letter to Daniel Halévy, he said that Péguy was worse than those who merely "describe everything [and] choose nothing," since he "writes down literally everything that passes through his head."[5] André Gide found in Péguy's alexandrines "the most botched that had been composed in any language."[6] While awarding the Estrade Delcros prize to Péguy for *The Mystery of Jeanne d'Arc's Love*, the representative of the Académie Française, Paul Thureau-Dangin, spoke of certain reservations about Péguy: "That the author has made of these repetitions a system, a mode that seems all too ready to become a mania, I regretfully agree."[7]

Gide's and Proust's (and the Académie's) judgments on Péguy's style were by no means unremittingly critical. While the Académie did not award Péguy its supreme literary prize, it did award him *a* prize, and Thureau-Dangin spoke of how those who read Péguy's poem "will feel themselves transported into realms to which contemporary literature rarely ascends."[8] In a postscript to his letter to Gide, Proust could not resist adding a word of praise for Péguy, telling Gide that Péguy had a "feel for the geometry of the land, of villages."[9] Upon reading *The Mystery of Jeanne d'Arc's Love*, in early 1910, Gide wrote the poet Francis Jammes to say that he was sending him a copy because "it is a very beautiful book."[10]

If even critics could find a kind word for Péguy's writing, it is nonetheless true that both appreciation and criticism of it abound. What about Péguy's style inspires such diverse and often visceral judgment?

Deleuze offered one answer; it sets Péguy's style within a metaphysical and theological trajectory of modern European culture, in which it represents both a great opportunity and a failure. Kierkegaard and Péguy "may be the great repeaters." But "they were not ready to pay the necessary price. They entrusted this supreme repetition, repetition as a category of the future, to faith." In this way, they are "the culmination of Kant," since "they realize Kantianism by entrusting to faith the task of overcoming the speculative death of God and healing the wound in the self." This recourse to faith makes both Kierkegaard and Péguy "the comedian of . . . [their own] ideal."[11]

One can let slide the latter phrase about serving as comedian of one's own ideal, which is an uncredited citation—or a very slightly altered repetition—of a passage in Nietzsche's *Beyond Good and Evil*.[12] But Deleuze has mishandled Péguy, not least by casually lumping Péguy's repetitions with Kant and with Kierkegaard. Péguy's poem *The Portal of the Mystery of Hope*—with its bold and manifold repetitions—is dedicated expressly to hope, and it is nothing other than the singularly beguiling guile of hope—often unmistakably earthy in nature—to induce human beings to repeat with great effort the same motion in an exponential approach toward divine infinity, not assumed to be speculatively dead (the Deleuzian accusation of playacting is an assertion about the ultimate nature of the real). For Péguy, we regularly feel that hope "deceives" us, but it is hope's indispensable task to sustain our relation to a living eternity.[13]

Furthermore, for Péguy it is precisely through the persistence of hope amid manifest *failures* to be a comedian of one's own ideal—either through awareness of temporal failures of desire, ambition, or one's moral failings—that it is possible to participate in the infinity of God, as well as with others and with creation.[14]

Péguy's treatment of these themes is clearly different from that of Kant and Kierkegaard. For Kierkegaard (or more precisely, for Constantin Constantius), repetition must not be confused with hope. "Hope is a lovely maiden who slips away between one's fingers . . . he who will merely hope is cowardly . . . hope is a beckoning fruit that does not satisfy . . . but repetition is the daily bread that satisfies with blessing."[15] The harrowing suffering of Job allows him to affirm repetition after "hope gradually vanishes."[16]

Péguy is more earthy and embodied than both Kant and Kierkegaard; that is, he is more willing to blend (as Hans Urs von Balthasar observed)[17] the aesthetic, ethical, and religious than Kierkegaard, and far more willing to countenance the worldly reconciliation of truth, goodness, and joy than Kant. For Péguy, resolutely temporal (or, to use his term, "terrestrial")[18] disappointments can serve as spiritual nourishment, but only if human beings continue to hope through and beyond the failure of their discrete hopes. These hopes are simultaneously carnal and spiritual; one hope does not "merely" dissolve into the other.

Péguy's repetition refers first to an infinitely creative abundance, superior to imagination and to desire, that language can only describe by exhausting itself in the act of description, at which point creation has only begun. Upon the creation of all things, for Péguy, God "saw the universe as an immense gift."[19] Language calls upon artistic imagination to express this gift, but, for Péguy, "it is infinitely more difficult to know an atom of the real world than to imagine universes and infinities of imaginations."[20] In a similar way, Péguy responds to an intellectual culture increasingly preoccupied—via Nietzsche and others—with perspectivalism, but he adds that it is not from mere perspective that the deepest sources of both disagreement and diversity come, since reality "would not be exhausted by a veritable infinity of perspectives."[21]

The perspectival vertigo that has consumed so many late modern and postmodern thinkers is, for a writer like Péguy, an often amusingly presumptuous attempt to encompass God's infinity intellectually, manifest in an inexhaustible creation, perpetually renewed in every instant. Péguy's style everywhere testifies to the importance of perspective, and the juxtaposition of words—often a near repetition—creates a manifold of perspectives and opens up spaces between them, as Deleuze rightly claims. But for Péguy this often expresses a continuous awakening to the presence of God's infinite abundance rather than simply an abstemious deferral of abundance.

For Péguy—speaking in the voice of God—human beings are indeed "monster[s] of anxiety," but this comes not from some condign existential dread in exile amidst a vale of tears, but from "ingratitude."[22]

Péguy's repetitive style explores how patient repetition with slight alterations—the infinite gradations of perspectival abundance—opens upon divine gifts, rather than leaving us too dizzy and confused to know which truth might possibly be worthy of our love and reason. To accomplish this artistic task, Péguy is particularly sensitive to the ways in which repetition enters into different kinds of daily conversation, manifests itself as liturgical speech, and can work within a profoundly modern aesthetic idiom.

In his prose writings, there are dialogical intervals where short repetitions emphasize an argument or a point of contention: his interlocutors can be friends (notably Daniel Halévy, as in his essay *Victor-Marie, Comte Hugo*), or allegorical figures (like Clio, the muse of history). In *Notre Jeunesse*, the argument is addressed to *"mon cher* Variot" or, once more, *"mon cher* Halévy."[23] Similarly, his poetry often takes the form of a dialogue—between Madame Gervaise, Jeanne's friend Hauviette, and Jeanne d'Arc, for example, as it does in *The Mystery of Jeanne d'Arc's Love.*

Péguy's thought is almost everywhere embodied and dialogical, dialogues sometimes overlapping or set within still other dialogues. Péguy here as elsewhere shows himself resolutely skeptical toward claims that thinking has somehow transcended the relation of body and mind, or of embodied persons speaking to other persons. Thinking takes the form of a free conversation because thinking is never complete, never a system, as it is for his opponents in the intellectual party. Here his decision to name his journal neither a *revue* nor an *année*, but a *cahier* (notebook) comes more sharply into focus.

Péguy complemented his commitment to dialogue with strikingly different forms of writing. In a conversation with Joseph Lotte in 1912, Péguy remarked: "Like *The Portal of the Mystery of Hope*, *The Mystery of the Innocents* is in the end from liturgy. You understand that I am one of those Catholics who would give all of Saint Thomas for the *Stabat Mater*, the *Magnificat*, the *Ave Maria* and the *Salve Regina*."[24]

In his poetry—particularly his late poetry—Péguy turns to repetition to recount the infinity of God, and human beings' search for God, in a manner reminiscent of the Psalms, or the passages of the Bible that ask to be heard as well as read. There are some liturgical passages in a poetic dialogue like *The Mystery of the Holy Innocents*, where one interlocutor (Madame Gervaise) calls out, "We are all children of one man," and Jeanne d'Arc responds, "We are all children of one God" followed by biblical passages from the Book of Genesis recounting the life of Joseph.[25] God repeatedly calls out to "night" in *The Mystery of the Holy Innocents*, as he does in *The Portal of the Mystery of Hope*, directing the reader to the fundamental experiences of life in the world—day, night, life, death—that is often a part of liturgical orienting, as in the opening to a common Roman Catholic Eucharistic Prayer, *a solis ortu usque ad occasum*, "from the rising of the sun to its setting."

Yet these liturgical cadences and biblical references are not, for Péguy, a simple recapitulation of a formal, high Christian liturgy. Instead, the God of Majesty appears in Péguy's poetry as a peasant father, drawn from Péguy's own peasant ancestry and modest artisan background, speaking in blunt, gentle, terse sentences. For example, God talks of "my girls, my children" when he talks of the three supernatural virtues (Faith, Hope, and Love).[26] In *The Portal of the Mystery of Hope*, Péguy relates, in the way of a peasant speaking common sense:

> Charity, says God, that doesn't surprise me.
> It's not surprising.
> These poor creatures are so unhappy that unless
> they had a heart of stone, how would they not have
> charity for one another.[27]

This very simple, informal language, sometimes placed in a liturgical register, is an indispensable portion of Péguy's aesthetic. Yet Péguy often also requires his readers to consider very carefully the printed page before them and the characters fixed upon it; for him, text too must call attention to the kind of materiality it has, perhaps especially when it is most spiritually exalted. Here and elsewhere, he participates in early modernist poetic experimentation.

His first poem included blank pages, intended to allow the reader time for reflection as he told the story of Jeanne d'Arc's life. In his later poetry, he was prone to italicize some words and to place others in bold type. In *The Portal of the Mystery of Hope*, for example, he speaks of hope throughout the poem, but his changes in typeface allow for hope (*Espérance*) to pop out next to faith and charity when they are placed alongside one another, or for "earth" (*terre*) to become intensely present at the moment of the Crucifixion, rather than a mere accompaniment to a disembodied, "purely spiritual" event. Typography that called attention to print as print was for Péguy a way to use his craft on behalf of the images of poetry, a craft for which he was a convinced advocate.[28]

Péguy's repetitions bear an affinity to the repetitions of Monet's haystack paintings (or his water lilies, or as Péguy refers to them, "this great modern, contemporary painter who made twenty-seven or thirty-five times his celebrated water lilies").[29] Nor is his work without connection to Debussy's repetitions of chords in a limited and often unresolved melodic sequence, say, in an opera like *Pelléas and Mélisande* of 1902, with its whole-tone scale that allows for a sense of suspended, continuous time to flow through the opera. Musical themes associated with characters and emotions appear and reappear again and again in subtly altered variations of harmony and timbre; the effect is emotionally powerful, but it derives its power from a repeated sounding of interior depths by myriad variations that, as it were, *explore* time patiently, and to cumulative effect.

For Péguy, this kind of early modernist repetition expresses the particulars of creation relating to the divine. For example, the references to "and God himself" that begin a series of quatrains in *Ève* allows Péguy to integrate experiences of time and space, of a particular village life, of youth, of night and day, of small corners of nature, and gather the reasoned and passionate, particular and universal instances of humanity's relation to the world under the attentive gaze of God.[30] Such is God's tribute to night at the end of *The Portal of the Mystery of Hope*, where God apostrophizes Night, his "daughter."[31]

Péguy refers not only to the grandeur of Night in space, but also to repeatedly to an "ocean" of wheat[32] in countless fields receding to the horizon, or to the impassively massive ocean itself, in many of his poems, and in prose as well. In contrast to these organic immensities, he is entirely unimpressed by encounters with industrial and technological power and immensity.[33]

In historical terms, Péguy's aesthetic is superficially similar to that of near-contemporary work, like Mallarmé's evocations of infinite space in a poem like "Les Fenêtres." For both Mallarmé and Péguy, the infinite is intensely desired but beyond possession; but Mallarmé's penchant for, among other things, synaesthesia indicates an abiding disjunction in his poetry between infinite desire, human experience, and a present and real infinite, which Péguy rarely finds compelling. In a still more striking contrast, Rimbaud's frantic call for a "dérèglement de tous les sens"[34] could not be more foreign to Péguy's lyrical sensibilities. The fields of wheat are an ocean tended and cultivated by God's human creature, but while they exceed any single human act or plan, human reason and labor allow for their magnificent organic arrangement. For Péguy, work complements no less the recognition of the gift of the carnal, the vulnerable, and the mortal in the midst of nature's immensity.

Péguy thus finds God's presence in an immense vault of creation that also houses a shockingly fragile but ultimately insuperable vitality. Nowhere is this sense of creation more clear than in *Ève* where "lost, the child was sleeping in this frail vessel / . . . for he was going to be thrown upon the enormous Ocean / the imperishable ship [*nef*, which also means the nave of a church], this fragile cradle."[35] A baby—including, as here, the infant Christ— is for Péguy the proper figure for humanity's relationship to the vastness of time and space. Here and elsewhere, Péguy's poetic language is a daring return to and reconfiguration of Pascal.

The cold, infinite spaces of Pascal's universe are inhabited carnally and relationally in Péguy's poetry, in a creation emanating from God's gently wry, loving word, always vulnerable life secure amid an awesomely immense yet infinite differentiation of space. Péguy's account of nature's grandeur within and beyond the earth not only reconfigures Pascal's "terror" before infinite spaces as an opportunity for loving and confident trust but also moves decisively away from the imperatives of the Kantian sublime. There is no question in Péguy that these immensities are enjoyed as a species of rational mastery by the beholder; rather the grandeur and terror of nature and space are transformed by an act of at once awed and loving delight in the infinite love of their ultimate origin and end.

For Péguy, in contrast to the particular loves and organic immensity of creation, technology seeks within it a monotonous, factitious regularity that can be entirely controlled on behalf of endlessly immanent desiring, however elaborate its technical innovation. So "it will not be these telephonographies / that will put us into the roots of being."[36]

An amazed acknowledgment at the sheer gratuity and diversity of being, in which "all is other / all is different,"[37] becomes for Péguy the fresh, authentic way of inhabiting creation, in which selves and beings are both uniquely themselves and participate in God's infinity. It is not reason alone that points to a possible transcendence of nature, but also our relationship with nature itself, which includes a patient trust, capable of a joyous, cooperative, and reasoned originality.

This turn in Péguy also discloses a stark contrast with the work of his contemporary, the French Catholic poet Paul Claudel. Claudel's poetry repeatedly turns to a language of ecstatic, erotic desire in search of some numinous power that in some sense overwhelms or cancels the self and material creation, replete with vehement speech that expresses the "invasion of poetic intoxication."[38] Claudel the poet can cry out, "Free me from the slavery and the weight of this inert matter" and "Blessed be my God, who has delivered me from myself."[39] When reviewing the idols that might tempt him, Claudel includes not just "progress" but also "truth" and "justice."[40] For Péguy, the carnal is not simply inert or opposed to God, God appears to transfigure rather than separate the unique self from itself, and following the ancient Christian notion of divine simplicity (in which God's attributes cannot be separated from one another or from his essence), for Péguy, God, among other things, *is* truth and justice.

For Péguy, the image of organic immensity and our fragile but continuing relation to it express divine love through all creation. To give thanks for that is an antidote to modern ingratitude. It invites the reader to love the earthy grandeur of the world and, perhaps above all, to wonder that anything—and everything—is.

From the beginning to the end of his life as an author, Péguy found artistic inspiration not only in the vault of the heavens or the organic immensity of earthly nature, but in a single human subject as well, a history that fascinated so many of his contemporaries in the Belle Époque: the life of Jeanne d'Arc.

At the turn of the last century, France—and, to a lesser extent, many other historically Christian societies—saw variously and intensely in Jeanne a specific series of meaningful possibilities, all of which had some force in the ambient culture and its various subcultures. She could serve as a model for modern young women, and as a nationalist icon; a martyr to religious persecution, and a saint who suffered quite specifically political violence; a naïve and perhaps deluded peasant girl who belonged to a superstitious age, and an all too lucid peasant girl who represented the people and their well-being against the educated and wealthy interests that continuously exploited the people, and thus inevitably betrayed and condemned her as a champion of the people.[41]

Péguy does not exactly "take a side" among these possibilities. He finds nearly all of them in Jeanne's life (for Péguy Jeanne is certainly not deluded, though she can be both naïve and painfully lucid). She loves all of France[42] yet is devoted supremely to God,[43] and would rather France lose its battle against the English than that French soldiers commit crimes of war, including pillage and rape.[44] She is an unlettered if sharp peasant woman condemned by clerics, who are also credentialed learned persons and often university professors, the willing tools of powerful politicians and political interests.[45] In keeping with Péguy's expansive account of metaphysical modernity, her judges are members of a "perpetual intellectual party."[46]

Jeanne is feminine, but she will not apologize for wearing men's clothes when her mission requires it: "It is our Lord God who ordered me to the work for which I had to wear men's clothes. As long as that work is incomplete, I won't stop wearing men's clothing."[47]

For Péguy, Jeanne embodies above all a radical openness to acting in the world in a new and unexpected way, prompted by grace, that is faithful to the past without seeking to lifelessly repeat it, and this in turn allows him to think his way into the question of evil in the world, and the relation of good and evil to repetition. It is not simply that Jeanne is a saint or a hero but that for him she is *both* a saint and hero, and thus occupies "a unique point of intersection in the history of humanity."[48]

The abiding question that Péguy explored through Jeanne's life can be put this way: How can sanctity and heroism be embodied in a painfully flawed world that includes predictable iterations and reiterations of evil, including on one's own "side"?

The poetry is itself a startling hybrid of novelty through tradition, both historical and artistic. Péguy's original *Jeanne d'Arc* contains many directions indicating her "silence," as well as the blank pages already mentioned. If this stylistic decision intimates a creative early-modernist awareness of the materiality of artistic space, it is also clear that Péguy took his history seriously. As preparation for writing about Jeanne, he immersed himself in her complete trial transcripts, compiled in five volumes by Jules Quicherat in the 1840s, as well as histories by Edmond Richer, Henri Wallon, Siméon Luce, and Jules Michelet.[49]

Throughout his writing on Jeanne, the historical and the creative are carefully entwined with one another. His Jeanne sometimes speaks precisely the words she said during her trial,[50] and she is in many ways the recognizably historical Jeanne: earthy and practical in peasant fashion in her dealings with historically identifiable others, respectful but vinegary toward her judges, and very reluctant to talk about the particulars of the voices she had heard. She is both calmly convinced of her communion with God and in anguish after being abandoned by her former allies. Péguy's Jeanne is thus not a free creation seized from a hazily grasped history (thanks to the trial of Jeanne and to the proceedings for her rehabilitation, the historical record of her life is exceptional in quantity and quality for a medieval person, man or woman). This history is put in dialogue with Péguy's distinctive stylistic and intellectual commitments.

Péguy's first poem about Jeanne is dedicated to "all those who will have lived their human life . . . trying to remedy universal human evil."[51] Yet in both *Jeanne d'Arc* and *The Mystery of Jeanne d'Arc's Love*, Jeanne's moral heroism is accompanied by a searing consciousness of a possible "exhaustion of history" and with it, *corrupt* repetition.

In the poems about Jeanne, repetition is very often not God's speech but the world's interminable parody of that speech. In *Jeanne d'Arc*, Raoul de Gaucourt tells her: "Men aren't worth much, Madame Jeanne; men are impious, men are cruel, looters, thieves, and liars; they love gluttonous feasts."[52] True piety cannot enter into effective temporal repetition; it is "too beautiful to last."[53] In *The Mystery of Jeanne d'Arc's Love*, the sheer weight of accumulated generations since the Christian Incarnation without a transfiguration of the world by love is a great burden. Christianity, Jeanne tells God himself in prayer, has had fourteen centuries since God sent his son, and then countless saints, but "fourteen centuries of Christianity, alas, since the birth, and death, and preaching [of Jesus]. And nothing, nothing, always nothing."[54]

For the nonbelieving Péguy, writing in the late 1890s, Jeanne enters history through a concession to this ongoing corruption: she persuades her uncle to tell a lie to her father so that she can leave her home and begin her mission. She participates in evil in order to act, but does not hide or explain away her own evil from herself or from God, and hence it does not diminish her faith in God and his universal love.

Jeanne continues to seek peace first, and only then war, despite the "wasted time" of which her friend complains.[55] At one point she has two masses said before battle and the English depart the field: she issues an order to let them leave in peace.[56] She does not want to carry a sword into the battles she leads, only her standard.[57] She cradles the head of a dying English soldier, cries at his death, and has him carried from the field;[58] she is dismayed when she learns that French soldiers have committed war crimes.[59] Her soldiers are often inspired by her to be both courageous and merciful, but are not entirely transformed. For a time her soldiers "hardly pillage anymore," and they go to confession.[60] As for Jeanne, she says simply to her learned judges, "I hate no one."[61]

At all times, she knows that God has not given her immunity from suffering and failure: "I am not protected against injury; I am not protected against prison; and I am not protected against death.”[62] She cannot count on God's protection for herself or her mission: “My voices have not told me that I would succeed.”[63]

Indeed, Jeanne is not successful in an immediate way: she is wounded, she is imprisoned, her trial is a sham, and, for all her resistance, she is convicted of heresy by the professorial and clerical minions of England's king and burned alive. With her condemnation, she wonders if she herself will be damned; but if so, she wants above all to comfort one of the damned, still hoping that God might save all.[64]

In *Jeanne d'Arc*, Jeanne is both a hero and a saint because she is willing to suffer and to act assertively in a flawed, ambiguous, and painful world of power and violence on behalf of her own people (as a hero), yet also to understand and embody an eternal love as a saint would; that is, she will make a total sacrifice of herself—not for “her people” or “the nation” but for a single damned soul, in an act of universal human solidarity.

In *The Mystery of Jeanne d'Arc's Love* (1910), the demoralizing, enervating persistence of evil in the world weighs again upon Jeanne. But in this poem, the question is above all how one's carnal spirit expresses God's love in the world, and how to understand the relation of time to justice and truth.

At the outset of the poem, Jeanne says the words that accompany the sign of the cross (“in the name of the Father, and of the Son, and of the Holy Spirit”), but she does not make the sign of the cross with her hands upon her body. She says the Our Father but breaks the rhythm of the prayer to tell God that his will is not done, that our daily bread is not given, that forgiveness is missing amid ineffective resistance to temptation and evil.[65]

Here the resurrection—the full redemption of the body—is missing, just as the physical sign of the cross is missing. Jeanne perceives and experiences the consequences of this apparent failure: either apostasy or despair. Even among the faithful, there is not only evil but the “infinitely worse” temptation to believe that “you have abandoned them.”[66]

Jeanne is very nearly accusing God in her despair. “You know what we are missing. We would perhaps need something new, something that would never have been seen before . . . after so many saints . . . after so many martyrs, after the Passion and death of your son.” At this point, Jeanne begins to spin thread. Then comes a single sentence: “In the end what we would need, my God, it would be necessary to send us a woman saint (*une sainte*) . . . who succeeds.”[67]

In a phrase, the prayer has been answered. As she begins both to pray and to work rather than separating prayer and work, we see the simultaneously present (manifest at a unique, given moment) and eternal (in origin) insight that will lead Jeanne to serve as the new *sainte*, one who succeeds. Jeanne herself will carry out her prayer through spiritually embodied action.

For Péguy, the mystery of love is not complete, and Jeanne is tempted to abandon her vocation and to continue her life as before. Her friend Hauviette asks why she wants to be like everyone else; Jeanne confesses she is scared. Fear is leading her toward corrupt repetition, to forsake her mission in order to seem safely the same. Yet once more she says there must be "new saintes."[68]

As she labors to understand human suffering from within God's eternal love—with a spiritual intensity and precision beyond Hauviette's—her specifically temporal horizons narrow. Hauviette sees time as a repetitive round of generally predictable failings and problems that inevitably emerge in linear time, to which the best answer is a slightly sad, slightly indifferent resignation. But the temporal focus of Jeanne is no longer upon the "fourteen centuries" of perdition since the Incarnation she had spoken of earlier, but of times within living memory: it is for "forty years" that there has been so much loss.[69] The experience of time moves from a line beginning at the Crucifixion and ending with the present (in which, to speak precisely, Jeanne sees history as "one damned thing after another") to an experience of an extended time, in which the plenitude of eternity can enter a unique specific historical moment—the age in which she lives. Soon Jeanne is focused on a still more immediate present than that of her general historical moment: many in France lack both "carnal bread" and "spiritual bread"—now.[70]

In Péguy's thought, this meeting of an immediate present with embodied, spiritual action is open to shocking gifts from an ultimate and eternal origin, and thus to an active and surprising originality that integrates different pasts with the present, in relation to eternity. The past can inspire, since, with a continuous relation to eternity, it can enact a faithful repetition that is not an interminable repeat of what has gone before.

Soon afterward, a nun named Madame Gervaise begins to speak, and in a sense she will show herself to *understand* Christianity better than Jeanne, even as she makes what were for Péguy the temporal errors characteristic of Christian "traditionalists" and "modernists" alike, ones that preclude Jeanne's openness to embodying the mystery of charity.

The temporal turn begins with Jeanne's radical solidarity with those who suffer. She tells Madame Gervaise that she is willing to be damned herself in order to save the damned from "the eternal Absence."[71] Madame Gervaise tells her that she has blasphemed.[72] Human beings in general and women in particular must accept their fate in time with passivity: "Women know only to cry."[73]

Jeanne responds—with convincingly youthful fervor—that the apostles should have resisted Jesus's arrest. Gervaise begins to chastise her further. "You do not speak like a little girl," she says, and urges her to share her struggle against pride, for "we are made like the others."[74] She is, without realizing, tempting Jeanne to enter into bad repetition, and with it a falsely humble conformity.

The dramatic turn in the poem is at once subtle and infinite. If one simply assumes that Jeanne is Péguy's omniscient hero and speaks for Péguy, the poem seems to issue into a kind of insurgent romanticism of the will.

Yet in *The Mystery of Jeanne d'Arc's Love*, the reader is not meant to find in Jeanne's words an unwavering guide to Péguy's own views about Christianity, especially since Jeanne's account of time and the body undergo striking changes within the poem as a result of both prayer and conversation. Gervaise will also become the narrator of what is possibly Péguy's best poem, *The Portal of the Mystery of Hope*, in which she gives an account of hope for which Péguy expresses the deepest sympathy.

For Péguy, Jeanne is both wrong and right, but the level of her propositional error is more superficial than the level of her profound and saintly receptivity. What he upholds in her is not her unerring discernment of Christian teaching about the Passion of Jesus, and whether knights should have rushed Golgotha on Good Friday, but her blunt and passionate devotion to the truth of her perceptions combined with an openness to deeper understanding.

Péguy had already signaled this receptivity in her opening improvisations alongside the Our Father, in which Jeanne incorporated her own words, speaking aloud before the divine the chasm between her lived experience and the prayer she is reciting. If she had said the Our Father dutifully but without allowing it to enter into and challenge her honest sense of the world's profound corruption and brokenness, she would never have been open to the suggestion of the need for a woman saint, and that *sainte* being herself. Her vocation is disclosed through an uncompromising devotion to the truth, very different from the lie that begins the journey from Domrémy in the first *Jeanne d'Arc*. In this poem, Jeanne says, "I cannot lie. I do not want to lie. I say what is."[75]

In theological terms, Gervaise is surely right that Jeanne is at risk of turning the Passion into a chivalric melodrama. Yet Gervaise now reveals her own spiritual weakness in relation to Jeanne. She still believes herself to be unworthy of the original apostles, but she believes that the cumulative movement of *linear historical time* entitles her to know more, to rest easy, and thus to be more spiritually confident and assured than they were—not by any effort of her own but simply by living many centuries after them. Jesus's original apostles "did not suspect their history, their own history, the grandeur of their history . . . we, we have received thirteen centuries of warnings . . . of practice . . . of existence."[76]

For Péguy, faith is given essential form by a correct understanding developed through time *and* is a living, embodied relation between a given present and eternity; the course of the poem strongly impels the reader toward a reading of Jeanne in which her youthful understanding is obviously flawed, but the freshness and directness of her relation to truth and to God's eternity will carry her beyond her elders' superior (but in form, two-dimensionally linear, and hence often reductive and at times complacent) understanding.

At the end of the poem, Jeanne concludes that as she speaks, Christianity itself is in this instant threatened with perdition. Her manner of speaking is blunt. Something, Jeanne implies, must be done by embodying love in the world. Gervaise tells her once more that we should "let the will of God come."[77] Jeanne, "a little abruptly" takes her leave, but commending her interlocutor to God, and Gervaise does the same.[78]

Péguy's Jeanne thus ends the poem as a bold and honest peasant girl given a commission by God that she does not yet fully understand, and that she can only understand by living it out. For Péguy, her vital love of the truth—her love, as the title indicates—is not amenable to definition: it is a "mystery." But it is a mystery that will work through a body open to living without reserve an eternally present love and justice, and love of justice.

That a peasant girl would lead the troops of France into battle to end generations of war was entirely unexpected, yet it was also simultaneously faithful to the demands of the immediate present (a desperate one in which unconventional proposals would be heard) and to a past that included the action of Saint Geneviève, defender of Paris.

As Péguy understood, while her sanctity and heroism will be a success, it is also true that in a certain sense Jeanne failed. She does not end war. Couldn't Péguy's readers rightly add to her lament that fourteen centuries of Christianity had brought "nothing, always nothing"—and that the five centuries that followed Jeanne up to Péguy's lifetime had done the same?

The question ignores the transformation at the heart of the poem, in which the question of suffering in God's creation is best understood in a dialogue between the present and the eternal that *then* makes sense of one's past and the future time available for *one's own* action.

In Péguy's account, of course the human world will always include evil; other epochs will have to pose the question of defeating evil anew in their own circumstances, accepting that all responses or work undertaken as a result of posing that question will be provisional and imperfect, and will be eventually subject to corruption, as mysticism gives way to politics, and as faithful repetition gives way to corrupt repetition. Yet for Péguy "perdition" is only definitive when the conversation between an immediate present and eternity—along with creative possibilities drawn from very different pasts—are neglected and abandoned, and the contemporary alone (a point in an inexorable sequence) is considered "relevant" and "real." "Bad repetition" in a purely linear time loses the sense of possibilities endowed with an original (in every sense) creative strength; repetition becomes constrictive, predictable, exhausting, propositional, and politicized.

Neither of Péguy's poems about Jeanne explores the question of how the persistence of "universal evil"[79] and other human failings and vulnerabilities might not just be resisted, but also energetically borne without being a visible hero or a saint. It was the patience for that task that Péguy believed—among other things—had been lost in Christianity, especially modern Christianity. That task would stand among the supreme tasks of Péguy's own work, another moment in an ongoing "Christian Revolution."[80]

CHAPTER 10

The Christian Revolution

In his final years, the erstwhile atheist Péguy grew certain that he, like Jeanne, had a unique mission. He told his friend Joseph Lotte, "A Catholic Renaissance is making its way through me."[1]

Little is known about Péguy's return to Catholic Christianity in 1907. He spoke very little about it, and acknowledged it (separately) to his friends Jacques Maritain and Lotte as an event that had already occurred.[2] Most of what is known about his return to Catholicism involves the impatience of his Catholic friends, notably Maritain, urging him to return to regular Mass attendance and the sacraments, accompanied by exhortations for him to baptize his children. Since his wife was not a believer and did not want them baptized, his children remained unbaptized. As his marriage was not a sacramental marriage, and because of his entirely unchanged anticlericalism, he remained outside the sacramental life of the church until—perhaps—the final days of his life, as he and his company traveled to the Front in 1914.[3]

Yet for all that, Péguy had returned to Christianity, distant from its institutional forms but without spiritual reserve. He prayed in the streets, he wrote in lively terms of his devotion to God, to Jesus, to the communion of saints. Yet the "renaissance" that worked "through" him implies that something had died or had been prevented from being born.

Péguy readily acknowledged that many obstacles to Christian rebirth in his own time were not necessarily unique. Since the time of Christ, "all temporal ages are situated equally on the same level" under "a law of love" that can be denied but not changed.[4] For Péguy, a genuinely Christian life of love is a difficult achievement in any century, since "all these twenty centuries have been . . . bad Christian centuries."[5] All times belong to God,[6] but saints are very often misunderstood by their Christian contemporaries, just as prophets (ancient and modern) were misunderstood by their contemporaries.[7]

Though his concern about that continuous temporal estrangement was real, Péguy also devoted attention to more immediate obstacles to a Christian renaissance; he believed that some of these were new and ominous, since "dechristianization" was quite different from mediocre or bad Christianity. That other ages of Christianity had, or would have, other problems did not, in his mind, recommend complacency toward the problems and questions placed before him. Among these immediate obstacles, was a factitious experience of nature, of life, and of the world that he found expanding in late modern culture, with reference to second creations and "decreations."[8]

These ersatz creations were nowhere to be found in Christianity's first efflorescence among the pagan peoples of late antiquity. "Their gods were false gods, but their world . . . was not a false world."[9] Paganism's relationship to the divine was filled with a strange ascending and descending motion, of human reverence for the gods that stood alongside a sense of superiority toward them. Toward the gods, for Péguy, Homer and others clearly felt—even if it was mixed or founded upon envy—"a certain contempt." In their Olympian deathlessness, the gods knew nothing of the "triple grandeur of men": that is, "mortality, deprivation [misère], risk." In particular, they do not know the embodied adventure of living an "irreversible" life.[10]

For Péguy, moderns have replaced the particularities of mythic stories with the abstractions of mythic ideas and "systems."[11] Systematizers often rely on an imagination unfaithful to reality,[12] but, as we have seen, for him imagination is open to but (in itself) infinitely less than infinite reality. The modern dwelling in mythic systems is, in Péguy's account, positioned very differently in relation to Christianity from the way paganism was. Péguy emphasized that both paganism and Christianity were founded upon vulnerability and even misfortune, with a need for profound meditation upon misfortune,[13] whereas modernity was founded upon power, control, and prosperity. Modern societies, in contrast to both Christian and pagan cultures, wanted the form of human life to become progressively less organic, and to pursue comprehensive orders of marketized, homogenizing abstraction[14] in service of skeptical self-possession.[15] Yet, as we shall see, the obstacles to Christian rebirth in late modern culture were for Péguy clearly not primarily "secular" but attributable above all to specifically Christian failures.

There were historical grounds for what would become Péguy's critique of Christian practice and education. Many Christian institutions remained fixed in practices, formal and informal expectations, doctrinal emphases, and counsels given form by the Protestant and Catholic Reformations in early modern Europe. These could put at the center of Christian life an exacting moral rectitude and an adherence to moral rules, at times almost for their own sake. In a quasi-Jansenist modern Catholicism in particular, this took the form of positing a chasmic disjunction between nature and the supernatural.

Through its imposing educational presence, institutional French Catholicism leaned heavily upon the heritage of scholasticism in particular. Catholic schools and universities tended to teach Christian theology with a great emphasis upon argumentation and Christian reasoning about God, moral life, and the life of the church (for example, the theology of the sacraments). These were given renewed impetus by the formal exhortation by the pope to place Thomism at the center of Catholic learning and theology in the 1879 encyclical *Aeterni Patris*. Imperatives like these gave Catholic Christianity a sometimes markedly intellectualized presence in educated, bourgeois French culture, in which syllogistic argumentation and catechetical precision were highly prized. The church also offered preemptive educational direction in the life of the faithful, and so the Index of Forbidden Books was a going concern in early twentieth-century Catholicism.

Yet even as Catholics and Christians developed a demanding and abstract language for thinking about theology, morality, and much else besides, that language often appeared distant from the language and practices of the times, without a full and charitable account of that distance. Persecuted during the French Revolution, their faith rejected by many secular republicans, a number of French Catholics in particular began to oppose modernity as such, even when movements within modern cultures drew upon Christian notions of charity to develop accounts of social justice for those dispossessed and exploited by the Industrial Revolution. Some French Catholics—by no means all, but their numbers were considerable—loudly sided with *rentiers* and other prosperous bourgeois on questions of political economy.

As we have seen, sometimes these and other Catholics called upon long-standing anti-Semitic preoccupations in Christian cultures to sustain a certain demagogic presence in an emerging mass culture, without challenging the prevailing social and economic order. They employed anti-Semitic invective to "explain" the uncertain situation and ambivalent relation of Christianity to modern cultures, and both to elicit and flatter prejudices in a time of extraordinary social, economic, and cultural change. In this way Jews were often scapegoated, most visibly during the Dreyfus affair. They were often accused of being carnal, legalistic, and Judas figures, "betraying Jesus."

For some, including Léon Bloy, anti-Semitic animus veered toward a certain kind of medieval and early modern Christian anti-Semitism connected to Good Friday, in which Jews bore direct responsibility for the death of Jesus, and did so continuously up to the present age.[16]

For others, it was Jewish "legalism" that was most at issue. In modern philosophy, as far back as Kant—and for many neo-Kantians after him—Judaism is simply a legal or constitutional system rather than a religion or authentically spiritual way of life.[17]

Yet in the minds of their detractors, an allegedly narrow legality did not preclude Jews from being disturbingly embodied and a "fleshly" people. The anti-Semite Édouard Drumont claimed that Jews smelled, and he cited another author wondering whether their alleged odor came from "their immoderate appetite for the flesh of goats and the flesh of geese."[18] In any case, their "odor" announced their carnality. A critical review of Drumont's *La France Juive* in the prestigious conservative journal *Revue des deux mondes* in May 1886 by its editor, Ferdinand Brunetière, could refer casually and repeatedly to an allegedly "carnal ideal of Judaism" among Jews and the "carnal dream of their fathers."[19] This could give a striking inflection to Christianity's relation to Judaism. Bloy put it in vivid terms meant to convey the paradoxical situation in which he found himself as an avowedly anti-Semitic Christian: in a letter to Raïssa Maritain, he wrote: "I eat, every morning, a Jew named Jesus Christ."[20]

French Jews were regularly accused of avarice. Scandals that exposed financial corruption in the Third Republic often emphasized any Jewish connection to the scandal, as if that corruption came from a "Jewish" source, even though the scandals were predominately the responsibility of non-Jews. Throughout the Dreyfus affair, Alfred Dreyfus was tirelessly presented as another Judas, an archetypal Jewish "traitor."[21]

Similar prejudices surface over and over in European and specifically French anti-Semitism. Drumont was particularly adept at blending together a toxic amalgam of anti-Semitic tropes; in a short approving note about Swedenborg's anti-Semitism, he quoted remarks about Jews having an odor (again), being "sordidement avares," and "confirmed" in "the life of the body" because they do not recognize "the New Jerusalem."[22]

As one form of French Catholicism became not traditional but self-consciously traditionalist—and at least partially politicized—another developed into theological modernism. The movement was associated above all with the priest, theologian, and biblical scholar Alfred Loisy. He went beyond John Henry Newman's argument that doctrine could undergo historical development from its origin;[23] even as Loisy had strongly disagreed with a theological liberal Protestant like Adolf von Harnack about the historical legitimacy of Catholicism,[24] in several writings he appeared to approach the theological liberalism of nineteenth-century Protestantism, in which the Bible and church doctrine respond primarily to historical circumstances, as part of an ongoing "evolution"[25] putting God in accord with recent scholarship—though what he called the "science of religions" was just beginning.[26] Loisy and other modernists tended to place theology under history in the order of disciplines. This move often appeared to suggest an at least semi-Hegelian account of Christianity, in which its revelation needed to be understood symbolically in order to express the dynamic spirit and inner logic of history, one that would cumulatively advance specifically human understanding and ethics toward a more complete and "rational" fulfillment.

The condemnation of theological modernism by Pope Pius X in 1907 marginalized Loisy in turn, who at first struggled with being deprived of his priestly ministry before settling into a kind of Deism. Throughout his career, Loisy had influential allies in French academic life, including sociologists like Durkheim, who sought to secure for him a major academic position. In 1909, he received an appointment to the Collège de France.[27]

There were of course other possibilities in French Catholicism—above all, those associated with Maurice Blondel's book *L'Action* of 1893—but they were not yet culturally influential, nor were they yet part of Catholic education.

Ultimately, for Péguy the tendencies within modern Christianity, and especially Catholicism—both traditionalist and modernist in form—emerged from a very deep and ongoing tendency within the history of Christianity as a whole; upon reflection, immediate obstacles to faith and Christian origins were closely connected. Most strikingly, for him there was an *impatience* in Christianity that appeared in its very early days. As Péguy wrote in one memorably provocative passage, "Jesus was able to graft Jewish anxiety into the Christian body." But "Jesus was not able (or did not want) to graft Jewish patience into the Christian body."[28]

Given his path of thinking and living, for Péguy it would be faithless and dishonest to gaze upon the obstacles to Christian life in the early twentieth century or upon the impatience in the history of Christianity, and to decide that his task would be to calculate how these obstacles might be sidestepped by "adjusting" or "reducing" Christianity to that which would not offend the sensibilities of the respectable, comfortable, metaphysically modern bourgeois. For Péguy, Christianity is for those who are in some sense not filled or secure, for "Jesus is . . . essentially the God of the poor, of the suffering, of workers . . . heaven is a heaven of common people [*petites gens*]."[29]

Instead, Péguy would confront the obstacles to living fully in the present as a Christian by going more deeply into the ultimate origin of Christianity, as some of his contemporaries had variously sought to do with analyses of "religion" as a general category, or with polemics about the origins of good and evil. Péguy coined the term for this movement in Christian theology a "return to the sources," or "ressourcement," toward a new, energetic (yet also primal, patient, ancient, and continuous) life.[30]

For Péguy, the *Wesen des Christentums* is devastatingly, scandalously simple: "God sacrificed himself for me."[31] This sacrifice of the infinite out of love for the finite initiated a great overturning in human history, the placing of the infinite within the finite: Christianity *"put the infinite everywhere."*[32] God's "infinite, eternal love"[33] for human beings came with the shock of something uncanny. Yet this decisive act of God's infinite love for human beings means that the failings of human beings matter infinitely to an infinite God, so that finite human beings can create a "wound" in God.[34]

In Péguy's account, it is this transformation in human being, of finitude and infinity, that is "the Christian Revolution."[35] Careful attention to this revolution will then open the way to a revolution in late modern Christianity.

For example, in Christianity, God is incarnate; the first datum of Christian revelation is that the one true and infinite God has freely assumed human flesh. What, then, is Christian about a rejection of the body and carnal life?

Péguy's prose and poetry is hence full of loving references to the "carnal,"[36] and to the ways in which the spiritual and the carnal complement and fulfill one another: Jesus himself lives a carnal life. Péguy pointedly observes that Jesus was a God-man and man-God, not an angel.[37] For Péguy it is an enormous mistake to neglect the carnality not just of Jesus but of saints as well, and thus, in his words, to "confuse the angel and the saint."[38] Both Incarnation and Resurrection are themselves both fully embodied and mystical for Péguy,[39] and Jesus "became our carnal brother."[40] For him, carnal and mystical are not opposites but natural and necessary complements in a material creation that testifies to the goodness of God its Creator: for "the supernatural is itself carnal."[41]

The stark division between the spiritual and the carnal Péguy observed around him is drawn from many sources, but French Jansenism figures prominently among them. Péguy appears to be an unlikely candidate for dispelling the lingering power of Jansenism in French Catholicism. Even as a religious skeptic, he had drawn upon the Jansenist-sympathizing Pascal for his account of modern metaphysics.

Yet Péguy was intrigued by Pascal's willingness to identify affinities rather than simply contrasts between Judaism and Christianity,[42] and how Pascal, as a Christian, retained his respect for pagan antiquity.[43] Pascal also allowed Péguy to develop or renew from an unexpected source an orthodox Catholic account of human carnality, original and faithful to an origin—not through, say, a Protestant turn *ad fontes* against the ongoing flow of Christian living and thinking in history but allowing an origin to disclose a continuous stream of fidelity of that origin occluded from view (often for reasons of *politique*).

In particular, to reflect upon the carnality of Christianity, Péguy meditated creatively upon a single fragment from Pascal: "Man is neither angel nor beast, and the worst of it is that he who would play the angel plays the beast."[44]

For Péguy, human beings become less than they are if they conceive of themselves as pure spirit (angels) or primarily creatures of material appetite or of pack-like social cohesion (beasts). Furthermore, the temptation to live as pure spirit begets the descent toward a purely material life.[45] Péguy intimates—without quite saying it explicitly—that a metaphysical modernity within or after Christianity compulsively inverts late medieval and early modern religious aspirations: ambitions to achieve an abstemiously "pure" human being that condescend to or lovelessly mortify the body become ambitions to achieve purely materialist, loveless explanations for carnal human being.[46]

Yet it was not simply a denial of the body that Péguy found still lingering from Reformation-era Christianity, particularly from Jansenism. For if the decisive, revolutionary event in the Christian revolution is a relationship of love—between God and creation, God and persons, persons for one another—how has this relationship become not accompanied by but subordinated to moral rules? Does a relationship of love nourish and sustain moral commitments, or have moral commitments substituted themselves for a relationship of love?

It is hardly the case that virtue and sin do not remain important for Péguy. Sin, he says, is a habitual hardening that slowly seals off the heart from the vivifying gift of grace.[47] Rather, it is that an exalted devotion to moralism above all else can itself be a form of hardening. Grace requires an openness and vulnerability that a thoroughgoing moralism either suspects to be weakness or has already proudly refused. Péguy's intense dislike for reflections on the possibility of persons being damned is in part because it contributes to such a hardening of the person who desires damnation for anyone; Péguy's Jeanne d'Arc will be free of it and will experience damnation for anyone as an agony for all human beings.[48]

Yet rather than move from a theological "conservatism" that is tempted to valorize moral rectitude above all to a theological "liberalism" that is tempted to reduce or pass over it, Péguy becomes an advocate for a "supple" morality, precisely because it demands *more* of those who practice it, just as a supple reason does: "It is obvious . . . that it is supple methods, supple logics, supple moralities that are more severe, being more strict." For Péguy,

> a stiff logic can let the recesses of error escape. A stiff method can let the recesses of ignorance escape. A stiff morality can let the recesses of sin escape, whereas in contrast supple morality will marry, denounce, pursue the sinuous paths of escape. . . .
>
> Stiffness it essentially unfaithful, and it is suppleness that is faithful . . . it is stiffness that cheats, it is stiffness that lies. And it is not only that suppleness doesn't cheat, not only that it doesn't lie, but that it does not permit cheating and lying. . . .
>
> It is supple moralities . . . that demand a perpetually ready heart. A heart perpetually pure. . . . It is supple moralities, supple methods, supple logics that exert uncompromising restraint. It is for this reason that the most honest man is not the one who stays within visible rules [*règles apparentes*]. It is the one who stays in his place, works, is in pain, and remains silent.[49]

Péguy's "supple morality" is a transformation of the heart, which in turn directs a lucid, patient, relentless attention to the whole of one's life, and prepares the way for action, often radical action (that is often also an action of steadfast fidelity, that is, "one who stays in his place"). A stiff morality is one that, having fulfilled certain obligations or checked off certain duties, can then leave the heart unchanged, and thus fails to attend to all that needs to be done through or in excess of rules; it allows the "recesses" of sin to remain where they are, to take energy and attention away from other people and from God. For Péguy it requires more sacrifice and more energy to live by supple morality than stiff morality, although stiff morality is more voluble about its accomplishments than supple morality: supple morality rarely "flashes out" into the world; it lives a life of quiet, faithful action.

There is in Péguy's account of an extremely demanding and living, sup-ple morality—set loose from mechanical formulations, or historicizing, or positivist, or clericalist calcification—an unmistakable debt to Bergson. In his own case, Péguy had good reason to claim in 1914 that Bergson had, as he put it, allowed "us . . . literally to find again the Christian position."[50] But Péguy brings to this position his own distinctive incarnational sensibility, and with it a skepticism about Christianity as a moralism and moral rules not because that morality is too strict but because it is too easy. For him, it must be re-membered that to be Christian is to enter into a relationship of love that seeks positively the good, rather than simply seeks to keep the self within fixed boundaries, unsoiled by the world.

Thoughts like these had powerful implications for how Christians relate to one another. In Péguy's account, the carnal and spiritual life of Jesus does not imply a divine intention that human beings should become angels but should live fully human lives in a "communion" that includes *both* sinners and saints. The communion implies a reaching out of "the hand"—the sinner to the saint, the saint to the sinner—in mutual help, in a vast "chain" of bodies and hands that reaches to Christ. To fail to be Christian is not to break a series of moral rules but not to be willing to enter a communion, not to extend one's hand to sinners and saints alike.[51] Péguy's communion of persons in Christianity is reminiscent of Bergson's integrative freedom, one that generously includes all states past and present, with the implicit exception of those states premised upon the refusal of that free and creative (and here, sacred) integration.

In this way, to be Christian is not to be set at a "certain moral, intellectual or even spiritual level."[52] Moralism demands that Christians be "graded" and set in line according to behavior; but for Péguy, "when a man can accomplish the highest action in the world without having been dipped in grace, that man is a stoic, not a Christian."[53] In one important respect, an exalted moralism—even a dedication to specifically Christian morality—calcifies souls, keeping lives buffered and sealed off from God: "Even God's love can-not put a dressing on the one who has no wounds."[54] Worse still for Péguy, "morality makes us owners of our poor virtues," whereas "grace makes us sons of God and brothers of Jesus Christ."[55] For "morality was invented by the sickly. And Christian life was invented by Jesus Christ."[56]

The social revolution, as Péguy famously observed, must be moral, and there is no sense here or elsewhere that he sought any rejection of morality. But for him a supernatural revolution exceeds moral rules in order to energize and deepen human beings' living relation to the divine source of goodness.

In his thoughts about carnality and a relation of love that exceeds the demands of moralism—written in very blunt, plainspoken language—Péguy drew upon several origins simultaneously. He returned to the sources of Christianity in the carnality of the Incarnation, he read Pascal anew, and he drew once more upon a fading but robustly embodied peasant culture, largely unwritten.

For Péguy, for many centuries so much of Catholic life—including its earthy, peasant piety—lived beyond the printed page. As he put it, "The Jew is a man who has been literate since forever, the Protestant [is a man who has been literate] since Calvin, and the Catholic since Ferry"[57] (that is, the late nineteenth-century advocate of universal education in France, Jules Ferry). But Péguy—with his peasant grandmother and peasant ancestors, with his artisan's childhood—transposed that earthy, unwritten way of expressing a relation to an incarnate God onto the printed page.

Péguy was insistent that by undertaking this work he was not initiating some original "break" or "transgression" in relation to the past—certainly not the Christian past—but rather remaining faithful to the ultimate origin of Christianity itself, and its continuous practice among the faithful. For, "the insertion of the spiritual in the carnal and the insertion of the eternal in the temporal, to put it directly, that is the mystery of the Incarnation."[58] A practical, embodied, peasant piety had been present for centuries, but often dormant or overshadowed, and certainly less respectable than the rigors of Protestant and Catholic Reformation soteriology, ecclesiology, and so on. In a bourgeois world of ubiquitous textual reference, this carnal piety had now to be written down. Péguy took up this task at the very moment when this sort of culture was still alive, but rapidly shrinking and increasingly intermingled with mass and elite cultures. In Europe, it would die out entirely within the lifetimes of his children.

In Péguy's account, the late modern "writing down" of an earthy peasant piety is entirely faithful to the Gospels themselves. Jesus's genealogy, for example—through a prostitute, liars, and the progeny of illicit affairs as well as of royal marriages—is "frightening," but the evangelist Matthew, with "that distinctively peasant honesty," is sure not to hide it.[59] For Péguy, Christianity must be understood as an "event" in time that encompasses and gives life to systems and thinking rather than being produced from them.[60] In this way, there is a distinctively blunt worker's modesty to be found in the origins of the Christian event: "all Christianity begins with this rough cradle that is a crèche."[61]

If Péguy found a way through an exalted if brittle moralism and a denial of authentic Christian carnality, it was also a way through the spiritual and the temporal divisions that had turned some Christians toward politics as a substitute for participation in the life of God. In his account, these political divisions find their origin in a separation of the temporal and the eternal.

For Péguy, whatever "side" is exalted at the cost of the other, any Christian separation of the eternal and the temporal is a catastrophe.[62] According to him, it is "the temptation of great souls" to deny the meaningfulness of temporality and matter (here one recalls his admiration for Plato). It is, Péguy writes, a "beautiful," "noble," and "aristocratic" way of thinking about one's experience,[63] where an immaculate empyrean alone truly exists while we live in a world of vain shadows. But then creation has no purpose, and for him it is a "great heresy" to claim that God created the world "to no effect."[64] The Incarnation expresses God's desire to save the world by participating in it bodily, to affirm the carnal world but not to dominate it, and certainly not to repudiate the world he created.[65]

While a certain kind of Christian falls into an incorporeal, atemporal angelism—and with it descends into an infertile rejection of the present— Péguy has no sympathy for Christians who dispense with or simply avoid the supernatural and a living, ongoing reciprocity between the temporal and eternal,[66] often in favor of politics and purely temporal concerns within a given historical moment.

This increasingly exclusive temporality could take the form of a conservative clericalism, and Péguy wrote not only of what "clerical politics did to Christian mysticism"[67] but of a "modernism of the heart" that had created "a religion of the bourgeois, a religion of the rich, a kind of superior religion for the superior classes of society." But this faith, for Christians entirely at peace with the world of power and money as they found it, was supremely "superficial" and even in a certain sense "nonexistent," since it ignored, among other things, the holy poverty at the origin of Christianity: to find the comfortable Christianity of the powerful and the rich in contradiction with its origin, "it suffices to refer to any text of the Gospels."[68]

Yet for Péguy the inclination toward the temporal could also take the form of a theological liberalism that attenuated the eternal and supernatural dimensions of Christianity. For example, when his poem *The Mystery of Jeanne d'Arc's Love* was critically reviewed in *La Revue hebdomadaire* in June 1911, Péguy memorably quarreled with the editor of the journal, Fernand Laudet, about the review's theologically liberal and modernist assumptions. The review assumed a stark division, without argument, between "history" and what Laudet called "legend."[69] It strongly implied that Jeanne had not had visions but had had hallucinations; that was more or less to say, Péguy observed, that Jeanne was "a crazy woman."[70] The review claimed that we have access only to the public life of Jesus (that is, his ministry) and the saints. Péguy observed that this argument logically led to the conclusion that not only countless lives of saints were inaccessible to Christians, but also the Incarnation itself.[71]

Péguy immediately acknowledged that many atheists write and speak honestly about their beliefs, citing Anatole France as an example. But, he said, Anatole France made no claim to believe in God. Laudet brought naturalistic and atheistic metaphysical assumptions into Christian thinking, Péguy said, because he was embarrassed by his own faith and wanted to signal his sympathies for a much more commodious, metaphysically modern commitment, kept at minimal distance from respectable opinion and prestigious institutions. Péguy concluded that "evidently the saints can appear contemptible when one has the honor of being the editor of *La Revue hebdomadaire*."[72] He went further: the man "who sells his God (for a smile, I mean to not fall under the smile of an augur from the intellectual party) . . . this man who sells his God sells Christianity as well."[73]

On the question of theological progress, Péguy always affirmed the possibility of drawing new and original things from a patient fidelity to the origins and history of faith, but he says of those "who want to improve Christianity" in itself (that is, rather than drawing from its origin and course faithful possibilities for its expression), that it is "a little, it is even entirely as if one wanted to improve the direction of the North."[74] Jesus came as Messiah for all centuries and is not reduced by modernity or anything else.[75] For Péguy, to make time and history the judge of all things appeals strongly to those who wish to escape the daunting challenge of embodying the temporal and eternal together. Seeking a purely temporal vindication for their propositions, they lack all mystical patience.

For Péguy, the Christian Revolution would not be an accommodation of divine revelation to modern, temporal impatience (either "reactionary" or "progressive" in form). Rather it would be a radically patient fidelity that brings centuries of thinking and action creatively together in strikingly new situations. If the church presumed to declare what free persons could read, for example, for Péguy it sufficed to observe that his own catechism "had no Index" of Forbidden Books,[76] any more than the Gospels did, or many centuries of Catholic Christianity. Where an often brutal and extreme capitalism holds sway, the simple living out of the words "and forgive us our debts, as we forgive those indebted to us," from the Our Father would, "taken seriously," constitute "the greatest revolution that there could now be, for it would be a revolution within the reign of money."[77]

Christian impatience and its secular descendants, Péguy claimed, led both "reactionaries" and "progressives" to idolize an abstract sequence of ideological propositions (that is, politique) rather than to inhabit patiently the truth of God's infinite love and live it out in their bodies, however difficult that may be. In passages like these, Péguy turns the language of sin away from a fear of personal damnation, but not to claim that sin is no longer a meaningful category. Rather, in keeping with centuries of Christian reflection (even if occasionally set in shadow), sin should be avoided not only out of fear but also by a positive desire to do good for others.[78]

As with a turn toward a certain metaphysics (none of which can conclusively demonstrate themselves), for Péguy, as we have seen, a life of this kind requires "a wager." With this wager, it "depends on us /that the great does not lack the small / . . . that the eternal does not lack the perishable." It is the "terrifying freedom of man" that "the wisdom of God can fail through us."[79]

Even as God puts his wisdom in our hands, for Péguy Christians must put themselves into God's hands. This often takes the form, in image and metaphor, of trusting one's self to Night, a darkness God creates and loves. In the words of The Portal of the Mystery of Hope, "O ma nuit étoilée, je t'ai créé la première" (O my starry night, I created you first). So God speaks to his "daughter" who offers a "luminous silence."[80]

Each human being is a "monster of anxiety"[81] who refuses the gift of sleep and rest from Night, refusing to abandon control, because they lack the courage both to work wholeheartedly and to find rest, "the courage to do nothing."[82]

Night's rest, however, is not the repose of death. As Péguy tells it, God loves her for her fertile capacity for life: hers is an expansive, even musical "silence" that allows the days of one's life to "join together . . . as if in a beautiful dance."[83] The dance is a figure of perichoresis—the participatory love of the Trinity in Christianity—in which day and night are entwined with one another in a continual celebration of creation, but a celebration perceptible only when one perceives the ways in which all the days are joined by night, "the fabric of time, the reserve of being."[84] Days become "different" through night, without which days would be an interminable, homogenous Day. It is in abandoning one's self to this reserve of being that one enters into the Night and recognizes it as the domain of hope and charity, what God calls "my great dark light."[85]

This abandonment requires trust, however, and for Péguy it is evident that he and other human beings resist God. This does not prompt him to move toward a rhetoric of "sinners in the hands of an angry God," either in the manner of Jonathan Edwards, or the similarly urgent French Catholic homiletic warnings about death and damnation in the early modern period, documented long ago by Bernard Groethuysen.[86] Instead, Péguy presents God gently playing among human beings like a father playing with his young children. He wants to let them win salvation and find their happiness. But the games of salvation are different, since

> I play often against man, says God, but it is
> he who wants to lose, the imbecile, and it is me who wants
> him to win.
> And sometimes I succeed
> so he wins.[87]

God will let human beings lose, according to Péguy—that is part of our freedom. But in Péguy's decided break from certain strains in early modern Christianity in particular, God takes no satisfaction in his justice if they insist on losing; he has only a parent's frustration with children who cannot recognize their true hope.

These abundant references in Péguy to God's love, to first creation, origins, ultimate origins, and attention to origins seem to pass rather lightly over something obvious. Christianity finds its origin in Jesus, and Jesus was Jewish. What does patient attention to the origin of Christianity allow one to understand about its own original relation to Judaism?

Surrounded by accusations that Jews as a group were "different" and, in particular, legalistic, carnal, and treacherous, Péguy found in all this anti-Semitism a source of bewilderment issued from diverse absurdities, refuted by observation of daily life and by honest meditation upon Christian origins.

First, he says, some French Jews, for the sake of their own safety or comfort, can take the route of politique. But in that, they, like everyone else, partake of the human condition and "are like all peoples." When Péguy writes of Jewish "politique" in *Notre Jeunesse*, he repeatedly refers that politique to the politique of humanity as a whole: "The great majority of Jews are like the great majority of (other) voters." Hence Jewish politique, "like all politiques," avoids and fears mysticism. Jews fear violence and the mystical power of the prophets that provokes controversy and fidelity to difficult callings, because, in ordinary circumstances, they seek to avoid the extraordinary—once more, because "the people of Israel are like all peoples."[88] If Jews stood out in any way for Péguy, it was because of a burden that was also a blessing: they continued to be God's exemplary people, charged to bring truth and justice to the world, at the very least through the prophetic office of Judaism (practiced by both believing and nonbelieving Jews, like Bernard-Lazare) on behalf of universal justice.

There is for Péguy a particular "anxiety" that comes with the cost of that task, amid the universal human or "modern" anxiety[89] (we have already seen that he finds Christians under the burden of a unique impatience).[90] His understanding of Judaism's role as a continuing collective body of God's truth is not supersessionist (that is, assuming Christianity simply "replaces" any role for Judaism in the world).

Furthermore, as we have seen, while Jews were for Péguy a people, that did not make them any less French than French gentiles.[91] Given his poverty and obscurity despite his intellectual gifts, it was more than clear that Bernard-Lazare was not irresistibly drawn to money. For Péguy it is obvious that greed is part of the human condition and in no way "Jewish" in kind or degree. Péguy, being poor, knew plenty of poor Jewish people: "I shall bear witness," he writes, "for poor Jews," with whom he has lived in "common poverty" but also a mutual "fidelity" and "solidity" and "unshakable friendship."[92] Among the wealthy, he is less expert, but remarks, "The only one of my creditors who behaved toward me not only like a usurer, but . . . like a usurer from Balzac . . . who treated me with . . . the hardness, with the cruelty of a usurer in Balzac was not a Jew." He was, Péguy remarks with pointed irony, "a Frenchman," he was "a Christian." Péguy then puts a question in italics, but with a period to punctuate a known answer: "*What would be said if he had been Jewish.*"[93]

The prejudice against Jews, Péguy says, is very much like an "optical illusion" where a white square on black "appears much larger" than the same-sized black square on white. For "every action, every operation, every square *Jewish on Christian* appears to us, we see it as being much bigger than the same square *Christian on Jew.*"[94]

To correct the illusion, and to "reestablish justice," Péguy repeats the phrase "what would be said if he was Jewish" several times, commending it to his readers as a test in specific cases, once more in italics: "*What would be said if Jaurès was Jewish. What would be said if . . .* [the then-pacifist and antinationalist] *Hervé was Jewish.*"[95]

Accompanying this deep quotidian prejudice was a profound religious in-comprehension. While Péguy was not a scholar of Judaism and did not know Hebrew, among his Jewish friends were several interested in Jewish history and culture, including Edmond-Maurice Lévy. Lazare Prajs records that he "often read the Psalms and other sacred texts in Hebrew to Péguy."[96] From these encounters and from his own reading, it seemed ridiculous to Péguy to claim that Judaism was a form of legalism, as many anti-Semites claimed: it was a "mysticism,"[97] with its own distinctive spiritual vocation.

As we have seen, it was the indispensable cooperation of Jewish, Chris-tian, and French mystique that for Péguy resisted the persecution and wrong-ful conviction of Dreyfus.[98] Nor did he find in this cooperation a kind of supersessionism, where Jews were merely "legal" in their devotion to the cause. The mystical prophet of the Dreyfus affair is not a Christian but rather Bernard-Lazare, and he attends to legal and many other matters from what is for Péguy a much more comprehensive way of understanding. Furthermore, as we have seen, Jews, Christians, and secular French republicans, their iden-tities variously configured, engaged in a process of "coming together"[99] in which their members brought out their unique mysticism through mutual testing rather than a hierarchical order of precedence.

Jews were unjustly censured for Péguy, and profoundly so: their flaws were the flaws of all human beings, exaggerated by the illusions of prejudice that also obscured their virtues, the same prejudice that led many of his contem-poraries to miss entirely the mystical dimension of Judaism.

Furthermore, it was simply not true that Jesus' arrest, trial and condem-nation (and with them Judas) was the decisive point of relation between Ju-daism and Christianity, and with it the alleged "betrayal" of Jesus by "the Jews."

Péguy rejected the notion that "the Jews" were in any way responsible for Jesus's death. In the Eucharist and elsewhere, Christians are "in the presence of the Passion of Jesus." In fact, Clio tells Péguy, speaking of Christians as such, "You are always put in the presence of Jesus." Péguy goes further: in the Mass and "in sin" it is "the crucifixion that recommences eternally in the world."[100] For Christians, their own sins lead to the Crucifixion of Christ: it is "Jesus that you wound, Jesus that you wrong. Jesus that you crucify."[101]

If Jesus is wounded and crucified by human sin, especially Christian sin, then the vital connection between Judaism and Christianity—of great mo-ment for Péguy—happens elsewhere, specifically in the Incarnation and the Resurrection. For Péguy, the Incarnation and the Resurrection are free acts of God that, like all acts of freedom, do not break from the past but daringly and creatively draw ever more deeply from their origin.

We have seen that for Péguy's mentor Bergson, freedom is a state in which the "self lets itself live, when it abstains from establishing a separation between the present and anterior states."[102] In Bergson's philosophy, "a free act" occurs when "the self alone [is] the author of it, since it will express the entire self."[103] In this Bergsonian way, for Péguy Judaism and Christianity are neither disembodied essences nor contingent representations eternally subject to the discontinuous flux of becoming. Instead, they draw faithfully from the past to produce what is radical (in the true etymological sense of radical, that is, "from the root") and are thus faithful, continuous, and always new. In this way, Jesus's Incarnation itself expresses its originality through fidelity to its Jewish root, something that becomes visible in the work of Péguy through his reflections on Jeanne d'Arc.

We have seen that in *The Mystery of Jeanne d'Arc's Love*, when Jeanne is approaching despair, she claims that "fourteen centuries of Christianity . . . and nothing, nothing, always nothing. And what reigns over the face of the earth [is] nothing, nothing, it is nothing but perdition."[104]

As Jeanne reflects on her impatience with evil and uncertainty, her own recognition of Jesus's Incarnation and Resurrection is exiguous, if not entirely absent—and with it, Judaism is absent. Early in the poem, she refers to Jesus's Crucifixion as a sacrifice, but not as an explicitly carnal sacrifice or as a victorious sacrifice—the embodied reality of Jesus's life, death, and especially Resurrection are absent. But then she says, "We need perhaps something new, something that has never been seen before."[105]

As she begins to understand her life as a radical commitment to the living relation between embodied temporality and eternity, Jeanne begins to speak powerfully not only about crucifixion and loss, but also about Jesus's resurrected body. That body was "human in its humanity, in our common humanity." This resurrected body enters into a fully embodied eternity with the Ascension, bringing human being into an unprecedented communion with time-transcendent reality.[106] Following hard upon that insight—not in spite but because of it—the embodied relation of Jesus to the Jewish people becomes visible to Jeanne with extraordinary sharpness: "Jesus who was Jewish, a Jew among you; race that received the greatest grace, and one that was refused to all Christian people, mystery of grace; elected race . . . we are brothers of Jesus in our humanity. But you, the Jewish people, you were his brothers in his very family."[107]

The affirmation of Incarnation and Resurrection is in this way decidedly not an affirmation that implies the *denial* of fraternity with Judaism; rather, it is precisely through a full, radically patient Christian fidelity to the Incarnation and Resurrection that Christians can *enter* into true fraternity with Judaism, one that does not deny or sublate their differences but allows these differences to relate to one another freely. For Péguy, Christians and Jews are in different ways both particular and universal, both particular collective bodies in which God's universal truth dwells and lives in the world. It was precisely the honor of Judaism to be a "carnal" religion, and the same was true for Christianity. For Péguy, the embodied carnal particularity of Judaism among and for all the peoples of the world, as God's people, opens the way to the embodied carnal particularity of Christ among and for the persons of the world. When Christians deny that continuity, Jews become scapegoats and Christianity is immediately cut off from its own origins, betrays itself—and becomes a politique.

For all that, the distinction Péguy drew between Jewish and Christian revelation remains, one that Péguy attributed not to his historical moment but to almost two thousand years of Christian life in the world—the problem of Jewish "patience" and Christian "impatience," and of how "Jesus was able to graft Jewish anxiety" into "the Christian body" but not "Jewish patience."[108]

At first, Péguy's thought about Christian impatience is strikingly reminiscent of Franz Rosenzweig's reflections on Judaism and Christianity in *The Star of Redemption*, in which (to state the matter with starkly simplifying brevity) Christians live in a stretched, sometimes unstable linear time of adoptive eschatological expectation, whereas Jews dwell within a vital and immediate relation to eternity.[109] But Péguy's thought takes a very different turn, since "it is by the deepest internal logic of language itself that *patience* is the virtue of the *passion*,"[110] a logic incarnated not just in the suffering of Jesus but also in the lives of saints that live Christ's passion anew.[111]

It is the forgetting of this passion of Christian patience—which Jesus *embodied* rather than propositionally taught or offered as a technique—that for Péguy intensifies or even opens the way to many of the flaws of modern culture; these include a passive-aggressive and cumulative hollowing out of all mysticism, as well as a reactionary, bitter, and violent particularism, with anti-Semitism as its supreme expression. But properly referred to Jesus's passion, Christian faith finds its distinctive patience.

As Péguy writes in *The Portal of the Mystery of Hope*, Christians must live their hope and its partial but inevitable disappointments from the perspective of eternity as well as from within time. His poem is attuned to the ways in which an embodied life becomes set in a given time and place, but that life is always bound up not only with the past but with multiple pasts, with the present, and even multiple presents (both the present as a discrete moment and as an ongoing, proximate continuity of experience), entwined in turn with diverse futures and with eternity. Péguy explores this multidimensional temporality poetically through a woodcutter, the peasant husband and father whose consciousness Péguy explores in the poem. It is the protagonist's capacity to inhabit these diverse temporal dimensions that makes Christian patience possible—and it is precisely this temporal multiplicity that finds its origin in the Passion.

The woodcutter lives in the immediate present, describing his daily life, feeling the full force of a cold winter day as his teeth chatter and icicles stick to his beard.[112] This present of immediate experience works within his attachment both to a local, intimate place and to ways of life that continue in an extended present. They are not only "rooted" but organically grow into the future. "The peasantry must continue,"[113] just as local regions and communities like Lorraine and Vaucouleurs and Jeanne d'Arc's native village Domrémy must continue.[114]

The woodcutter knows that continuity must move forward in historical time—but without him. He reflects upon how with each day he moves closer toward not only his death but his own oblivion as well. He acknowledges that a time will come when his sons will have his name, and that name will no longer refer to himself but his sons: "He thinks with tenderness of the time where there will be no need for him / and where everything will be fine all the same." Or again, more viscerally, of his own gathering annihilation in the memory of the world: "He thinks with tenderness of the time when he will no longer be even a remark."[115] The intimate, irenic tenderness that accompanies his consciousness of death—and, as we shall see, the sense of a humble flourishing for his community beyond his own life—are striking. There is no Heideggerean *Entschlossenheit* in Péguy's woodcutter.

He reflects upon the days when his children will have his tools, and those days will signal "the reign of his children."[116] Those days he will never see, those days when he will be gradually forgotten, will be days of goodness and good fortune: "His children will fare better than he, of course. / And the world will get on better. /Later. / He is not jealous of it. / On the contrary / . . . what lunatic would be jealous of his sons and the sons of his sons."[117]

The woodcutter knows that when he dies, his body will be placed beside "his father and his grandfather whom he knew" and will in a certain sense enter a near past. But it will also enter different, more distant pasts, "with all the old men and all the old women" he never knew. Their community will continue into the future through their descendants, and the descendants of their descendants—but those descendants and their descendants will also die, and eventually so will all his people.

Upon a hasty reading of this passage, Péguy might sound like a late modern apologist for traditional "peoples" and "kin" as a purveyor of ersatz immortality; but his prefatory remark is of utmost importance for understanding his actual thinking about collective bodies and their survival. Here as elsewhere in Péguy's writing, there is precisely no eternity or immortality in a "race," or a nation, or a people, any more than in an individual life: "for the race itself and the blood are perishable and will perish."[118]

For Péguy it is spiritually indispensable to belong to a people, just as it is to live an embodied individual life, but only if one relates to that people as flawed and mortal—like one's self, and other selves. Yet even as all persons and peoples join in a succession of pasts that successively become obscure and unknown, their lives and loves remain entwined with an ultimate continuity and an end to time, "awaiting the resurrection of the body."[119] The woodcutter says that amid the inevitable death of all persons and all peoples, it is "the blood of Jesus" that does not perish.[120]

All time—multiple pasts, presents, and futures—eventually flow into eternity. Yet the present (both immediate and continuous) has its own responsibility to eternity. This is why God has put "his eternal hope / in our transitory hands / in our sinful hands."[121]

The present work of sinful hands manifests itself supremely in different kinds of work—the work of eternity that is present to the work of tools and hands, the work of minds, with the cooperation of mind and body to reproduce, in every sense. By reproducing rather than repeating, there is a surprising fidelity in difference—and surprising difference in fidelity—to the past. The father and mother are not the children, yet the children allow some small portion of their being into the world beyond their deaths; the tools will have new owners, will be used very differently, yet will draw upon their origins, and innovations will be occasioned by unexpected possibilities in the past.

The "wager" to work for temporal futures that will certainly not include or remember ourselves has little appeal for those seeking personal vindication and imperishable historical "results." As Péguy's Jeanne says at the beginning of *The Mystery of Jeanne d'Arc's Love*, the world is always full of injustice, evil is never decisively defeated in history, and it appears obvious to Péguy that some purely human futurity will never definitively defeat it; it will simply change its forms, as it has always done.

In *The Mystery of Jeanne d'Arc's Love*, Jeanne began to realize that it is she who must act on behalf of life and love against corrupt repetition as both a hero and a saint, to love the good and boldly confront the evils of her moment. It is a woman who takes this active, heroic, and assertive role in Péguy's Christian writings, while a man must remain humble and quiet. The woodcutter must cultivate patience, a patience that must reckon with both the power and failure of hope. In fact, in Péguy's *Portal of the Mystery of Hope*, trust in "hope" reliably fails, with a superficially dispiriting constancy.

How can this be understood? In the poem, Hope, personified as a little girl, may surprise God and humans alike, but for Péguy she goes wherever she wants and does not pay attention to what it costs human beings to follow her. Hope "makes us go twenty times to the same place / which is generally a place of deception / (earthly) / It's all the same to her. She is like a child. She is a child."[122] She acts as if human beings have all their lives before them, with nothing having been lost and nothing to lose, without the marks of past and present suffering.

If their faith is understood only in relation to an empty, homogenous linear time of past, present and future (as it is in standard modern notions of time), Christian hope dissolves either into an impatient, increasingly politicized frustration or a kind of vaporous abnegation of the world. But for Péguy true Christian hope counts failure faithfully, as God does *beyond* time, where fidelity and newness, origins and difference are reconciled:

For the wisdom of God
Nothing is ever nothing. All is new. All is other.
All is different.
In the eyes of God nothing is repeated.
These twenty times that she [that is, hope] makes us take the
    same way
to arrive at the same point
in vain.
For human eyes it is the same point, the same way, these are the
    same twenty times.
But this is mistaken.
This is the wrong reckoning, and false accounting. . . .
If the way is a way of holiness

In the eyes of God, a way of trials
the one who took it two times, is two times more holy
in the eyes of God and the one who took it three times
three times more holy, and the one who did it
twenty times, twenty times more holy. That is the way God
counts.[123]

For Péguy, the appearance of faithful, good, yet in some sense failed repetition is a source of grace and wisdom: hope does not count the cost, and it
is only through hope that human beings also learn not to count the cost, to
wager upon an uncertain future after hard falls and inevitable, repeated
disappointments, with others and with themselves, and still remain open to
hope, and to the promise of eternity that nourishes human beings through
time, toward their infinite end.

For Péguy, human beings see failure to reach temporal goals as a kind of
imprisoning, repetitive finitude, where failures sequentially resemble one
another interminably, and the experience of success is distinct: one has either
"arrived" somewhere—or not. History does not appear to "arrive" anywhere—
in this late work, Péguy's talk about an "age of competence" to succeed modern metaphysics falls away—since history is filled with injustice and fragile
improvements that are easily undone, and our own personal "arrivals" (if they
arrive), fall increasingly under the shadow of our approaching deaths. But, for
Péguy, God works not sequentially but exponentially, in a dimension of transcendent time beyond the line of past, present, and future.

To continually open one's self toward following what is good and just and
rightly lovable—to engage in work that makes one vulnerable and repeatedly
fail, or reach what one sought only to understand it is not an end, and to remain open to trying again faithfully for what is good and just and rightly
lovable—that is to find one's self transformed by hope in ways that would never
have happened if one had "arrived," suitably buffered and secure at some end
point that would be the basis for further temporal success, understood as the
next temporal goal.

For Péguy, the monotonous or even ghastly repetition that the metaphysically modern dispirited Christian (or the metaphysically modern dispirited
secular person) finds in history and in the general run of human experience is
only two-dimensional. One sees that "the point" has not been reached by the
line in time, and concludes that "there is no point." But for Péguy, each time
the line is traveled, the person who travels it (and works through it honestly)

gains in depth—the path becomes transformed through time, in many dimensions—and there are always richer and unexpected ways through which the grace of God can move, and human beings can relate to time and to eternity. In *The Portal of the Mystery of Hope*, Péguy does not seek to denounce the inevitable human desire to "arrive" in the world but seeks to magnify and transform it with patience. It requires trust, open to darkness and uncertainty as one makes one's way.

It is in abandoning one's self to a divine reserve of being that one enters into the Night and recognizes it as the domain of hope and charity, the "great dark light."[124]At the conclusion of the poem, God experiences time through Night in the death of his son, and as a bereaved father. Jesus is unburied, and

> I alone at that instant, father after so many fathers,
> I alone could not bury my son.
> But then, O Night, you came.
> O my dear daughter among them all, and I see it still and
> I will see it in my eternity
> It is then O Night that you came and in a large shroud
> you buried
> The Centurion and his Roman men,
> The Virgin and the holy women,
> And this mountain, and this valley, upon which Night descended,
> And my people of Israel and the sinners together with the one
>   who died, had died for them
> And the men of Joseph of Arimathea who were already
>   approaching,
> carrying the white shroud.[125]

Night for Péguy is precisely what the "second creation" he saw taking shape in the early twentieth century sought to suppress. For him, its ambitions toward comprehensive and global enlightenment (where there is no "Night") concealed a deep hostility to what is given and uncontrolled, that which requires trust in what is not immediately visible and not subjected to human will through instrumental reason. Through Night, the beginning (what God "created . . . first") comes to make all things new, summoning all things to a more certain relation of trust with their origin in eternity.

The Christian collective "body" in history has tended to impatience, often disastrously. But, for Péguy, to return in hope to the Christian origin of redemption—the Passion—opens the way to an infinitely original and embodied patience. In this way, in a moment of profound understanding, Madame Gervaise tells Jeanne in *The Mystery* that when Christ was on the cross, "The whole past was present to him. The whole present was present to him. All the future, the whole future was present. All eternity was present to him. Together and separately."[126]

For Péguy, the late modern person, Christian or not, generally experiences time in profound contrast to the time patiently opened within the Passion, the time in which the woodcutter also participates. Instead there is an empty linearity that impatiently demands deliverance from itself in the form of a new creation, one subject to our control. This can take the form of a politicized, secular ideological eschaton, or a politicized faith (on the "Left" or the "Right"), or a tidal flood of technology and frantic activity (as Péguy called it, a world of "graphies," "scopies," and "-phones," with "tele-")[127] that relieve human beings of the boredom, anxiety and chronic, at times dangerous impatience that living in two-dimensional, one-speed cumulative time inevitably brings with it. In that time, nothing is new except more of the same, especially further advancements toward a more complete "second creation"—and nothing is other.

Péguy's peasant embodies patience beyond a denuded linear time, a patient, integrative temporality that approaches the patience of the Passion where "all is new. All is other." He simultaneously inhabits a time of pasts and futures. But he also inhabits a present in contact with eternity when Christian "waiting" is no longer the basis for an impatient fraying and intensification of linear time or a despairing emptiness of time, but rather a fullness of time. Hope awakens desire and instructs it in patience, and with it a steady movement—at once linear and cyclical, from courageous rest to carnal work and back again—a movement that revolves in suffering and joy to encounter a fructifying, exponentially expansive peace.

For Péguy, a Christianity without a living relation to different pasts and futures, an immediate present in contact with an infinitely transcendent eternity, will become empty and destructive. But a Christianity that affirms life through multiple temporal dimensions can with confident fidelity dispatch an unchristian aversion to the carnal. A living relation of this kind would be able to demand a more rigorous and sacrificial goodness by reducing the preeminence of moral rules in order to demand a more exacting and less compromising relation to the good among Christians; sin and evil remain monotonously the same, but the good is not merely an opposing rule, but an opening to what is infinitely alive. Such a Christianity can recognize its true and ineradicable root in Judaism, resisting the temporal dispersion of sacred energies into interminable, sterile political and religious animosities. It was to this task that Péguy felt called, not as a saint but as an avowed sinner.[128]

Given its habitation in diverse forms of writing and its abiding affirmation of multiplicity, Péguy's work did not complete itself, in the manner of a system. There is, for example, in the notion of God's vulnerability to human sin and suffering a hint of what would come to be called process theology. If God "*needs* us, God *needs* his creature,"[129] that need could open up the notion that Péguy so opposed, that our understanding of God could evolve in time and thus "improve," as he dryly put it, the "direction of the North." But Péguy never developed his thought in that direction and, especially in his poetry, shows how that "vulnerability" expresses an unchanging and infinite divine love for creation.

Whatever was left undone in his writing, what Péguy had done was considerable. At the turn of the last century, he encountered a still somewhat Jansenist, moralizing, politicized Christianity, polarized by allegiances to secular preoccupations on the Left and the Right, often anti-Semitic, often trapped in an empty linear time, opposed by a theological modernism that regularly insinuated modern metaphysics into Christianity, and ingratiatingly implied that its claims to truth could be winsomely and continuously evacuated. He revolved all of it in simultaneously new and ancient terms through ultimate Christian origins: that is, the Incarnation, the Crucifixion, and the Resurrection. In this way, he participated in a faithful revolution (in every sense) of Christian practice and language.

His writings had cost him a great deal. He was, Péguy told his friend Lotte in the fall of 1913, going to be poor for the rest of his life. Yet as Péguy himself had said, poverty and marginality were also a form of freedom, a gift inviting deeper, more faithful, more honorable, and more creatively original ventures into the questions that mattered most to him. He told Lotte he had "inconceivable trials in the order of private life, immense graces for my work." In the end, "only I can say certain things, so I say them."[130]

CHAPTER II

Despair and Exaltation

In the years immediately after his return to Catholicism in 1907, financial debts, emotional turmoil, and intellectual isolation weighed heavily upon Péguy. But with the success in 1910 of both *The Mystery of Jeanne d'Arc's Love* and *Notre Jeunesse*, he began to hope that his writing might at last be recognized.

Profiles of Péguy and his work began to be published in mainstream journals—some by his friends, like the Tharauds, who found editors willing to publish them. *L'Éclair* and *La Nouvelle Revue Française* devoted articles to Péguy; newspapers like *L'Action Française* often disagreed with him, but no longer ignored him.[1] Péguy read them all: his archives show a terse "Vu" (seen, read) in his handwriting near the headline of each article.

Word of Péguy's late renown soon spread over the Alps, the Channel, and the Rhine. From 1910 forward, references to and articles about Péguy's work appeared in newspapers and reviews published in Geneva, Madrid, Krakow, Rome, and London.[2] In 1912, Péguy was the subject of a lecture in Glasgow.[3] German intellectuals also read him; a survey of the *Cahiers* appeared in the German literary magazine *Das literarische Echo*.[4] The German Expressionist poet Ernst Stadler wrote a piece entitled "Die neue französische Lyrik" in *Der lose Vogel*, in which he lavished praise on Péguy for prose "without model and without equal."[5] Across the Atlantic, there was a similar turn: at the end of June 1910, readers of the *New York Times* were told that Charles Péguy "seems destined to acquire a wider fame and a larger following" in the wake of *The Mystery of Jeanne d'Arc's Love*.[6]

There was some reason to believe that Péguy would be able to secure a still modest but more secure income for his family. In particular, he began to hope that *The Mystery* would win a prize from the Académie Française. Maurice

Barrès—a member of the Academy—promised to help him, and Péguy, for the first time, began to court tentatively the opinion of powerful and influential people, even if they disagreed with him on politics, religion, and art, as Barrès certainly did.

It was not to be. Péguy had crossed too many political and religious boundaries in the Third Republic—and made too many enemies—for a prize awarded by consensus to be an easy prospect, and his lobbying was predictably awkward. The situation was made still worse when his friend and collaborator Romain Rolland was nominated for the same prize; his nomination may well have been an attempt to divide the votes of those sympathetic to the *Cahiers*. Péguy's old Sorbonnard antagonist Ernest Lavisse cuttingly remarked during the deliberations that Péguy had recently "put some holy water in his Communard gasoline,"[7] and the bon mot was widely circulated among intellectuals in Paris. After an initial round of close voting, the major prize was not awarded.

In the end, Péguy was given a smaller prize, and his resentment was palpable and sufficiently prolix to be exhausting to his friends.[8] In America, the *New York Times* reported his loss, concluding that "the real reason" for his defeat was his "open antagonism to the methods and tendencies of the Sorbonne."[9]

Nonetheless, encouraged by the praise of Rolland, Barrès, Gide, and others, Péguy continued to write poetry: some of it very powerful, including *The Portal of the Mystery of Hope,* which would soon be continuously in print. At first it sold poorly, but Péguy had begun to fascinate readers, including some of his friends. In 1912, Rolland wrote in his journal, "I can read nothing after Péguy. All the rest is literature. How today's best sound hollow next to him! He is the most honest and brilliant force in all European literature."[10]

For all that, Péguy's life appeared to him a failure. His marriage was still difficult, and while he approved and encouraged the match, his love Blanche Raphaël had married. His ruptures with friends and associates continued, although sometimes made on behalf of other friends. Georges Sorel and he had become more distant since Péguy had dissented from Sorel's politics in *Notre Jeunesse.* When it appeared to Péguy that Sorel had convinced friends on the jury of the Goncourt Prize in 1912 not to support a work by his friend (and antinationalist, anti-Bergsonian) Julien Benda[11] on the grounds of anti-Semitism (Benda was Jewish), Péguy broke with him entirely.[12]

Péguy had a gift for friendship, however, even if he did not always have a gift for keeping friends in his stormy life. He remained loyal to Lotte, to the

Tharauds, and to Bergson. He was soon close to the young novelist Alain-Fournier, who said of Péguy: "Not since Dostoevsky has there been a man who was so clearly a man of God."[13]

As war with Germany approached, Péguy became more reticent—though not silent—about the evils of European imperialism, and he did not retract what he had written and published before. In personal terms, he did not prosper. In 1913, he published his poem *Ève*, a work of hundreds of pages in which Christ speaks to the first woman in the Garden of Eden for hundreds of lines before the poem begins in Péguy's own authorial voice. Péguy thought it his masterpiece and sent copies of it to prominent members of the Académie Française; he suggested to Lotte that it be sent to the Catholic bishops of Belgium and Canada as well.[14] In private conversation, he indulged in grandiose comparisons, comparing *Ève* favorably to Dante's *Paradiso*.[15]

Its immediate reception was disastrous. It sold only two copies upon its initial release,[16] and more than a hundred of Péguy's subscribers cancelled their subscriptions to the *Cahiers* in the six weeks after it was published.[17] Many of his friends—including the Tharaud brothers—thought it a mess, and struggled to defend Péguy against his many critics. Péguy himself remarked that the poem had fallen into a "total silence."[18]

Throughout these years, Péguy continued to write both poetry and prose—the latter most memorably in his reflections on French literature and reading in *Victor-Marie, Comte Hugo*, and on the failings of modern capitalism and the culture (and metaphysics) it expressed in *L'Argent* and *L'Argent suite*. These were read widely and with interest. Péguy's audience grew, even if the subscribers to the *Cahiers* still numbered little more than a thousand in its final years—at most thirteen hundred or fourteen hundred people and institutions.[19]

Péguy now occupied a unique and in some ways bizarre position in the intellectual world of Paris. Even as he began to attract notice in a wider world of letters, fame and marginality appeared to increase at the same time, and Péguy continued to a pay a price for his unique path through the controversies of the age. Renan's grandson, the soldier Ernest Psichari, dedicated his homage to the soldier's life, *L'Appel des armes,* to Péguy. Yet they too came to fall out over, among other things, the reluctance of Péguy to take the sacraments and become a fully practicing Catholic.[20] Psichari had also moved closer to the thinking of Charles Maurras, for whom Péguy had no sympathy.

Péguy was openly mistrusted by virtually every significant faction in French intellectual life, while at the same moment artists, writers, and philosophers intensely admired different aspects of his work. Among many Catholic intellectuals and clergy, his anticlericalism and evident independence elicited mistrust. Yet if Péguy remained an object of suspicion for the guardians of Catholic orthodoxy in Paris, the partisans of theological liberalism and modernism had no sympathy for him. He was totally unapologetic about the supernatural dimensions of Christianity, and made no effort to disguise his skepticism about their capacious, continuous accommodations to modern metaphysics and bourgeois respectability.

Similar problems bedeviled his political position. Péguy never ceased to be a socialist—and to the end, his critiques of capitalist exploitation and the marketization of human experience in Europe and America lost none of their force—but his affiliations with Herr, Jaurès, and other leaders of the institutional Socialist Party had been broken definitively at the beginning of the century. His arguments about the likelihood and desirability of a coming defensive war against a German invasion did not help. After the imbroglio surrounding the start of the *Cahiers*, prominent academic socialists and sociologists like Marcel Mauss simply hated him.[21] On the Right, several disciples of Maurras had anticipated a turn to their camp after *The Mystery of Jeanne d'Arc's Love*, but Péguy would have none of it: he continued to argue that Maurras and his followers and allies were destructive reactionaries.[22]

In the closing years of his life, Péguy was thus a singular and isolated man. His worries at home intensified, especially when one of his sons was taken seriously ill. After several doctors were consulted on the case, in June 1912 Péguy decided to go on pilgrimage to Chartres Cathedral, accompanied by Alain-Fournier. He walked more than eighty miles in three days. At Chartres, he entrusted his children to Saint Mary and prayed for the sick child of a friend with whom he had stayed on the way. It appears that there he also found a way to renounce his lingering passion for Blanche Raphaël. Strikingly, he found in his pilgrimage a great peace; he told Lotte: "It was an ecstasy . . . all my impurities suddenly fell away. I was another man . . . I was able to pray for my enemies, [and] that had never happened before."[23]

Though his fatigue was mounting, the *Cahiers* continued, and he continued to publish those with whom he disagreed. In his final years, Péguy published a critique of Bergson by Benda, as well as work by the pacifist and anti-nationalist Rolland.[24]

It was not simply his own struggles that troubled him. In early 1914, he was disheartened at the virulence of attacks against Bergson, and shocked to learn that Bergson's writings—long under fire from the French Reactionary

Right—might be placed on the Index of Forbidden Books by the Catholic Church.

In March 1914, Péguy wrote Bergson, offering to spring to his defense: "I alone have a pen strong enough to cut a Maurras down to size, I alone have sufficient strength of hand simultaneously to drive back the anti-Semites and the fanatics."[25] He offered Bergson his services as a student of philosophy who would fight his politicized opponents, once more in the intellectual space of the fortnight, between philosophy and theology on the one hand and politics and contemporary culture on the other. To the end of his life, Péguy's "Catholic Renaissance" would not countenance a condemnation of Bergson. There would be a rapprochement neither with the defenders of the Index nor with anti-Semites.

Péguy persisted as writer and editor, commuting to the Parisian suburb Bourg-la-Reine on the train from Paris. He defended Bergson, more philosophically than his rather pugnacious offer to Bergson implied, publishing a *Note on Bergson and Bergsonian Philosophy* in April 1914. His defense of Bergson would be followed by clerical accusations against Péguy himself. It seemed that officials within the church were considering placing his own writings on the Index, since offense had been taken at his recent affirmation of "supple" as opposed to "stiff" morality.[26]

In his quotidian round, friends like Rolland still found the predilections Péguy had for anger and free-floating criticism exasperating, and the Tharaud brothers observed that his repeated fallings out with friends were like a trail of "broken glass" in his life.[27] Rolland assumed that Péguy was exhausted after "fifteen years" of "inhuman labor and venomous battles."[28] The remark of Péguy's Clio that Péguy did not see himself "celebrating the fiftieth anniversary of the *Cahiers*"[29] appeared very much on his mind, as he interpreted small happenings in his final years as omens of his approaching death. A man entered his bookshop and remarked that after a poem like *Ève*, one could die. Péguy took the remark as uncanny,[30] and repeated it to friends.

The Austrian Archduke Franz Ferdinand was assassinated at the end of June 1914. Péguy's life received a new élan from the preparations for war that followed, and he supported the order for mobilization. He still saw the war as a just one that would bring about a general and even final peace, telling Geneviève Favre that he left for the Front as "a soldier of the Republic, for general disarmament and the last of wars."[31] Long a reserve lieutenant in the 276th Reserve Infantry Regiment (of the Sixth Army),[32] he expected to see battle soon—and on his native soil.

As Péguy undertook his preparations for war, his ongoing defense of Bergson came to an abrupt end in high summer 1914—his final manuscript, the *Note conjointe sur M. Descartes,* stops in mid-sentence.[33] When Geneviève Favre asked him on August 3 what would become of his manuscripts, he said he hadn't thought about it, since what he was about to see was more important than anything he had written.[34]

Yet there had recently been one altogether immediate reason to reflect on what he had written, even as the forty-one-year-old prepared for war. On July 31, 1914, Jean Jaurès was assassinated in the Café du Croissant by a nationalist. Péguy, whose hatred for Jaurès had assumed ugly proportions—and who had written that in time of war, Jaurès would have to go to the guillotine— had ambiguous and almost entirely silent reactions to the news that quickly spread around the capital. According to Daniel Halévy, upon learning of Jaurès's assassination, Péguy moved with a flinch of "wild exultation."[35] But Geneviève Favre claimed that he looked burdened with sadness about Jaurès's death soon afterward.[36]

It is certainly possible, as Rolland thought, that both of these wordless reactions were true.[37] Péguy the militant preparing for war, beset by a feeling of suppressed resentment and grievance, exulted without words; but memories of Jaurès the human being who had never wished him ill, and who had been working for peace, soon brought him to grieve for him—and possibly to regret the invective he had directed his way.[38]

As war became more and more likely, Péguy worried for his children, who would suffer without the modest support of their father's income. He hoped and expected that the war would end soon, so that his oldest son (who turned sixteen that year) would not have to fight in it.[39] As he told his friend Jules Riby: "Since it's going to happen, I would much rather it be me than my children."[40] He asked Bergson to help provide for his children if he did not survive the war. Bergson agreed.[41]

It was in these days that Péguy's pregnant (and still religiously skeptical) wife asked him whether the child should be baptized when he or she was born. Péguy told her to think about it, and offered no instructions.[42]

Péguy spent his final days in Paris staying at Geneviève Favre's residence, reconciling with all those in Paris with whom he had argued or spoken shortly. His poem *Ève* from the previous year, as Halévy later remarked, seemed to confess a need to resolve the struggle between anger and grace in his writing in favor of grace, a resolution that he now sought in his life:

Another will erase from the oak bark
The trace of the only name we have loved.
Another will erase from our books of hate
The trace of twitch grass, the grain of wild mustard
Another will erase from the ash bark
The trace of the only name that we have carved.
But no one will erase from our books of pain
The trace of a *Pater* or an *Ave*.[43]

His reaching out to others included people from every moment of his life in Paris, including Léon Blum, with whom Péguy reconciled. He also tried to see Lucien Herr, who was on vacation.[44] He spoke in friendly terms to the housemaid in Favre's residence with whom he had had a quarrel, and they embraced.[45] He also met with old and constant friends. Several of them commented that Péguy seemed freer than he had been in a very long time: one remarked that finally he was not preoccupied with "the next *Cahier*."[46]

As battle approached, Péguy sang songs that expressed his unflagging hope of bringing different pasts together in a living whole: he sang a battle cry of the ancien régime, along with the old republican song *La Carmagnole*.[47] He joined his troops at the Front and wrote repeatedly of peace. He wrote letters to his wife, to his mother, to Geneviève Favre, and to Blanche Raphaël.[48] To his wife, Charlotte, he wrote of how much he loved her, and asked her: "Live in peace as we [that is, his fellow soldiers] do."[49] Those same soldiers gave him the nickname *pion* (the word for a schoolteacher, proctor, or monitor at the time, although it is also the French word for a pawn in chess).[50] Péguy took the teasing in good humor—"Joke, joke, my friends"—claiming that his soldiers nonetheless would want to see "your pion" in battle.[51]

Péguy had longed to live in what he called an "epoch" (that is, a time of exemplary and spectacular crises, with fundamental principles of justice at stake) rather than a "period" (ages of stability with a certain indifference to principle and often blithely, even cynically accommodating to accumulating injustice).[52] At last he was living out his hope. Yet his late dialogues with Clio repeatedly and insistently observe the ultimate incapacity of history alone to bear the weight of any human desire for unifying, fulfilling purpose and meaning. One can assume that Péguy wrote of both the desire and the incapacity from experience, and did not entirely transcend his yearning to find his own serene wholeness in "epochal" historical experiences.

The German Army made rapid progress through France and moved toward Paris. Péguy had already concluded that it was an opportunity for a greater victory: the situation in early September 1914 would allow French soldiers to do what the armies of the French Revolution had done in 1793.[53]

Early in September 1914, Péguy and his fellow officers slept in a chapel, and he adorned a statue of Saint Mary with flowers.[54] Within a day, every man sleeping in the chapel was dead.[55]

On September 5, Péguy's company engaged German troops near Villeroy, about thirty miles northeast of Paris. The bullets zipped from and toward them amid the rumble and roar of artillery. Late in the afternoon, Péguy urged his troops forward, standing up under fire. He cried out, "Shoot, shoot for God's sake . . . keep shooting!"[56] just before he was shot in the head. He died instantly.

CONCLUSION

Through Péguy's encounter with his own historical moment, the world of Belle Époque France—and of the modern West before its great twentieth-century catastrophes—opens up anew. We find there possibilities of culture, politics, theology, literature, philosophy, and the multiplicity of time that ask for understanding on their own terms. Those possibilities were clearly not limited to those associated with the partisans of immanent becoming and the partisans of arrested immanence and reaction. Through Bergson, Poincaré, Duhem, Boutroux, and the unique circumstances of his embodied life, Péguy found his way to a much more tensile and expansive range of possible understanding and experience.

One finds in Péguy both the unmistakable impress of a unique history, and a creative exploration of diverse pasts opened up through it. He is the student of Bergson, and also the original reader of Pascal. He is the young provincial in Paris, animated by the quintessentially Belle Époque student dream of founding a journal that will speak truth to the world, but also, unlike the vast majority of his contemporaries, the defiant scourge of advertising and institutional parties, as well as expedient alliances—that is, the self-conscious practitioner of courage and honor in the manner of a Cornelian hero.

Péguy was an anti-Marxist French socialist, but also the inheritor of a centuries-old, fast-fading peasant culture. He was simultaneously a practitioner of a robust and earthy, embodied Catholic piety and a supporter of the secular French Republic. He learned something invaluable about the origins of his Christian faith from the conversation and example of his Jewish friends and colleagues, joined the fight against anti-Semitism, and continued in it to his last days. He also inhabited the provincial artisanal culture of the late nineteenth century as well as the early twentieth-century artistic and philosophical worlds of Paris, and loved them both.

His work was often inspired by a hope of returning to ultimate origins to express something continuously original, in service to an exactly rigorous, demanding, and unsentimental love. He could draw freely from time and history in the direction of integration: the universal and the particular, early modernism and premodern religious ritual, and—creatively drawing upon Jeanne d'Arc as well as Pascal—both steadfast anticlericalism and devoted Catholicism.

In all of these commitments, he sought revolution in the fullest sense— that is, to seek substantial change, to open the way to orbital revolutions of thought in which he found an intimation of eternity, to achieve a reconciliation of origins and originality in motion, and to encourage a patient, organic cultivation that opens the way to new growth.

Because Péguy refused to yield either to the metaphysics of immanent becoming, or to the particularist reaction that tries to pull that rote linearity backward, he was able to free himself from the great late modern metaphysics of inhumanity. Reaction is often immediately and viscerally inhuman, requiring immediate and visceral opposition; immanent, unending becoming is often gradually and procedurally inhuman, requiring the work of patient, relentless argument and persuasion. Péguy returns, advances, and transcends them both on behalf of the human.

Péguy belongs differently to his different futures: to the Great War, to the interwar years, to the Second World War and the postwar decades, and to the late twentieth century. All of those futures are important; I will address them in a separate work. In this Conclusion, however, let us focus simply on what Péguy gives to this future, to our time, inflected but not identical with the futures that proceed from him, and the pasts that proceed from us toward him.

Some discrete correspondences are immediately apparent. Accompanied by the reign of money and its technological apparatus, prevailing approaches to the humanities and their characteristic metaphysics—related to the ones that incurred Péguy's objections—have presided over an ever more rapid diminution of interest in and respect for the humanities. He would not be surprised to learn that many academic guardians and advocates of these metaphysics congratulate one another for producing argumentative variations within their metaphysical traditions, even as classrooms empty and indispensable books go unread.

In these same years, complicity in hideous evil has deprived many religious leaders—above all in Péguy's own Catholic Church—of both their moral and spiritual credibility. Hence for believers, his commitment to anticlerical fidelity can be prescient and instructive.

In a more subtly pervasive way, lived experiences of time have been drastically constricted by the turn toward a comprehensively technological society, dominated by mass media and an almost inescapable global market. An age of ubiquitous electronic screens has diminished our embodied, relational bonds to work, leisure, the natural world, and—above all—to other people. It has also become more difficult to experience the present's living connection with different pasts, and to hope for a living and mobile, dynamic continuity between past, present, and surprisingly various possible futures, as well as to inhabit simultaneously in mind and body both the particular and the universal. These are realities that require more patience and effort to experience than they did even two or three generations ago.

Changes to our common speech—the comparative fullness of shared reference, the mutual words of truth, justice, nature, civic freedom, and faith—testify to this relentless narrowing in different precincts of culture, politics, and thinking. As recently as the middle decades of the twentieth century, for example, in a very different age and culture from Péguy's, Martin Luther King Jr. offered his distinctively embodied, spiritual, universal language of justice to his country and to the world. It is certainly very different from Péguy's language of justice, faith, and politics, but in some important ways, closer to his than to our own. King did indeed sometimes speak of an arc of history; this was a powerful expression of hope, and given our own obsession with the procession of linear time, these words are often remembered. But he also—and now this is less often remembered—declared a love of universal justice that drew generously from a profound attachment to the unique particulars of his nation's physical territory, its founding charters (that allowed him to repudiate injustice in original ways without repudiating a shared origin), and a unique, ancient, transcendent, and animating faith, accompanied by philosophical arguments drawn from ancient, medieval, early modern, and modern sources. Precisely *because* of those particular and transcendent attachments and that integrative, historical, philosophical, and spiritual language, he led those with ears to hear to a deeper respect and desire for universal love and justice.[1]

In educated society throughout the West, it is increasingly difficult to speak and write in King's language, or Péguy's, or anything related to them. It is replaced by prose bleached of the particular and of a living universality alike. It is almost considered affected or presumptuous to speak or write now as they variously did, though confronting a burgeoning oligarchy—an expansive reign of money with ambitions to achieve a second creation—begs for words in living, deep continuity with those languages.

Our common tongue—but we don't say "tongue" for language anymore, it's too close to embodied life—yields increasingly to relentless and vacuous abstraction. These abstractions do not disclose a compelling inner logic, or stimulate conceptual precision, but are cavernous and unattended warehouses of language. They emerge from the metaphysics underwriting capitalism and technology, and in academic life (as Péguy observed), an ostensibly separate and antagonistic but often congruent language of ready-made abstractions.

This language of markets and learning (and marketized learning) is uniform and appalling: "constructed narratives" and "empowerment," "human capital," "innovative strategies," and "deft interventions" that "theorize" all "binaries" and "centrisms" as part of a "critique" that quietly exempts its own ultimate commitments from criticism, accompanied by "professional development" amid "sites" and "nodes" and "networks" fashioned by "power relationships" endowed with "resources" beside "consumers" in "interpersonal relationships," within "discourses" with "vectors" "interfacing" with "imaginaries" and "imagined communities" in a history that makes its way by "negotiating" and "evolving."

The language of moral reasoning is subject to the same evacuation: ethical negations are (tellingly) much more easily expressed than affirmations, and even there, works of malice and awkward manners alike are habitually consigned to the terminal murk of the "problematic" and "inappropriate." This language expresses an expansive, controlling, implicit metaphysics that calcifies and empties all it surveys, refusing to touch the quickening particulars (and think the precisely reasoned relations) of unique things, events, and persons.

Such is the dead, unreasoned, inattentive, ready-made language spoken by so many young and old, not only by marketers but easily and often by authors and artists, professors, teachers, persons of God: that is, the people who one would naturally hope would resist this consuming linguistic destitution. It reliably, preemptively concedes the next inexorable step in a predictable procession of nouns turning into strangely lifeless verbs, the reduction of being into a kind of borderless devitalized becoming: a cumulatively abstracted, monetized, publicized, historicized, metaphysically monochromatic procession of linear time.

Transformative, unforeseen events—for Péguy, "the event"—inevitably thwart the insistent ambitions underwriting this expansive destitution. In our own time, we see a familiar reaction trying to exploit these ruptures around us. Far too often it is the familiar politicized reaction, often with the same false-hoods and malice, the same contempt for truth, the assertion of a mythic amal-gam from the past inserted mechanically into the present, the delight in conflict and the humiliation of fellow human beings, the bigotry and spiteful rejection of universal humanity and universal justice, accompanied by demagoguery and an ill-concealed sympathy for authoritarianism. In late modernity, eco-nomic, cultural, political, and social traumas often lead to a reemergence of reaction; their opponents conclude in turn that the world requires nothing but still more comprehensively immanent, devitalized becoming. Their partisans turn and turn, interminably sterile and exhausting antagonists.

Is there not something better than this march of inhuman, vacuously ab-stractive becoming and embittered, enraged, inhuman reaction parading around us? Even now—especially now—may we hope for a surprising, clari-fying, and vivifying renewal?

Whenever these questions are raised, Péguy becomes invaluable. He is not without flaws; in his own words about the French, far from it. Often irascible, his intellectual shortcomings often arise from (fittingly, if ironically) a meta-physical confusion. He perceived and reflected upon—but worked out more poetically than philosophically and theologically—the distinction between the Bergsonian notion of an absolute cumulatively growing in time on the one hand, and, on the other, God's transcendence of space and time as eter-nal source and perpetual ground of all being, who manifests himself in the time and space he both creates and sustains. Whatever his suggestive reservations about Bergson's *Creative Evolution*,[2] this ambiguity in argument (though not in art) would leave in turn an ambiguous legacy, even as Péguy always remains open both to a gathering of temporal possibilities in time, and transcendence beyond time.

Metaphysical imprecision has consequences for thinking about practical questions, as Péguy well understood. In this way, his rich thinking on par-ticularity and its entwinement with a flawed and mortal nation—or simply a "place in time"—can occasionally move toward a blinkered fascination with his own nation-state, in which he does not explore the embodiment of the spiritual, but turned toward language that risks being read as a blurring of the temporal with the eternal; this was his old friend Julien Benda's sharpest criticism of Péguy.[3]

Another instance of Péguy's incomplete thinking about history's relation to what transcends time was his attachment to eighteenth-century notions of war as a force of sudden, expansive transformation; those found within a certain turn of Kant's political thought, for example—and very often among Girondins and Jacobins during the French Revolution. He spoke of the historical parallel between the invasion of France in 1914 and the revolutionary battles of 1793 just before his own death in battle, hoping for a quick, chivalrous war that would secure a just, lasting, and final peace. This is obviously not the same as a fascist fascination with mass war, industrial violence, and domination for its own sake, and with it, war divorced from universal justice; for Péguy it is always the case that those soldiers are happy who "died for the carnal earth, provided it was a just war." But on questions leading to the war of 1914 as nowhere else, he was right to admit what a soldier had once told him: that he had a visionary's sight for things distant, and not for things closest to him.[4]

Yet living in that approaching distance, we cannot content ourselves with comforting observations about historical and conceptual ironies. We need a thinker who can write clearly that human beings are always metaphysical beings: "Everyone has a metaphysics. Manifest or latent."[5] A comprehensive metaphysical consensus in history can only be impersonated or, put bluntly, faked by an elite consensus of different varieties. Even if one finds the voluble "modesty" of the advocates for a given consensus—in Péguy's time and our own—rather poignant, claims to have set "aside" or left "behind" or gone "beyond" metaphysics exempt a currently prominent and often expedient metaphysics from free questioning, and deprive other human beings of their metaphysical freedom. Freely made metaphysical wagers, if they acknowledge the freedom of others to make other wagers, are infinitely better. Such a wager may bring gifts beyond reciprocation.

To this end, Péguy's notion of "metaphysical federalism" would limit the excesses of a constrictive metaphysical hegemony in contemporary culture. Often the partisans of immanent becoming—who broadly tend to align themselves with philosophical liberalism, though not always, and it is not necessarily their ultimate end—fail to acknowledge that without some recognition of substantively different metaphysical possibilities, liberal orders become corrupt for reasons liberalism itself has understood for a very long time. Undivided, unchecked, comprehensive power in a given order of culture or politics tends to become self-seeking, complacent, and intolerant. In Péguy's phrase, advocates of a modern metaphysics that enjoy this preeminence cease to practice the liberal arts and become what Péguy calls "modernist." Refusing to engage with or acknowledge legitimate metaphysical differences becomes the necessary means to secure a final and illiberally "liberated" future, with freedom curiously conceived not as free will, agency, or substantive creativity, but as an ever more comprehensive repudiation of different pasts, above all those open to the transcendence of time.

Rather than fleeing from and suppressing honest metaphysical differences, it is worth attending to Bergson's argument that true and lasting tolerance is best secured by those with a passion for truth and justice rather than a devotion to prefabricated ideological formulae of any variety—and with it, Péguy's argument that mysticisms more easily share a given present with other mysticisms than mysticisms that have decayed into politics are willing to do. There is no avoiding this often painful relation between mysticism and politics: politics always partakes in mysticism as its ultimate "creditor," just as mysticisms inevitably do descend into politics, and the only way through that corruption is a still greater and more original mystical fidelity.

In our time, we need no less a thinker who relates creatively and faithfully to origins, who affirms an originality more promising and real than another predictable "transgression." We need a thinker who upholds the legitimacy of embodied and particular lives, individual and communal, as well as the demands of universal justice and the dignity of all human beings.

Not least, Péguy helps us to encounter time differently—writing in the present in "fortnights" that can both integrate and distinguish time and eternity, relating them to different dimensions of philosophical, theological, literary, and historical enquiry. Popular appeals to the "vindication of history," safely bland calls among scholars for "recasting" the "social imaginary" (whether understood "subjectively" or "objectively" it is another stillborn phrase extracted from a metaphysics without hope) are entirely inadequate substitutes for this fullness. Their failure intimates that as metaphysical creatures, one of the temporal possibilities that human beings seek—with the full freedom to reject it—is the specifically eternal dimension of experience, manifest in but transcending time.

That is what at least a century of steadily accelerating and ever more pervasive metaphysical exhortation, in higher education and cultural programming alike, has claimed we must reject above all. The acolytes of this metaphysics labor to recreate (or decreate) a world; they are inclined to repudiate not only the past but the transcendence of time in all forms (Platonic and otherwise), and above all God. Péguy recognized this gathering imperative already in Renan, then in the bourgeois intellectual culture of the early twentieth century. Much closer to our own time, Richard Rorty acknowledged the ongoing prominence of this campaign over the course of the last century: "The objective is de-divinization." That is, "to de-divinize nature, de-divinize language; de-divinize science; de-divinize society."[6]

Yet in Renan and many after him, the death of God and "de-divinization" does not end with itself; it is often assumed that it incurs the death of human being. A time without agency or hope, interminably linear and supersessive rather than integrated or open to anything beyond itself, moves toward a complete repudiation aimed not only at all metaphysical alternatives to itself, but at ourselves as well.

Happily, the language of convergent modern intellectual ambitions is not the whole of language, still less of life; in Péguy's terms, the map is not the territory. Yet one can find these affiliated repudiations today in the garrulous contributions of post-humanists, antihumanists, and transhumanists, as well as in portentous "interventions" against a somehow invariably "naïve" humanism. Without and within them, we find inhuman intimations in the imperatives of our language, in comprehensive markets and technologies and the metaphysics to which they habituate us, surrounding yet dogged by seething, frequently vicious reactionaries. Amid all the powers that reject the full dimensions of human being, it seems nothing less than a divine love and rational infinity can turn the advocates of modern metaphysics from a persistent if persistently frustrated ambition to be "true" to the repudiation of loving the truth, amid a dual destitution of language and time. To use the language of crisis (and all ages have their own great crises) it is this crisis of destitution that Péguy saw gathering around him—metaphysical in origin, manifest in language and time, expressed through the most varied aspects of our lives. It is with us still.

Péguy offers us a different way, for in our world, time and language are never spent. The multiplicity of time grows into the present, even as different times abide, pasts and futures and eternity coming together in all the perpetually vanishing presents when we act. A patient and mystical courage allows us to live, act, speak, and write freely in those presents, relating to pasts, presents, futures, and the transcendence of time neither as moderns nor as antimoderns, but integratively, as amoderns—that is, to love, lucidly, whenever and wherever we meet what is worthy of love. That love includes the real and ongoing goods of late modernity, but is not bound by supersessive and linear historical time. There are insights and actions from very different human pasts, richer than many of our histories, ready to give themselves to us; there are very different human futures that will not acknowledge us in the slightest—and that need us to offer them whatever good we can. As participants in that revolution, once more attuned to the integrative plenitude of time, we can listen anew to the native tongues of a universal hope.

NOTES

INTRODUCTION

1. For example, Charles Maurras supported the traditional authority of Catholicism without any religious faith. This would be the ground for the condemnation of his movement Action Française by the Vatican in 1926.

2. This is close to but somewhat different from Péguy's "mécontemporains." That term emphasizes the independence of Péguy and others from their contemporaries, rather than placing the emphasis (as Péguy certainly does in different passages throughout his work) upon an independence of judgment in relation to the imperatives of modern culture and its preeminent "construals," either progressive or reactionary in nature. For the reference to "mécontemporains," see Charles Péguy, *Oeuvres complètes*, ed. Robert Burac, 4 vols. (Paris: Gallimard, Bibliothèque de la Pléiade, 1987–1992), vol. III, "Les Amis des cahiers," p. 344. Henceforth this source will be designated "OC," followed by volume number, manuscript title, and page number. Unless otherwise noted, all translations by all authors are my own. It is from this passage that Alain Finkielkraut drew the title for his book about Péguy, *Le Mécontemporain* (Paris: Gallimard, 1991).

3. See Walter Benjamin, "On the Image of Proust" (1929), in *Selected Writings, 1927–1930*, trans. Rodney Livingstone and others, ed. Michael W. Jennings, Howard Eiland, and Gary Smith (Cambridge, MA: Harvard University Press, 2005), vol. 2, part 1, p. 245. For the long-standing interest of Benjamin in Péguy's writing, see his letters to Ernst Schoen, Gershom Scholem, and Hugo von Hofmannsthal between 1919 and 1927, published in *L'Amitié Charles Péguy*, no. 9, January–March 1980.

4. See Walter Benjamin, "The Present Social Situation of the French Writer" (1934), in *Selected Writings, 1931–1934*, vol. 2, part 2, p. 750. Benjamin adds that the phrase that begins with "enemies of the laws" is a reference to the title of a book by Maurice Barrès.

5. Gershom Scholem, *Fidélité et utopie* (Paris: Calmann-Lévy, 1978), p. 90. See *L'Amitié Charles Péguy*, no. 9, January–March 1980. A translated version of the same general argument about Péguy can be found in an article adapted from a lecture given by Scholem to the World Jewish Congress in 1966, printed in *Commentary*, November 1966.

6. See Hans Urs von Balthasar, *The Glory of the Lord: A Theological Aesthetics*, vol. III: *Studies in Theological Style: Lay Styles*, trans. Andrew Louth, John Saward, Martin Simon, and Rowan Williams (San Francisco: Ignatius Press, 1986), in particular the chapter devoted to Péguy, pp. 400–517.

7. See Henri de Lubac, *The Drama of Atheist Humanism*, trans. Edith Riley and Anne Nash (San Francisco: Ignatius, 1995), p. 92. Originally published as *Le Drame de l'humanisme athée*, Paris, 1944.

8. Charles Taylor, *A Secular Age* (Cambridge, MA: Harvard University Press, 2007), p. 745.

9. See Julian Jackson, *De Gaulle* (London: Haus, 2003), p. 10. See also de Gaulle's remarks to Alain Peyrefitte on September 9, 1964, published in *L'Amitié Charles Péguy*, no. 53, January–March 1991, pp. 42–43, in which it is clear that this primacy of influence continued throughout his life.

10. See Léopold Senghor, "Charles Péguy et Léopold Sédar Senghor," in *Péguy-Senghor: La Parole et le monde*, ed. Jean Bastaire and Jean-François Durant (Paris: Harmattan, 1996), pp. 13–15.

11. Hannah Arendt, "Christianity and Revolution," *Nation*, 161, no. 12, September 22, 1945. Reprinted in *Essays in Understanding, 1930–1954* (New York: Schocken Books, 1994), p. 152.

12. Rachel Bespaloff, "The Humanism of Péguy," *Review of Politics*, December 1946, p. 92.

13. See Giles Deleuze, *Difference and Repetition*, trans. Paul Patton (New York: Columbia University Press, 1994).

14. Christopher Forth, *The Dreyfus Affair and the Crisis of French Manhood* (Baltimore: Johns Hopkins University Press, 2004), p. 241.

15. Ibid.

16. Ibid., p. 87.

17. Ibid., p. 136.

18. Ibid., p. 206.

19. The connections between Dreyfusism and antifascist resistance (or collaboration) were indeed quite complicated, but not in the way Forth assumes. For a careful study of the subject, see Simon Epstein, *Les Dreyfusards sous l'Occupation* (Paris: Albin Michel, 2001).

20. See OC, III, *Notre Jeunesse*, pp. 63–64.

21. Ibid., p. 57.

22. See, for example, *Oeuvres poétiques*, *"Le Mystère de la charité de Jeanne d'Arc,"* p. 426.

23. Vladimir Nabokov, *Lectures on Literature* (New York: Harcourt, 1980), p. 1. Nabokov's remarks about the nonsequential joys of painting over the temporal ones of, say, music are not mine; but the importance of exacting work with specific details and the need for passionate yet patient attention to them are in no way dependent upon this preference.

24. For a recent example of several historians working with this model, see *Confronting Modernity in Fin-de-Siècle France: Bodies, Minds and Gender*, ed. Christopher Forth and Elinor Accampo (New York: Palgrave Macmillan, 2010). While the contributors vary in emphasis and argument, there are abundant reference to crises and "anxieties" about traditional gender roles, social hierarchy, and sexuality throughout the text, and in some especially assertive passages by Elizabeth Williams, the epoch as a whole is said to be beset by, e.g., "high gender panic" (see p. 105, and a reference to "gender panic" on p. 91). Acknowledging the general explanatory model, in *Sexing the Citizen: Morality and Masculinity in France* (Ithaca, NY: Cornell University Press, 2006), Judith Surkis writes of how she intends to "displace the causal framework of 'crisis' that has been operative in much historical writing about gender and sexuality in turn-of-the-century France and fin-de-siècle European culture more generally" (p. 11). Yet the perception of "crisis" (and related "anxieties") within the Belle Époque is a central part of Surkis's argument, even if the word is, at least at first, often used with scare quotes that distance the author from the assessments of contemporaries reported to the reader with great regularity: see pp. 30, 43, 58–59, 60, 61, 63, 68, 75, 89, 102, 116, 121, etc. More important, even

as Surkis presumably hopes to leave behind or critique the contemporary *perception* of crisis, she subsequently endorses an account of crisis and anxiety, e.g., her discussion of "political and financial crisis" in the late nineteenth century in which, at the same moment, as "historians have well indicated . . . the 'new woman' embodied a perceived threat to a well-organized and regulated social order," and furthermore, "anxieties" about homosexuality were entwined with "the socialization of . . . citizens" (pp. 70–72). "Anxiety" subsequently appears as a way for Surkis to describe and even to explain the interest in reforming education (followed by the now traditional claim that two opposed groups moved within a matrix of anxieties that gave boundaries to a debate without its participants being aware of it—see p. 103), and other anxieties appear elsewhere, including ones about depopulation and unmarried men (see pp. 113 and 121). Surkis rightly acknowledges that much of the standard model has become tired, but her own approach does little more than suggest a slightly altered configuration of the cultural and political background for the long-standing account of crises and anxieties connected to identity, in particular sexual identities, at the turn of the last century. It should be said that all ages have their crises, including the Belle Époque; but these crises were not precisely what many historians have assumed them to be, nor were their "solutions" as clear as they imagine.

25. See Peter Gordon's response to Brad Gregory's *Unintended Reformation* entitled, "Has Modernity Failed?" at *Imminent Frame*, September 12, 2013: http://blogs.ssrc.org/tif/2013/09/12 /has-modernity-failed/?disp=print.

26. This has never received a more didactic, polemical formulation than in Foucault's *Preface to Anti-Oedipus*, though of course it also found expression in Lyotard's *Postmodern Condition*. These texts obviously no longer command the partisan energies that they once did, but that is precisely my point: this general sensibility (rather than specifically Foucaultian, Deleuzeian, and Lyotardian claims) has been assimilated into a standard model that takes this background for granted. That someone like Foucault emphasizes that knowledge and power produce subjects is a decidedly unpersuasive objection to this claim; with the partial exception of his late lectures at the Collège de France, a Foucaultian account makes the subject a perishable artifact of power and knowledge in time, that can abolish or cancel the subject it itself so recently and fortuitously produced.

27. George Steiner, "Drumming on the Doors," *Times Literary Supplement*, no. 4682, December 25, 1992.

28. See Sarah Hammerschlag, *The Figural Jew: Politics and Identity in Postwar French Thought* (Chicago: University of Chicago Press, 2010), pp. 55–62; quote on p. 57.

29. Ibid., p. 59.

30. See the reference to "la plupart des Juifs aussi firent leur devoir de solidarité," OC, I, *L'Épreuve*, p. 52.

31. OC, III, *Notre Jeunesse*, pp. 50–51. Annette Aronowicz has argued this point very persuasively. See *Jews and Christians on Time and Eternity* (Stanford, CA: Stanford University Press, 1998).

32. From OC, *Oeuvres poétiques*, *Le Porche du mystère de la deuxième vertu*, p. 666. One indication of its renown is its presence on the opening page of the excerpt from Péguy in the 1990s *Penguin Book of French Poetry, 1820–1950* (London: Penguin, 1991).

33. OC, III, *Note conjointe*, p. 1293.

34. See the reference in the book's concluding sentence to the need to "develop a hospitable politics that does not depend on the homogenizing rhetoric of humanism." Hammerschlag, p. 267.

35. OC, III, *Notre Jeunesse*, p. 50.

36. Ibid., p. 135.

37. Ibid., p. 74.

38. Hammerschlag, p. 65. OC, III, *Notre Jeunesse*, p. 64.

39. OC, III, *Notre Jeunesse*, pp. 93 and 95. For more on the cited passage on p. 95, see Chapter 7, footnote 30.

40. For example, for Péguy, mysticism is "the invincible strength of the weak" (OC, III, *Notre Jeunesse*, p. 66). For Péguy's account of Bernard-Lazare's religious convictions, see *Notre Jeunesse*, p. 64; Péguy's own attitude toward the explicitly political positions (i.e., not related to doctrine) of many Catholic clergy can be found on p. 21.

41. OC, III, *Notre Jeunesse*, p. 40. Italics in original text.

42. Ibid., pp. 82 (on universal justice) and 95 (its specific application to both Muslim and Christian societies). The very partial interpretation Hammerschlag offers of Péguy also omits the intense and explicit admiration for him expressed by one of her book's heroes, Maurice Blanchot. For Blanchot in turn, it is Péguy who is a hero; in Blanchot's words, Péguy is a "peerless writer" and a "master and a model of greatness." See Blanchot's article in *Journal des débats*, May 4, 1941, in a collection of Blanchot's writing, Maurice Blanchot, *Into Disaster: Chronicles of Intellectual Life, 1941*, trans. Michael Holland (New York: Fordham University Press, 2014), p. 20. Given that Blanchot wrote and published this encomium to Péguy during the war (when the Resistance and to some extent groups within the Vichy Regime were both trying to claim Péguy as their own), it is of course possible that this was an attempt to make his way through a complicated period in literary politics rather than to express a sincerely held intellectual conviction. Yet the precise manner in which Blanchot singled out Péguy for praise shows that he admired him, and further, for qualities that lead Hammerschlag to commend Blanchot to her readers. For Blanchot, as he wrote in the *Journal des débats* in the summer of 1941, Péguy reveals movement and multiple perspectives at once. His "very complicated" life is like a page that "must be turned and read on both sides." That life is "double but without the least trace of duplicity." In Blanchot's account, this is nowhere more evident than in Péguy's penchant for leaving blank spaces in his writing, always leaving more writing to be done, leaving space for silence that "invites" the presence of the inaccessible (as Blanchot observes, for the late Péguy this is the space for revelation). Péguy is patiently at peace with the "multiplication of signs" and is at once a writer capable of personal identification (writing robustly in the first person would be just one example) and of standing both within and outside his identity as a person and as a writer. See, for these passages, Maurice Blanchot, "Solitudes de Péguy," *Journal des débats*, June 30–July 1, 1941.

43. See Jules Isaac, *Jésus et Israël* (Paris: Albin Michel, 1948).

44. John Connelly, *From Enemy to Brother: The Revolution in Catholic Teaching on the Jews, 1933–1965* (Cambridge, MA: Harvard University Press, 2012), p. 143. Connelly offers no citation of this letter. No other writing by or about Péguy is cited in the book.

45. OC, III, *Dialogue de l'histoire et de l'âme charnelle*, p. 778.

46. Romain Rolland, *Péguy*, vol. II (Paris: Albin Michel, 1944), pp. 249–250.

47. Connelly, p. 182.

48. Ibid.

49. Ibid., p. 183.

50. Lazare Prajs, *Péguy et Israël* (Paris: Editions A.-G. Nizet, 1970), pp. 162–163. Prajs acknowledges Bloy's and Péguy's shared interest in the relationship of Judaism and Christianity, but unlike Connelly, he precisely sets forth the many ways in which the two men starkly differed, both personally and intellectually.

NOTES TO PAGES 18–28

51. *Charles Péguy: Lettres et entretiens*, ed. Marcel Péguy (Paris: Éditions de Paris, 1954), p. 144.

52. William C. Wimsatt, *Re-Engineering Philosophy for Limited Beings: Piecewise Approximations to Reality* (Cambridge, MA: Harvard University Press, 2007), p. 339.

53. See Rebecca Goldstein, *Incompleteness: The Proof and Paradox of Kurt Gödel* (New York: Norton, 2005).

54. See Loren Graham and Jean-Michel Kantor, *Naming Infinity* (Cambridge, MA: Harvard University Press, 2009).

55. The term appears in OC, *Oeuvres poétiques*, *Le Porche*, p. 633.

56. For more on Marxism and non-Marxist French socialism, see Tony Judt, *Marxism and the French Left* (New York: New York University Press, 2011).

57. All of these names can be found on the pages of subscriber's lists in the Archives Charles Péguy; Péguy handwrote *Notre Jeunesse* on the back of them. See the handwritten manuscript of *Notre Jeunesse*, Archives Charles Péguy, Orléans, France.

58. OC, II, *Par Ce Demi-clair Matin*, p. 92. The list appears with some modifications on p. 95. For example, northern Italy is there considered free but the south less so, and parts of the United States are free but others less so (this may well be a reference to the Jim Crow South, but there is no clarification in the text).

59. See Charles Péguy to Henri Bergson, March 2, 1914; quoted in Prajs, pp. 200–201.

60. Péguy spoke of a "deepening" of his thinking but not a rupture or an "evolution." See OC, III, *Un Nouveau Théologien*, pp. 549–550. See also, in the same volume, *Notre Jeunesse*, p. 42 and pp. 66–67.

61. Hence Péguy writes of revolution as a continual "deepening," a "renewal" and an integrative movement: see OC, I, *Avertissement*, from the *Cahiers*, March 1904, pp. 1305–1307.

62. Metaphysics is of course a term variously defined, from Aristotle to Thomas Aquinas to Kant and Heidegger. For Péguy and others, it refers to questions of ultimate origins and ends, including questions of meaning, being, value, good and evil, and truth, i.e., what is "after" or "beyond" the domain of scientific and demonstrable knowledge. He believes it is simply not possible to think and live with no assumptions and conclusions about these questions; nor is it possible to have certain and secure (rather than probabilistic) foundations for one's conclusions, whether they are "positive" or "negative," "high" or "low."

63. I am grateful to David Beecher for our conversations about the relation between origins and originality.

CHAPTER 1

1. See William Sewell, *Work and Revolution in France* (Cambridge: Cambridge University Press, 1980), p. 269.

2. Émile Durkheim, *On Morality and Society*, ed. Robert Bellah (Chicago: University of Chicago Press, 1973), p. 12, from *Sociology in France in the Nineteenth Century*. Originally published in the *Revue Bleue*, 4th series, 13, no. 20, 1900.

3. Ibid., "The Division of Labor in Society," pp. 145–146.

4. Ibid.

5. Raoul Frary, *La Question du Latin* (Paris: Cerf, 1885), pp. 2–15; quotation on p. 15.

6. *Lettres aux instituteurs: Jean Jaurès, François Guizot, Jules Ferry* (Paris: Calmann-Lévy, 2007), p. 23.

7. Ibid., pp. 33–37.

8. Ibid., pp. 35–40.

9. Jean Jaurès, "Le Socialisme et le radicalisme en 1885," *Discours parlementaires* (Paris: Cornély, 1904), p. 28. Quoted in Pierre Barral, "Ferry et Gambetta face au positivisme," *Romantisme*, 8, 1978, no. 21–22, p. 153.

10. See Barral, no. 21–22, pp. 151–155. Quote on p. 152.

11. Michael Gane, *French Social Theory* (Los Angeles: Sage, 2003), pp. 37–38.

12. Terry Clark, *Prophets and Patrons: The French University and the Emergence of the Social Sciences* (Cambridge, MA: Harvard University Press, 1973), p. 103.

13. For Durkheim, Comte's stages of history, for example, lacked "the slightest causal relationship," and his third positive stage was "purely arbitrary." See Durkheim, *The Rules of Sociological Method*, in *The Rules of Sociological Method and Selected Texts on Sociology and Its Method*, ed. Steven Lukes, trans. W. D. Halls (New York: Macmillan, 1983), p. 140.

14. Jacqueline Lalouette, *La France de la Belle Époque* (Paris: Tallandier, 2013), p. 19.

15. See OC, I, *Réponse brève à Jaurès*, p. 555.

16. OC, II, *Il ne faut pas dire* (written in 1906), p. 566.

17. OC, II, *Un Poète l'a dit*, 828.

18. Ernest Renan, *L'Avenir de la science* (Paris: Flammarion, 1995), pp. 89–90.

19. Ibid., pp. 164, 237–238, 241–242, 299.

20. Ibid., pp. 96, 105–107. See also p. 164. Capital letters removed from a phrase within the quoted passage.

21. Ibid., p. 166.

22. Ibid., p. 117.

23. Ibid., pp. 127–128, 136–137.

24. Ibid., p. 122.

25. Ibid., pp. 291, 360, 370–371, and 375.

26. Ibid., pp. 114, 333–336.

27. Ibid., pp. 256–257.

28. Ibid., pp. 127–128.

29. Ibid., pp. 269–278. Quoted passage on p. 276.

30. Ibid., p. 275.

31. Ibid., p. 304, 197–198.

32. Ibid., pp. 490–491.

33. Ibid., pp. 247–253.

34. Ibid., p. 229.

35. Ibid., p. 402.

36. *Émile Durkheim: On Morality and Society*, ed. Robert Bellah, p. 22, from *Sociology in the Nineteenth Century*.

37. Durkheim, *The Rules of Sociological Method* in Lukes, ed., p. 72. Italics removed from original.

38. For respectful, critical references to Descartes in coverage of neuroscience in the Belle Époque, see Alfred Dastre, "Le Système nerveux: Doctrines et théories récentes," *Revue des deux mondes*, April 1900, pp. 682 and 685. For the poem addressed to Descartes, see Sully Prudhomme, "Descartes," *Revue de métaphysique et de morale*, 5, no. 1, January 1897, pp. 1–4.

39. René Descartes, *Oeuvres et lettres*, ed. André Bridoux (Paris: Gallimard, Pléiade, 1953), *Discours de la méthode*, pp. 132–138, 168–169.

40. "The Contribution of Sociology to Psychology and Philosophy," from *Revue de métaphysique et de morale*, 17, 1909, pp. 754–58. Included in Durkheim, *The Rules of Sociological Method and Selected Texts on Sociology and Its Method*, esp. 237.

41. Ibid.

42. Quoted in Fabien Robertson, "Durkheim: Entre religion et morale" in *Revue de Mauss*, no. 2, 2003, pp. 126–143, paragraph 2. Available online at https://www.cairn.info/revue-du-mauss-2003-2-page-126.htm. The quote is taken from Durkheim's *Cours de science sociale*.

43. Émile Durkheim, "The Division of Labor in Society," in *On Morality and Society*, ed. Robert Bellah (Chicago: University of Chicago Press, 1973), pp. 123 and 137.

44. "Debate on Explanation in History and Sociology" (1908), in Durkheim, *The Rules of Sociological Method and Selected Texts on Sociology and Its Method*, p. 212. Durkheim believes these causes can be determined "after the event" but not in the manner of Bergson and Péguy; rather he seeks answers through what he understands to be objective scientific investigation.

45. OC, III, *L'Argent*, p. 788.

46. Ibid.

47. See Peter Dear, *Revolutionizing the Sciences: European Knowledge and Its Ambitions, 1500–1700* (Princeton: Princeton University 2001), p. 61.

48. Descartes, *Discours de la méthode*, p. 168.

49. Julien Offroy de La Mettrie, *L'Homme-Machine* (Paris: Denoël, 1981), pp. 212–213.

50. See Immanuel Kant, *Kritik der praktischen Vernunft* (Frankfurt: Suhrkamp, 1974), especially the short chapter "Die Unsterblichkeit der Seele" with its references to an "unendliche Progressus" and an "unendliche gehenden Fortschritte" on pages 252–254.

51. Immanuel Kant, "The End of All Things," in *Perpetual Peace and Other Essays*, trans. Ted Humphrey (Indianapolis: Hackett, 1983), p. 103.

52. See Ludwig Feuerbach, *Das Wesen des Christentums* (Stuttgart: Reclam, 1969), especially the concluding peroration on pp. 400–411, where the sacred confers lasting meaning upon matter, as an atheistic religion of humanity is upheld throughout.

53. See Marilynne Robinson, *Absence of Mind* (New Haven: Yale University Press, 2010), pp. 38–42, and the chapter devoted to Comte in Henri de Lubac's *Drama of Atheist Humanism*, trans. Edith Riley, Anne Nash, and Mark Sebanc (London: Sheed and Ward, 1949).

54. See Friedrich Nietzsche, *Posthumous Fragments*, Summer–Fall 1884, 26 (412), http://www.nietzschesource.org/#eKGWB/NF-1884,26[412].

55. See Robertson, quotation from "Durkheim," paragraph 4. Italics in original.

56. See Durkheim, *The Rules of Sociological Method*, ed. Lukes, pp. 36 and 72. Italics removed.

57. See Célestin Bouglé, Introduction to *Émile Durkheim: Sociologie et philosophie* (Paris: Presses Universitaires de France, 2014), pp. xlviii. Originally published in 1924. Bouglé was well known for qualifying certain Durkheimian ideas: see W. Paul Vogt, "Un Durkheimien Ambivalent: Célestin Bouglé," in *Revue française de sociologie*, 20, no. 1, 1979, pp. 123–139.

58. Émile Durkheim, *The Elementary Forms of Religious Life*, trans. Carol Cosman (Oxford: Oxford World's Classics, 2001), p. 5.

59. François Simiand, "Méthode historique et science sociale," *Revue de synthèse historique*, 1903. The entire text can be found at http://www.uqac.uquebec.ca/zone30/Classiques_des_sciences_sociales/index.html: page numbers are taken from this edition, pp. 1–22; citation from p. 13.

60. See the "Debate on Explanation in History and Sociology," with Durkheim, Seigno-bos, Bouglé, and others as participants, in Durkheim, *The Rules of Sociological Method and Selected Texts on Sociology and its Method*, pp. 211–228.

61. Simiand, pp. 9–10.

62. Ibid.

63. Ibid., p. 13. Italics removed.

64. Ibid., pp. 14–17, especially pp. 16–17; italics removed.

65. Ibid., p. 19.

66. Ibid., pp. 19–20.

67. Ibid., pp. 20.

68. See Léon Walras, *Études de l'économie sociale* (Paris: Pichou, 1896), pp. 8–16.

69. The quote appears in ibid., p. 29; for similar remarks, see also pp. 49 and 140.

70. See Gustave Lanson, *L'Université et la société moderne* (Paris: Armand Colin, 1902), p. 58; on Langlois and Seignobos, see Glenn Roe, *The Passion of Charles Péguy* (Oxford: Oxford University Press, 2014), p. 116.

71. Lanson, p. 98. For an implicit reference to the security of the nation vis-à-vis Germany, see p. 7.

72. Gustave Lanson, "L'Histoire littéraire et la sociologie," *Revue de métaphysique et de morale*, 12, 1904, p. 622. Quoted in Roe, p. 147.

73. Alfred Dastre, "Le Système nerveux," *Revue des deux mondes*, April 1900, pp. 669–670.

74. Ibid., pp. 671–672.

75. Ibid., p. 664.

76. Ibid., pp. 678–679.

77. Théodule Ribot, *Les maladies de la mémoire* (Paris, 1881).

78. Théodule Ribot, *Les maladies de la mémoire*, 18th ed. (Paris: Alcan, 1906).

79. See Dastre's references to researchers from many countries working on neurological questions, e.g., pp. 677, 680 (including Wilhelm Wundt), 683, 687, and 688.

80. Clark, p. 29.

81. Ibid., pp. 45–47.

82. Ibid., pp. 166–169.

83. Ibid., p. 169.

84. Ibid., p. 27.

85. See Émile Durkheim, *L'Évolution pédagogique en France*, introduction by Maurice Halbwachs (Paris: Presses Universitaires de France, 2014), p. 1. See also Roe, p. 60.

86. See Lukes's introduction to *Durkheim: The Rules of Sociological Method and Selected Texts on Sociology and Its Method*, p. 9.

87. Fritz Ringer, *Fields of Knowledge: French Academic Culture in Comparative Perspective 1890–1920* (Cambridge: Cambridge University Press, 1992), pp. 43–47.

88. See Marcel Fournier, *Marcel Mauss*, trans. Jane Marie Todd (Princeton: Princeton University Press, 2006), pp. 65–67.

89. Voltaire, *Lettres Philosophiques*; critical edition with an introduction and commentary by Gustave Lanson, vol. I (Paris: Cornély, 1909), introduction, p. l; italics in original text. For a further discussion of the controversy about Lanson's methods and this edition of Voltaire in particular, see Ringer, pp. 240 and 244.

90. Ringer, pp. 178–179, 187–188.

91. Quoted in ibid., p. 125.

92. Quoted in Fournier, p. 140. Massis was occasionally associated with Péguy as well, but ultimately joined the anti-Bergsonian, broadly Maurrasian current in French intellectual life. See Burac, pp. 257 and 289. While the authors (and their interviewees) praise Péguy in their book, they include an anti-Semitic reference to the "Jewish party" becoming ascendant after the Dreyfus Affair (not at all Péguy's interpretation of the same event), along with the admiring references to Maurras. See "Agathon," *Les Jeunes Gens d'aujourd'hui* (Paris: Plon, 1913), p. 234.

93. *France and the Dreyfus Affair: A Documentary History*, ed. Michael Burns (Boston: Bedford/St. Martin's, 1999), p. 8.

94. Ibid., p. 8; speech by Maurice Barrès, November 1, 1898. From Maurice Barrès, *Scènes et doctrines du nationalisme* (Paris: Juven, 1902), 432–434. Trans. Michael Burns.

95. It might be, as one historian has argued, that "Judeophobia" and "anti-Semitism" were not as politically influential in this period as some had previously thought, but certainly as *both* shared assumptions among radical right-wing movements with an ominous future, and as increasingly visible and toxic forces in French literary culture, it is impossible to deny their power. See Steven Englund, "Antisemitism, Judeophobia, and the Republic," in *The French Republic: History, Values, Debates*, ed. E. Berenson, V. Duclert, and C. Porochasson (Ithaca, NY: Cornell University Press, 2011), pp. 278–288.

96. See William D. Irvine, *The Boulanger Affair Reconsidered: Royalism, Boulangism, and the Origins of the Radical Right in France* (Oxford: Oxford University Press, 1989).

97. As stated in *La Libre Parole*, May 23, 1892. In Burns, p. 11.

98. See Paula Hyman, *The Jews of Modern France* (Berkeley: University of California Press, 1998), p. 96.

99. See Édouard Drumont, *La France Juive* (Paris: Marpon and Flammarion, 1886), pp. 5–7.

100. Drumont, pp. 51, 190, and 422.

101. Charles Maurras, *L'Avenir de l'intelligence*, 2nd ed. (Paris: Albert Fontemoing, 1905), p. 135–37.

102. Ibid., p. 22.

103. Ibid., pp. 222, 233.

104. Ibid., p. 222.

105. Ibid., pp. 71–73, 77, 87, and 84.

106. Ibid., p. 54.

107. Ibid., p. 98.

108. Ibid., p. 235. See the readings of poems by Renée Vivien, the Comtesse de Noailles, Madame de Régnier, and Lucie Delarue-Mardus on pp. 157–221. Maurras is aesthetically sensitive to their talents—at one point, he claims that Vivien's poetry is in some ways superior to Baudelaire's (see pp. 173 and 177)—but there is no doubt that for Maurras (with a partial exception for Régnier) all these poets express the cultural sensibility he decries.

109. Ibid., p. 302.

110. Ibid., p. 15.

111. Ibid., p. 104.

112. Ibid., pp. 120–121.

113. Ibid., p. 105.

114. Ibid., pp. 115–116.

115. Ibid.

116. Ibid., p. 135.

117. Ibid., pp. 122–132, especially 124–125.

118. Ibid., p. 135.

119. Gaston Milhaud, "La Science rationelle," *Revue de métaphysique et de morale*, 4, no. 3, May 1896, pp. 280–281.

120. Ibid., p. 288.

121. See Alan Burdick, *Why Time Flies* (New York: Simon and Schuster, 2017), pp. 10–14.

122. Milhaud, p. 282. Italics in original.

123. Ibid., pp. 285–286.

124. Ibid., p. 292.

125. Ibid., pp. 286.

126. Ibid., p. 298.

127. Ibid, p. 293.

128. Ibid., p. 302.

129. Ibid., pp. 301 and 292.

130. Ibid., p. 301.

131. See Peter Galison, *Einstein's Clocks, Poincaré's Maps* (New York: Norton, 2003), pp. 62–75.

132. Henri Poincaré, "Sur les Principes de la mécanique," from *Bibliothèque du Congrès International de philosophie* III (Paris, 1901), pp. 457–494, in Galison, pp. 199–200. As Galison points out, the passage in altered form would find its way into Poincaré's *La Science et l'hypothèse*.

133. Henri Poincaré, *La Science et l'hypothèse* (Paris: Flammarion, 1968), pp. 64–65. Originally published in 1902.

134. Ibid., p. 65.

135. Ibid., pp. 25 (for quoted passage) and 245–250.

136. Ibid., p. 158.

137. Pierre Duhem, *La Théorie physique: Son Objet, sa structure* (Paris: Brouzeng, 1906), pp. 221–222. Italics in original. Quoted in Anastasios Brenner, *Les Origines françaises de la philosophie des sciences* (Paris: Presses Universitaires de France, 2003), p. 53.

138. Ibid., p. 197. Italics in original. Cited (including quoted passage) in Brenner, p. 54.

139. Pierre Duhem, *L'Expérience de physique,* in *La Théorie physique: Son Objet, sa structure* online (Lyon: ENS Éditions, 2016), part I, paragraph 1: http://books.openedition.org/enseditions/6921. Italics in original.

140. Brenner, p. 85.

141. On Péguy's admiration for Poincaré, see, e.g., OC, III, *Note conjointe*, p. 1470. For Poincaré and Péguy living close to one another, see OC, III, p. 1545, note for p. 201.

142. See Péguy's assessment of Duhem's work in OC, II, *Cahiers de la quinzaine*, February 3, 1907, pp. 652–653.

143. See Durkheim's account of his influences from November 1907 in ed. Lukes, p. 259. Translated from Émile Durkheim, and Simon Deploige, "A Propos Du Conflit de la morale et de la sociologie," *Revue Néo-scolastique* 14, no. 56 (1907): 606–21, esp. pp. 606–607 and 612–614.

144. Émile Boutroux, *Pascal* (Paris: Hachette, 1900), pp. 43–46.

145. Ibid.

146. Ibid., pp. 62, 145.

147. See Henri Bergson, *La Philosophie française* (Rennes: Éditions la Part Commune, 2017), pp. 37–38. Originally published in 1915.

148. Félix Ravaisson, "La Philosophie de Pascal," *Revue des deux mondes*, 80, 1887, pp. 399–428. Translated in *Félix Ravaisson*, ed. and trans. Mark Sinclair (London: Bloomsbury, 2016), p. 258.

149. Ravaisson, "La Philosophie de Pascal," in Sinclair, p. 267.

150. Ibid., p. 266.

151. Félix Ravaisson, "Testament philosophique," *Révue de métaphysique et de morale*, 1901, pp. 1–31, expanded edition of 1933, trans. Jeremy Dunham and Mark Sinclair, in Sinclair, p. 304.

152. Ravaisson, "Metaphysics and Morals," *Révue de métaphysique et de morale*, 1893, pp. 6–25, in Sinclair, p. 279.

153. Ravaisson, "Testament philosophique," in Sinclair, p. 315.

154. Ibid., p. 316.

155. Ravaisson, "Metaphysics and Morals," p. 290.

156. OC, III, *Note sur M. Bergson*, p. 1253.

157. Romain Rolland, *Péguy*, vol. I (Paris: Albin Michel, 1944), p. 38.

158. Henri Bergson to Horace Kallen, trans. Tony Nuspl. See *The Reception of Pragmatism in France and the Rise of Roman Catholic Modernism, 1890–1914*, ed. David G. Schultenover, S.J. (Washington, DC: Catholic University Press, 2009), pp. 217–218.

159. For more on this notion, see Henri Gouhier, *Bergson dans l'histoire de la pensée occidentale* (Paris: Jean Vrin, 1989), pp. 29–33. For Bergson's account of how consciousness evolved for action, see *L'Évolution créatrice*, in *Oeuvres,* ed. André Robinet (Paris: Presses Universitaires de France, 1959). Upon the question of the ways in which this orientation toward action distorts our understanding of living reality, see p. 635, where we are "only at ease in the discontinuous, in the immobile, in the dead. *The intellect is characterized by a natural incomprehension of life.*" Italics in original.

160. Henri Bergson, *La Pensée et le mouvant*, in *Oeuvres*, ed. Robinet, pp. 1271–1272.

161. Henri Bergson to Horace Kallen, ed. Schultenover, p. 218.

162. Henri Bergson, *Essai sur les données immédiates de la conscience*, in *Oeuvres*, ed. Robinet, pp. 67 68.

163. See OC, III, *Note conjointe*, p. 1323; OC, II, *Un Poète l'a dit*, pp. 810, 887, and 1481, note 2 to p. 810.

164. Henri Bergson, *Matter and Memory*, trans. Nancy Paul and W. Scott Palmer (New York: Zone Books, 1996), p. 54. Here I use the English translation, because Bergson himself read and amended it (he was a native speaker of English by way of his English mother).

165. Ibid., p. 72.

166. Ibid., p. 94.

167. Ibid., p. 120.

168. See Alva Noë, *Out of Our Heads: Why You Are Not Your Brain and Other Lessons from the Biology of Consciousness* (New York: Hill and Wang, 2010). See also the broader review of some of the more extravagant claims made by cognitive neuroscientists in David Bentley Hart, *The Experience of God* (New Haven: Yale University Press, 2014).

169. Bergson, *Matter and Memory*, pp. 119–121.

170. Ibid., p. 126.

171. Ibid., p. 198.

172. Ibid., p. 103.

173. Ibid., p. 150.

174. Ibid., p. 205.

175. Ibid., p. 177.

176. Ibid., p. 227.

177. Ibid., p. 240.

178. Ibid., p. 231.

179. Ibid., p. 218.

180. Ibid., p. 244.

181. For more on Bergsonian intuition, see OC, Bergson, *La Pensée et le mouvant*, pp. 1271–1277. See also Frédéric Worms, "James and Bergson: Reciprocal Readings," in *The Reception of Pragmatism in France and the Rise of Roman Catholic Modernism, 1890–1914*, pp. 76–92, and Leszek Kolakowki, *Bergson* (Oxford: Oxford University Press, 1985), pp. 24–36.

182. OC, Bergson, *Essai sur les données immédiates de la conscience*, p. 85.

183. Ibid., p. 67.

184. Ibid., p. 109 and p. 113 for quoted passages (for a broader discussion of freedom and separation from conventional demarcations, temporal and otherwise, see pp. 109–113). For Bergson, habits and accounts of mind that insist upon the separation of "present" and "anterior"—or deny the existence of an integrating self—obscure this freedom.

185. Bergson, *Matter and Memory*, p. 249.

186. Ibid., pp. 222–223, 239, 249.

187. For further reflection on Bergson's claim about freedom, see Frédéric Worms, *Le Vocabulaire de Bergson* (Paris: Ellipses, 2013), pp. 60–63.

188. Lanson, *L'Université et la société moderne*, p. 48. In this passage, Lanson does express concern that these gifted scholars struggle to set appropriate academic expectations for students.

189. Henri Bergson, "La Spécialité," speech given on Prize Day at the Lycée d'Angers, August 3, 1882. Published in *La Politesse* (Paris: Rivages, 2014), pp. 45–54.

190. Jean Jaurès, *Histoire socialiste de la révolution française* (Paris: Éditions de la Librairie de l'Humanité, 1901–1908).

191. Ruth Harris, *The Dreyfus Affair: Politics, Emotion, and the Scandal of the Century* (New York: Henry Holt, 2010), p. 189.

192. The manifesto was published in *Le Matin* as "Un Appel pour la culture classique." See *Le Matin*, August 24, 1911.

193. Henri Poincaré, *Les Sciences et les humanités* (Paris: Fayard, 1911), pp. 7–13.

194. Ibid, pp. 21–24.

195. Ibid., pp. 25–32.

196. It was a speech for the occasion marking the "Prix du Concours général" in summer 1895. See Henri Bergson, "Le bon sens et les études classiques," in "La Politesse" (Paris: Éditions Payot et Rivages, 2014), p. 56.

197. Ibid., pp. 69.

198. Ibid., pp. 70.

199. Ibid., pp. 70–71.

200. Ibid., pp 61 and 68.

201. Ibid., p 73.

202. Ibid., pp. 71–72.

203. Ibid. pp. 74–77 (p. 77 includes the quoted passage).

204. Ibid., p. 77.

205. Ibid., pp. 74–76.

206. See Edward Berenson, *The Trial of Madame Caillaux* (Berkeley: University of California Press, 1993), pp. 227–232.

207. Michael B. Palmer, *Des Petits Journaux aux grandes agences: Naissance du journalisme moderne, 1863–1914* (Paris: Aubier, 1983), table 3, pp. 324–328. Totals tabulated from a table indicating circulation figures for French newspapers in November 1910.

208. Gustave Flaubert, *L'Éducation sentimentale* (Paris: Pocket, 1998). Originally published in 1869.

209. Maurice Barrès, *Les Déracinés* (Paris: Émile Paul, 1911). Originally published in 1897.

CHAPTER 2

1. OC, II, *De la Situation faite au parti intellectuel dans le monde moderne devant les accidents de la gloire temporelle,* pp. 765–766.

2. Géraldi Leroi, *Péguy entre l'ordre et la révolution* (Paris: Presses de la Fondation Nationale des Sciences Politiques, 1981), p. 29.

3. Marjorie Villiers, *Charles Péguy* (London: Collins, 1965), first illustration (a reproduction of a watercolor by Péguy), facing page 33.

4. Ibid., 19–20.

5. Félicien Challaye, *Péguy socialiste* (Paris: Amiot-Dumont, 1954), 15. See OC, Péguy, *Oeuvres poétiques,* 330.

6. Villiers, 19–20.

7. See Challaye, p. 15.

8. OC, III, *Note conjointe,* p. 1304.

9. Challaye, p. 15.

10. See Eugen Weber, *My France: Politics, Culture, Myth* (Cambridge, MA: Harvard University Press, 1991), pp. 227–229.

11. Jérôme et Jean Tharaud, *Notre Cher Péguy* (Paris: Plon, 1926), vol. I, p. 33.

12. OC, III, *L'Argent,* p. 817.

13. On Péguy's knowledge of German, see OC, III, p. 1565, note 1.

14. OC, III, *L'Argent,* p. 817.

15. For more on this history, see Archives Municipales: Histoires d'Orléans, "Orléans: d'une gare à l'autre," http://archives.orleans-metropole.fr/r/245/orleans-d-une-gare-a-l-autre/.

16. See the entry "Joan of Arc" in the *Catholic Encyclopedia* of 1917. Found at http://www.newadvent.org/cathen/08409c.htm.

17. See Owen Chadwick, *A History of the Popes, 1830–1914* (Oxford: Oxford University Press, 2003), p. 178.

18. See Félix Doupanloup, *Le Catéchisme chrétien ou un exposé de la doctrine de Jésus-Christ offert aux hommes du monde* (Paris: Blanchard, 1865). For Péguy's turning to this catechism late in life, see OC, III, *Un Nouveau Théologien* (1911), p. 399. For more on the catechism, see Prajs, pp. 21–28.

19. Dupanloup, *Le Catéchisme chrétien.*

20. See Pierre Birnbaum, *The Anti-Semitic Moment,* trans. Jane Marie Todd (Chicago: University of Chicago Press, 2003), pp. 74–82.

21. For Péguy's account of this similarity in difference, see OC, III, *L'Argent,* p. 810.

22. G. Bruno (the pseudonym of Augustine Fouillée), *Le Tour de France par deux enfants: Devoir et patrie* (Paris: Eugène Belin, 1888). First edition published in 1877.

23. Villiers, pp. 36–37.

24. Ibid., pp. 37–38.

25. Centre Charles Péguy, Folder Number 909. "La Morale est-elle indépendante de la métaphysique?" Essay at Lycée Lakanal, 1891–1892.

26. Robert Burac, *Péguy: La Révolution et la grâce* (Paris: Laffont, 1994), p. 73.

27. Péguy expresses this point in an early *Cahier*: see OC, I, *Réponse brève à Jaurès*, p. 550.

28. OC, I, *Cahiers de la quinzaine*, April 4, 1901, p. 729. The structure of Péguy's phrase took on a life of its own up to the present, and quoted freely or adapted to different situations, is frequently quoted by journalists and activists.

29. Challaye, *Péguy socialiste*, pp. 29–30, 40.

30. Tharaud, vol. I, pp. 64–65.

31. Quotes taken from a letter from Péguy to Paul Collier, May 11, 1895, quoted in Challaye, p. 38. Description of student activities taken from Burac, pp. 62–64.

32. Ibid., p. 41.

33. See John Stanley, *The Sociology of Virtue: The Political and Social Theories of George Sorel* (Berkeley: University of California Press, 1981), esp. p. 278.

34. OC, I, extracts from Jaurès in *La Préparation du congrès socialiste national*, p. 385.

35. Jean Jaurès, "De la Réalité du monde sensible," in *Rallumer tous les soleils*, ed. Jean-Pierre Rioux (Paris: Omnibus, 2006) pp. 133–134.

36. OC, I, extracts from Jaurès in *La Préparation du congrès socialiste national*, p. 385.

37. For more on Cousin's influence in nineteenth-century French education, see Jan Goldstein, *The Post-Revolutionary Self* (Cambridge, MA: Harvard University Press, 2005).

38. OC, I, extracts from Jaurès in *La Préparation du congrès socialiste national*, p. 385.

39. See Tharaud, vol. I, pp. 73–137, recounting Péguy's friendships in an often heroizing mode during his student days, prior to his involvement in the Dreyfus affair; for another example, see Péguy's meeting with Jules Isaac in Villiers, pp. 46–47.

40. In fact, Péguy loved Corneille's *Polyeucte* in particular. His interest will be discussed at greater length later.

41. Quoted in Villiers, p. 71.

42. Tharaud, vol. I, pp. 145–147.

43. Challaye, p. 87.

44. Burac, p. 78.

45. As noted in Peter J. Bernardi, *Maurice Blondel, Social Catholicism and Action Française* (Washington, DC: Catholic University Press, 2009), p. 13, note 23.

46. Interview with Pope Leo XIII, *Le Figaro*, March 15, 1899, p. 1. The pope described Dreyfus's situation this way: "Fortunate is the victim that God recognizes as sufficiently just to liken his case to that of his own sacrificed Son."

47. Bernardi, pp. 9–28, especially pp. 9–15.

48. See Robert Gildea, *Children of the Revolution: The French, 1799–1914* (Cambridge, MA: Harvard University Press, 2008), p. 362.

49. See Frédéric Gugelot, *La Conversion des intellectuels au catholicisme en France, 1885–1935* (Paris: CNRS, 2010).

50. Burac, p. 91; Villiers, pp. 96–99.

51. Tharaud, vol. I, pp. 162–166.

52. Burac. p. 91. OC, *Oeuvres poétiques, Jeanne d'Arc*, p. 27.

53. OC, *Oeuvres poétiques, Jeanne d'Arc*, p. 27.

54. OC, I, *Marcel, De la Cité harmonieuse*, p. 56. See also OC, III, *Notre jeunesse*, p. 104.

55. OC, I, *Marcel, De la Cité harmonieuse*, p. 95. For more on the connection between Péguy and these distinctively French socialisms, see Géraldi Leroy, *Péguy entre ordre et la révolution* (Paris: Presses de la Fondation Nationale des Sciences Politiques, 1981), pp. 82–85.

56. OC, I, "Les Récentes Oeuvres de Zola," *Le Mouvement socialiste*, November 1–15, 1899, pp. 260–263.

57. OC, I, "Compte rendu de congrès," p. 790.

58. Ibid., pp. 796.

59. For the reference to women and children, see Tharaud, vol. I, pp. 29–30.

60. OC, I, from Péguy's handwritten notes (mid-1890s), p. cxxv.

61. Ibid.

62. Ibid., p. cxxvi.

63. OC, I, *De la Grippe*, p. 404.

64. OC, II, *Par Ce Demi-clair Matin*, p. 196.

65. Anatole France, as related to Émile Faguet. Quoted in Burac, p. 128.

66. Boutroux, prefatory note (unnumbered page).

67. Ibid., p. 18.

68. See, e.g., ibid., pp. 114–115.

69. Ibid.

70. Ibid., pp. 114 and 165–166.

71. See, e.g., ibid., p. 137.

72. Ibid., pp. 101 and 134.

73. OC, I, *Marcel, De la Cité harmonieuse*, p. 56.

74. Thauraud, vol. I, p. 184.

75. Ibid., p. 190.

76. Ibid., pp. 192–194.

77. The issues available at the Centre Charles Péguy in Orléans testify to this commitment: the paper is thick and remarkably durable more than a century after publication—impressive for a book, let alone a periodical without heavy binding. The fonts are also meant to be read, complemented by considerable space between words and lines (and with those spaces, higher printing costs).

78. See OC, I, *Encore de la Grippe*, p. 431.

79. On Albert Baudouin and Bernard-Lazare's financial support, see Villiers, pp. 99 and 153; for Bergson's, see Frantisek Laichter, *Péguy et ses Cahiers de la quinzaine* (Paris: Maison des Sciences de l'Homme, 1995), p. 269. On G. Favre, see Romain Rolland, *Péguy*, vol. I (Paris: Albin Michel, 1944), p. 122.

80. Laichter, p. 269.

81. In 1905, Romain Rolland's novel *Jean-Christophe*, serialized in the *Cahiers*, was later sold by Péguy to a publisher without Rolland's consent. Péguy eventually conceded Rolland's rights—and Rolland continued his friendship with Péguy and his writing for the *Cahiers*—but Péguy had allowed himself an act of striking editorial presumption. See Rolland, vol. I, pp. 125–129.

82. See Burac, pp. 289–290. See also Annette Aronowicz, *Jews and Christians on Time and Eternity* (Stanford: Stanford University Press, 1998), p. 4.

83. Péguy describes these meetings in *Notre Jeunesse*, p. 61. According to the Tharauds, Halévy rarely attended. Tharaud, vol. 2, p. 152. For Benda's presence, see Laichter, p. 269.

CHAPTER 3

1. For Descartes, see René Descartes, *Discours de la Méthode*, in *Oeuvres complètes*, ed. André Bridoux (Paris: Gallimard, Bibliothèque de la Pléiade, 1953), pp. 168–169, 179.

2. For a rather severe account of the inexorable progress of the modern in Rousseau, see Jean-Jacques Rousseau, *Rousseau, Juge de Jean-Jacques*, in *Oeuvres complètes*, vol. I, ed. Bernard Gagnebin and Marcel Raymond (Paris: Bibliothèque de la Pléiade, 1959–1995), pp. 890–891.

3. See Alexis de Tocqueville, *De la Démocratie en Amérique* in *Oeuvres complètes*, ed. André Jardin, vol. II (Paris: Bibliothèque de la Pléiade, 1992), pp. 848, 852–853.

4. Friedrich Nietzsche, *Götzen-Dämmerung*, fragment 43. See http://www .nietzschesource.org/#eKGWB/GD-Streifzuege-43.

5. OC, III, *Notre Jeunesse*, p. 132.

6. OC, III, *Notre Jeunesse*, pp. 22–23.

7. OC, III, *Notre Jeunesse*, p. 22. See also *L'Argent*, p. 809.

8. OC, III, *Note conjointe sur M. Descartes*, p. 1448.

9. For Euripides, see OC, III, *Victor-Marie, comte Hugo*, p. 303; for Charles VII, see ibid., *Note conjointe*, p. 1353.

10. OC, II, *Par Ce Demi-clair Matin*, p. 163.

11. OC, III, *Clio, Dialogue de l'histoire et de l'âme païenne*, p. 1124. See also OC, II, post-humous manuscript, written in February 1906, p. 473.

12. OC, II, *Il ne faut pas dire*, p. 566.

13. OC, II, *De la Situation faite au parti intellectuel dans le monde moderne*, pp. 562–563.

14. OC, III, *L'Argent*, pp. 808–809.

15. OC, III, *Note conjointe sur M. Descartes*, p. 1448.

16. OC, III, *Notre Jeunesse*, p. 131.

17. OC, III, *L'Argent*, p. 797.

18. Among many examples, see OC, I, *Encore de la Grippe*, p. 423; *Avertissement*, Cahiers, March 1, 1904, 1298–1299, and OC, III, *Notre Jeunesse*, pp. 21–22.

19. OC, II, *Notre Patrie*, p. 42.

20. OC, III, *Note conjointe sur M. Descartes*, pp. 1448–1449.

21. OC, II, untitled posthumous manuscript, written in February 1906, p. 473.

22. OC, III, *Victor-Marie, Comte Hugo*, p. 303.

23. OC, III, *Note conjointe sur M. Descartes*, pp. 1353–1354.

24. OC, I, *De Jean Coste*, pp. 1032–1038. See also the references to hospitality and supplication in ancient religion, and how this religion shares a sense of communion with Christianity, in OC, III, *Clio, Dialogue de l'histoire et de l'âme païenne*, pp. 1158–1159. Social-ism during the Dreyfus affair is presented as a similar kind of communion based on a deeply Christian "charity" and a "vocation" for "temporal poverty" in OC, III, *Notre Jeunesse*, pp. 84–85.

25. See the parody of Marxist conferences and disputation in OC, II, *Heureux les systé-matiques*, pp. 223–311, especially 240–262, as well as the reference to "socialisme parlemen-taire" in OC, III, *Notre Jeunesse*, p. 85.

26. OC, III, *Notre Jeunesse*, p. 51.

27. OC, III, *Notre Jeunesse*, pp. 131–132.

28. OC, II, *Par Ce Demi-clair Matin*, p. 209. The Pascalian resonance is immediately confirmed by the italicized quote that follows, directly from the *Pensées*: "*Il est encore dangereux de lui trop faire voir sa grandeur sans sa bassesse. Pourtant c'est ce qu'a fait tout le monde moderne, parce que tel était l'intérêt, et la secrète aspiration du monde moderne.*" Italics in original text.

29. See Blaise Pascal, *Oeuvres Complètes*, ed. Jacques Chevalier (Paris: Gallimard, Bibliothèque de la Pléiade, 1954), *Pensées*, pp. 1341–1342.

30. OC, III, *Note conjointe sur M. Descartes*, p. 1429 and 1453; OC, Péguy, II, *Notes pour une thèse*, p. 1100.

31. OC, II, *Notes pour une thèse*, p. 1100.

32. OC, II, *Notes pour une thèse*, p. 1102; on utilitarianism, see also *Cahiers de la quinzaine*, February 3, 1907, p. 670.

33. OC, III, *Dialogue de l'histoire et de l'âme charnelle*, p. 595.

34. See, for examples, OC, III, *L'Argent*, pp. 841–843; *Clio, Dialogue de l'histoire et de l'âme païenne*, pp. 1174–1179, 1183–1184.

35. OC, III, *Clio, Dialogue de l'histoire et de l'âme païenne*, p. 1084.

36. See, Friedrich Nietzsche, *Morgenröthe*, book III, fragments 203 and 204. Available at nietzschesource.org. See, e.g., http://www.nietzschesource.org/#eKGWB/M-203.

37. OC, III, *L'Argent*, p. 824; OC, II, *Cahiers de la quinzaine*, January 28, 1906, pp. 405–407.

38. OC, II, *Cahiers de la quinzaine*, December 31, 1905, p. 397.

39. OC, II, *De la Situation faite au parti intellectuel dans le monde moderne*, p. 543.

40. OC, III, *Note conjointe sur M. Descartes*, p. 1418. On the power of habit in the realm of ideas, see *Note sur M. Bergson et la philosophie bergsonienne*, pp. 1252–1253.

41. OC, III, *Note conjointe sur M. Descartes*, pp. 1429–1430.

42. OC, III, *L'Argent*, p. 813.

43. OC, III, *Note conjointe sur M. Descartes*, p. 1431.

44. On technological and economic progress, see OC, II, *Cahiers de la quinzaine*, February 3, 1907. The progress of justice is less certain, but the repeated description by Péguy of Charles Maurras and Action Française as reactionary as well as his repeated praise for the Declaration of the Rights of Man and Citizen and its historical consequences strongly suggest progress in the extension of universal legal rights. See also his remark about the rights in OC, III, *Notre Jeunesse*, p. 104, where he writes of "the legitimate rights of nations" and "the most legitimate rights of peoples" with reference to the ends of socialism, which would preserve the rights of self-determination of different peoples, rather than annulling them.

45. OC, III, *Clio, Dialogue de l'histoire et de l'âme païenne*, e.g., p. 1129.

46. Ibid., p. 1033.

47. Ibid. See also OC, III, *Note conjointe sur M. Descartes*, p. 1458.

48. OC, III, *Notre Jeunesse*, p. 133.

49. OC, III, *Note conjointe sur M. Descartes*, p. 1418.

50. OC, III, *Notre Jeunesse*, pp. 10–11. For Péguy, this metaphysically modern self is no longer open to learning as a source of wonder and attunement to a reality that transcends the self. For Péguy on the dangers of security as a kind of existential imperative that trumps justice, see OC, II, *Par Ce Demi-clair Matin*, p. 122.

51. On the distancing from religious and national differences (which he argues makes internationalism strictly speaking impossible), see Péguy with reference to Jaurès as representative of

this sensibility: OC, III, *Notre Jeunesse*, pp. 95–96. On the enduring power of social rank and class, see OC, III, *Notre Jeunesse*, p. 129. He adds that the same persons who rejected the possibility of orders of distinction among, say, exemplary lives, or among poets and philosophers, or historical epochs and events, often assigned real worth to the prevailing intellectual hierarchy particular to their own professional circumstances. See, e.g., OC, III, *L'Argent*, p. 838, and *L'Argent suite*, pp. 882, 896.

52. OC, II, *Notes pour une thèse*, p. 1100.

53. OC, III, *Note conjointe sur M. Descartes*, p. 1306.

54. OC, II, *Un Poète l'a dit*, pp. 855; OC, III, *Note conjointe sur M. Descartes*, p. 1306, OC, II, *Brunetière*, p. 639.

55. OC, II, *Brunetière*, p. 625.

56. OC, II, *Par Ce Demi-clair Matin,* p. 126.

57. OC, II, *Un Poète l'a dit*, p. 855.

58. OC, III, *Note conjointe sur M. Descartes*, p. 1307.

59. OC, III, *Notre Jeunesse*, p. 23.

CHAPTER 4

1. Renan uses the term very frequently to designate his method and his ambitions for the future. See Ernest Renan, *L'Avenir de la science* (Paris: Flammarion, 1995), pp. 113–114, 117, 127–128, 187–189, 197–198, 241–242, 256–257, 306–307, and 336.

2. OC, III, *L'Argent suite*, p. 883.

3. Ibid.

4. See OC, II, *Cahiers de la quinzaine*, December 31, 1905, p. 400; *Un Poète l'a dit*, p. 842, for "the great cry of the modern world;" for "what one opposes," see *Notes pour une thèse*, 1101.

5. OC, II, *Brunetière*, p. 626–627.

6. OC, II, *Cahiers de la quinzaine*, February 3, 1907, p. 647.

7. OC, II, *De la Situation faite au parti intellectuel*, pp. 560–561.

8. For example, see OC, III, *L'Argent suite*, p. 871.

9. To this end, note the rapid move from "modern intellectual metaphysics" to "the modern intellectual party" in the *Cahier* of February 3, 1907 (OC, II, p. 646).

10. OC, II, *De la Situation faite au parti intellectuel,* p. 547.

11. OC, II, *Cahiers de la quinzaine*, February 3, 1907, p. 646.

12. Ibid.

13. OC, II, *Notes pour une thèse*, p. 1058.

14. Ibid., pp. 1098 and 1059 (for quoted passage).

15. OC, II, *Il ne faut pas dire*, pp. 569–571.

16. OC, II, *Un Poète l'a dit*, p. 849, OC III, *Notre Jeunesse,* p. 124.

17. OC, III, *L'Argent suite*, p. 878.

18. Voltaire, *Lettres philosophiques*, critical edition with an introduction and commentary by Gustave Lanson, vol. I (Paris: Cornély, 1909). For a further discussion of the controversy about Lanson's methods and this edition of Voltaire in particular, see Fritz Ringer, *Fields of Knowledge: French Academic Culture in Comparative Perspective 1890–1920* (Cambridge: Cambridge University Press, 1992), pp. 240 and 244.

19. See OC, III, *Notre Jeunesse*, pp. 22–23, and OC, II, *De la Situation faite au parti intellectuel*, pp. 712–713.

20. OC, II, *Un Poète l'a dit,* pp. 848–851.

21. See, e.g., OC, I, *Zangwill,* p. 1439.

22. See OC, III, *Un Nouveau Théologien, Cahiers,* September 24, 1911, p. 490, where Péguy places Michelet's name alongside that of those thinkers and writers he most admires, including Plato, Hugo, Pascal, Lamartine, Sophocles, Descartes, and others. See also *L'Argent,* pp. 788–789.

23. Hence Péguy's respectful skepticism vis-à-vis Durkheim's arguments about suicide. See Péguy's review of *Le Suicide* in OC, I, *La Revue socialiste,* November 15 1897, pp. 39–40, and OC, II, *Heureux les systématiques,* pp. 268–269.

24. OC, III, *L'Argent suite,* p. 877.

25. Ibid., p. 878.

26. Ibid., p. 959.

27. Ibid., pp. 880–881.

28. OC, III, *L'Argent,* pp. 842–843.

29. Ibid., pp. 843–844.

30. OC, III, *Clio, Dialogue de l'histoire et de l'âme païenne,* p. 1191.

31. Ibid., pp. 1190–1192.

32. Ibid.

33. Ibid., p. 1182.

34. Ibid., pp. 1177. Italics in original text.

35. Ibid, p. 1190.

36. Ibid., p. 1178; OC, II, *De la Situation faite à l'histoire et à la sociologie dans les temps modernes,* p. 486.

37. OC, III, *Clio, Dialogue de l'histoire et de l'âme païenne,* p. 1182.

38. See Badiou's remarks about Péguy in *Europe,* August–September 2014, nos. 1024–1025.

39. For Péguy, "a metaphysics, a philosophy, an art, a people, a race [in Péguy's sense—see Chapter 5] a culture" all belong to the "order of the event." See OC, II, *Cahiers de la quinzaine,* February 3, 1907, p. 664.

40. OC, III, *Notre Jeunesse,* p. 124.

41. Ibid. See also OC, II, *Heureux les systématiques,* pp. 268–277.

42. OC, I, *Casse-cou,* pp. 714–716.

43. OC, I, *Cahiers,* October 1, 1901, *Compte rendu,* p. 791.

44. OC, III, *Clio, Dialogue de l'histoire et de l'âme païenne,* pp. 1114–1115.

45. Ibid., p. 1122.

46. Ibid., pp. 1120–1121.

47. Ibid., p. 1120.

48. Ibid., pp. 1114–1115.

49. Ibid., p. 1124. Italics in original text.

50. Ibid., pp. 1120, 1124–1125.

51. OC, III, *Clio, Dialogue de l'histoire et de l'âme païenne,* p. 1129.

52. OC, II, *Notes pour une thèse,* pp. 1098 and 1059.

53. OC, I, "M. Léon Walras," *La Revue socialiste,* February 15, 1897, pp. 3–18.

54. Ibid., esp. pp. 12–18.

55. OC, II, *Brunetière,* p. 587.

56. Ibid.

57. OC, II, *Un Poète l'a dit,* pp. 880–881. Italics in original text.

58. Ibid.

59. Ibid., pp. 834–835.

60. For Durkheim as patron, see OC, III, *L'Argent suite*, p. 873. Italics in original text. For Péguy's characterization of Durkheim's methods, see OC, II, *Heureux les systématiques*, p. 261.

61. OC, I, review of Durkheim's *Le Suicide* in *La Revue socialiste*, no. 155, November 15, 1897, pp. 39–40.

62. OC, II, *Un Poète l'a dit*, pp. 904–905.

63. OC, II, *Brunetière*, p. 619.

64. OC, II, *L'Argent suite*, p. 873. Italics in original text.

65. OC, II, *De la Situation faite au parti intellectuel,* pp. 560–561.

66. OC, II, *Il ne faut pas dire*, p. 571.

67. OC, I, *Zangwill*, p. 1397.

68. From Virginia Woolf, "Mr. Bennett and Mrs. Brown" (London: Hogarth Press, 1924), pp. 4–5.

69. OC, II, *Cahiers*, February 3, 1907, p. 651: "Rien n'est aussi difficile que de faire comprendre à celui qui ne le veut pas qu'on a beau nier, qu'on fait tout de même de la métaphysique, et tout de même de la philosophie, et tout de même de la religion—que généralement ne pas prendre certain positions, ne pas occuper certain situations, c'est infailliblement en prendre et en occuper d'autres."

70. Ibid., p. 672.

71. Ibid. Italics in original text.

72. OC, II, *De la Situation faite au parti intellectuel dans le monde moderne*, pp. 562–563.

73. OC, II, *De la Situation faite à l'histoire et à la sociologie dans les temps modernes,* pp. 513–515.

74. OC, III, *L'Argent*, p. 821.

75. OC, II, *De la Situation faite au parti intellectuel dans le monde moderne*, pp. 562.

76. OC, III, *Notre Jeunesse*, p. 22.

77. OC, II, *Notes pour une thèse*, p. 1230.

78. OC, III, *Victor-Marie, Comte Hugo*, p. 314; *Un Nouveau Théologien*, pp. 493–94.

79. OC, II, *De la Situation faite au parti intellectuel dans le monde moderne devant les accidents de la gloire temporelle*, pp. 716–717.

80. OC, II, *De la Situation faite au parti intellectuel*, pp. 562–563.

81. OC, III, *L'Argent suite*, p. 877–881.

82. OC, III, *Victor-Marie, Comte Hugo*, p. 313.

83. OC, III, *Note conjointe sur M. Descartes*, pp. 1455–1458. Italics in original text.

84. Ibid., p. 1460.

85. OC, III, *Victor-Marie, Comte Hugo*, p. 313.

86. OC, II, *Brunetière*, p. 617.

87. OC, II, *Par Ce Demi-clair Matin*, pp. 173. See also Ibid., *Un Poète l'a dit*, p. 890.

88. OC, III, *Clio, Dialogue de l'histoire et de l'âme païenne*, p. 1152.

89. OC, III, *Un Poète l'a dit*, p. 824.

90. OC, II, *Les Suppliants parallèles*, p. 375.

91. OC, II, *Brunetière*, p. 629.

92. OC, II, *De la Situation faite à l'histoire et à la sociologie dans les temps modernes*, p. 495.

93. OC, III, *Note sur M. Bergson et la philosophie Bergsonienne*, pp. 1263–64.

94. OC, II, *Brunetière*, p. 623.

95. Ibid., p. 629.

96. OC, III, *Dialogue de l'histoire et de l'âme charnelle,* pp. 764–765.

97. OC, II, *Brunetière,* p. 588.

98. OC, III, *Note conjointe sur M. Descartes,* p. 1348.

99. OC, III, *Dialogue de l'histoire et de l'âme charnelle,* p. 765; *Note conjointe sur M. Descartes,* pp. 1364–1365.

100. OC, II, *Cahiers,* February 3, 1907, pp. 656–657.

101. Ibid., p. 659.

102. OC, II, *Un Poète l'a dit,* p. 806. This intensely personal mode of reading has a long history (of which Péguy was unaware) in thoughts about reading in nineteenth- and twentieth-century theology, especially in Søren Kierkegaard and Karl Barth.

103. See OC, II, *De la Situation faite à l'histoire et à la sociologie dans les temps modernes,* p. 486.

104. OC, III, *Clio, Dialogue de l'histoire et de l'âme païenne,* pp. 1008 and 1020.

105. Ibid., p. 1009.

106. Ibid., p. 1159.

107. Ibid., p. 1160.

108. OC, II, *De la Situation faite à l'histoire et à la sociologie dans les temps modernes,* p. 486; OC, III, *Notre Jeunesse,* pp. 5–7.

109. OC, III, *Notre Jeunesse,* pp. 5–7.

110. Ibid. Italics in original text.

111. See, among many other examples, OC, III, *Un Nouveau Théologien,* pp. 490–491; *L'Argent suite,* p. 959. See also the claims of Simiand and others about historical laws and individual agency in Chapter 1.

112. OC, III, *Clio, Dialogue de l'histoire et de l'âme païenne,* p. 1171.

113. Ibid., pp. 1009–1010.

114. Ibid., p. 1014.

115. Ibid., pp. 1006–1007.

116. OC, III, *Note sur M. Bergson et la philosophie bergsonienne,* p. 1255.

117. OC, III, *Notre Jeunesse,* p. 34.

118. OC, III, *L'Argent,* p. 842.

119. Péguy's account of aging is explored in the next chapter.

120. OC, II, *Cahiers,* February 3, 1907, p. 668.

121. OC, II, *De la Situation faite au parti intellectuel dans le monde moderne devant les accidents de la gloire temporelle,* pp. 700–701.

122. Ibid., pp. 702–704.

123. Ibid., p. 703.

124. Ibid., p. 704.

125. Ibid., p. 705.

126. OC, II, *Un Poète l'a dit,* pp. 816–817.

127. Ibid., pp. 812–817.

CHAPTER 5

1. See, among many others, *Confronting Modernity in Fin-de-Siècle France: Bodies, Minds and Gender,* ed. Christopher Forth and Elinor Accampo (New York: Palgrave Macmillan,

2010), *Histoire du Corps, Volume II: De la Révolution à la Grande Guerre*, ed. Alain Corbin (Paris: Seuil, 2005), and Judith Surkis, *Sexing the Citizen: Morality and Masculinity in France, 1870–1920* (Ithaca, NY: Cornell University Press, 2006).

2. OC, II, *Heureux les systématiques*, p. 264.

3. OC, II, *De la Situation faite au parti intellectuel dans le monde moderne devant les accidents de la gloire temporelle*, pp. 702–704.

4. OC, II, *Heureux les systématiques*, pp. 264–265.

5. OC, *Oeuvres poétiques*, *Ève*, p. 949.

6. One thinks of the gratitude that the woodcutter in *Le Porche* feels when thinking of the time when he is dead and quickly forgotten, and his children live without him. See OC, *Oeuvres poétiques*, *Le Porche*, p. 548.

7. See Milan Kundera, *The Unbearable Lightness of Being*, trans. Michael Heim (New York: Harper and Row, 1984).

8. OC, III, *Clio, Dialogue de l'histoire et de l'âme païenne*, p. 1175.

9. Ibid., p. 1132.

10. Ibid., p. 1134.

11. Ibid.

12. OC, *Oeuvres poétiques*, *Le Porche*, pp. 545–548.

13. Ibid., p. 546.

14. Ibid., p. 545.

15. The term was Francis of Assisi's affectionate nickname for his own body.

16. OC, III, *Dialogue de l'histoire et de l'âme charnelle*, p. 637.

17. Ibid., *Clio, Dialogue de l'histoire et de l'âme païenne*, p. 1154.

18. Ibid.

19. See Paul Fussell, *The Great War and Modern Memory* (Oxford: Oxford University Press, 1975).

20. OC, II, "Louis de Gonzague," *Cahiers*, December 31, 1905, p. 378.

21. Ibid., pp. 378–379.

22. OC, III, *Notre Jeunesse*, p. 74.

23. OC, II, *Louis de Gonzague*, p. 378.

24. OC, II, *Les Suppliants parallèles*, p. 372.

25. OC, II, *De la Situation faite à l'histoire et à la sociologie dans les temps modernes*, p. 493.

26. OC, II, *Hervé traître*, p. 447.

27. OC, II, *Cahiers de la quinzaine*, January 28, 1906, p. 421.

28. OC, II, *Heureux les systématiques*, p. 307.

29. OC, I, *De la Grippe*, p. 404.

30. Ibid.

31. Ibid., pp. 402–404.

32. Ibid., p. 402.

33. Ibid., pp. 404–406.

34. The contribution of a certain kind of Christian to this situation is discussed in Chapter 10, "The Christian Revolution," especially with reference to Jesus being a man and not an angel.

35. OC, *Oeuvres poétiques*, *Le Porche*, p. 604.

36. OC, III, *L'Argent suite*, p. 910; *Clio, Dialogue de l'histoire et de l'âme païenne*, p. 1154.

37. OC, *Oeuvres poétiques*, *Ève*, p. 969.

38. Ibid., *Le Porche*, p. 542.

39. OC, III, *Victor-Marie, Comte Hugo,* p. 177.

40. Ibid., pp. 163–165.

41. OC, II, *De la Situation faite au parti intellectuel dans le monde moderne devants les accidents de la gloire temporelle,* pp. 728–731.

42. OC, III, *Notre Jeunesse,* pp. 103 and 105.

43. OC, II, *Cahiers,* Feburary 3, 1907, p. 668.

44. OC, II, *Par Ce Demi-clair Matin,* p. 126.

45. OC, II, *Brunetière,* p. 576. Italics from the biblical quotation (Genesis 2:23) have been removed.

46. OC, III, *Clio, Dialogue de l'histoire et de l'âme païenne,* p. 1033.

47. OC, III, *Victor-Marie, Comte Hugo,* pp. 331–332. Capitals and italics in original.

48. OC, III, *L'Argent,* pp. 794–795.

49. Ibid., pp. 787 and 790.

50. Ibid., p. 795. Italics in original text.

51. Ibid., p. 823.

52. Ibid., pp. 823–824.

53. Ibid.

54. OC, III, *Note conjointe sur M. Descartes,* p. 1418.

55. Ibid.

56. Ibid., p. 1420.

57. OC, *Notre Jeunesse,* p. 103.

58. See, e.g., OC, I, *De Jean Coste,* p. 1033.

59. He introduces the difference between poverty and destitution as early as 1902 in *De Jean Coste* but returns explicitly to his treatment of the terms in his *L'Argent* of 1913 (for the latter reference to poverty and misery as he wrote about them in *De Jean Coste,* see OC, III, *L'Argent,* p. 814).

60. OC, I, *De Jean Coste,* pp. 1035–1036.

61. Ibid., p. 1022.

62. OC, I, *De Jean Coste,* p. 1033.

63. OC, III, *L'Argent,* p. 812.

64. Ibid., p. 813.

65. Ibid., p. 812.

66. Ibid., p. 815.

67. See ibid., pp. 813–815. The meanings of "jouer" and "jeu"—meaning both "to play" and "game" respectively, but also terms often used with particular reference to gambling and bets—are difficult to reproduce in English.

68. See, e.g., OC, III, *Dialogue de l'histoire et de l'âme charnelle,* p. 764–765. See also the discussion of the "glorious incertitude" of metaphysics in Chapter 4.

69. OC, I, *De Jean Coste,* p. 1034.

70. Ibid.

71. Ibid.

72. Ibid., pp. 1033–1035.

73. Ibid., pp. 1034–1035.

74. OC, II, *Notes pour une thèse,* p. 1169–1171.

75. Ibid., pp. 1200–1201; see also pp. 1214–1215.

76. Ibid., p. 1174.

77. Ibid., pp. 1175–1177. Péguy thought a deathless life (not the same as dwelling in eternity) undesirable. See the reflection on pagan contempt for the deathless pagan gods in OC, III, *Clio, Dialogue de l'histoire et de l'âme païenne*, pp. 1163–1164.

78. OC, II, *Notes pour une thèse*, pp. 1175.

79. OC, III, *Notre Jeunesse*, p. 97. Italics in original.

CHAPTER 6

1. See Fénelon, *Telemachus*, ed. and trans. Patrick Riley (Cambridge: Cambridge University Press, 1994), book 10, p. 170. Quoted in Michael Sonenscher, *Sans-Culottes* (Princeton: Princeton University Press, 2008), p. 218.

2. David Bell, *The First Total War* (Boston: Houghton Mifflin, 2007), p. 111.

3. Madame Roland to Bancal, June 25, 1791, in Marie-Jeanne Roland, *Lettres de Madame Roland*, ed. Claude Perroud, 2 vols. (Paris: Imprimerie Nationale, 1900–1902), vol. II, p. 313. Quoted in Bell, p. 117.

4. Immanuel Kant, *Kritik der Urteilskraft, Akademie Ausgabe*, vol. V, p. 263, lines 2–8. The passage was called to my attention (where it appeared in shorter form and with a different translation) in Bell, p. 81.

5. Bell, p. 140.

6. Quoted from Wilhelm von Clausewitz, "Bekenntnisdenkschrift," in *Schriften—Aufsätze—Studien—Briefe*, ed. Werner Hahlweg, 2 vols. (Göttingen: Vandenhoek and Ruprecht, 1966), pp. 749–750. Quoted in Bell, p. 241.

7. For a general treatment of this theme, see Albert O. Hirschman, *The Passions and the Interests: Political Arguments for Capitalism Before Its Triumph* (Princeton: Princeton University Press, 1977). For Benjamin Constant, see Benjamin Constant, "De la Liberté des Anciens comparée à celle des Modernes," in *Oeuvres politiques de Benjamin Constant* (Paris: Charpentier, 1874), pp. 258–286.

8. See Norman Angell, *Europe's Optical Illusion* (London: Simpkin, Marshall, Hamilton, Kent, 1909). This is the first edition of the book; subsequent editions used the title *The Great Illusion*.

9. For more on von Suttner, see Brigitte Hamann, *Bertha von Suttner: A Life for Peace* (Syracuse, NY: Syracuse University Press, 1996).

10. Norman Ingram, "Pacifism," in *The Columbia History of Twentieth-Century French Thought*, ed. Lawrence D. Kritzman (New York: Columbia University Press, 2006), p. 76.

11. Ibid.

12. For more on Mathiez's political convictions, see *Amitié Charles Péguy*, October 1, 1972, "Péguy et Albert Mathiez," by James Friguglietti, pp. 2–16, esp. p. 15.

13. Ingram, p. 76.

14. Marie-Claire Bancquart, *Paris "Belle Époque" par ses écrivains* (Paris: Adam Biro, 1997), p. 12.

15. G. Bruno, *Le Tour de France par deux enfants: Devoir et patrie* (Paris: Eugène Belin, 1888), p. 308.

16. Ernest Psichari, *L'Appel des armes* (Paris: Oudin, no date provided; 31st printing), p. 33. Originally published in 1913.

17. Alain, *Propos sur le bonheur* (Paris: Gallimard, 1928), p. 109. The essay, entitled "L'Égoïsme," was originally written in February 1913.

18. Alain, pp. 102–106, in particular p. 103. These remarks are included in the essays "Agir" of April 1911 and "Hommes d'action" of February 1910.

19. OC, II, *Par Ce Demi-clair Matin*, p. 139.

20. OC, I, *Marcel, De la cité harmonieuse*, pp. 90–91.

21. OC, II, *Par Ce Demi-clair Matin*, p. 97.

22. See Raoul Allier, *L'Enseignement primaire des indigènes à Madagascar, Cahiers*, 6th series, 1904–1905, no. 4.

23. See E. D. Morel and Pierre Mille, "Le Congo Léopoldien," *Cahiers*, 7th series, 1905–1906, no. 6. See also Félicien Challaye, "Le Congo français," series 7, 1905–1906, no. 12, and Pierre Mille and Félicien Challaye, "Les Deux Congos," series 7, 1905–1906, no. 16.

24. See *Oeuvres poétiques, Jeanne d'Arc*, pp. 171–173.

25. OC, II, *Notre Patrie*, p. 60.

26. Ibid., p. 59.

27. Ibid., p. 37.

28. OC, III, *Note conjointe sur M. Descartes*, pp. 1343–1344.

29. Ibid., p. 1343.

30. See OC, II, *Par Ce Demi-clair Matin*, p. 175, and III, *Note conjointe sur M. Descartes*, p. 1342–1343.

31. OC, III, *Note conjointe sur M. Descartes*, pp. 1344–1345.

32. OC, II, *Par Ce Demi-clair Matin*, p. 174.

33. See, e.g., OC, II, *Par Ce Demi-clair Matin*, p. 175, and III, *Note conjointe sur M. Descartes*, pp. 1343–1346, esp. p. 1345.

34. OC, III, *Note conjointe sur M. Descartes*, p. 1345.

35. Ibid., p. 1344.

36. OC, II, *Par Ce Demi-clair Matin*, p. 174.

37. OC, III, *Note conjointe sur M. Descartes*, p. 1345.

38. OC, II, *À Nos Amis, à nos abonnés, Cahiers*, June 20, 1909, p. 1307.

39. Charles Péguy to Alexandre Millerand, January 15, 1912. Quoted in *Amitié Charles Péguy*, no. 180, Correpondance Péguy–Millerand, August 1972, pp. 2–3.

40. OC, III, *Note conjointe sur M. Descartes*, p. 1413. Italics in original text.

41. Ibid., p. 1346.

42. Ibid., p. 1348.

43. OC, III, *L'Argent suite*, p. 924.

44. Ibid., pp. 936–937.

45. OC, II, *À Nos Amis, à nos abonnés*, p. 1307.

46. *Oeuvres poétiques, Ève*, p. 1028.

47. Ibid. Italics added.

48. OC, III, *L'Argent suite*, p. 915. Italics in original text.

49. OC, II, *Notre Patrie*, pp. 41–42.

50. OC, II, *Les Suppliants parallèles*, December 17, 1905, p. 363.

51. See Alexis de Tocqueville, *Oeuvres complètes*, ed. André Jardin (Paris: Bibliothèque de la Pléaide 1992), vol. I, *Travail sur l'Algérie*, pp. 704–705. See also Tocqueville, *Oeuvres complètes*, ed. J. P. Mayer (Paris: Gallimard, 1959–), vol. XIII, part II, letter from Tocqueville to Mme. Louis de Kergorlay, May 1848, p. 220. On Mill, see Uday Singh Mehta, *Liberalism and Imperialism* (Chicago: University of Chicago Press, 1999).

52. OC, II, *Un Poète l'a dit*, p. 928.

53. Villiers, p. 377. See also Leroi, p. 245.

54. Tharaud, vol. II, p. 244.

55. Joseph Letaconnoux, "Le Départ de Péguy," *Le Crapouillot*, August 1918. Quoted in Burac, p. 304.

56. OC, II, *De la Situation faite au parti intellectuel dans le monde moderne*, p. 748. The words "scientific" and "scientifically" are used in a critical sense more than a dozen times in a single paragraph.

57. OC, III, *Notre Jeunesse*, p. 139.

58. See Robert A. Nye, *Masculinity and Male Codes of Honor in Modern France* (New York: Oxford University Press, 1993), p. 186.

59. Ruth Harris, *Dreyfus: Politics, Emotion and the Scandal of the Century* (New York: Henry Holt, 2010), 94.

60. Nye, p. 187.

61. Piers Paul Read, *The Dreyfus Affair* (London: Bloomsbury, 2012), 41.

62. Patrice Higonnet, *Paris: Capital of the World* (Cambridge, MA: Harvard University Press, 2002), p. 315.

63. See http://www.youtube.com/watch?v=9uvxXgm2TWs.

64. Venita Datta, *Heroes and Legends of Fin-de-Siècle France: Gender, Politics and National Identity* (Cambridge: Cambridge University Press, 2011), p. 17.

65. See Edward Berenson, *The Trial of Madame Caillaux* (Berkeley: University of California Press, 1992).

66. Nye, p. 184.

67. OC, III, *L'Argent suite*, p. 934. Italics in original text.

68. *Polyeucte* appears throughout Péguy's work. For a sense of how highly he thought of the play, see OC, III, *Victor-Marie, Comte Hugo*, pp. 295–299.

69. Ibid., p. 295.

70. Ibid., pp. 276–279; 282–285; 296.

71. Ibid., pp. 299–302.

72. OC, III, *L'Argent*, p. 820.

73. Ibid., p. 821.

74. OC, III, *Notre Jeunesse*, pp. 66 and 148.

75. See the references to the integrity (and continuity) of his socialism and Christianity in ibid., p. 85, and the rejection of Action Française on p. 122.

76. The reference to a Dreyfusard honor, remaining intact after years of difficulty despite the threat to careers, property, and life, can be found in ibid., p. 48 and p. 89.

77. Ibid., pp. 120–121.

78. Ibid. p. 151. Quotation italics removed.

79. Specifically, Pierre Corneille, *Le Cid*, act I, scene VI, verse 344. See OC, III, p. 1526, note 1.

80. OC, III, *Notre Jeunesse*, p. 151.

81. OC, II, *De la Situation faite à l'histoire et à la sociologie dans les temps modernes*, pp. 508–509.

82. OC, III, *L'Argent*, p. 838.

83. OC, III, *L'Argent suite*, pp. 880–881.

84. OC, III, *Notre Jeunesse*, p. 103.

85. OC, II, *Cahiers*, October 1, 1905, p. 3.

86. OC, III, *L'Argent*, p. 821.

87. Ibid.

88. Ibid.

89. OC, II, *Cahiers*, January 28, 1906, p. 418. In *Personnalités* (OC, I, p. 918), Péguy had estimated that the number of readers offended by each issue should be "at least a third."

90. OC, III, *L'Argent*, p. 821.

91. See OC, II, *Un Poète l'a dit*, pp. 911–914. Péguy and Sangnier were both committed to social justice, but it seems that Sangnier was, to Péguy's mind, too willing to work within French politics as currently constituted and did not think deeply enough about Catholicism and modernity. For Péguy's disappointment at Dreyfus accepting a pardon, see OC, III, *Notre Jeunesse*, p. 46.

92. Ibid., pp. 70–76; 91–92.

93. Ibid., p. 89.

94. Ibid., pp. 115–116.

95. OC, III, *L'Argent suite*, p. 924.

96. OC, II, *Hervé traitre*, p. 452.

97. OC, III, *Notre Jeunesse*, pp. 138–139.

98. OC, III, *L'Argent*, pp. 829–831.

99. OC, III, *L'Argent*, p. 829.

100. OC, III, *Un Nouveau Théologien*, p. 510.

101. OC, III, *L'Argent*, p. 809.

102. Burac, pp. 188–189.

103. Ibid., p. 250.

104. Villiers, pp. 238–239. As Villiers observes, Péguy appeared to agree with his mother's assessment: when told in confidence of her son's extramarital passion by Geneviève Favre, Péguy's mother exclaimed: "My son is a married man and that's that!"

105. Charles Péguy to Geneviève Favre, August 22, 1914. In *Amitié Charles Péguy*, no. 66, April–June 1994, p. 88.

106. Ibid., pp. 117–118.

CHAPTER 7

1. See Günter Arnold, Kurt Kloocke, and Ernest A. Menze, "Herder's Reception and Influence," in *A Companion to the Works of Johann Gottfried Herder*, ed. Hans Adler and Wulf Kopeke (Rochester, NY: Camden House, 2009), p. 410.

2. Ernest Renan, *Qu'est-ce qu'une nation?* (Paris: Mille et une Nuits, 1997), p. 33. Péguy also made use of this "concert" image with reference to philosophical differences (see Chapter 4).

3. In strict philosophical terms, Hegel would appear first in any history of these projects that entwined the particular and the universal. Yet until the mid-twentieth century, Hegel was less influential in France than elsewhere in Europe. He had some appreciative French readers (most notably Victor Cousin), but his complete works were translated into French only in the second half of the nineteenth century, and were not always understood on the occasions when they were read. French readers in the Belle Époque generally depended upon Augusto Véra's translation of Hegel's major works (he published the first French translation of Hegel's *Logic*, for example, in 1859, and the *Phenomenology of Spirit* in 1867–1869).

4. On Mazzini's hopes for this kind of change, see Denis Mack Smith, *Mazzini* (New Haven: Yale University Press, 1994), pp. 11–12.

5. Cited in Patrice Higonnet, *Paris: Capital of the World* (Cambridge, MA: Harvard University Press, 2002), p. 68.

6. One witness to this sense of humiliation was Alfred Dreyfus. As he wrote to his wife, Lucie, in December 1894, "Do you remember I told you that, finding myself in Mulhouse about ten years ago in September, I heard passing under our windows a German band celebrating the anniversary of Sedan? I felt so very distressed that I cried from rage, bit my sheets in anger and swore to dedicate all my strength and intelligence to serve my country against those who thus insulted the grief of all Alsatians." See Alfred and Lucie Dreyfus, "Écris-moi souvent, écris-moi longuement," in *Correspondance de l'île du Diable*, ed. Vincent Duclert (Paris: Mille et une nuits, 2005), p. 72. This passage quoted in Ruth Harris, *Dreyfus: Politics, Emotion and the Scandal of the Century* (New York: Henry Holt, 2010), p. 23.

7. Renan, p. 32.

8. Ibid., pp. 30–34.

9. Ibid., p. 32.

10. Ibid., p. 15.

11. Ibid., pp. 13, 24.

12. Ibid., p. 13.

13. Ibid., p. 33.

14. See Friedrich Nietzsche, *Jenseits von Gut und Böse*, fragment 207. http://www .nietzschesource.org/#eKGWB/JGB-207.

15. For more on some of these tendencies in French anarchism, see John Merriman, *The Dynamite Club* (Boston: Houghton Mifflin, 2009).

16. Quoted in Eric Cahm, "Péguy et le nationalisme français de l'Affaire Dreyfus à la Grande Guerre," *Cahiers de l'Amitié Charles Péguy*, 25, 1972, pp. 29–30. Quoted in Robert Gildea, *Children of the Revolution* (Cambridge: Harvard University Press, 2008), p. 426.

17. Jean Maitron, *Le Mouvement anarchiste en France* (Paris: Maspéro, 1975), vol. 1, p. 371 note. Quoted in Gildea, p. 426.

18. OC, II, *Par Ce Demi-clair Matin*, p. 143.

19. OC, II, *Oeuvres poétiques, Le Mystère des saints innocents*, pp. 693–694.

20. OC, III, *Note conjointe sur M. Descartes*, p. 1350.

21. Victor Hugo, *Les Misérables*, trans. Christine Donougher (London: Penguin, 2013), p. 336.

22. OC, II, *Oeuvres poétiques, Le Mystère des saints innocents*, pp. 741–742.

23. See OC, III, p. 1713, note 2 to p. 937.

24. OC, III, *L'Argent suite*, p. 937. Italics removed from the opening portion of the quote.

25. Ibid., p. 934.

26. OC, III, *Notre Jeunesse*, pp. 104 and 151.

27. OC, III, *L'Argent suite*, pp. 921–922.

28. Ibid., p. 915.

29. OC, II, *Les Suppliants parallèles*, p. 363.

30. OC, III, *Notre Jeunesse*, p. 95. Péguy adds "Israel excepted" but this does not mean a kind of "partisan" injustice (as the surrounding remarks make clear), and Péguy adds a reference to how "French" Bernard-Lazare was on the same page. It probably refers to the young anarchist Bernard-Lazare's "teasing" Zionists (Bernard-Lazare himself became a Zionist) mentioned on p. 65, even as Bernard-Lazare defended persecuted Jews everywhere (pp. 64–65), with heroism and considerable sanctity (p. 94).

31. Ibid.

32. Ibid., p. 155. In the passage, Péguy will not allow either republican freedoms or Christian freedoms to be set aside, or to prevent he and others from affirming both of them at once.

33. Ibid., pp. 15–20, esp. p. 19.

34. OC, II, *Par Ce Demi-clair Matin*, pp. 92 and 95.

35. *Lettres et Entretiens*, ed. Marcel Péguy (Paris: Éditions de Paris, 1954), pp. 147. This conversation also alludes briefly to one side of Péguy's ongoing equivocations about colonialism in his final years.

36. Ibid., pp. 146–147.

37. OC, III, *L'Argent*, p. 821.

38. Ibid. "Life" is italicized in the original.

39. OC, III, *L'Argent suite*, Cahiers, p. 945.

40. OC, II, *Un Poète l'a dit*, p. 890.

41. OC, III, *Notre Jeunesse*, p. 104

42. OC, III, *L'Argent suite*, p. 938.

43. Ibid., pp. 936–937.

44. Ibid., pp. 925–926. This is a defensible if remarkably generous account of the National Convention up to the early days of 1793, and perhaps once more after 9 Thermidor. Despite recent efforts at its rehabilitation (notably by Slavoj Zizek and Sophie Wahnich), to write broadly of the National Convention's ultimate "gentleness" and "tenderness" in the days of the Committee of Public Safety, the arrest of the Girondins, the Law of Suspects, the Dechristianization Campaign, the execution of the Indulgents, the Law of 22 Prairial, and more—on the grounds that it prevented future bloodshed—is wildly speculative and implausible.

45. OC, III, *Clio, Dialogue de l'histoire et de l'âme païenne*, pp. 1170–1173.

46. OC, II, *À Nos Amis, à nos abonnés*, p. 1314.

47. OC, III, *Clio, Dialogue de l'histoire et de l'âme païenne*, pp. 1171–1172.

48. Ibid., p. 1170.

49. OC, III, *Note conjointe sur M. Descartes*, p. 1350.

50. OC, II, *Par Ce Demi-clair Matin*, p. 92.

51. OC, III, *Notre Jeunesse*, pp. 111–113.

52. Ibid., pp. 111–112, and p. 47 for the shared commitments of different kinds of Dreyfusards.

53. OC, III, *Note conjointe sur M. Descartes*, p. 1331.

54. See Péguy's account of the scapegoating, lies and illusions practiced and disseminated by anti-Semites in Chapter 10.

55. OC, III, *Notre Jeunesse*, pp. 157–158.

56. See the discussion of Jaurèssian mysticism in Chapter 2.

CHAPTER 8

1. Ernest Renan, *L'Avenir de la science* (Paris: Flammarion, 1995), pp. 370–371.

2. See Chapter 2.

3. OC, III, *Notre Jeunesse*, p. 20.

4. See, e.g., OC, I, *De Jean Coste*, p. 1044, where the absence of mysticism testifies to a failure to encounter reality in full.

5. OC, I, *Avertissement, Cahiers*, March 1, 1904, pp. 1289–1290.

6. See Daniel Halévy, *Apologie pour notre passé*, 11th series 1909–1910, no. 10.

7. OC, III, *Notre Jeunesse*, pp. 14, 17–18.

8. Ibid, pp. 17–18.

9. Ibid., p. 104.

10. Ibid., p. 92.

11. Ibid., pp. 157–158.

12. Ibid., pp. 48 and 157–158.

13. *City of God*, book XIX, 24 and 25. Translation from Augustine, *City of God*, trans. Henry Bettenson (London: Penguin, 2003), pp. 890–891.

14. OC, III, *Notre Jeunesse*, p. 30.

15. Ibid., p. 66.

16. Ibid, pp. 82 and 95.

17. Ibid., p. 82.

18. See the regular reference by Péguy to a general human tendency to avoid patient sacrifice—"comme toutes les politiques" and "comme la grande majorité des (autres) électeurs"—in his discussion of the Dreyfus Affair (ibid., pp. 50–51). He adds that Jews and Christians both misunderstand their prophets and saints even as they are sustained by prophets and saints (p. 56). The flaws—and declining devotion—of French republicans can be found at several points in the essay, including on p. 10.

19. Ibid., p. 146. Italics removed from "all the virtues."

20. Ibid., pp. 47; 50; 84–86; 64–65; 94–95.

21. Ibid., p. 50.

22. Ibid., p. 135.

23. Ibid., pp. 74 and 95.

24. Ibid., p. 37.

25. Ibid.

26. See Friedrich Nietzsche, *Der Antichrist* (Frankfurt: Insel, 1986), p. 41, #23.

27. See, e.g., *Notre Jeunesse*, p. 21.

28. Ibid., p. 77.

29. In addition to the persistent presence of this theme in *Notre Jeunesse*, see OC, II, *De la Situation faite à l'histoire et à la sociologie dans les temps modernes*, p. 509.

30. OC, III, *Notre Jeunesse*, p. 10. Italics in original text.

31. Ibid., p. 46.

32. There are Vichian resonances to this turn in the argument, but Péguy does not cite Vico here (he cites him elsewhere, e.g., via Michelet in OC II, *Par ce Demi-Clair Matin*, pp. 210–212).

33. OC, III, *Notre Jeunesse*, p. 156.

34. Ibid., p. 10. Italics in original text.

35. Ibid., p. 11.

36. Ibid., p. 21.

37. OC, I, *Les Élections*, p. 990.

38. OC, III, *Notre Jeunesse*, pp. 68–75, and 90.

39. Ibid., pp. 151–152.

40. Ibid., p. 20. Capitals in original text.

41. Ibid., pp. 28–29.

42. Ibid., p. 41. This notion of inescapable indebtedness to a source that exceeds the demonstrable is no doubt uncomfortable to some readers. Yet it remains a powerful argument,

broadly familiar in contemporary terms to readers of Jürgen Habermas, who has argued that Western philosophy is decisively shaped by its history of drawing conceptual innovations from Christian sources. The affinity is broad and inexact because it is precisely the living embodiment of this inheritance that concerns Péguy, rather than a speculative process of "rationalization"; but both notions share a conviction that the future rests not with an imperative to transgress, but a simultaneously dynamic and enduring attention to a transcendent source. See Jürgen Habermas and Joseph Ratzinger, *Dialektik der Säkularisierung: Über Vernunft und Religion* (Freiburg: Herder, 2007).

43. OC, III, *Notre Jeunesse*, p. 22.

44. Ibid., p. 29.

45. Ibid., p. 30.

46. OC, II, *De la Situation faite à l'histoire et à la sociologie dans les temps modernes*, p. 513.

47. OC, III, *Notre Jeunesse*, pp. 156 and 29.

48. John Rawls, *Political Liberalism*, expanded ed. (New York: Columbia University Press, 2005), p. 135, from the section entitled "Lecture IV: The Idea of an Overlapping Consensus."

49. Ibid., p. 159.

50. Ibid., p. 160.

51. Ibid., p. 163.

52. OC, III, *Notre Jeunesse*, p. 151.

53. OC, II, *Par Ce Demi-clair Matin*, p. 209.

54. OC, III, *Notre Jeunesse*, p. 147.

55. Ibid., p. 148.

56. See Péguy's remarks on Action Française in OC, III, *Notre Jeunesse*, p. 158; see also *Note conjointe sur M. Descartes*, pp. 1331 and 1453.

CHAPTER 9

1. Gilles Deleuze, *Difference and Repetition*, trans. Paul Patton (New York: Columbia University Press, 1994), p. 5.

2. Ibid., p. 22.

3. Interview of Charles de Gaulle by Alain Peyrefitte, September 9, 1964, ed. Jean Bastaire, in *L'Amitié Charles Péguy*, no. 53, January–March 1991, pp. 42–43. Peyrefitte was minister of information at the time of the interview.

4. Bruno Latour, "Trains of Thought: Piaget, Formalism and the Fifth Dimension," *Common Knowledge*, 6, no. 3, p. 179. Quoted in Henning Schmidgen, "The Materiality of Things? Bruno Latour, Charles Péguy, and the History of Science," *History of the Human Sciences*, February 13, 2013, p. 6.

5. Marcel Proust to Daniel Halévy, written in 1907 or 1908, in Jean Bastaire, "Péguy vu par Proust," in *L'Amitié Charles Péguy*, no. 35, July–September 1986, p. 185.

6. André Gide, quoted in Julie Sabiani, "Péguy," *Dictionnaire de Poésie: De Baudelaire à nos jours*, ed. Michel Jarrety (Paris: Presses Universitaires de France, 2001), p. 574.

7. Statement by Thureau-Dangin for Académie Française, 1911, in *L'Amitié Charles Péguy*, no. 29, September 1952, p. 13.

8. Ibid.

9. Bastaire, "Péguy vu par Proust," p. 185.

10. André Gide to Francis Jammes, February 15, 1910, and May 3, 1910. In "Correspondance André Gide–Péguy," compiled by Alfred Saffrey, *Feuillets de L'amitié Charles Péguy,* no. 65, June 1958, pp. 24–25.

11. Deleuze, pp. 94–95.

12. See Nietzsche, *Jenseits von Gut und Böse,* fragment 97. "What? A great man? I always see only the play-actor of his own ideals." http://www.nietzschesource.org/#eKGWB /JGB-97.

13. *Oeuvres poétiques, Le Porche,* pp. 650–651.

14. This latter theme—with reference to the communion of sinners and saints—is discussed in the next chapter.

15. Søren Kierkegaard, *Repetition,* trans. Howard and Edna Hong (Princeton: Princeton University Press, 1983), p. 132.

16. Ibid., p. 212.

17. See Urs von Balthasar, pp. 400–517.

18. *Oeuvres poétiques, Le Porche,* p. 650.

19. Ibid., *Ève,* p. 943.

20. OC, II, *Brunetière,* p. 612.

21. OC, II, *À Nos Amis, à nos abonnés,* p. 1298.

22. *Oeuvres poétiques, Le Porche,* pp. 666, 659, and 661–62.

23. OC, III, *Notre Jeunesse,* p. 19 and 45.

24. *Charles Péguy: Lettres et Entretiens,* ed. Marcel Péguy (Paris: Éditions de Paris, 1954), p. 120.

25. See *Oeuvres poétiques, Le Mystère des saints innocents,* pp. 758–769. Italics removed.

26. Ibid., *Le Porche,* p. 535.

27. Ibid., *Le Porche,* p. 534.

28. Ibid., pp. 569 and 584. For more on Péguy's exceptional care with the editing and production of the *Cahiers,* see Burac, pp. 121–122.

29. OC, III, *Clio, Dialogue de l'histoire et de l'âme païenne,* p. 1026.

30. *Oeuvres poétiques, Ève,* pp. 939–943.

31. Ibid., *Le Porche,* pp. 665–667.

32. Ibid., "La Tapisserie de Notre Dame," p. 896.

33. See, e.g., OC, II, *Cahiers de la quinzaine,* February 3, 1907, p. 668.

34. See Stéphane Mallarmé, "Les Fenêtres," in *Collected Poems* (Berkeley: University of California Press, 1994). See also Arthur Rimbaud, "Lettre du voyant," letter to Paul Demeny, May 15, 1871, at http://poetes.com/rimbaud/voyant.htm.

35. *Oeuvres poétiques, Ève,* p. 1065.

36. Ibid., *Ève,* p. 1141.

37. Ibid., *Le Porche,* p. 651.

38. Paul Claudel, *Cinq Grandes Odes* (Bruges: St. Catherine's Press, 1913), p. 115.

39. Ibid., pp. 63 and 98.

40. Ibid., p. 85.

41. See, e.g., the "Thalamas" controversy and the speech of Jaurès prompted by it in *L'Humanité,* I, no. 229, December 2,1904, first page; Jules Michelet, *Jeanne d'Arc* (Paris: Hachette, 1853); St. Thérèse de Lisieux, *Essential Writings,* trans. and ed. Mary Frohlich (Maryknoll, NY: Orbis, 2003), pp. 88–106; G. Bruno (Augustine Fouillée), *Le tour de France par deux enfants* (Paris: Belin, 1888), pp. 59–61; Anatole France, *Vie de Jeanne d'Arc* (Paris:

Calmann-Lévy, 1908); Solange Leibovici, "Ceci n'est pas une femme: La Jeanne de l'extrême droite," in *Jeanne d'Arc entre les nations*, ed. Ton Hoenselaars and Jelle Koopmans (Amsterdam: CRIN, 1998), pp. 135–136. Archbishop Dupanloup's enthusiasm for Jeanne's beatification is naturally part of this history as well.

42. *Oeuvres poétiques, Jeanne d'Arc*, p. 130.

43. See ibid., p. 122, where Jeanne comforts a mortally wounded English soldier, and Jeanne's final prayer in the poem on pp. 325–326.

44. Ibid., pp. 170–173.

45. Ibid., pp. 223–225, 233, 245, and 255.

46. OC, III, *Un Nouveau Théologien*, p. 560.

47. *Oeuvres poétiques, Jeanne d'Arc*, p. 266.

48. OC, III, *Un Nouveau Théologien*, p. 569.

49. See OC, III, p. 1620, note 2.

50. See, e.g., Jeanne's famous response to the "trap" question of whether she thinks she is in a state of grace, reported accurately in *Oeuvres poétiques, Jeanne d'Arc*, pp. 278–279. The question is intended to force Jeanne to confess either her guilt (she is not in a state of grace) or her culpable presumption (she presumes to know God's ultimate judgment upon her soul). Jeanne's riposte doubtless stunned her accusers: "If I am, may God keep me there; if I am not, may God put me there."

51. Ibid., *Jeanne d'Arc*, p. 27.

52. Ibid., p. 173.

53. Ibid., p. 145.

54. Ibid., *Le Mystère de la charité de Jeanne d'Arc*, p. 370.

55. Ibid. *Jeanne d'Arc*, pp. 68–69.

56. Ibid., pp. 141–142.

57. Ibid., p. 264.

58. Ibid., pp. 122–123.

59. Ibid., pp. 158–159.

60. Ibid., p. 144.

61. Ibid., p. 267.

62. Ibid., p. 129.

63. Ibid., p. 200.

64. Ibid., pp. 312–313 and 326.

65. *Oeuvres poétiques, Le Mystère de la charité de Jeanne d'Arc*, pp. 369–370.

66. Ibid., pp. 371–372.

67. Ibid., p. 372.

68. Ibid., pp. 378–381.

69. Ibid., p. 399.

70. Ibid., p. 400.

71. Ibid., p. 426.

72. Ibid., p. 426.

73. Ibid., p. 452.

74. Ibid., p. 491.

75. Ibid., p. 503.

76. Ibid., p. 516.

77. Ibid., p. 524.

78. Ibid., p. 525.

79. *Oeuvres poétiques, Jeanne d'Arc,* p. 27.

80. OC, III, *Note conjointe sur M. Descartes,* p. 1318.

CHAPTER 10

1. *Charles Péguy: Lettres et entretiens,* ed. Marcel Péguy (Paris: Éditions de Paris, 1954), p. 142.

2. For Maritain, see *Péguy au porche de l'Église: Correspondance inédite Jacques Maritain–Dom Louis Baillet,* ed. René Mougel and Robert Burac (Paris: Cerf, 1997), p. 30. The book also includes a detailed account and record of the personal and familial controversies that attended Péguy's return to Christianity. For Lotte—who learned of Péguy's return to Christianity in 1908—see *Lettres et entretiens,* ed. Marcel Péguy, pp. 57–58.

3. The best account of the ambiguous evidence on this question can be found in Marjorie Villiers, *Charles Péguy* (New York: Harper and Row, 1965), pp. 374–375.

4. OC, III, *Un Nouveau Théologien,* p. 458.

5. OC, III, *Dialogue de l'histoire et de l'âme charnelle,* pp. 690.

6. Ibid., p. 648.

7. OC, III, *Notre Jeunesse,* p. 56. For Péguy, this is not a supersessionist account of the relationship between Judaism and Christianity. Bernard-Lazare was rejected and ignored by many of his Jewish contemporaries. Similarly, Péguy's "Catholic Renaissance" was, Péguy thought, largely ignored and rejected by the official Catholicism around him.

8. On dechristianization, see OC, III, *Dialogue de l'histoire et de l'âme charnelle,* p. 690. "Second creation" and "decreation" were discussed in Chapter 3.

9. OC, III, *Clio, Dialogue de l'histoire et de l'âme païenne,* p. 1159.

10. Ibid., pp. 1163–1164.

11. OC, II, *Par Ce Demi-clair Matin,* p. 126.

12. OC, II, *Heureux les sytématiques,* p. 228.

13. OC, III, *Dialogue de l'histoire et de l'âme charnelle,* p. 782.

14. OC, III, *Clio, Dialogue de l'histoire et de l'âme païenne,* p. 1033.

15. See, e.g., the reference to moderns as "those who have nothing more to learn . . . who devote themselves, and who sacrifice themselves to nothing," in OC, III, *Notre Jeunesse,* p. 10.

16. Léon Bloy, *Le Salut par les Juifs* (Paris: A. Demay, 1892), pp 34–35.

17. See Yirmiyahu Yovel, *Dark Riddle: Hegel, Nietzsche, and the Jews* (State College, PA: Penn State University Press, 1998), p. 17; Robert Erlewine, *Monotheism and Tolerance: Recovering a Religion of Reason* (Bloomington: Indiana University Press, 2010), p. 110, and Jayne Svenungsson, "Enlightened Prejudices: Anti-Jewish Tropes in Modern Philosophy," in *Conceptualizing History: Essays on History, Memory and Representation,* ed. Andrus Ers and Hans Ruin (Huddinge: Södertörn University, 2011), pp. 279–290.

18. Édouard Drumont, *La France juive: Essai d'histoire contemporaine* (Paris: C. Marpon and E. Flammarion, 1886), p. 105.

19. Ferdinand Brunetière, review of *La France juive, Revue des deux mondes,* May 1886, pp. 700–701.

20. Quoted in Richard D. E. Burton, *Holy Tears, Holy Blood: Women, Catholicism and the Culture of Suffering in France, 1840–1970* (Ithaca, NY: Cornell University Press, 2004), pp. 80–81.

21. For many examples, see Michael Burns, *France and the Dreyfus Affair: A Documentary History* (Boston: Bedford/St. Martin's, 1999).

22. Drumont, *La France Juive*, p. 130, note 2.

23. Though he repeatedly referred to Newman in hopes of presenting his views in more moderate fashion: see Alfred Loisy, *L'Évangile et l'Église* (Paris: Picard, 1902), pp. 161–163, 195–196, 213, and 231.

24. See ibid., pp. xvii, xix, 118, and 120.

25. See Loisy, *L'Évangile et l'Église*, p. XXIII.

26. Alfred Loisy, *À propos d'histoire des religions* (Paris: Nourry, 1911), p. 9. Quoted in C. J. T. Talar, "Innovation and Biblical Interpretation," in Darrell Jodock, ed., *Catholicism Contending with Modernity* (Cambridge: Cambridge University Press, 2000) p. 208.

27. Ibid.

28. OC, III, *Note conjointe sur M. Descartes*, p. 1293.

29. OC, III, *Un NouveauThéologien*, p. 409.

30. The term appears in *Oeuvres poétiques, Le Porche*, p. 633.

31. OC, III, *Dialogue de l'histoire et de l'âme charnelle*, pp. 676 and 679.

32. Ibid., pp. 703–704. Italics in original text.

33. Ibid., p. 740.

34. Ibid., p. 676.

35. OC, III, *Note conjointe sur M. Descartes*, p. 1318.

36. Evident in the very titles of works like *Dialogue de l'histoire et de l'âme charnelle*, and references to the carnal in, e.g., *Oeuvres poètiques, Ève*, p. 1041.

37. OC, III, *Dialogue de l'histoire et de l'âme charnelle*, p. 679.

38. Ibid.

39. Ibid., pp. 679 and 728.

40. OC, *Oeuvres poètiques, Le Porche*, p. 589.

41. *Oeuvres poétiques, Ève*, p. 1041.

42. OC, III, *Note conjointe sur M. Descartes*, p. 1290.

43. Ibid., p. 1372.

44. See Blaise Pascal, *Oeuvres Complètes*, ed. Jacques Chevalier (Paris: Gallimard, Bibliothèque de la Pléiade, 1954), *Pensées*, p. 1170.

45. OC, III, *Dialogue de l'histoire et de l'âme charnelle*, pp. 677–679. Note the use of materialism and mechanical terms, as well as phrases like "metaphysically, religiously inanimate," in Péguy's account of what it means for human beings to become "beasts" upon failing to be angels.

46. Ibid.

47. OC, III, *Note sur M. Bergson et la philosophie bergsonienne*, pp. 1254–1255; *Note conjointe sur M. Descartes*, pp. 1321–1323.

48. See, e.g., *Oeuvres poétiques, Le Mystère de la charité de Jeanne d'Arc*, p. 426.

49. OC, III, *Note sur M. Bergson et la philosophie bergsonienne*, pp. 1276–1277.

50. OC, III, *Note conjointe sur M. Descartes*, p. 1444.

51. OC, III, *Un Nouveau Théologien*, p. 573.

52. Ibid.

53. Ibid.

54. OC, III, *Note conjointe sur M. Descartes*, p. 1311.

55. OC, III, *Note conjointe sur M. Descartes*, p. 1313.

56. OC, III, *L'Argent suite*, p. 929.

57. OC, III, *Note conjointe sur M. Descartes*, p. 1297.

58. OC, III, *L'Argent suite*, p. 955.

59. OC, III, *Victor-Marie, Comte Hugo*, pp. 238–239.

60. OC, I, *Cahiers de la quinzaine*, March 15, 1904, pp. 1331–1332.

61. OC, III, *Un Nouveau Théologien*, p. 450.

62. OC, III, *Dialogue de l'histoire et de l'âme charnelle*, pp. 652–654.

63. Ibid., p. 671.

64. Ibid., pp. 641–642

65. Ibid., pp. 653–654.

66. Ibid., p. 674.

67. OC, III, *Notre Jeunesse*, p. 21.

68. Ibid., p. 100.

69. OC, III, *Un Nouveau Théologien*, p. 400.

70. Ibid., p. 452.

71. Ibid., pp. 400–402.

72. Ibid., pp. 394–395, 407, 453.

73. Ibid., p. 454.

74. OC, III, *Dialogue de l'histoire et de l'âme charnelle*, p. 686.

75. OC, III, *Un Nouveau Théologien*, pp. 473–474.

76. OC, III, *Note conjointe sur M. Descartes*, p. 1464.

77. OC, III, *Note sur M. Bergson et la philosophie bergsonienne*, p. 1273.

78. Here, Péguy was transposing into the language of human motives a very old Christian penitential vocabulary that distinguished attrition (repentance drawn not from a love of God but from, say, fear of disgrace and punishment) from contrition (repentance inspired by love of God).

79. *Oeuvres poétiques*, *Le Porche*, pp. 597 and 616.

80. Ibid., pp. 666–667.

81. Ibid.

82. Ibid., p. 658.

83. Ibid., p. 661.

84. Ibid, p. 663.

85. Ibid., pp. 663–664.

86. See Bernard Groethuysen, *The Bourgeois: Catholicism vs. Capitalism in Eighteenth-Century France*, trans. Mary Ilford (London: Barrie and Rockliff, 1968).

87. *Oeuvres poétiques*, *Le Mystère des Saints Innocents*, p. 707.

88. OC, III, *Notre Jeunesse*, pp. 50–51. The parentheses are Péguy's. Annette Aronowicz has particularly interesting observations on this theme: see *Jews and Christians on Time and Eternity: Charles Péguy's Portrait of Bernard-Lazare* (Stanford: Stanford University Press, 1998).

89. OC, III, *Notre Jeunesse*, p. 133.

90. In one passage, Péguy claims that Jewish anxiety has been "grafted" into Christianity as well, by Jesus himself (see OC, III, *Note conjointe*, p. 1293).

91. OC, III, *Notre Jeunesse*, p. 74.

92. Ibid., p. 135.

93. Ibid., p. 136.

94. Ibid., p. 138.

95. Ibid., pp. 138–139.

96. Prajs, pp. 93–94.

97. OC, III, *Notre Jeunesse*, p. 47.

98. Ibid., pp. 47; 84–86; 64–65.

99. Ibid., p. 50.

100. OC, III, *Dialogue de l'histoire de l'âme charnelle*, pp. 778.

101. Ibid.

102. Henri Bergson, *Oeuvres*, ed. Robinet, *Essai sur les données immédiates de la conscience*, p. 67.

103. Ibid., p. 109 (for a broader discussion of freedom and separation from conventional demarcations, temporal and otherwise, see pp. 109–113).

104. *Oeuvres poétiques*, *Le Mystère de la charité de Jeanne d'Arc*, p. 370.

105. Ibid., p. 372.

106. Ibid., p. 404.

107. Ibid., pp. 410–411.

108. OC, III, *Note conjointe sur M. Descartes*, p. 1293.

109. See Franz Rosenzweig, *The Star of Redemption*, trans. William Hallo (Notre Dame, IN: University of Notre Dame Press, 1985).

110. OC, III, *Un Nouveau Théologien*, p. 420. Italics in original text.

111. Ibid.

112. *Oeuvres poétiques*, *Le Porche*, p. 541.

113. Ibid., p. 544.

114. Ibid., p. 594.

115. Ibid., pp. 546–547.

116. Ibid., p. 547.

117. Ibid., p. 546.

118. Ibid., pp. 545 and 543.

119. Ibid., p. 545.

120. Ibid., p. 543.

121. Ibid., p. 604.

122. Ibid., *Le Porche*, p. 648.

123. Ibid., p. 651.

124. Ibid., pp. 663–664.

125. Ibid., pp. 670.

126. *Oeuvres poétiques*, *Le Mystère de la charité de Jeanne d'Arc*, p. 488.

127. OC, II, *Cahiers de la quinzaine*, February 3, 1907, p. 668.

128. *Lettres et entretiens*, ed. Marcel Péguy, p. 173.

129. *Oeuvres poétiques*, *Le Porche*, p. 615. The italics are Péguy's.

130. *Lettres et entretiens*, ed. Marcel Péguy, p. 172.

CHAPTER 11

1. See Jérôme and Jean Tharaud, "Le Nouvel État d'esprit: Charles Péguy," *L'Éclair*, August 7, 1910; Michel Arnauld, review of *Notre Jeunesse* in *La Nouvelle Revue Française*, September 1, 1910; "La Décomposition Dreyfusienne," *L'Action Française* (unsigned article), October 25, 1910. See also Henri Vaugeois, "Péguy," *L'Action Française*, June 12, 1911.

2. See "La Pensée et le style de Charles Péguy," *Journal de Genève* (written by "J.E.R."), June 11, 1911; "Paris: La retórica del Anuncio," in *El Liberal*, July 18, 1911; "Grand-prix de littérature,"

Czas (Krakow), June 17, 1913; Francesco Ruella, "Un Francescano," *Gazetta di Romano*, June 16, 1914; Valéry Larbuad, "From Abroad," *New Weekly* (London), June 13, 1914.

3. As recounted in the *Glasgow Herald*, March 13, 1912; the lecture was given to the Franco-Scottish Society.

4. See Henri Guilbeaux, "Die 'Cahiers de la Quinzaine,'" *Das literarische Echo*, June 1, 1912.

5. Ernst Sadler, "Die neue französische Lyrik," *Der lose Vogel*, no. 5, 1912. The complete article can be found at https://www.uni-due.de/lyriktheorie/texte/1912_stadler.html.

6. Alvan F. Sanborn, "Literary Notes from Paris," *New York Times*, June 25, 1910.

7. See Burac, *Péguy: La Révolution et la grâce*, p. 258.

8. For an account of the situation surrounding the prize competition, see ibid., pp. 258–259; see also Marjorie Villiers, *Charles Péguy* (London: Collins, 1965), pp. 269–271.

9. Alvan F. Sanborn, "Literary Notes from France," *New York Times*, July 23, 1911.

10. Romain Rolland, *Péguy*, vol. I (Paris: Albin Michel, 1944), p. 8.

11. See Isaiah Berlin, "Georges Sorel," in *Against the Current* (Princeton: Princeton University Press, 2013), p. 410. Originally published in 1979.

12. Burac, *Péguy: La Révolution et la grâce*, pp. 279–280.

13. Quoted in Villiers, p. 236.

14. *Lettres et entretiens*, ed. Péguy, pp. 178–181.

15. Ibid., p. 173.

16. Villiers, p. 342.

17. Burac, *Péguy: La Révolution et la grâce*, p. 289.

18. *Lettres et entretiens*, ed. Péguy, p. 210.

19. Burac, *Péguy: La Révolution et la grâce*, pp. 289–290. See also Annette Aronowicz, *Jews and Christians on Time and Eternity* (Stanford: Stanford University Press, 1998), p. 4.

20. See Ernest Psichari, *L'Appel des armes* (Paris: Oudin, 1913), dedicatory page. For Péguy's quarrel with Psichari, see Burac, *Péguy: La Révolution et la grâce*, p. 289. See also Frédérique Neau-Dufour, *Ernest Psichari: L'Ordre et l'errance* (Paris: Cerf, 2001), pp. 81 and 235, and Tharaud, *Notre Cher Péguy*, vol. II (Paris: Plon, 1926), pp. 179–182.

21. See Marcel Fournier, *Marcel Mauss*, trans. Jane Marie Todd (Princeton: Princeton University Press, 2006), pp. 98–99.

22. See OC, III, *Notre Jeunesse*, pp. 21–22, 158; *L'Argent*, p. 809.

23. Quoted in Burac, *Péguy: La Révolution et la grâce*, pp. 270–273.

24. Both Rolland and Benda were published in the 14th series of the *Cahiers*, in 1912–1913. Benda's critique of Bergson, entitled "Un philosophie pathétique," was published as a *Cahier* later in 1913.

25. See Péguy to Bergson, March 2, 1914, in Lazare Prajs, *Péguy et Israël* (Paris: Éditions A. G. Nizet, 1970), pp. 200–201.

26. Burac, *Péguy: La Révolution et la grâce*, pp. 292–293 and 297; Villiers, 352.

27. Tharaud, *Notre Cher Péguy*, vol. II, pp. 210–211.

28. Rolland, vol. II, p. 116.

29. OC, III, *Clio, Dialogue de l'histoire et de l'âme païenne*, p. 1214.

30. Tharaud, *Notre Cher Péguy*, vol. II, pp. 233–234.

31. Ibid., p. 244.

32. Robert Gildea, *Children of the Revolution: The French, 1799–1914* (Cambridge, MA: Harvard University Press, 2008), p. 437.

33. OC, III, *Note conjointe sur M. Descartes,* p. 1477.

34. Rolland, vol. II, p. 179.

35. Daniel Halévy, *Péguy et les Cahiers de la quinzaine* (Paris: Puriel, 1979), p. 399. Quoted in Burac, *Péguy: La Révolution et la grâce,* p. 301.

36. Villiers, p. 371.

37. Rolland, vol. II, pp. 180–182.

38. The Tharaud brothers report a remark to Péguy's friend Charles de Pesloüan broadly congruent with this reading, at least with reference to Péguy's regret that Jaurès had been murdered, and Péguy's sense that it was not altogether a misfortune in time of war: Péguy said he had been "obliged to say" to the radicals of his acquaintance that Jaurès's assassination was "abominable," but added to his friend that Jaurès did have a "power of capitulation" that would have been dangerous if France lost the war. See Tharaud, *Notre Cher Péguy,* vol. II, pp. 237–238.

39. Villiers, p. 377.

40. Cited in Géraldi Leroi, *Péguy entre l'ordre et la révolution* (Paris: Presses de la Fondation Nationale des Sciences Politiques, 1981), p. 245.

41. Villiers, p. 372.

42. Ibid., p. 370.

43. *Oeuvres poétiques,* p. 1102. An edited version of this passage, with a different translation, appears in Daniel Halévy, *Péguy and the Cahiers de la quinzaine* (New York: Longmans, 1947), p. 297.

44. Leroi, p. 258.

45. Villiers, p. 373.

46. Ibid., p. 372.

47. Ibid., p. 13 and p. 373; Burac *Péguy: La Révolution et la grâce,* p. 304.

48. See his remarks to that effect in Charles Péguy to Geneviève Favre, August 22, 1914. Published in *Amitié Charles Péguy,* no. 66, April–June 1994, p. 88.

49. Charles to Charlotte Péguy, August 7, 1914, in Victor Boudon, *Avec Charles Péguy de la Lorraine à la Marne, aôut–septembre 1914* (Paris: Hachette, 1916), p. 164.

50. Ibid., p. 60.

51. Gildea, p. 439.

52. See OC, III, *Notre Jeunesse,* p. 16.

53. Joseph Letaconnoux, "Le Départ de Péguy," *Le Crapouillot,* August 1918. Quoted in Burac, *Péguy: La Révolution et la grâce,* p. 304.

54. Claude to Simone Casimir-Perier, October 8, 1914, printed in Boudon, p. 193. See also Burac, *Péguy: La Révolution et la grâce,* p. 310, and Villiers, p. 380.

55. Halévy, p. 286.

56. Boudon, pp. 145–146.

CONCLUSION

1. Among many possible examples, one thinks of the references to Augustine and Aquinas in the Letter from Birmingham City Jail; the images of America's land and landscape in the "I Have a Dream" speech, as well as the references to the American Constitution and the Declaration of Independence; references in King's speeches and writings to

Jesus and Saint Paul, W. E. B. Du Bois, Shakespeare, Malcolm X, Plato, Martin Buber, Frederick Douglass, Kant, Lord Acton, and Gandhi; the closing of his speech to sanitation workers in Memphis the night before King was killed, with both its abundant biblical and distinctively American references to the Constitution and the "Battle Hymn of the Republic," as well as his speech on Vietnam in April 1967. See *A Testament of Hope: The Essential Writings and Speeches of Martin Luther King, Jr.*, ed. James M. Washington (New York: HarperCollins, 1986).

2. See OC, II, *Un Poète l'a dit*, pp. 810 and 1481, note 2.

3. See Julien Benda, *The Treason of the Intellectuals*, trans. Richard Aldington (New York: Norton, 1928), pp. 46–47.

4. OC, I, *Réponse brève à Jaurès*, p. 575.

5. OC, III, *L'Argent*, p. 805.

6. Quoted in Mark Edmundson, "When I Was Young at Yale,'" *Chronicle of Higher Education*, January 27, 2014. Rorty apparently included himself in this trajectory, but the earliest figures mentioned by Edmundson became prominent early in the last century, e.g., John Dewey.

INDEX

abstraction, in modernity, 92, 102, 103, 124, 192, 227
Académie Française, 59, 67, 176–77, 216–18
Action Française, 43, 74, 148, 150, 154, 158, 162, 165, 249n44
L'Action Française (newspaper), 216
Agathon (pseudonym of Henri Massis and Alfred de Tarde), 41
aging, 118–19
Alain (pseudonym of Émile Auguste Chartier), 135
Alain-Fournier (pseudonym of Henri-Alban Fournier), 218, 219
Algeria, 140
Alsace-Lorraine, 133, 152, 157, 159
amodernity, 6, 231
anarchists, 154
Angell, Norman, 133
Angola, 157
Année sociologique (journal), 40
anticlericalism, 15, 22, 73, 169, 191, 219, 225
antihumanism, 15, 98, 231
Antimilitarist Association, 154
antimodernism: Catholic, 67; and French Revolution, 84; Péguy and, 83, 85
anti-Semitism: Catholic, 43, 73–74, 193–94; Christian, 16, 193–94, 204; Dreyfus affair and, 42–43; as modern, 84–85, 86; in nineteenth-century France, 5, 42, 45, 68, 194; in Orléans, 68; Péguy and, 8–9, 14, 16–18, 22, 76, 217, 220; of reactionaries, 42; science as basis of, 42. *See also* Jews and Judaism: stereotyping and scapegoating of
anxiety: Christian, 203, 268n90; historiographical accounts of, 6, 11, 234n24; Jewish, 205, 268n90; Péguy's conception of, 15, 91; of the self, 91
Arendt, Hannah, 7

Aristotle, 60, 84, 85, 87
Aryans, 42, 121
"as if" metaphysical principles, 103, 109
Association de la Paix, 133
atheism, 34, 69–72, 78, 191, 202
Augustine, Saint, 56, 155, 166–67; *City of God*, 166
Aulard, Alphonse, 75

Bacon, Francis, 32, 34
Badiou, Alain, 100
Baillet, Louis, 70
Balthasar, Hans Urs von, 7, 20, 178
Barrès, Maurice, 42, 43, 154, 216–17; *The Uprooted*, 63, 77
Barth, Karl, 253n102
Baudelaire, Charles, 26
Baudouin, Charlotte (Charlotte Péguy), 73, 75, 80, 81, 149, 191, 221–22
Baudouin, Marcel, 73
Bell, David, 132–33, 139
Bellais, Georges, 75
Benda, Julien, 21, 82, 217, 219, 228
Benjamin, Walter, 7, 20
Bergson, Henri, 18, 51–61, 64, 84, 87; anti-Semitic attacks on, 22, 219–20; *Creative Evolution*, 54, 228; Durkheim vs., 103–4; on education, 58–61; *Essay on the Immediate Data of Consciousness*, 57; and evolution, 52, 55, 57–58, 243n159; and freedom, 54, 56–58, 114, 199, 207; "Good Sense and Classical Education," 59; *Introduction to Metaphysics*, 82; *Matter and Memory*, 54, 57; on mind and matter, 54–57; Péguy and, 20–22, 51, 69, 76–78, 81–82, 103–4, 199, 218–21, 224, 228; psychology of, 76–77; Ravaisson and, 50; and space, 52, 98; and time, 52–53, 55–58; on tolerance, 60, 230

Bernardin de Saint Pierre, Jacques-Henri, *Paul et Virginie*, 117
Bespaloff, Rachel, 7, 20
Bismarck, Otto von, 152–53
Blanchot, Maurice, 14, 236n42
Blondel, Maurice, *L'Action*, 195
Bloy, Léon, 18, 194
Blum, Léon, 79, 222
body, 117–31; Bergson's conception of, 56; bourgeois culture in opposition to, 124; denial of, 196–97; earthy, 119; late nineteenth-century conceptions of, 117, 120; limits and vulnerability of, 122; medical perspective on, 120, 126; modern conception of, 116, 120, 122–24; peasant, 118, 119; Péguy's conception of, 117–18, 120, 122; scholarship on, 117; soul in relation to, 117; and violence over questions of honor, 143; work performed with, 123, 131, 182. *See also* the carnal
bourgeois culture: avoidance of conflict by, 159; critique of, 77, 125, 127–30; denial of the body by, 124; as feature of modernity, 123–25; money and the market linked to, 124, 126; the press and, 77–78; universality of, 77, 125; work and, 123–29
Boutroux, Émile, 20, 49–51, 78–79, 224
brain, 38–39, 55–56
Brenner, Anastasios, 49
Briand, Aristide, 158
Brunetière, Ferdinand, 194

Cahiers de la quinzaine (Fortnightly Notebooks), 21, 61, 64, 71, 79–82, 122, 123, 132, 134, 135, 140, 142, 146–49, 150, 179, 216–20, 222
Caillaux, Henriette, 143
Caillaux, Joseph, 142
Calvin, John, 200
capitalism, 43, 107, 202–3, 218, 219, 227. *See also* money and the market
the carnal: Christianity grounded in, 196–97, 199–201, 207–8; denial of, 120, 122–24, 196–97; earthiness of, 23, 120, 122–23, 139, 229; Jewish stereotyping concerning, 194; Judaism grounded in, 208; in Pascal's orders of human being, 87; Péguy and, 23, 196; shared life in, 160; the spiritual in relation to, 119–20, 122–23, 183, 196–97; war and, 137–39. *See also* body

Cassagmac, Paul de, 142
Catholicism: antimodernism of, 193; and anti-Semitism, 43, 73–74, 193–94; conversion to, 75; critique of, 193; in French culture, 26; and Judaism, 16–18; liberal, 198, 201–2, 219; modernist, 194–95, 219; Pascal and, 79; Péguy and, 22, 67–70, 74, 149–50, 165, 169, 179, 191, 216, 218–20, 225, 266n7; right vs. left, 74, 193–95; and secularism, 74; social movements of, 74; Ultramontane, 67–68, 74. *See also* Index of Forbidden Books
Cavour, Camillo, 152–53
certainty/uncertainty, 32, 45–48, 109–11, 213
Charcot, Jean-Martin, 120
charity, 34, 50–51, 180. *See also* love
Charles VII, 84, 86
Chartres Cathedral, 219
Chaucer, Geoffrey, 118
Christianity, 191–215; and anti-Semitism, 16, 193–94, 204; anxiety associated with, 203, 268n90; carnal nature of, 196–97, 199–201, 207–8; community as basis of, 199; corruption of, 172; critique of, 192–93, 196–202, 208; individuals' relationship to, 203–4; Jewish aspects in, 15, 195, 197, 204, 206–8, 215, 268n90; love as essential to, 191, 196, 197, 199, 203; morality and, 34–35, 197–200, 214–15, 220; obstacles to belief in, 191–92, 195–96; patience as significant aspect of, 182, 190, 191, 195, 198, 202–3, 208–9, 213–14; in Péguy's works about Jeanne d'Arc, 183–90, 207; and politics, 201; *ressourcement* of, 196–97, 200, 204, 207–8, 213–14; revolutionary character of, 197, 202, 215; risk and vulnerability in, 203, 212; and time, 201, 209–11, 214. *See also* Catholicism; Protestantism
cities, 124
classical education, 22, 41, 59–60, 66–67, 106
Claudel, Paul, 18, 75, 182–83
Clausewitz, Wilhelm von, 133, 141
Clemenceau, Georges, 21, 142
Clio, muse of history, 84, 99, 102, 112, 119, 120, 160–61, 179, 206, 220, 222
Collège de France, 78, 195
Collège de Sainte-Barbe, 69
Collier, Paul, 70
colonialism, 136, 261n35. *See also* imperialism

Combes, Émile, 147
competence, Péguy's vision of the age of, 130–31, 212
Comte, Auguste, 26, 28–29, 31–35, 43–46, 50, 52, 71, 83, 104, 117, 130
Condorcet, Nicolas de Caritat, marquis de, 132
Connelly, John, *From Enemy to Brother*, 16–18
consciousness, 38, 54–55, 76
Constant, Benjamin, 35, 133, 151
Corneille, Pierre, 72, 110, 111, 143–46, 161, 224; *Le Cid*, 145; *Polyeucte*, 143–44
countries, 160–62. *See also* nations and nation-states
courage, 9–10, 145
Cousin, Victor, 26–27, 72, 259n3
critique: defined, 30; as ground of freedom, 39; in late nineteenth-century thought, 39; Péguy's critique of, 94–116; Renan's advocacy of, 30–31, 94. *See also* reading and interpretation
La Croix (*The Cross*) (newspaper), 43
Crucifixion, 180, 187, 206, 207, 215

Dante Alighieri, *Paradiso*, 218
Darwin, Charles, 52, 102
Dastre, Alfred, 38, 51
death: aging as harbinger of, 118; denial of, 120; thoughts on contemplation of one's approaching, 119, 209–10
Debussy, Claude, 22, 181
Dechristianization Campaign, 74
Declaration of the Rights of Man, 90, 138, 159, 249n44
decreations. *See* second creations
de Gaulle, Charles, 7, 20, 176
Deism, 34, 195
Delescluze, Charles, 152
Deleuze, Gilles, 7–8, 16, 20, 176, 177, 179
democracy, 43
Déroulède, Paul, *Chants de soldat*, 134
Descartes, René, 31–32, 34, 79, 83, 109–10
destitution, 126–27, 129, 255n59
determinism, 2, 58
Diaghilev, Serge, 65
Dreyfus, Alfred, 5, 8–9, 14–16, 21, 42–43, 73–77, 145, 147, 154, 162, 168, 194
Dreyfus affair, 5, 9, 15–16, 42–43, 73–77, 96, 100, 145, 154, 159, 165, 167–68, 172, 175, 206
Dreyfusards, 8–10, 14, 18, 21, 43, 73, 75–77, 96, 145, 158, 167–68, 172

Drumont, Édouard, 121, 194; *La France juive*, 42
duels: Péguy and, 73, 142; resurgence of, 142–43; war conceived on the model of, 132–33, 136, 141
Duhem, Pierre, 48–49, 61, 94, 224
Dupanloup, Félix, 67–68
durée (duration), 53, 56–57, 61
Durkheim, Émile, 7, 18, 27, 29, 31–33, 35–36, 39–41, 45, 47, 49–50, 52, 60, 84, 87, 95, 103–4, 195; *Suicide*, 103

earthiness: of the carnal, 23, 120, 122–23, 139, 229; of Catholicism, 200, 224; denial of, 122–23; of experience, 103, 110; hope and, 177, 180, 211; of Jeanne d'Arc, 184; of nature, 118; of peasants, 22, 118, 119, 184, 200; in Péguy's work, 22, 23, 178, 183, 200, 224; piety and, 183, 200
L'Éclair (journal), 216
eclecticism, 26–27
École des Beaux-Arts, 26
École Normale Supérieure, 40, 69–70, 72, 75, 80, 146
École Pratique des Hautes Études, 40
education: Christian, 192–93; classical, 22, 41, 59–60, 66–67, 106; as cultivation of mind, 58–61, 66–67, 106–7; Ferry reforms of, 27–28, 106–7; in late nineteenth-century France, 25, 27–28, 58–61, 66–69, 106–7; Péguy's, 66–70, 80; role of humanities in, 59–60; secularism in, 28, 31, 68, 84. *See also* learning; teachers
Edwards, Jonathan, 204
1848 Revolution, 26, 63, 74, 152
Einstein, Albert, 47
Enlightenment, 132
equality, 126, 129
ethics, 33
Euripides, 84, 85
events, 100, 102, 200, 227–28
evolution, 52, 57–58, 102, 243n159

fascism, 8–11; self in relation to, 13; and war, 134, 140, 229
fatras (jumble, messiness), 115, 118
Favre, Geneviève, 81, 149, 220–22
Favre, Jules, 149
feminism, 43
Fénelon, François, 132
Fermat, Pierre de, 79

Ferry, Jules, 28, 68, 200
Ferry Laws (1880), 106
Feuerbach, Ludwig, 34–35
Le Figaro (newspaper), 74, 142
First Moroccan Crisis (1905, 1906), 136, 140
Flaubert, Gustave, A Sentimental Education, 63, 77
Forth, Christopher, The Dreyfus Affair and the Crisis of French Manhood, 8–11
Foucault, Michel, 12, 13, 235n26
France: anti-Semitism in, 5, 42, 45, 68, 194; Catholicism in, 26; culture of, 25–27; education in, 25, 27–28; and modernity, 26–27; as nation, 155; Péguy's view of, 155–59; Third Republic, 27–43, 58–69; war fascination in, 134–35
France, Anatole, 21, 29, 78, 202
Franco-Prussian War, 25–27, 68–69, 152
Franz Ferdinand, Archduke, 220
Frary, Raoul, 27–28, 41
fraternity, 129–30
freedom: Bergson's conception of, 54, 56, 57–58, 61, 114, 199, 207; critique as ground of, 39; God's, 207; memory as affordance of, 57, 114; modernism vs., 1, 105, 144–45; particularism as ground of, 159, 161–62; Péguy's conception of, 6, 158–59; the self and, 207; uncertainty as basis of, 111, 115, 118. See also individuals: agency of
French Revolution, 22, 26, 58, 69, 74, 84, 97, 100, 129, 132, 133, 138, 141, 155, 160, 172, 193, 229, 261n44
Freud, Sigmund, 95
Fussell, Paul, 120
Futurism, 134

Gambetta, Léon, 28–29
Gauguin, Paul, 10
Germany, 133, 136–37, 140, 152, 153, 157–59, 218, 223
Gide, André, 21, 176, 217
gift, 19
Gillet, Louis, 72
Girondins, 132, 155, 229
Global Positioning System, 45
Gobineau, Arthur de, 42
God: death of, 177, 231; in Descartes's thought, 34; freedom of, 207; in Kant's thought, 34; love shown by, 196, 203–4; in modernist thought, 91, 101, 171; Péguy's conception of, 111, 178–80, 182–83, 191,

196, 200, 204, 210, 212–13, 215; in Péguy's poetry, 155, 156, 179–81, 185–86, 189, 204, 213; in positivist thought, 30, 31; relation of world to, 178, 181–83, 196–97, 201; in socialist thought, 28; vulnerability of, 215
Gödel, Kurt, 21
Goncourt Prize, 217
Gordon, Peter, 13
grace, 159, 184, 197, 199, 212–13
gratitude, 182–83
Great War, 21, 134, 139, 141, 191, 220–23, 229
Gregory of Tours, 155
Greuze, Jean-Baptiste, 118
Groethuysen, Bernard, 204
La Guerre sociale (newspaper), 154
Guizot, François, 28, 151

Habermas, Jürgen, 262n42
habit, limitations imposed by, 56–57, 60, 89–93, 107, 125
Halévy, Daniel, 165, 176, 179, 221
Hammerschlag, Sarah, The Figural Jew, 14–17
happiness, 118–19. See also humanity and human being: fulfillment of
Harmonious City, in Péguy's writings, 75–76, 79, 135, 154, 156
Harnack, Adolf von, 195
heartland, 4
Hébertists, 132
Hegel, G.W.F., 35, 93, 170, 195, 259n3
Heidegger, Martin, 209
Herder, Johann Gottfried von, 151–52
heroism, 8–10, 184–89
Herr, Lucien, 70–72, 79, 80, 219, 222
Hervé, Gustave, 154, 162, 205
higher education. See scholars and universities
Hilbert, David, 21
historicism, 15, 19–20, 25, 88, 97–98, 109
history and historiography: as arbiter of value, 90–91, 101–2, 202, 222; critique of models of, 13–14, 19–20, 25, 40–41, 96–104, 112–13; events in, 100, 102, 200, 227–28; interpretation of/in, 111–14; memory vs., 99–100; normative frameworks underlying, 12–13; Péguy's conception of, 96–104, 112–13; positivist, 40–41; roles of individuals and structural circumstances in, 13–14, 19–20, 98, 113; theology in relation to, 195. See also historicism

Hobbes, Thomas, 60, 170
Hofmannsthal, Hugo von, 10, 65
Homer, 109, 112–13, 136, 161, 192
honor: *Cahiers* as expression of, 146–48, 150; Dreyfus affair and, 145; dueling and, 142–43; justice associated with, 145–46; Péguy's notion of, 142–50; sacrifice associated with, 142, 144–45; war and, 136–37, 141
hope, 101, 113, 119, 120, 123, 177–78, 180, 208, 210–14, 226, 232
Hugo, Victor, 109, 140, 155
humanities, 37, 59, 225
humanity and human being: aging as essential feature of, 118–19; fulfillment of, 34, 72, 119 (*see also* happiness); fundamental experiences of, 110; and inhumanity of modernisms, 5; limits and vulnerability of, 118–19, 122; modernity's conception of, 104–5; Pascal's orders of, 87, 173–74; Pascal's religious understanding of, 197; religion of humanity, 26, 29, 34–35, 44; scientific studies of, 38–39; and specialization, 58; transcendence/disappearance of, 3, 31, 39, 103; universalist opposition to, 3, 5; values of, 89–90. *See also* antihumanism; body; the carnal; soul; the spiritual
Huysmans, J. K., 75

idealism, 54, 56
Ignatius of Loyola, 42
immanent becoming, 1–5, 13, 31, 33, 45, 225, 229
imperialism, 138, 140, 157, 172, 218. *See also* colonialism
Incarnation, 100, 185, 187, 196, 200–202, 206–8, 215
Index of Forbidden Books, 193, 202, 220; Vatican, 22
individuals: agency of, 14, 19, 33, 36–37, 98, 113; the social in relation to, 1, 27, 30, 33
intellect. *See* mind/intellect
intellectual coalition, 39–41, 43–44, 47, 49, 57–59
intellectual history, 13–14
intellectual party, 5, 29, 93, 95–99, 101–4, 106–7, 109, 116, 144, 146, 184
internationalism, 77, 152, 158, 159, 172
interpretation. *See* reading and interpretation

Isaac, Jules, 16
Italy, 152

Jacobins, 76, 84, 155, 229
James, Henry, 10
James, William, 52
Jammes, Francis, 177
Jansenism, 79, 193, 196–97
Jaurès, Jean, 28, 58, 71–72, 76, 79, 133, 138, 142, 147–48, 163, 165, 205, 219, 221, 271n38
Jeanne d'Arc, 10, 15, 67, 72, 84–86, 123, 136, 180, 183–90, 198, 202, 207, 210–11, 214, 225
Jesus: carnal nature of, 196, 199; essential Christian role of, 202, 208, 210; God's relationship to, 213; incorporation of Jewishness into Christianity by, 15, 195, 204, 206–8, 268n90; Jews' responsibility for death of, 17, 68, 194, 206; particular circumstances of, 113, 161; Péguy's faith and, 191; in Péguy's work, 185, 188–89; the poor and vulnerable associated with, 129, 196, 199; war associated with, 138. *See also* Crucifixion; Incarnation; Passion; Resurrection
Jews and Judaism: anxiety and, 205, 268n90; carnal nature of, 208; Catholicism and, 16–18; and the Dreyfus affair, 14–15; exemplary status of, 205; Jesus and, 15, 17, 68, 194, 195, 204, 206–8, 268n90; patience characteristic of, 195, 208; Péguy and, 14–17, 204–6; stereotyping and scapegoating of, 194, 204–6, 208. *See also* anti-Semitism
Joinville, Jean de, 15
journalism and newspapers: and dueling, 142; as expression of truth, 63, 77, 79, 146–47, 150; importance of, 62–63; Péguy and, 61, 64, 77–78, 80–81, 93
Judaism. *See* Jews and Judaism
Jünger, Ernst, 139
justice: 10, 16, 18, 34, 74, 76, 90, 91, 94, 120, 126; classical education and, 60; Dreyfus affair and, 14–15; fraternity linked to, 129–30; God as, 183; honor associated with, 145–46; mysticism in relation to, 163, 166–69, 172, 174–75; particularism as ground of, 159, 161–62, 175; universal, 3, 9, 77, 129, 138, 158, 162–63, 167–68, 175, 226; value of, 60, 122, 130, 139; war and, 139, 140

Kallen, Horace, 52
Kant, Immanuel, 27, 34, 54–55, 63, 70, 107,
    111, 124–25, 132, 140, 177–78, 182, 194, 229.
    See also neo-Kantianism
Kierkegaard, Søren, 176–78, 253n102
King, Martin Luther, Jr., 226, 271n1
kitsch, 118
Klimt, Gustav, 10
knowledge: modern, 85; neo-Kantian
    conceptions of, 50–51. See also mind/
    intellect
Kraus, Karl, 62, 65
Kundera, Milan, 118

La Mettrie, Julien Offroy de, 34
Langlois, Charles, 37, 98, 148
language, in twenty-first century, 226–27
Lanson, Gustave, 37, 41, 47, 58, 95, 97
Lapie, Paul, 40
late modernity, conventional view of, 11–13
Latour, Bruno, 176
Laudet, Fernand, 201–2
Lavisse, Ernest, 60, 95, 100, 217
Lazare, Bernard, 9, 14–17, 73, 81, 121, 158,
    167–69, 205–6, 260n30, 266n7
learning, 58–61, 111–15. See also teachers
Le Bon, Gustave, 164; Psychology of Crowds,
    134
Leo XIII, Pope, 74; Aeterni Patris, 193; Au
    Milieu des sollicitudes, 74; Rerum
    Novarum, 74
Levinas, Emmanuel, 14, 111
Lévy, Albert, 69
Lévy, Edmond-Maurice, 206
liberalism, political, 114, 139, 144–45, 152,
    158, 174, 229
liberalism, theological, 195, 198, 201–3, 219
La Libre parole (Free Speech) (newspaper), 42
Ligue pour la culture française, 59
Littré, Émile, 29, 35, 44, 67, 71
Lobachevsky, Nikolai, 47
Loire River, 65
Loisy, Alfred, 195
Der lose Vogel (journal), 216
Lotte, Joseph, 18, 158, 179, 191, 215, 217–18,
    219
Louis-Napoleon, 67
Louis XIV, 84, 137
love: Christian, 191, 196, 197, 199, 203, 215;
    God's, 111, 196, 203–4; in modern
    thought, 29, 34–35, 50–51, 62, 86, 87, 95;

moralism in relation to, 197–200;
    morality grounded in, 50–51; mysticism
    and, 166–69, 172, 174–75, 231;
    particularism as ground of, 162, 163, 166;
    in Pascal's orders of human being, 87; and
    politics, 156, 159, 166–67, 171, 172, 174–75,
    226; transcendent nature of, 51, 166; work
    and reading as expression of, 113, 123,
    125, 131
Lubac, Henri de, 7
Luce, Siméon, 184
Lukes, Steven, 40
Luther, Martin, 42
Ly, Arria, 142
Lycée d'Orléans, 66
Lycée Lakanal, 69, 133
Lycée Louis-le-Grand, 69, 78

Machiavelli, Niccolò, 170
Maistre, Joseph de, 84, 164
Mallarmé, Stéphane, 181
Marinetti, Filippo Tommaso, 134, 139
Maritain, Jacques, 18, 75, 191
Maritain, Raïssa, 75, 194
market. See money and the market
Marx, Karl, and Marxism, 8, 12, 21, 72, 86,
    108, 164, 224; The German Ideology, 70
masculinism, 8–10
Massis, Henri, 41, 241n92
materialism, 38, 54–56, 71, 76
Mathiez, Albert, 69, 133, 159
Maurras, Charles, 43–45, 47, 74, 85, 142, 154,
    164, 218–20, 233n1, 249n44; The Future of
    Intelligence, 43–44
Mauss, Marcel, 7, 18, 19, 33, 47, 60, 95, 219
Mazzini, Giuseppe, 152, 172
memory, 38, 50, 54–57, 99–100, 114
metaphysics: critiques of, 31, 39, 94–95,
    102–3, 105, 110, 229; defined, 237n62;
    federalism of, 115, 229; homogeneity vs.
    diversity in, 88, 90–91, 96–98, 107–9,
    112–15; incomplete, unpredictable, and
    risky character of, 110–11, 113, 115, 128–29;
    of the intellectual party, 95–96, 98, 101,
    103–4, 106, 109, 116; modern, 84, 86–109,
    114–16, 120, 123, 139, 170–71, 173, 175, 212,
    219, 229–31; Péguy's conception of,
    110–14. See also philosophy
Michelet, Jules, 98–100, 151, 155, 184
Milhaud, Gaston, 45–49, 94
Mill, John Stuart, 140

Millerand, Alexandre, 137

mind/intellect: Bergson's conception of, 54, 56–57; materialistic conception of, 38; and modernity, 87–88, 103, 175; in Pascal's orders of human being, 87. *See also* knowledge

misery. *See* destitution

modernity: anti-Semitism and, 84–86; and the body, 116, 120, 122–24; bourgeois culture in, 123–25; Catholic embrace of, 194–95, 219; Catholic opposition to, 193; dual nature of, 1; France and, 26–27; freedom and, 1, 105, 144–45; God in, 91, 101, 171; and human being, 104–5; identity and, 3; as immanent becoming, 1–3, 13; the market as key characteristic of, 89–93, 107–9, 115; mechanical, systematic, controlling character of, 85–88, 91, 115, 175, 182, 192; metaphysics associated with, 84, 86–109, 114–16, 120, 123, 139, 170–71, 173, 175, 212, 219, 229–31; mind/intellect and, 87–88, 103, 175; mysticism shunned by, 170–71; new or transformative character of, 83–84, 88, 104–5, 107; oppositional, particularist strand of, 3–5; Péguy's conception of, 1, 5–6, 83–93; Péguy's speculative future of, 130–31; scholarship on, 11–13; second creations of, 92–93, 97, 120, 192, 213–14; the self in, 91–93, 170–71, 249n50; sovereign character of, 107–8; technology in, 1, 114, 115, 130–31, 141, 181–82, 214, 226; time in, 91; war in, 136–37, 139, 141. *See also* antimodernism; late modernity

Monet, Claude, 22, 181

money and the market: bourgeois culture and, 124–25; modern life shaped by, 88–93, 107–9, 114–15, 219; in twenty-first-century experience, 227; war in relation to, 133

morality: Christianity as basis for, 34–35; Christian moralism as perversion of, 197–200, 214–15, 220; Péguy on, 69, 198–99, 220; science in relation to, 50; in twenty-first-century experience, 227

Morel, E. D., 21–22, 136

Le Mouvement socialiste (journal), 76

Mozart, Wolfgang Amadeus, 89

Müller, R. F., 55

mysticism: anti-institutional conditions for, 16, 169–70; corruption of, 171–72, 174, 190, 201; Dreyfus affair and, 15–16, 165, 167, 175, 206; Jaurès and, 71–72, 165; Jews and, 206; justice and truth in relation to, 162, 163, 166–69, 172, 174–75; love and, 166–69, 172, 174–75; modernity's shunning of, 170–71; participants in, 167–68; Péguy and, 71, 165; politics and, 71–72, 164–75; relations among forms of, 168–69, 173, 174, 230; scientific opposition to, 35–36; suffering in relation to, 166

Nabokov, Vladimir, 11

Napoleon Bonaparte, 138

Napoleon III, 26–27, 67, 152

National Convention, 138, 159–60, 261n44

nationalism: imperialism and, 172; internationalism in relation to, 77; Péguy and, 155–57, 160; universalism and, 42, 152, 154; and war fascination, 134

National Socialism, 140

nations and nation-states, 33, 140, 151–53. *See also* countries

nature, 117–18, 182, 193

Naudy, Théophile, 66–67

neo-Kantianism, 41, 48–50, 78, 194

Neoplatonism, 52

neo-Thomism, 85

Newman, John Henry, 195

New Sorbonne, 37–38, 40, 58, 95, 97–100, 109, 165

New York Times (newspaper), 216, 217

Nicole, Pierre, 79

Nietzsche, Friedrich, 7, 35, 81, 83, 89, 95, 139, 153, 166, 169, 170, 176–78

night, as Christian metaphor, 203–4, 213

non-Euclidean geometry, 47–48

La Nouvelle Revue Française (journal), 216

the organic: modern disdain for, 86–87, 91, 99, 124, 181–82, 192; Péguy's affirmation of, 23, 114, 123, 130; real and genuine nature of, 86–87, 91, 98, 103, 114, 131, 182–83; social sciences' disdain for, 36

Orléans, 65–68

pacifism, 132–36, 140, 148

paganism, 192

Papal States, 152

parents, 125

Paris, 124

Paris Commune (1871), 73, 74, 152

Parmenides, 53

particularism: abstraction vs., 92; anger characteristic of, 4; characteristics of, 3–5; freedom grounded in, 159, 161–62; justice grounded in, 159, 161–62, 166, 175; love grounded in, 163, 166; as opponent of immanent becoming, 3–5, 225; opposition to, 5, 154; Péguy and, 157, 159–63; reactionary political championing of, 4–5, 42–43, 154, 162; self-contradictions of, 4–5; universalism in relation to, 151–54, 159, 162, 259n3

party, as term of opprobrium, 95–96

Pascal, Blaise: Boutroux's lectures on, 50, 78–79; and Catholicism, 79; Descartes vs., 110; and Judaism, 197; on knowledge, 50–51; and orders of experience/the human being, 87, 173–74; Péguy and, 20, 50, 78–79, 87, 110–11, 122, 182, 197, 200, 224–25; as subject of *Cahiers* essays, 81; writing of, 79

Passion, 17, 186, 188–89, 206, 208–9, 214

past: Bergson's conception of, 56; particularist conception and use of, 4; the present in relation to, 21; as possibilities for the present and future, 39

patience: characteristic of love and mysticism, 168, 171, 173, 195; as essential to Christianity, 182, 190, 198, 202–3, 207–9, 213–14; Jewish, 195, 208

Paul, Émile, 112

peasants and peasant culture: body of, 118, 119; earthiness of, 22, 184; exemplary qualities of, 183–84, 189, 200, 209, 214; God depicted as, 156, 180; Jeanne d'Arc associated with, 184, 189; modernity's destruction of, 128; Péguy's affinity for, 22, 66–67, 69, 118, 127, 156, 180, 200, 224; piety of, 200; time sense of, 214

Péguy, Charles: and Bergson, 20, 22, 50–52, 54, 69, 76–78, 81–82; bookshop of, 8, 9, 75, 79–80, 82, 220; children of, 141, 149, 191, 219, 221; death of, 21, 22, 223; extramarital passion of, 149, 217, 219; finances of, 75, 80–82, 215–17; friendships of, 69–73, 79, 217–18, 220–22; intellectual commitments of, 21–23; marriage of, 73, 149, 191, 217; and mécontemporains, 233n2; and modernity, 1, 5–6; poverty of, 21; prize awarded to, 217; relevance and significance of, 6–8, 23–24, 61–62, 225–32;

scholarship on, 8–11, 14–20; and science, 49–50; social position of, 21, 216–18; on violence and war, 8–10; youth of, 65–82

Péguy, Charles, writings of: *L'Argent*, 144–45, 159, 218; *L'Argent suite*, 157, 218; *Clio, Dialogue of History with the Carnal Soul*, 17, 84, 99, 102, 112, 119, 120, 160–61; *Clio, Dialogue of History with the Pagan Soul*, 84, 99–102, 111, 113, 118–20, 124, 160, 161, 192; *Ève*, 123, 181–82, 218, 220–22; "The Flu Again," 122; *Jeanne d'Arc*, 72, 75, 136, 184–86, 188; *Marcel: First Dialogue of the Harmonious City*, 75–76, 135; *The Mystery of Jeanne d'Arc's Love*, 17, 150, 176–77, 179, 185–89, 201–2, 207, 210–11, 214, 216, 219; *The Mystery of the Holy Innocents*, 155–57, 179–80; *Note conjointe sur M. Descartes*, 107, 139, 221; *Note on Bergson and Bergsonian Philosophy*, 220; *Notre Jeunesse* ("Our Youth"), 9, 16, 17, 121, 131, 147, 157–58, 165, 167, 169, 179, 204–5, 216, 217; "On the Flu," 122; *On the Situation Made for the Intellectual Party in the Modern World*, 106; *The Portal of the Mystery of Hope*, 123, 177, 179–81, 188, 203, 208–9, 211–13, 217; reception of, 176–78, 216–18; "Still More on the Flu," 122; style of, 176–81; *Victor-Marie, Comte Hugo*, 123, 179, 218. See also *Cahiers de la quinzaine*

philosophy: change in, 100; differences within, 111; positivist attack on, 51; sociology vs., 33, 103–4. *See also* metaphysics

Pius IX, Pope, 26; *Syllabus of Errors*, 67

Pius X, Pope, 74, 195

Plato, and Platonism, 21, 51, 94, 95, 107, 111, 113, 114, 161, 201, 230

Poincaré, Henri, 18, 20, 47–49, 51, 59, 94, 224; *Science and Hypothesis*, 47; *The Sciences and the Humanities*, 59

Poincaré, Raymond, 21

politics: Christianity and, 201; love and, 166–67, 174–75; modern, 170–71; mysticism and, 71–72, 164–75; Péguy and, 7, 73, 75, 77, 135, 158–60, 164–75, 219; reactionary, 41–43; scientific vs. irrational, 164; in twenty-first-century experience, 228

the poor. *See* poverty and the poor

Portugal, 157

positivism, 26, 28–29, 35, 40, 44–46, 71, 76, 130
poverty and the poor, 126–29, 144–45, 167, 169, 175, 255n59
Prajs, Lazare, 206
present: Bergson's conception of, 55–56; the past in relation to, 21; Péguy's conception of, 81, 190
Pressensé, Francis de, 157, 159
process theology, 215
progress, 90
Protestantism, 195, 200
Proust, Marcel, 7, 21, 52, 65, 142, 176, 177
Prudhomme, Sully, "Descartes," 32
Psichari, Ernest, 75; L'Appel des armes, 134–35, 218
psychology, 76

Quicherat, Jules, 184
Quinet, Edgar, 151, 152

Rabelais, François, 110
race, 120–21
Racine, Jean, 84, 144
Raphaël, Blanche, 149–50, 217, 219, 222
rationality. See mind/intellect; science
Ravaisson, Félix, 50–51
Rawls, John, 174
reaction, political, 5, 24, 41–45, 84, 85, 108, 154, 162, 164, 165, 202, 208, 219
reading and interpretation, 111–14, 253n102
reason. See knowledge; mind/intellect; science
reductionism, 88
Reinach, Joseph, 142
Reinach, Salomon and Théodore, 58
religion: critiques of, 29–31, 39, 71–72; positive aspects of, 71–72; religion of humanity, 26, 29, 34–35, 44; sociological study of, 35–36, 40. See also Catholicism; Christianity; Protestantism
Renan, Ernest, 29–33, 39, 45, 52, 67, 75, 81, 84, 97, 106, 121, 134, 151–52, 166, 218, 230–31; The Future of Science, 29–31, 83, 87, 94, 164; La Vie de Jésus, 29; Qu'est-ce qu'une Nation, 153
repetition: Christian meaning of failures of, 212–13; limitations imposed by, 190; in Péguy's works, 176–81, 185; science and, 48. See also habit
replica creations. See second creations

respect, 105, 145–48
ressourcement (going back to the sources), 21, 196, 200, 204, 207–8, 213–14
Resurrection, 186, 196, 206–8, 210, 215
revolution: Christian, 197, 202, 215; connotations of, 23; Péguy and, 23, 225
La Revue blanche (journal), 73
Revue de métaphysique et de morale (journal), 32
Revue des deux mondes (journal), 38, 194
La Revue socialiste (journal), 102, 103
Ribot, Théodore, 38, 54–55
Ribot's Law, 55
Riby, Jules, 221
Richelieu, Armand Jean du Plessis, Cardinal, 137
Richer, Edmond, 184
Richet, Charles, 140, 148
Riemann, Bernhard, 47
Rimbaud, Arthur, 181
risk and wagering, 91, 99, 109–11, 113, 115, 128–29, 203. See also sacrifice
Roland, Madame, 132, 140
Rolland, Romain, 17, 21, 81, 82, 134, 148, 217, 219–21; Jean-Christophe, 247n81
romanticism, 43, 117, 188
Rops, Félicien, 10
Roques, Mario, 79
Rorty, Richard, 231
Rosenzweig, Franz, 208
Rousseau, Jean-Jacques, 43, 83, 84, 117, 118, 170
Roy, Henri, 66, 69
Russell, Bertrand, 65

sacrifice: Christianity based on, 196; courage associated with, 9–10; honor associated with, 142, 144–45; Jeanne d'Arc and, 186; modernity and, 86, 91; nations unified by, 153; particularists' willingness to, 4; Péguy and, 110, 123, 141–42, 148; truth associated with, 63, 110, 135. See also risk and wagering
Sangnier, Marc, 72, 74, 147, 259n91
Scheler, Max, 65
scholars and universities: as advocates of immanent becoming, 2–3, 8; critique of, 2–3, 6, 8–9, 11–20, 29, 92–93, 95–97, 103–9, 146, 225, 227; late nineteenth-century principles governing, 39–41; modern, 92–93; opposition to, 4; reactionary forces, 41–45; Renan's recommendations for, 30–31; and specialization, 58

Scholem, Gershom, 7, 16
Schwarz, Ottilie, 18
science: anti-Semitism buttressed by, 42; as
    basis of cultural advancement, 27, 29–33,
    44, 130; change in, 100; critique of science
    by, 45–51; and the human being, 38–39;
    and the humanities, 37; Péguy's vision for,
    130–31; politics and, 164; social sciences
    and, 32–33, 35–38, 44, 102; status of, in
    late nineteenth century, 36–39, 41, 109
secondary education, 41, 59, 66, 106
second creations, 92–93, 97, 120, 192, 213–14
Second Moroccan Crisis (1911), 136
Second Vatican Council, *Nostra Aetate*, 16
secularism: Catholicism and, 74; in French
    education, 28, 31, 68, 84; Jews blamed for,
    73; Péguy's education and, 68
security, personal, 8, 56, 88, 91, 99, 126–28
Seelisburg conference (1947), 16
Seignobos, Charles, 37, 47, 75, 95
self: anxieties of, 91; Bergson's conception of,
    57; fascism in relation to, 13; and freedom,
    207; modern, 91–93, 170–71, 249n50;
    vulnerability of, 212
self-giving, 170–71
self-interest, 86, 88, 89, 124
semaines sociales (discussion sessions), 74
Senghor, Léopold, 7, 20
Sillon, 74
Simiand, François, 36–37, 44, 45, 47, 48, 59,
    60, 79, 80
sin, 17, 197–98, 203, 206, 214, 215
socialism: and the Dreyfus affair, 75;
    embourgeoisement of, 125, 129; of Jaurès,
    71, 76; and pacifism, 133–34; Péguy and,
    21, 69–71, 73, 75–76, 78–80, 127, 131,
    150, 219
Socialist Party, 71, 80–81, 129, 219
sociology and social sciences: critique of, 21,
    102–4, 106; in French universities, 40, 96;
    nature as conceived by, 118; vs.
    philosophy, 33, 103–4; of religion, 35–36,
    40; scientific basis of, 32–33, 35–38, 44, 102
Sorbonne, 40, 41, 59, 75, 78, 94, 104, 107,
    217. *See also* New Sorbonne
Sorel, Georges, 71, 82, 139, 164, 217;
    Reflections on Violence, 134
soul: Bergson's conception of, 56; body in
    relation to, 117; materialist account of, 38;
    and Pascal's orders of human being, 87.
    See also the spiritual

space: Bergson's conception of, 56; Poincaré's
    conception of, 47–48; time in relation to,
    52–53, 98
the spiritual: the carnal in relation to,
    119–20, 122–23, 183, 196–97; denial of,
    120, 122–23. *See also* soul
Stadler, Ernst, 216
Staël, Madame de, 43
St. Bartholomew's Day Massacre, 153
Stein, Gertrude, 65
Steiner, George, 14
Strauss, Richard, 10
St. Vincent de Paul Society, 69
sublime, 182
suffering: associated with aging, 118–19; of
    the destitute, 127; existential question of,
    190; honor associated with, 144; Jeanne
    d'Arc and, 186; mysticism in relation to,
    166; nations unified by, 153
Surkis, Judith, 234n24
Suttner, Bertha von, 133

Taleb, Nassim, 100
Tarde, Alfred de, 41
Taylor, Charles, 7
teachers, 125
technology, 1, 114, 115, 130–31, 141, 181–82,
    214, 226
texts: reading and interpretation of, 109–14,
    253n102; dangers of unthinking reverence
    for, 112–13
Thatcher, Margaret, 8
Thauraud, Jérôme and Jean, 75, 216, 218,
    220, 271n38
Thérèse de Lisieux, 65
Thomism, 193
Thureau-Dangin, Paul, 176–77
time: Bergson's conception of, 52–53, 55–58;
    Christian conception of, 201, 202, 207–14;
    as consensus among measurements, 45–46;
    as durée (duration), 53, 56–57, 61; in early
    twentieth-century thought, 18–19, 61–62;
    education and, 60–61; and eternity, 52;
    in late nineteenth-century thought, 39;
    linear conception of, 39, 61; modern, 91;
    Péguy's conception of, 6, 21; Poincaré's
    conception of, 47–48, 61; space in relation
    to, 52–53, 98; in twenty-first-century
    experience, 226
Tocqueville, Alexis de, 83, 140
Tolstoy, Leo, 81

Le Tour de France par deux enfants
    (textbook), 68–69, 134
transcendence: human desire for, 230–32;
    immanence vs., 1; love and, 51, 166;
    modernity opposed to, 95, 230–31; of
    nature, 182; particularist conception of, 4;
    as source of indebtedness, 262n42; war
    associated with, 132–34
trust, 127, 182, 203–4, 213
truth: certitude as criterion of, 94, 109; God
    as, 183, 203; honor associated with,
    144–45, 150; journalism as expression of,
    63, 77, 79, 146–47, 150; modern relation
    to, 37, 48, 56, 86, 91, 126, 146, 179, 215, 218,
    231; mysticism in relation to, 71, 166–69,
    171–75; Péguy's conception of, 6, 9,
    110–12, 144, 186–89, 205, 208; sacrifice/
    risk associated with, 63, 110–12, 135,
    162–63

Ultramontane Catholicism, 67–68, 74
Universal Coordinated Time, 46
universalism: embourgeoisement as false,
    77–78; of immanent becoming, 3–4;
    justice grounded in, 3, 9, 77, 129, 138,
    158, 162–63, 167–68, 175, 226; nationalism
    and, 42, 152, 154; opposition to, 3–5,
    42, 154; particularism in relation to,
    151–54, 159, 162, 259n3; Péguy and, 154,
    157–63
Universal Peace Congresses, 133
universities. *See* scholars and universities
urban life, 124

Vaihinger, Hans, 103
Vallès, Jules, 152
Veuillot, Louis, 67
Villiers de l'Isle-Adam, Auguste, 10
violence. *See* war and violence
Voltaire, 162; *Lettres philosophiques*, 41;
    Philosophical Dictionary, 70

wagering. *See* risk and wagering
Wallon, Henri, 184
Walras, Léon, 37, 102
war and violence: ancient vs. modern,
    132–33, 136–37, 139, 141; the carnal and,
    137–39; the duel as model of, 132–33, 136,
    141; Enlightenment perspectives on,
    132–33; fascination with, 132–40, 229;
    honor and, 136–37, 141–43; Jeanne d'Arc
    and, 136, 183–85, 189; justice and, 139, 140;
    Péguy's views on, 9, 10, 135–42, 228–29
Weber, Max, 7, 95
Williams, Elizabeth, 234n24
Wimsatt, William, 20
women: Christian role of, 211; conceptions
    and representations of, 10; Jeanne d'Arc as
    model for, 183–84, 186–87, 211; as model for
    nature, 117–18; and violence over questions
    of honor, 142–43. *See also* feminism
Woolf, Virginia, 104
work, 123, 125–29, 131, 182, 210
Wundt, Wilhelm, 38

Zeno of Elea, 53
Zola, Émile, 22, 73, 76–77; *J'accuse*, 73, 76

ACKNOWLEDGMENTS

This book took shape over some time. I will offer only a short list of acknowledgments here, one that must stand for thanks intended for a much larger group of generous and helpful people.

First, I am grateful for all the assistance given by the staff members of the Archives Charles Péguy in Orléans. Their enthusiasm and patience with my questions and requests are deeply appreciated.

I am also thankful for the help of all the staff at the University of Pennsylvania Press, especially for the work of my editor, Damon Linker, whose exemplary professionalism, support, and advice have been indispensable. I'm particularly grateful for the remarks of the manuscript's evaluator (whose critical care was extraordinary) and other anonymous commenters for Penn Press.

Portions of the book were presented in earlier form at Georgetown University, Harvard University, the University of Durham, and the University of Toronto (the latter at a meeting of the International Society for Intellectual History). The comments and questions I received were sharp and helpful. I'm especially grateful to Boston College and the University of Texas at Austin for the opportunity to give invited lectures on themes and questions drawn from this project.

I am also thankful for the assistance and academic hospitality of the Bibliothèque Nationale de France, Regenstein Library, Widener Library, the University of Bamberg, as well as various public libraries and coffee shops in Chicago and elsewhere that generously afforded me time and space to write.

Numerous colleagues and friends provided insight, encouragement, and suggestions about this book, as well as invaluable practical and administrative support for research. Among many others, I would like to thank Fred Baumann, David Beecher, Jeff Bowman, Michael Budde, Amber Carpenter, Emanuele Colombo, Sylvie Coulibaly, Hugo Duhayon, Tom Foster, Fabian Geier, Patrice and Margaret Higonnet, Christian Illies, Christopher Kelly, Thomas

Levergood, Josh Levithan, Jonathan Ray, Julie Sabiani, Christian Schäfer, Devin Stauffer, Valentina Tikoff, and David Williams.

Special thanks go to my parents, Thomas and Beatrice Maguire, and my brother, Tom Maguire, for listening to an inordinate number of conversations about this project.

For all the gifts of time, encouragement, criticism, and expertise given to this book and its author, I offer my sincere thanks.